The Uses Of Wild Plants

The Uses Of Wild Plants

Using and growing the wild plants of the
United States and Canada

Frank Tozer

Green Man Publishing
Santa Cruz

ISBN: 0-9773489-0-3

Library of Congress Control Number: 2005936078

First published in 2007

Green Man Publishing
Santa Cruz
P.O. Box 1546
Felton
CA 95018

Greenmansantacruz.com

Caution

This book is for educational purposes only, and does not endorse the actual use of any plant for any purpose. The plants described in this book have been widely used in the past, but this does not in any way guarantee that they are totally safe. The interactions between plants and the human body are too complex for you eat any wild plant without considering the potential dangers. Any plant can potentially cause serious problems. The publisher and author accept no liability for any injury or ill effects that may result from the use of any of the plants described herein.

For Elsie and David

My parents

Introduction

The uses of wild plants is one of the oldest branches of human knowledge. For most of our history wild plants have fed us, clothed us, sheltered us, kept us warm, helped us protect ourselves, healed our injuries and even allowed us to talk with the gods. Survival once largely depended upon an extensive knowledge of plants; where to find them, how to identify them, how to use them, what parts to use, and when to gather them. Our hunter-gatherer forbears survived on wild plants for countless generations and accumulated a vast amount of knowledge on their uses. How they worked out how to make certain poisonous plants safe to eat remains a mystery, as does how they discovered that certain plants could cure specific diseases. They knew the uses of wild plants better than we could ever hope to, and I have drawn heavily on their knowledge for this book.

An extensive knowledge of wild plants was also very important for farming peoples. For many centuries peasant farmers around the world have lived more or less self sufficiently on small farms, depending upon what they could grow, supplemented by what they could gather from the wild, and many still do. These people have been another major source of information for this book. They used plants in many different ways; not only as a supplemental food source, but also for beer, medicines, tools, building materials, roofing, animal feed, lighting, charcoal, paint, fencing, fertilizer, and many other things that made life easier. Often they would sell or trade products they had gathered, as a source of income.

As rural economies developed and became more diverse, many people began to specialize in various crafts. These people still frequently looked to wild plants for their raw materials, using them to make baskets, furniture, houses, cloth, footwear, rope and cord, nets, fish traps, dyes, musical instruments and much more. Wild plants were also important as sources of raw materials for fledgling industries. These included rosin, charcoal, potash, pitch, turpentine, tannins, oils, alcohol, waxes, alginates and creosote. Of course wild plants have long been important to the medical profession, as painkillers, antiseptics, sedatives, and medicines for specific diseases, pregnancy and other health issues. As the population increased it became necessary to domesticate many wild plants to meet the demand for their products. In densely populated areas these cultivated plants sometimes became an important part of the landscape, in the form of woodlots, hedgerows, orchards, groves and coppiced woodland.

Wild plants are still important today, and find their way into our lives in many different ways, though we rarely go out and gather them for ourselves. Most important are the trees that provide our lumber and paper. These form the basis of a huge industry, and their products, directly or indirectly, employ millions of people. Trees are also widely used for firewood, a renewable source of energy that doesn't contribute to global warming. Many drugs are directly derived from wild plants, others are synthesized using natural plant chemicals as templates, or as starting materials. These are now an important part of a multi-billion dollar industry. At the same time much of the world still depends almost entirely on plants for their medicines, because they simply can't afford the cost of modern drugs. The herb industry is another large scale user of wild plants; in medicines, food supplements, cosmetics and teas. A few wild foods are gathered commercially on a large scale (Wild-Rice, Pine Nuts, Blueberries, Black Walnuts), others are occasionally collected commercially for sale to gourmet restaurants, or to meet local demands (Fiddleheads, Pokeweed, Juneberries). The foliage of quite a few plants is gathered in quantity from the wild, for use by florists. Alginates, gathered from wild seaweeds, find their way into a surprising variety of foods, cosmetics and other products.

Many people in the developed world today know little of the wild plants that surround them, and feel no connection to them, or the natural world. Plants that were once an integral part of our lives are now pretty much invisible, or are even thought of as a nuisance for invading our garden space.

The Uses Of Wild Plants

This is unfortunate because we are just as dependent upon plants for our survival as we ever were. The only difference is that the plants grow where we can't see them, often hundreds, or even thousands, of miles away. It is my hope that this book will help to raise awareness of the value of wild plants, how much they have given us in the past, and how much more they might give us in the future.

If you grew up in a suburban, or rural, area you probably already know a little about the uses of a few wild plants. Children tend to be closer to the earth than adults, and Blackberries, Wild Strawberries, Chestnuts, Wood Sorrel, Spearmint and other plants have long been a part of country children's lives. As a teenager growing up in Britain, I was fascinated to learn that many other plants had uses too, and that humans had already investigated all of the plants I found growing around me (and in pretty much every area of the planet). Information on edible and useful plants wasn't readily available in Britain at that time, so I began to seek out this knowledge. The process of learning everything I could about the uses of plants continued after I moved to the United States, and has now been ongoing for over twenty five years. For much of this time I have also been growing many of the plants discussed here. I wrote this book for others like me, people who are curious about the wild plants around them, and want to know more about them. I might say that I have written the book I would have loved to have been able to read when I was fifteen years old.

Recreational foragers, adventurous gourmets and outdoors cooks will find a wealth of information on interesting edible plants in this book. In many countries wild plants are still widely used for food, and not just by the very poor. Many traditional recipes call for specific plants, so that French, Greek, Italian, Mexican, Chinese and other great cuisines offer many interesting ways to use wild plants. Much is sometimes made of the fact that wild edible plants are organic, and free for the gathering, and this is certainly a bonus.

Some people are interested in wild foods for survival, believing that in an uncertain world they may one day be important once more. There is certainly no guarantee that life will always be as easy as it is at the moment. In many parts of the world wild foods have been vital in times of scarcity, brought on by intermittent wars, famine, disease, revolution and other social upheavals. In such times people have turned to the woods and hedgerows to supplement scarce food supplies, or even as their sole means of survival. This happened as recently as the war in Bosnia. The knowledge of how to use wild plants could help to give you a greater sense of independence and self-sufficiency.

Using wild plants can have a positive effect on you health, by providing the most nutritious foods available. Many conventionally grown crops are becoming devitalized by chemical farming and often contain significantly fewer nutrients than they did fifty years ago. I use wild plants because I believe that eating a wide variety of foods helps to provide superior nutrition. I prefer to get my extra vitamins and minerals from living plants rather than from chemical plants; they are also cheaper. Many wild plants are very rich in vitamins, minerals, bioflavinoids, antioxidants, anthocyanins, enzymes, essential fatty acids, and probably other nutrients we haven't even discovered yet. Just as they can help to heal the earth of scars caused by industrial human use, so they can help to heal bodies scarred by industrial foods and pollution. This is quite different from using plants as medicines, which is another aspect of plant use entirely.

I have incorporated many useful wild plants into my present garden in California, to make it more productive with little extra work. I mostly grow plants that aren't common in my area, or are not native, but that thrive in my climate and perpetuate themselves. I also grow improved cultivars of local plants, or their close relatives. In doing this I have many plants available literally at my doorstep. As I write this there are Chestnuts showering down on to the hammock in my front garden. Cultivating these plants opens up another dimension in wild plant use because we can select and improve the plants to suit our own purposes. Choosing individuals with traits more to our liking, such as better flavor, more productive, larger or earlier. I am particularly interested in forest gardening, where trees are grown as crops, along with productive shrubs, vines, perennial and annuals, in a highly productive, cultivated ecosystem.

I have mentioned quite a few reasons why I am interested in wild plants, but the most important reason is that using and growing them brings me an enormous amount of personal satisfaction. Having them around me rewards me as much on a psychological level as on a material one. It has been hypothesized that humans have a deep need to be surrounded by plants, that they are essential for psychological health and well-being. I certainly believe it.

Many of these plants could play a significant role in helping us to create a sustainable and non-destructive way for humans to live on the earth. I imagine a future where every house collects solar energy to provide most of the energy its inhabitants use. I imagine every house with a garden that recycles all of the nutrients its inhabitants use, and purifies all of their wastewater for re-use. A garden full of plants that provide for many of our daily needs; for food, drink, fuel, clean water, medicines, flavorings, wood, charcoal, animal feed, dyes, basket materials, plant supports and more. Such a garden could be very beautiful, and would provide for our psychological well-being as well as our physical health. I have much more to say about such gardens, but I must save it for another book.

Many of the plants described in this book could help us to reduce our demands upon the planet, but if they are ever to be used to meet our industrial scale needs they must be cultivated on a large scale. Some of the plants discussed here will doubtless become important crops, to provide us with food, fuel, medicines, building materials, animal feed, chemicals, fertilizers and other raw materials. They might be used for powering cars; admittedly an idea with limited value in a nation of over 150 million cars, and for treating sewage, neutralizing toxic wastes, cleaning polluted water, soil and air, recovering valuable pollutants, collecting solar energy or reducing noise. Algae have been found that can grow oil, using the carbon dioxide, and nitrous oxide, emitted from power plant smokestacks. We could use wild plants as crops in novel ways. Coppicing shrubs and trees on short rotations to quickly grow the materials to make structural wood panels, beams, wallboard and paper. Growing Hemp, Reed or Bamboo to make paper instead of using trees. Creating food producing forest farms that mimic natural ecosystems. Using deep-rooted perennial grain crops, in combination with nitrogen fixers, as long-term perennial food producing systems that don't require annual planting, fertilizing or disturbing the soil.

I have tried to make this book as comprehensive as possible, covering as many plants, and as wide a variety of potential uses ,as I could. Some of these uses will not be practical for a variety of reasons. Some plants have very strong flavors that don't suit pampered modern day tastes. Some plants need special techniques to make them useful, and may be too time consuming or labor intensive to be worthwhile. Many plants won't be economically practical as sources of fuel or chemicals until cheaper mined sources become much more expensive. A lot of the information on the best and easiest ways to use plants has been lost with the death of older generations, many of whom were the last to have direct experience of generations of subsistence farming. We need to rediscover how best to use many of these species before we can fully utilize them. Some of the uses I describe are relatively new, and much experimental work is needed before these can reach their full potential. On the other hand many of the uses I describe are perfectly practical already. They only await motivated individuals willing to work out the best ways of growing and using them.

Whenever a book such as this appears there are voices expressing concern that drawing attention to useful plants could cause an increase in gathering, so they eventually become less common. This concern does have some validity, as Ginseng, Damiana, Peyote and many other plants are much less common than they used to be because of over-gathering. This is also true of mature Redwoods, Cedars, Black Walnuts, White Pines, Douglas Firs, and countless other economically important plants. However this is rarely because of people gathering plants for their own use. It is

The Uses Of Wild Plants

nearly always because they are gathered for commercial purposes, with the sole aim being to make money. Of course this attitude is definitely incompatible with the conservation of anything and is to be deplored. Euell Gibbons, the best known wild food forager of modern times, used to argue that conservation does not mean non-use. Gathering wild plants doesn't have to be exploitive, it can be a symbiotic relationship, of mutual benefit to both plants and humans. Native Americans used the plants around them quite intensively, but rather than the plants becoming rarer, they often increased in abundance.

Human beings are an ingenious species, always trying to improve their situation. Hunter-gatherers around the world realized they didn't just have to take what nature offered. They could actually increase the amount of wild food available by managing the vegetation to suit their needs. They did this by careful observation and experimentation, and over many generations they played a significant role in shaping the landscape. What appeared to be a wilderness to the first European settlers, was often a carefully managed and sophisticated system, which enabled food to grow itself with minimal human effort.

Hunter gatherers managed the plants around them with the techniques that would later form the basis of agriculture; sowing, digging, irrigation, selecting superior seeds, weeding, coppicing, and especially burning. As every gardener knows, these simple techniques greatly increase the productivity and usefulness of plants, and this applies just as much to wild plants as it does to cultivated ones. In California primitive peoples sometimes burned the land annually, and then sowed part of their harvest of edible seed on the newly cleared ground. By doing this they were able to create enormous stands of edible seed-bearing annuals. They also burned underneath food bearing trees such as Oaks, Fan Palms and Mesquite, to reduce insect damage, and to make fruit gathering easier. Fire was also used to prevent tree encroachment, regenerate shrubs and to increase the amount of food available for edible wildlife (and to make it easier to hunt them). They cultivated, weeded and propagated beds of edible roots, and stands of fruit bearing shrubs, thereby increasing the quantity and quality of the food available. Plants that produced basket-making materials were weeded, coppiced and cared for, so they produced material far superior to that to be found growing naturally.

I have emphasized cultivation in this book because the growing human population is putting increasing pressure on wild places and plants. Many plants can be gathered from the wild without harm, but others are vulnerable, and could easily be harmed by over-harvesting. In such cases if you want to use a plant you should grow it yourself. If you don't have your own garden, you might try guerrilla gardening, growing the plants on waste ground, or scattering the seed of wild plants on suitable sites.

I feel I should probably apologize to any taxonomists out there for not keeping my botanical nomenclature as up to date as it could be. I don't doubt that quite a few of the plants I mention have been re-named recently, some probably more than once. However this book is not really intended for professional botanists. I am interested in the plants themselves, more than their Latin binomials, and if you the reader know what plants I am referring to, that is good enough for me.

The plants

The following plants are those I consider to be the most useful to be found growing wild in North America. All of them have something special to offer. They may have been staple foods of indigenous peoples. They might provide an abundance of tasty food (some are still gathered commercially from the wild), or be important flavorings. Quite a few of these plants are particularly nutritious, some have powerful medicinal properties, and a few contain unique chemicals. Some were once important for particular crafts and were the basis of major industries. A number have been cultivated as crops in the past, and many more could become important crops in the future.

Abies species / Firs

Throughout   *Pinaceae*
The Firs resemble the Spruces (*Picea*) in appearance and uses. They are sometimes known as Balsam Firs because their juvenile bark is pocked with small blisters full of aromatic resin. This resin has a number of special uses, and demand for it once supported a minor industry in some areas.

Chewing gum: The sugar-rich resin is edible and that of several species has been used as chewing gum. It is gathered and prepared like that of the Black Spruce (Picea). This gum has been called a "highly concentrated food", but its strong balsam flavor makes it rather unpalatable.

Famine: The inner cambium layer of bark is edible, but not very pleasant.

Medicine: The resin of the Balsam Fir (*A. balsamea*) is known to herbalists as Canada Balsam, and was once commonly used as a diuretic and laxative.

Native Americans mixed the resin with lard or fat to make an ointment for wounds (they covered the wound with clean material to prevent dirt sticking to it). It was used in the same way by European settlers, and soldiers of both sides during the civil war. A poultice of inner bark was also used to treat wounds.

Other uses: Canada Balsam resin has the same refractive index as glass, making it almost invisible when viewed through a microscope. This makes it useful as cement in the preparation of specimen slides. It is also quite aromatic and has been added to soaps and perfumes. It was once used for caulking bark canoes.

Wood: Generally the wood is too soft to be good for lumber, though there are a few exceptions. Wood from the better species is used for construction, crates, plywood and paneling. It was once used for food containers, as it has little odor. The Firs are most often used for making paper.

Fuel: These species are poor firewood, giving only about 13 million Btu per cord. The resinous bark makes good kindling, though of course you shouldn't take it from live trees.

Christmas Trees: The Firs are widely cultivated for use as Christmas trees and are also cut from the forest in large numbers for this. Such a practice is not necessarily as destructive as one might imagine, as there are usually many more young saplings than there is growing room and most would eventually die anyway. Cutting out the "inferior" saplings for Christmas trees leaves the rest to grow on under improved conditions. If you really don't want to kill a tree for Christmas you can just cut off the top, and leave the bottom branches to continue growing.

Beds: The old-time woodsmen used armloads of the boughs to make browse beds. They would chop down a few trees, trim off the branches and make a rough rectangular frame. This was then filled with the boughs, with their butts stuck in the ground to form a thick springy cushion. The end result is soft and aromatic, but rather destructive, unless the trees are to be cut anyway (See *Pinus* for an alternative).

Other uses: The aromatic evergreen boughs are widely used by florists for wreaths and floral decorations, and gathering them is a cottage industry in some areas.

Cultivation: These trees are popular ornamentals in some areas. The short-lived seed is gathered in September, before the cones open and planted in moist soil. If immediate planting is impractical, then stratify at 40 degrees for three months and plant in the spring.

Species include:
A. balsamea - **Balsam Fir**
This eastern species is the source of Canada balsam.

A. grandis - **Grand Fir**
This attractive tree is a popular ornamental in its native northwest and in mild wet climates around the world. It grows very fast and may reach 150 feet in height in only 50 years. It doesn't make good lumber, but is an important pulpwood tree.

A. procera - **Noble Fir**
This large tree is an important lumber producer.

Abronia latifolia / **Yellow Sand Verbena**

West coast   *Nyctaginaceae*
This plant is usually found on beaches. In many places it is getting less common, and shouldn't be used unless it is very abundant.

Food: The Chinook people cooked and ate the fleshy stems and large roots. They often dried these, and then ground them to flour for baking or gruel.

Cultivation: The plant has been cultivated as an ornamental, for its attractive and fragrant yellow flowers. It may be grown from seed or division, in well-drained soils.

Acacia greggii / **Catclaw Acacia**

Southwest   *Mimosaceae*
Many of the species in this large genus are adapted to grow in hot dry climates, and they can be found in desert

areas around the world. This species gets its common name from the hooked spines that protect it (it's also known as Devils Claw). These can inflict a nasty wound to the careless gatherer, so one must be cautious when gathering from the plants.

Seeds and pods: The seeds contain about 33% protein and 25% oil and were commonly eaten by the Pima, Cahuilla and other desert peoples. However they may also contain toxins, so should be used with caution.

The immature pods can be eaten raw, but are improved by boiling in a change of water to reduce their bitterness. The ripe seeds and pods were used like those of the closely related Mesquite (*Prosopis*). Usually they were parboiled to reduce their bitterness, then dried and ground to flour. The parboiled seeds can also be used like dry beans.

Wood: Acacia wood is hard and heavy and of little commercial importance. It is used locally for fence posts and as hot-burning firewood. Native Americans used it for bows and spears. The supple shoots were stripped of their thorns and used for basket weaving.

Wildlife food: The pods are food for many creatures, and the spiny branches provide a safe refuge from predators. The flowers produce copious nectar, which bees make into highly prized *uvalde* honey. Another creature that favors this plant is the Lac insect (*Tachardia lacca*), which produces lac. This substance has been used to make lacquer and paint. Native Americans used it for waterproofing baskets.

Gum: Resin from the plant has been used like Gum Arabic.

Cultivation: Seed can be collected from the ripe pods from late summer onward. The tough seed coat prevents rapid germination, and in the wild the seeds may lay dormant for years before sprouting. To hasten germination soak the seeds in acid, or nick them with a file (to allow water to penetrate) and then soak in water for 24 hours. The tree can also be propagated from semi-ripe cuttings, and this is usually easier. They will grow in most kinds of soil, even poor alkaline ones and need little attention once established. Generally they dislike cold and may die if the temperature drops below 20 degrees Fahrenheit. They are very drought tolerant, but grow more rapidly if irrigated.

The Acacias are typical pioneer species; fast growing and short lived. Like most members of the *Fabaceae* they are host to nitrogen-fixing bacteria in nodules on their roots, and consequently enrich the soil they grow in. They are sometimes used for erosion control, land reclamation and as spiny, stock proof hedges.

Related species:
A. farnesiana - Sweet Acacia
This species is cultivated in France for its sweet scented flowers. These are used in perfume and soap.

Acer saccharum / Sugar Maple
East   *Aceraceae*
The Maples were an important food source for the Chippewa, Winnebago and other northeastern tribes. The harvest of sugar from the huge trees of the primeval forest was limited only by their ability to remove the water from the sap by primitive means. The sugar was actually a staple food in some tribes; some individuals consuming as much as two pounds of it per week. The spring sugar harvest was an important annual celebration and feast, as it signaled the end of winter and its hardship.

Caution: Maple sugar is not really the healthy alternative to refined cane sugar that it is sometimes claimed to be; it is the same thing, sucrose. It would be interesting to study the diseases of the Native American tribes who ate large quantities of Maple sugar, to see if any modern ailments showed up.

Maple Syrup: The tapping of Maples for sugar is not purely a Native American discovery. The Norway Maple (*A. platanoides*) was tapped for sugar in Scandinavia long before Europeans discovered America. The first English settlers learned how to tap the Maples from Native Americans, and it quickly became an integral part of colonial pioneer life. It was an important trade item among Native Americans and European settlers, and occasionally even a substitute for money.

This tree is the most important source of commercial syrup, providing over 70% of the crop (the rest comes from various other species). Tapping the maples yields a familiar and tasty treat, but I can't recommend it unreservedly, because it is a refined sugar.

Sugaring is a fairly straightforward process if you have the right equipment and don't mind breathing steam. You don't even have to live in the northeast, as sugar-yielding Maples can be found over much of the country. Most syrup is produced commercially in the northeast, because the wide variation in night and day temperatures ensures a reliable flow of sap.

Gathering time: The sugaring season starts in late winter, when sap starts to run in the trees. Sap is produced most copiously when temperatures get up into the forties during the day, and drop down below freezing at night. The season ends when buds appear on the trees. The length of the season depends upon the weather. It may be as short as a week, or as long as a month.

The amount of sap yielded by a tree varies considerably with the amount of sun, wind and moisture it receives, and of course the length of the season. Some trees have been known to yield as much as 300 gallons of sap in a season, though 50 is probably average for a mature tree. It takes about 30 gallons of sap to make one of syrup.

Tapping methods: If you break a twig from a tree in late winter, or early spring, a watery sap oozes from the wound. Making Maple syrup begins with collecting this in sufficient quantity (which is easier said than done).

The earliest tapping method consisted of cutting a V shaped slit in the bark of the trunk (much as rubber trees are tapped) and putting a stick in the bottom of the V to lead the sap into a Birch bark container. This isn't very satisfactory, as it can lead to infection and rot in the tree.

The traditional tapping method is to drill a small half inch hole about two inches into the sapwood, about 3 feet off the ground. A small tube of slightly larger diameter (called a spile) is hammered into the hole to drain the sap. A bucket (now often a plastic milk jug) is hung from the spile to catch the sap, and covered to keep out dirt. Up to three holes can be drilled into a large tree without harm, though tapping kills the sapwood for an inch or so around the hole, so you can't use the same hole the following year. The sap must be collected frequently in warm weather, as it spoils quickly.

Tapping methods haven't changed much in the past 100 years, though now disposable plastic bags frequently replace buckets as containers. In larger operations plastic pipe is now often used to drain the sap directly to a central holding tank, and vacuum pumps may be used to speed up the flow.

Evaporating: Maple sap is mostly (about 95%) water, all of which must be removed to make sugar. This was a

problem for Native Americans because they didn't have metal pots for boiling. They removed some of the water by allowing the sap to freeze overnight (water freezes at a higher temperature than the sugar, so the ice is almost pure water) and then removing the ice. Alternatively they would let the sap freeze solid and then allow it to melt (the sugar melts first). The more concentrated sap was then boiled in bark or wood containers by dropping heated stones into it. This process isn't as inefficient as it sounds, but metal pots for boiling the sap were one of the first important trade items with Europeans.

Any pan can be used for evaporating, but wide shallow ones are best, as the large surface area allows for most efficient evaporation. Many kinds of evaporators are used for home sugaring, ranging from converted barbecues and oil drum stoves, to specially designed commercial evaporators with separate compartments for raw sap and finished syrup. You can't really use the indoor kitchen stove (unless you want to remove the wallpaper), as you will fill the house with steam. Serious sugar producers have a special sugaring shed out among the trees, so they can work comfortably in all weather.

The sap is strained to remove twigs, insects and dirt and then boiled until all the water is removed. As the water boils away, more sap is added to maintain a full evaporator. When the pan is full of thick syrup it must be watched very carefully, as it can easily stick to the bottom of the pan and burn, ruining the flavor. The traditional way to check when the syrup is done, is to pour a spoonful onto the snow and watch how it congeals. This is how Maple candy originated, it is simply syrup poured onto the snow to cool and eaten off of a stick. A more precise way to check it is a candy thermometer. When the syrup reaches 219 degrees Fahrenheit it is finished.

Uses: The uses of Maple syrup are too well known to describe here. It has also been fermented to make beer.

Greens: The small tender seedlings have been added to salads.

Wood: Sugar Maple wood is hard (it's sometimes called Hard Maple), strong and attractive. It works and finishes well and is commonly used for cabinetmaking, flooring and turning. A few trees produce figured wood such as Birds Eye Maple (its spots actually look like eyes) and Fiddleback Maple (from its use in violins). This is highly prized and so expensive it has led to the theft of trees by timber rustlers. They are even more destructive than most rustlers, as they may cut into many trees before finding one that has the desired curly grain.

Firewood: The wood is excellent fuel, giving about 24 million Btu per cord. The resulting ash is rich in potassium and was once shipped to Europe for making soap and glass. Maple charcoal was an important export to Britain in colonial times.

Animal food: Many birds and small animals eat the winged seeds. In winter rodents sometimes chew the bark to get at the sugar rich cambium layer.

Cultivation: The Sugar Maple grows to 125 feet in height, lives up to 250 years and puts on a spectacular display in fall when its leaves die and change color. It has long been prized as a shade tree. It is sensitive to air pollution and often doesn't thrive in urban areas.

In summer Maples often produce seed in such abundance it can be gathered by the bucketful. This should be planted immediately in rich, deep, well-drained soil. An easy way to get Maple trees is to carefully dig the seedlings from the wild. In spring they can often be transplanted from around mature trees or lawns.

The young seedlings prefer part shade, though mature trees need full sun. The trees respond well to fertilizer. When given an inch of sewage sludge weekly they grew four times faster than unfertilized trees.

Maples coppice well, and can be cut for firewood or pulpwood on a 10 - 25 year rotation.

Crop Use: Commercial Sugar Maples groves are generally made up of wild trees. Until recently very little breeding work had been done to improve their sugar producing qualities. This despite the fact that the sap of individual trees shows a considerable variation in sugar content. Some trees produce sap with as much as 12% sugar, yet most average only 3 - 4% sugar. Using select cultivars could give a 300% increase in yield with no extra work. It might also be possible to propagate curly Maple trees as a commercial lumber crop.

Fertilizer: The leaf mould and wood ash are excellent garden fertilizers.

Related species: Most species have been tapped for sap at one time or another, with varying success (the weather is usually the most important factor). The best include:

A. negundo - **Box Elder** Syn *Negundo aceroides*
A. saccarinum - **Silver Maple**

A. platanoides - **Norway Maple**
This European species is commonly planted as an ornamental. This is fortunate as it may be the best sugar producer of all the Maples.

A. macrophyllum - **Big leaf Maple**
This large West Coast tree can give excellent syrup.

Achillea lanulosa, A. millefolium / Yarrow

Throughout   *Asteraceae*

These two species are almost identical, so it's hard to differentiate between the two. *Achillea lanulosa* is the native American Yarrow, while *A. millefolium* is naturalized from Europe. Fortunately they are also identical in their uses.

Greens: The aromatic, tender young shoots, leaves and flowers are a minor salad ingredient, but too strongly flavored to eat in bulk. They have also been used as a potherb, either mixed with milder greens, or cooked in a change of water to reduce the strong flavor.

Drinks: I most often use Yarrow as a minor addition to green blender drinks (see Comfrey - *Symphytum*). It was once widely used for flavoring beer, but was eventually displaced by Hops.

Medicine: Yarrow has historically been most important as a wound herb, as indicated by such common names as Carpenters Grass, Herbe Militaris and Woundwort. According to myth, Cheiron the centaur taught the Greek warrior Achilles how to use the leaves to treat his wounded soldiers (hence the generic name *Achillea*). In the form of a wash, poultice or salve it continued to be an important military wound dressing even into the twentieth century. Among its active ingredients are tannin (which is astringent), an alkaloid called achilleine (which apparently helps blood to clot) and salicylic acid (which is antiseptic). It is also anti- inflammatory. See *Plantago* for how to use leaves as wound dressings.

Yarrow has been used to stop internal bleeding and to treat ulcers and insect bites. It is also used as an eyewash for tired or irritated eyes (often with Fennel (*Foeniculum*).

The plant was once officially in the USP as an emmenagogue and in large amounts has been used (unofficially) as an abortifacient. It was also used to stimulate the liver, help digestion, promote sweating (one of the best herbs for this), relieve toothache, treat diarrhea and lower blood pressure.

Hair treatment: A strong decoction of Yarrow leaves may be rubbed into the hair after shampooing. This was once considered so beneficial as to be able to prevent baldness. It was often mixed with other herbs, such as Nettle, Chamomile and Sage, and is still found in some high priced herbal shampoos.

Other Uses: Native Americans smoked dried Yarrow leaves and tops with other herbs. It was also powdered for use as incense and snuff (which is probably why a related species has the common name Sneezeweed). The stalks have been used in dried flower arrangements, and for throwing the I-ching.

Companion Plant: Most gardeners consider Yarrow to be a minor weed of lawns and flower borders, but biodynamic gardeners believe it to be one of the best of all companion plants. They say it stimulates the growth of nearby plants, increasing their disease resistance and content of essential oils. They sometimes even transplant Yarrow alongside ailing plants to revive them. Its scent is said to repel garden pests such as Japanese Beetles and ants. If any of these claims are true Yarrow deserves a little space in every garden.

Horticultural Uses: Yarrow is a fine lawn plant and has been planted along with Thyme, Chamomile and Clover as a low maintenance herbal lawn.

If you can get enough of the foliage it can be used to make an excellent liquid fertilizer (see Comfrey - *Symphytum).*

Cultivation: Yarrow is easily grown from seed, soft cuttings or division and thrives in almost any soil or situation. It spreads rapidly in good soil, and sometimes becomes a minor weed.

Related species:
A. ptarmica - Sneezeweed
This western species can be used as above. It is said that Native Americans used a poultice of the chewed roots as a local anesthetic.

Acorus calamus / Sweet Flag
East   *Araceae*
Sweet Flag or Calamus is found growing throughout the eastern United States, in shallow water or boggy ground. It is distinguished from the somewhat similar, but poisonous, Wild Irises by its light green color and pungent ginger-like taste and smell.

Caution: Sweet Flag contains asarone, which was banned from use as a food additive in the USA in 1968. In quantity it can cause central nervous system depression, intestinal tumors and low blood pressure.

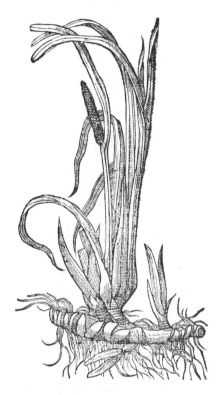

Some Native American tribes used Sweet Flag root to induce visions and considered it to be a sacred plant. They also chewed it to increase endurance and reduce fatigue, much as Coca leaves are chewed in South America. Apparently chewing a small 1 – 2 inch piece of root would increase endurance (runners described themselves as "running above the ground") and bring on a feeling of well-being. A larger 10 inch piece could induce visions (or hallucinations, depending on your view of reality). It was originally thought that asarone was responsible for the psychoactive effects (the body can convert it into tri-methoxy-amphetamine), but it is possible that another substance may be responsible.

Flavoring: The roots may be used for flavoring any time they are available, though they are best when dormant in winter (if hard to locate). They can be used as a substitute for Ginger in baking, and were once popular candied as a confection.

Shoots: The new spring shoots and succulent young leaves are a delicious minor addition to salads. They can also be cooked for a few minutes as a potherb, or added to soup.

Tea: Almost all parts can be used to make tea. The roots have been used in liqueurs, cordials and root beers.

Medicine: Sweet Flag root was once included in the USP as a stomachic, carminative and to treat hyperacidity. It has also been used as an antiseptic, and to kill parasites both internally and externally.

Aphrodisiac: The root has long had a reputation as an aphrodisiac, which might (with a little imagination) be linked to its vision inducing qualities.

Insect Repellant: In medieval Europe Calamus leaves were prized as a strewing herb (they were scattered on earthen floors to hide unpleasant smells), as they have a fine scent and insect repellant properties. Calamus oil, or synthetic asarone (the active ingredient), has been used to keep moths from clothes, to repel fleas and lice and as a non-toxic fumigant for grain. Ironically the oil actually attracts fruit flies and has been used as bait to catch them. It has been found that the roots secrete a substance that can kill harmful bacteria.

Other Uses: The powdered root was used in tooth powders (also used to relieve toothache), sachets and herbal smoking mixtures, and as a substitute for Orris. The essential oil was added to perfumes, and to bathwater to aid in relaxation.

Cultivation: This attractive plant is often grown as an ornamental in sunny wet places, ditches, lake margins and marshy ground. It can also be grown on dry land if watered frequently. Like many aquatic plants it grows rapidly, and may produce as much as 2000 pounds of root per acre annually. Propagate by root division, or ripe seed planted in a flat of rich soil and kept very wet. Transplant the young plants to a permanent site when several inches high

Horticultural Uses: Sweet flag has been planted in the garden, and around houses, to keep away ants and other pests. The powdered root has been used as a general garden insect repellant.

Aesculus species / Buckeyes
Throughout   *Sapindinaceae*
Caution: The large plump Buckeye nuts look like a valuable food source and they can be eaten if carefully prepared. They are poisonous when raw however, as they contain a toxic glycoside called aesculin, which destroys red blood cells and causes nausea, vomiting and

paralysis. Even when properly treated the nuts are not a particularly attractive food, and most Native American tribes ignored them unless the more palatable acorn crop failed. They are a potentially important survival food however, as they are often available in quantity, and contain as much as 11% protein, 5% fat and 70% carbohydrate. In Europe related species have been eaten by humans, but were most often used as animal feed, after treatment to remove their toxins.

Preparation: Aesculin is water-soluble, so the nuts can be leached in much the same way as acorns (see *Quercus*). The tough, leathery shells are harder to remove however and were soaked overnight to soften them and make removal easier. Native Americans often steamed them in a fire pit for up to 10 hours and then peeled and sliced the soft kernels. These were then leached like acorns in a stream for several days until sweet. Alternatively the steamed kernels were pounded to meal, which was then leached in a sand filter for 2 - 10 hours.

Uses: The leached meal was used like that of acorns, for baking, or to make gruel (which was eaten hot or cold). It was usually prepared as needed, as it doesn't keep very well.

Medicine: The bark of the California Buckeye (*A. californica*) has been used as a laxative like Cascara Sagrada (see *Rhamnus*).

Fish Poison: Probably while leaching the nuts Native Americans discovered another property of the nuts. The leachate stupefies fish, causing them to float, but without affecting their edibility. The leaves and flowers have been used in the same way.

Alcohol: The starchy nuts have been fermented to produce alcohol.

Animal food: European Horse Chestnuts (*A. hippocastanum*) were prepared as animal feed by crushing and soaking for 24 hours and then boiling for 30 minutes in fresh water.

Sunscreen: Apparently the juice from the plant has been used as a sunscreen and sunburn treatment. I haven't tried this, but it is the only plant I know of that has been suggested for this use.

Soap: Aesculin has a detergent effect and can be used to clean clothing (just crush the leaves and agitate them in water). It may even help protect them against insects such as moths.

Cordage: Native Americans used the fibrous inner bark of Buckeyes for cordage.

Cultivation: Generally these species are easily grown from ripe seed, planted immediately, or stratified at 40 degrees for four months (California Buckeye needs no stratification). They don't transplant well. Some shrubby species can also be propagated from suckers. Generally they prefer well-drained, fairly rich soil.

Horticultural Uses: Some *Aesculus* species are planted as ornamentals, the most important being the European Horse Chestnut.

Agastache foeniculum / Anise Hyssop
Syn *A. anethiodora*

East   *Lamiaceae*

Flavoring: As the common and specific names suggest this plant has an Anise / Fennel flavor. The leaves can be used sparingly in salads and as flavoring. Native Americans used them to flavor and sweeten many dishes.

Tea: Probably the best use of the plant is for tea.

Animal Food: The blue flower spikes are attractive to bees as a source of nectar and their long flowering season makes them especially useful. Many birds eat the seed.

Cultivation: This perennial is easily grown from seed or root division in moist soil, and is attractive enough to be grown as an ornamental. It self-seeds profusely, and might be considered a weed if it wasn't such a nice plant.

Related species:
A. urticifolia - Giant Hyssop
Native Americans used the mucilaginous seed of this western species like that of Chia (*Salvia*), for drinks, bread and gruel. Unlike most members of the Mint family Giant Hyssop is an important forage plant for animals.

A. neomexicana.
Used for tea and flavoring as above.

Agave species / Agaves
Southwest   *Agavaceae*
The Agaves are similar to their cousins the Yuccas (*Yucca*), though they are larger, less tolerant of cold and have small spines along the edges of their leaves. Like many desert plants they use Crassulacean acid metabolism or CAM (see *Cereus*), which helps them to conserve water. They can survive on as little as three inches of water a year.

These common plants were very important to Seri, Paiute, Apache and other desert peoples as a source of food and many other necessities of life. Families often owned gathering rights to certain areas, or made special trips to especially rich gathering grounds.

Agaves were once a hazard to people on horseback, as a horse walking into the sharp leaves might throw its rider and more than a few unfortunate people landed on the spiny plants. Today the sharp leaves sometimes puncture the tires of off road vehicles.

Caution: All Agaves are toxic raw. Internally they can damage the liver; externally their acrid sap may cause a rash in some individuals. Fortunately heat destroys the poisonous substances in the plant, so the cooked parts are edible.

Hearts: Agaves grow like Palm trees, from a single central growing point or heart. These are quite nutritious and were a staple food of some desert tribes, though they can cause stomach upset and diarrhea if eaten in excess. They are available from April onward, and vary in size according to species and growing conditions. Some are six inches in diameter, others almost two feet.

Native Americans removed the heart by hammering a sharp digging stick into the center of the plant and then prying it out. Don't put your hand into the plant's center, as the recurved spines can give a nasty cut when you remove your hand. Harvesting the heart in this way doesn't usually kill the plant, as it simply forms one or more new hearts. Harvesting may even extend its life by delaying flowering. An alternative method of gathering was to simply cut off all the leaves until you are left with the heart. However this may kill the plant.

Cooking: Native Americans wrapped the heart in its own outer leaves and baked it in a fire pit for 24 - 72 hours. These pits were sometimes twelve feet in diameter and four feet deep. See Camas (*Camassia*) for more on the construction and use of these pits. Baking converts much of the starch into sugar, so the cooked hearts are soft, brown and almost as sweet as molasses. Hearts that weren't eaten immediately would be made into cakes and dried for storage. They also made a drink by mixing them with water, which is probably how *pulque* originated.

If you want to cook the hearts in civilized surroundings, wrap them in aluminum foil, and bake in a 350-degree oven for 10 - 12 hours.

Flower Stems: The young flower stalks are also rich in sugar and were another valuable food for Native Americans. When only a few feet high they are tender and palatable, but if you take them the plant will not set seed and reproduce, so don't do it unless it is very common. You can cook the peeled stem by boiling, or by baking in a fire pit.

Other Foods: The leaves used to protect the baking hearts in the fire pit were also used for food. Their fleshy interiors were either scraped from the leaves and eaten, or simply chewed and their fibers spit out. They have also been boiled for several hours and then mashed to extract their sugar. The resulting liquid was then strained and boiled down to make sweet syrup.

The flowers (parboil if bitter), fruit (often infested with maggots) and seed are also edible. Native Americans dried the cooked flowers stems, hearts, fruits and leaves for later use.

Medicine: The Agaves were not important medicinally, though Native Americans used the sap as an antiseptic wound dressing.

Needle and thread: Native Americans obtained a needle and thread by pounding the pulp from a leaf, to leave the sharp spiny tip and several long tough threads. They removed all but the strongest and longest thread and used it for sewing.

Fiber: Agave leaf fibers are very strong and tough, and have been used for cord, rope, sandals, mats, thatch and bowstrings. The related species (*A. sisalana*) is cultivated to produce the hairy string called sisal. The Aztecs and early Spanish explorers used the outer leaves of some species for paper.

Alcoholic drinks

Agave hearts are used to make the alcoholic drinks pulque, tequila and mescal. The hearts are gathered as they begin to swell prior to flowering (at this time they are full of sugar), and are roasted in a fire pit, crushed in water and then fermented for about a week. The resulting liquid is known as pulque and is drunk like beer. This can then be distilled to make mescal and Tequila.

In the Mexican state of Sonora these drinks are a part of local culture (much as whiskey is in Tennessee and Kentucky) and a lot is produced illegally from wild plants.

Other Uses: The brown juice remaining in the fire pit after baking was used as face paint. A section of a dried leaf was folded in half, frayed at the ends and used as a brush for hair and paint. The flower stems have been used for tent and hut poles and walking sticks. The spiny tips were used as pins and awls.

Cultivation: Agaves can be grown from seed or offsets (known as pups). They prefer well-drained sunny locations and need little care once established. The main threats to the plants are humans and hard frosts.

Horticultural Uses: These striking plants are widely planted as low-maintenance ornamentals in areas with dry summers and mild winters. They are also cultivated commercially for fiber, drugs and to make tequila. They are sometimes planted as spiny fences to deter animal and human intruders. It is not a good idea to plant them too near to paths, or areas of other human activity, as the spiny tips are dangerously sharp.

A characteristic of Agaves is that the primary leaf cluster usually dies after flowering, as it takes so much energy and water to produce fruit. The plant often survives by producing offsets however.

Useful species include:
A. americana
A. desertii
A. utahensis
A. palmerii - **Palmer's Agave**
A. angustifolia
The last two species are prized for making tequila and mescal.

A. murpheyii

This rare species is usually found around the sites of ancient villages, and is probably a Native American cultivar. The flowering plant produces an abundance of pups so is easily propagated. It's too rare to use from the wild, but might be potentially valuable as a new crop for producing food or mescal.

Agropyron repens / Couch Grass

Throughout   *Poaceae*

This European native now grows almost all around the world, and is almost universally despised as one of the worst of all weeds. Its creeping roots spread aggressively and any fragment that breaks off will quickly grow into a new plant. The creeping shoots are incredibly tough and have been known to penetrate boards, tree roots and even road surfaces. If undisturbed for a season a single plant may grow four feet high and spread an inch per day to form a mat ten feet across. Under ideal conditions a two-year-old plant may have a total root length of over 300 miles. No wonder the Anglo-Saxons gave it the name Couch, which means vivacious.

As if its aggression and vigor weren't enough to condemn it, Couch Grass also secretes a substance that inhibits the growth of neighboring plants. This effect that may persist even after the plants are removed.

Roots: You might think eating the plant is going a little too far, the action of one who has done too much weeding, but the nutritious rhizomes have actually been sold in markets in parts of Europe. They contain up to 8% sugar, a form of starch called triticin, and are rich in the minerals iron, potassium and silica.

The roots are gathered while dormant from fall to spring, dried, ground to flour, and mixed with wheat flour for making bread and gruel. Flour could probably be extracted as for Kudzu (see *Pueraria*).

Drink: The roots have been used for tea with lemon and honey, and also roasted as a coffee substitute.

Seed: The seed has been used like that of the related Wheat (*Triticum*).

Medicine: The green juice from the plant has been used as a chlorophyll rich tonic (sick animals instinctively seek it out and chew it). A tea of the roots was used as a diuretic spring tonic, blood purifier, and for kidney and urinary problems such as cystitis and bladder infections.

Animal Food: Couch grass and its relatives are useful as forage plants on very poor soils. The starchy roots are a favorite food of pigs, and these animals have been used to eradicate it from fields. Many birds eat the seeds.

Horticultural Uses: No one who has fought a serious infestation of Couch grass would ever dream of planting it (except in a nightmare perhaps), but the plant does have some horticultural value. It is excellent for stabilizing bare soil and sand dunes, enriches poor soils with humus, and concentrates soil minerals in an easily utilized form.

The genes of *Agropyron* species have been incorporated into cultivated wheat varieties to improve disease resistance. Some species (*A. elongatum, A. intermedium, A. trachosporum, A. repens*) have been crossed with Wheat (*Triticum* sp) to produce perennial grain crops known as Agrotriticums. Some of these have a higher protein content than Wheat, and have produced up to 25 bushels per acre, but their yield gradually declines after the first year.

Eradication: You might feel like giving up when faced with a serious infestation of Couch Grass, but there are ways to remove it. A thick mulch of leaves, carpet, black plastic or cardboard can smother it. Large plants such as Sunflowers or African Marigolds (*Tagetes minuta*) can shade and choke it out, while pigs will happily dig it up and eat it. Several smother crops of Buckwheat may weaken it to the point where it can be removed.

Couch Grass can also be killed by repeated cultivation, the roots being chopped up as they produce new leaves in spring (and consume much of their food reserves). They are then cut again every time they sprout, until they are exhausted and die. Prevent re-infestation of cleared areas by digging a ditch somewhat deeper than the plant roots penetrate.

Related species:
A. acutum
A. junceum
A. pungens - **Coast Wheatgrass**
A. smithii - **Western Wheatgrass**
Use as above.

Akebia quinata / Chocolate Vine

Southeast   Lardizabalaceae

This species was originally introduced to North America as an ornamental, and is naturalized in the southeastern states.

Greens: The new shoots have been used in salads. The dried leaves have been used for tea.

Fruit: The juicy purple fruits are sold in markets in parts of Asia. They contain a tasty pulp that can be eaten fresh (it is often sprinkled with lemon juice) or used to make jelly. This pulp also makes a good drink when mixed with lemon juice.

The Uses Of Wild Plants

Horticultural Uses: This fast growing vine can be used to make an attractive deciduous screen, or to climb on wire fences (or any ugly object you wish to hide). You will need to plant two varieties (for cross-pollination) if you want to get fruit.

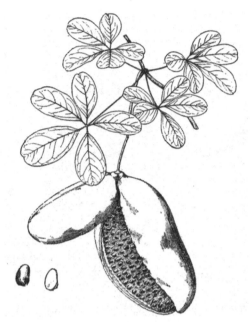

Cultivation: Chocolate Vine can be grown from seed, but more often layering or root cuttings are used. It likes rich soil and full sun. It is very vigorous, often growing 20 feet in a season, and is also fairly hardy.

Alaria esculenta / Kelp

Northeast coast   *Phaeophyta*
This is one of the most commercially important Seaweeds, and is harvested on a large scale for use as fertilizer, food and as a source of alginates.

Caution: When gathering any seaweed make sure the water isn't polluted.

Nutrients: Kelp is very rich in minerals, containing up to thirty different elements. An analysis of this seaweed also shows it to be rich in carbohydrates, but these are in a form that humans have difficulty in assimilating, and at best only 50% is actually digested. Apparently our ability to digest the plant improves if it becomes a regular part of the diet, as the stomach starts producing suitable enzymes. The dried plant is available in tablet form as a natural mineral supplement.

Gathering: This seaweed is always found underwater, so must be gathered by swimming or from a boat. When gathering any seaweed never uproot the whole plant, always leave part of it to regenerate. Sometimes storm cast weed is still good to eat.

Food: This species is very salty, so the dried powdered plant is often used as a salt substitute. It is available in health food stores for this.

The young fronds can be eaten while still tender. In Japan similar species are used in salads, soups, sauces, stir fry, and even tea (under the name wakame). The midribs are also edible raw or cooked. You can reduce their saltiness by soaking in water for a half hour before use (throw this water away).

Algin: The plant is a rich source of algin, and can be used like Irish Moss (*Chondrus*) as a gelatin substitute.

Medicine: Kelp tea is a good tonic and is a cure for most mineral deficiencies (especially iodine). It has also been used to hasten the healing of broken bones. Tibetan mountaineers are said to eat seaweed to combat fatigue, which sounds reasonable until you consider how far the sea is from Tibet.

Animal Food: Kelp was once widely fed to livestock, hence one common name Pig-weed.

Chemicals: The algin in Kelp is widely used by the chemical, food and pharmaceutical industries. See Giant Kelp (*Macrocystis)* for more on this.

Fertilizer: Kelp is an excellent garden fertilizer or green manure, and can often be gathered in quantity from the shore after storms. Gardeners who don't have access to fresh plants can buy dried Kelp powder or liquid seaweed concentrate. Again see *Macrocystis*.

Related Species:
 A. crispa
A. praelonga
A. marginata
A. taeniata
A. nana
Use as above.

Alliaria petiolata / Garlic Mustard

Northeast   Brassicaceae
This hardy member of the Mustard family often persists over the winter. It is a useful wild food because it is one of the first plants to start growing in spring, and so provides fresh greens very early in the year.

The young leaves have a distinctive mild Garlic odor, and add pungency to salads and sandwiches. They can also be used to flavor to soups and sauces. Older leaves and shoots can be used as a potherb until the flowers open, though you may need to change the cooking water once or twice to reduce their bitterness. The seeds can be used like those of Mustard (*Brassica*).

Medicine: The Leaves have been used as a wound poultice.

Cultivation: Garlic Mustard is easily grown from seed in moist soil, and self-sows freely.

Allium species / Wild Garlics, Wild Onions

Throughout   Amaryllidaceae

This genus can be roughly divided into those species that taste like Onion and those that taste like Garlic. Their value as flavoring varies considerably. Some are tasty raw, others are only good cooked, and some are so strongly flavored they can only be used for flavoring.

These are among the most valuable wild food plants for the forager. They are useful for flavoring blander foods, and are easily identified by their characteristic odor.

Caution: Though *Alliums* are very widely eaten throughout the world, they have been known to poison livestock, with symptoms of liver and kidney irritation, jaundice and anemia. No cases of serious human poisoning have occurred, though they can cause stomach upset when eaten in quantity, and may irritate the kidneys. They may also accumulate toxic selenium or nitrates from the soil, so use the green parts cautiously.

It is just about conceivable that you might confuse the bulbs with those of the poisonous Death Camas (*Zigadenus*), so use caution.

These species store their starch in the form of inulin, which is quite indigestible to humans (see Elecampane - *Inula*), and can cause flatulence and indigestion if eaten in quantity.

Rare: Some *Allium* species are quite rare and shouldn't be disturbed. Gather only the commoner species, after positive identification, and only when abundant.

Flavoring: The bulbs, bulblets, flower buds and green tops can be used to flavor wild greens, soups, salads and sandwiches.

Greens: Tender spring foliage can be added to salads. Older foliage is too tough to eat, but can be used as flavoring. Simply remove the tough parts after cooking.

Bulbs: Onion bulbs are at their best while dormant, from fall to early spring, though they may be hard to find at this time. Some bulbs can be uprooted by pulling on the tops, others must be carefully dug as the tops break off easily.

Native Americans roasted the whole bulbs in a fire pit in the same way as Camas (see *Camassia*), and ate the sweet interiors. You can emulate this by wrapping them in aluminum foil and baking in a 350-degree oven, or the ashes of a fire, for 45 minutes. They dried and stored large quantities of bulbs for winter use. The larger bulbs and bulbils can be pickled like cultivated Onions.

Medicine: *Allium* bulbs are antiseptic, and perhaps antibiotic, and have often been used to treat wounds and insect bites. They are also rich in vitamins A and C and have been used to cure scurvy. Cultivated Onions (and perhaps other species) may also help reduce cholesterol and blood pressure levels. Onion tea was once used as a spring tonic to cleanse and rejuvenate the body.

Insect Repellant: It is said that Native Americans used these pungent plants as insect repellants, by simply smearing them on their skin. This may also repel people though.

Animal Food: *Allium* flowers are attractive to bees and other insects.

Cultivation: These beautiful species are relatives of the Lilies, and (like those plants) they are often grown as ornamentals. Generally they prefer a rich moist soil with some sun, and are propagated from seed, bulbils or offsets. Once established they reproduce both vegetatively and by self-sowing.

Useful species include:
A. canadense - Wild Garlic
One of the best flavored *Alliums*, the bulbs were a staple food of some Native American tribes, and were gathered in large quantities for winter use. The leaves can be used as a potherb. Use like cultivated Onion or Garlic.

A. tricoccum - Ramp, Wild Leek
This is probably the best of the wild *Alliums*. It is said to have given its name to the city of Chicago. Apparently the plant was so plentiful there that it scented the air with its distinctive smell. This led Native Americans to name it Shik- ako, which meant "place of Skunks". In parts of the Appalachian Mountains gathering Ramps is an annual spring tradition, and "Ramp feeds" are social events in churches and firehouses.

The tender spring foliage can be eaten until the flowers appear. It can be used to add pungency to salads and soups, or it can be boiled for 5 - 10 minutes as a potherb. The bulbs are good boiled or baked.

A. cernuum - Nodding Wild Onion
A. stellatum - Autumn Wild Onion
The strongly flavored bulbs are good for flavoring, or can be eaten as a vegetable after cooking in a change of water. Lewis and Clark wrote that Native Americans ate them to remedy the flatulence caused by eating baked

Camas bulbs. Both of these species have been cultivated as ornamentals.

A. acuminatum - **Hooker's Onion**
A. drummondii – **Wild Onion**
A. falcifolium - **Wild Garlic**
A. geyerii – **Geyers Onion**
A. obtusum - **Sierra Garlic**
A. textile - **Prairie Onion**
A. validum - **Swamp Onion**
These species can be used like Nodding Wild Onions.

A. perdulce - **Frasers Onion**
This prairie species produces a large sweet bulb, and has been suggested as a potential new crop plant.

A. schoenoprasum - **Wild Chives**
This is the wild form of common garden Chives, though somewhat coarser and more strongly flavored.

A. sibiricum - **Siberian Chives**
Siberian Chives is very similar to Wild Chives, though somewhat larger. Some botanists consider it to be the same species.

A. ampeloprasum - **Wild Leek**
A. vineale - **Field Garlic**
These naturalized European species are common weeds on lawns and waste places. They are too pungent to eat raw, but can be used sparingly as flavoring.

Alnus species / Alders

Throughout   *Betulaceae*
Like their cousins the Birches (*Betula*), the Alders are pioneer trees, able to colonize disturbed ground rapidly. Since the arrival of white people and their disruptive and destructive habits, they have been able to expand their range considerably.

Food: These species are of little value as food, though the inner bark has been eaten in times of famine, and the immature catkins are said to be nutritious, if not very tasty. Apparently the Red Alder (*A. rubra*) has been tapped like Sugar Maple (*Acer*) to produce syrup and drinking water.

Medicine: Alder bark contains as much as 20% tannin, and is used medicinally as an astringent gargle for sore throats. Native Americans used a decoction or poultice of leaves or chewed bark for bruises, burns, wounds and even gangrene. Thoroughly dried and aged bark has been used to treat diarrhea. The fresh bark is emetic.

Wood: Most Alder species are of little importance as lumber because they don't grow big enough. They are used for plywood, fenceposts and pulpwood. Alder wood is durable if kept wet, and is often used for pilings and revetments.

The notable exception to this is the Red Alder, which is the most important commercial hardwood in the northwest. This species is widely used in cabinetmaking.

Fuel: The Alders vary considerably in their value as firewood; some are pretty good while others are poor. They are often widely used for fuel, because they are common, fast growing, and of little commercial value for anything else. Red Alder is the commonest firewood in parts of the Pacific Northwest, and is the wood most often used to smoke salmon in that area. European Alder was once coppiced to make charcoal for fuel and for making gunpowder.

Tooth powder: The dried bark was once mixed with Ginger, Sweet Flag, Bayberry and other herbs, to make a powder for cleaning the teeth.

Cultivation: Alder seed is gathered from the ripe cones in late summer and sown as soon as possible. It can also be stratified at 35 degrees for three months and planted the following spring. The trees may also be grown from suckers, hardwood cuttings or layering. They do well on wet soils, and once established they spread vegetatively.

Alders are able to fix atmospheric nitrogen by means of symbiotic actinomycete bacteria in nodules on their roots, so are valuable pioneer trees. An acre of the trees can add 150 pounds or more of nitrogen to the soil annually, mostly in the form of leaf litter.

The Red Alder is a good companion for Douglas Fir, as it supplies nitrogen to the tree, and helps it to resist attack by a lethal fungus disease (*Poria weirri*).

Horticultural uses: Because of their nitrogen fixing ability Alders are valued for reclaiming damaged land such as mine spoil heaps. They are sometimes planted as nurse trees to protect tender tree seedlings from climactic extremes, and are planted along watercourses to prevent erosion.

European Alder was once coppiced (on a 10 - 20 year rotation) to provide poles for various farm and home uses. It has recently been proposed that Alders be grown in energy plantations, the wood being used for firewood, or processed to produce charcoal, alcohol and wood gas.

Alternanthera philoxeroides / Alligator Weed

Southeast, S. California   *Amaranthaceae*
This vigorous aquatic plant was introduced from tropical America, and is now a serious pest in some warmer

areas. It grows and spreads rapidly, clogging waterways and impeding drainage and navigation.

Greens: Alligator Weed can be eaten as a salad or potherb. Like many members of the *Amaranthaceae* it contains oxalic acid, so should be eaten in moderation and preferably cooked (this removes much of the water soluble oxalates).

Animal food: Alligator Weed has been successfully used as fodder for domestic cattle. The animals will harvest it themselves, even swimming to get it, or it can be harvested and fed to them.

Water purification: Alligator Weed has been used like Water Hyacinth (*Eichornia*) to purify polluted water. It has been estimated that the plants could remove 650 pounds of nitrogen, 170 pounds of phosphorus and 180 pounds of potassium from an acre of water annually. It can also remove toxic heavy metals. The plant isn't as efficient as Water Hyacinth, but tolerates low nutrient levels much better. The abundant foliage can be used like that of *Eichornia* for fertilizer or energy. It can also be used to clean domestic greywater

Althaea officinalis / **Marshmallow**
Northeast   *Malvaceae*
Root: The white roots are rich in sugar, starch and mucilage, and were once toasted or candied to produce the original marshmallows. They can be peeled and eaten

raw in salads, or boiled as a vegetable, but are very slimy and not all that pleasant (frying the cooked roots reduces this quality). The slime can actually be put to use as a soup thickener.

Chewing stick: The clean dried root has been used as a toothbrush.

Medicine

The genus name *Althaea* means to heal and was given because of their importance to herbal medicine. The mucilaginous nature of the plant makes it useful as a soothing poultice or wash for skin problems, wounds and burns. The grated root is especially good and has even been used to treat gangrene. It has been taken internally to treat the entire digestive tract. The whole plant strengthens the immune system.

Other foods: The young leaves, seed pods and flowers are edible, and may be added to salads, used as a potherb, or made into tea.

Cultivation: As the name suggests Marshmallow likes marshes and wet ground. It is usually propagated by division, but seed works well also.

Amaranthus species / Pigweeds
Throughout   *Amaranthaceae*
These common weeds are considered fit only for pigs in this country, yet some species were a staple food crop for Native Americans. They were most widely cultivated in South America, where they became an important grain crop. The conquering Spaniards brutally suppressed its growth and use, considering it a symbol of paganism and native independence.

Amaranth seed has a better amino acid balance than almost any other common vegetable protein, and even contains the lysine and methionine often lacking in plant proteins. It is also rich in vitamins, and the minerals calcium, phosphorus and iron. The leaves are rich in protein, vitamins A and C, calcium and iron. The plant has made a comeback as a crop in recent years. Amaranth cereals and cookies are appearing in health food stores, and the seed can be found in garden catalogs

Caution: The leaves contain oxalic acid, so should be eaten in moderation. One must also be careful about gathering the plant where chemical fertilizers are used, as they may accumulate nitrates and become toxic. Fortunately when used as a potherb most of these toxins are leached out, so they are unlikely to be consumed in dangerous quantities.

Seed gathering: Gather the seed by bending the ripe heads into a bag and rubbing out the dry seeds. For larger quantities collect the whole heads and leave them on a sheet to dry out. When they are completely dry, beat or walk on them to thresh out the shiny black seed, winnow out the chaff and it's ready to use. Native American women used to do all this in one operation. The whole spike was stripped off into the hand, and the chaff was blown away to leave clean seed. If birds were a problem they would tie the ripening flower spikes together.

Seed use: Unlike many wild seeds, those of Pigweed need no preparation except cleaning. However toasting improves its flavor and causes it to pop like popcorn. This can be done in a hot pan in the same way as for popcorn (if it won't pop try sprinkling a little water onto the seed). If you have a large quantity of seed, spread it a half inch deep in a pan, and roast it at 350-degree oven for a half-hour, stirring occasionally.

The popped seed can be added whole to baked goods, ground to flour for baking and gruel, The whole raw seed can be sprouted like alfalfa until about one quarter inch long, and used in salads and sandwiches. It can also be boiled like millet in salt water. Some people soak it in water overnight before cooking.

Greens: The tender young spring leaves and growing tips are good until the flower appear, and may be used in salads, or boiled for 5 - 10 minutes as a potherb. Older leaves may be added to soup, or boiled as a potherb for 20 minutes.

The leaves are a useful addition to green drinks (see Comfrey - *Symphytum).*

Cooked Greens

Probably the best way to cook Pigweed greens is to sauté some onion and garlic in a pan and then add the washed greens. The water sticking to the leaves will be enough to cook them. If you plan to serve these to guests you might want to call them something other than Pigweed, maybe Chinese Spinach.

Medicine: The mildly astringent leaves have been used as a poultice for wounds, insect bites and stings. These wind-pollinated plants often cause hay fever.

Animal food: Wild Pigweeds are an important food source for many wild birds, and have been planted or encouraged to help feed domestic fowl. The foliage is a valuable feed for livestock.

Crop uses: Some *Amaranthus* species are becoming important crop plants once again. They originated in the tropics and use C4 photosynthesis, which makes them more efficient in the high heat and light intensities found there. Consequently they can produce a lot of food in a limited area. Individual seed heads from cultivated plants may weigh up to five pounds each, and the plants may yield up to two pounds of seed per square yard. Not many North American tribes cultivated Amaranths, but they did encourage them to grow nearby by scattering seed in suitable places. If you have the space this is still a good way to grow them. Some cultivated varieties have white seed instead of black.

A number of species are cultivated as warm weather substitutes for spinach. Look for the seeds under the names Tampala, Chinese Spinach or Hinn Choy.

Cultivation: Sow the seed directly in rich soil, after frost danger is past and the soil is warm. Once established they grow like weeds and produce ripe seed heads in 3 - 4 months. They self-sow readily.

Horticultural uses: These species are a mixed lot, with crop plants, ornamentals and weeds all represented. The ornamental species (Love-Lies-Bleeding, Joseph's' Coat) also produce edible leaves and seed. Amaranths are said to be good companions for Carrot, Radish, Pepper, Eggplant, Potato, Corn, Cucumber, Tomato and Onion.

Some species are serious agricultural weeds. They produce an abundance of long-lived (up to forty years) seed and can out-compete almost all crop plants.

Best species include:
A. diacanthus.
A. hybridus - **Green Pigweed**
A. palmeri. - **Palmers Pigweed**
A. powelli - **Powells Pigweed**
A. retroflexus - **Red Root Pigweed**
A. spinosus - **Thorny Pigweed**
A. cruentus - **Purple Amaranth**
A. hypochondriacus - **Princes Feather**
These last two species are sometimes cultivated.

Ambrosia trifida / **Giant Ragweed**
Throughout   *Asteraceae*
Seed: The wind pollinated Ragweeds produce lots of pollen and are notorious for causing late summer hay fever. Sufferers consider them a major pest. The plants also produce an abundance of oily edible seed (they contain almost 20% edible oil), which were a common food for some native peoples. The plants were sometimes cultivated as a seed crop and Native American plant breeders produced varieties with light colored seed, that was four or five times larger than wild seed. These varieties are probably all extinct, but the plant deserves attention for its potential as a crop plant.

Fiber: The stem bast fibers of this tall (up to 15 feet) plant have been used like those of Flax (*Linum*) for cordage and rope.

Animal food: Ragweed seed is an important food for some wild birds.

Garden uses: Grow from seed in rich moist soil. This fast growing annual could be useful as a green manure or compost plant for the garden. This should be cut, or dug into the soil before it sets seed.

Amelanchier species / Juneberries

Throughout   *Rosaceae*
Amelanchier species can be found growing across most of North America under the names Shadbush, Saskatoon berry and Serviceberry. The individual species are sometimes hard to distinguish because they hybridize easily, however no species is poisonous and all are safe to eat. The quality of the fruit varies considerably with climate, season and individuals, so you have to experiment to find the best-flavored berries.

Juneberries often produce wholesome fruit in abundance and are one of the best American wild fruits. Unfortunately this is not always the case. In some areas they are infested with small worms that render them unpalatable, and in other areas they don't produce much fruit.

Saskatoon (*A. alnifolia*) berries were very important to the Blackfoot and other plains tribes, and the harvest was an important annual event. Its primary use was for making a staple food, pemmican, which is a mixture of Buffalo meat, fat and the berries.

Caution: Use the berries in moderation, as excessive consumption may cause diarrhea.

Gathering: For a few days in spring the plants are covered in white blossoms and stand out like beacons. This is the best time to locate them, so you can return in early summer to gather the fruit. In a good location the fruits can quickly be gathered in quantity.

Uses: Though somewhat mealy or seedy, the berries are rich in vitamin C and carbohydrates. They are good raw or cooked, in the same ways as Blueberries, in jelly, pies and muffins. Some people say a little lemon juice improves the flavor of the cooked fruit. They can be preserved by drying like raisins, or by freezing the whole fruits.

Native Americans crushed the berries into flat cakes and dried them for winter use. Often they mixed them with wild grass seeds to make "bread". The Assiniboine made

a delicacy by mixing the fruit with mashed Indian Breadroot (*Psoreala*), The dried fruit was sometimes ground to meal and mixed with wheat flour for baking.

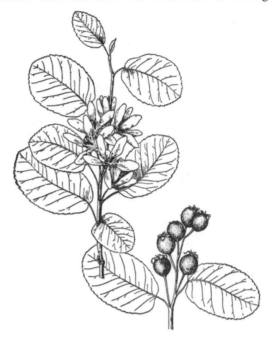

Drink: The berries can be used to make a drink like Manzanita cider (see *Arctostaphylos*). They are sometimes fermented to make wine.

Wood: Native Americans prized the supple shoots for making bows, arrows and spears.

Animal food: The fruit and foliage provide food for a wide variety of creatures. Deer browse on the leaves to an extent that the plant is considered an indicator of their population level. The more the plants in an area are damaged, the higher the population of deer.

Cultivation: *Amelanchier* species could become an important crop for northern areas, and superior cultivars of several species are already available. They are self-fertile, shade tolerant, very hardy and pretty enough to have been grown as spring flowering shrubs or hedges. Propagate by suckers (best), layering, softwood cuttings, division or seed (stratify for three months at 40 degrees). They prefer moist soil.

Species include:
A. arborea - **Downy Serviceberry**.
This is the only species large enough to be considered a tree. The berries are good, but hard to reach when forty feet up in the air. I looked unsuccessfully for Juneberry shrubs for several years in my neighborhood in Connecticut, and finally found one of these trees growing within ten feet of my house. All I ever saw was a smooth gray trunk and the spectacular, but ephemeral, white flowers (they only last a few days) high above.

The Uses Of Wild Plants

***A. alnifolia* – Saskatoonberry, Serviceberry**
This western species can be very productive and several improved cultivars are available.

Amphicarpa bracteata / Hog Peanut
Syn A. monoica
East   *Fabaceae*
The Hog peanut not only produces conventional Pea-like flowers, but also bears flowers like those of the Peanut. These burrow underground after fertilization, and form edible bean-like seeds about a half-inch long.

Gathering: The nutritious underground seeds form in October, and can be dug from fall until the following spring. The plants are relatively easy to locate, even in winter, because the persistent dead vines cling to surrounding vegetation. Under adverse conditions the yield of seed is pretty sparse, but in ideal conditions they produce abundantly, and were a staple of Native Americans.

Wild animals also prize the seed, and some hoard them for winter use (a Vole might hoard a pint of seed). Native Americans often obtained the seeds from rodent nests, believing that the animals were helping their human cousins by gathering the seed. They paid for the seeds by leaving other food in exchange. Not to pay for them was considered stealing.

Preparation: Native Americans removed the seeds from their leathery pods by soaking in a solution of wood ashes for about an hour, or by boiling them. They were then eaten raw, roasted like Peanuts, dried and ground to meal, cooked like beans or added to soup.

Other foods: The small seeds produced by the aboveground flowers are edible, but it's hard to get enough to be worthwhile.

Cultivation: It is said that Hog Peanuts were once cultivated for their seeds in the southeast, and they have potential as a food crop if improved varieties could be produced. They are easily grown from seed in rich soil.

Angelica atropurpurea / *American Angelica*
North and east   *Apiaceae*
This relative of the European Angelica (*A. archangelica*) is found in cooler areas of the northeast and Canada. Both the American and European species were considered magical plants by their respective native peoples. The characteristic odor and flavor of the plants is reminiscent of Juniper berries.

Caution: One must always be very careful about gathering any member of the *Apiaceae*, especially when they are not in flower, as a number of species are extremely poisonous. Young Angelica plants somewhat resemble the lethal Water Hemlocks (*Cicuta* species). Even the Angelicas are by no means completely harmless, in a few susceptible individuals their sap can cause photodermatitis, and they may be toxic if eaten in large amounts.

Greens: The young spring leaves can be used in salads or as flavoring.

Stems: The immature flower stems can be cooked as a vegetable, though you will have to change the cooking water at least once to reduce their strong flavor. The candied, cooked stems of garden Angelica were once a popular confection.

Drink: All parts of the plant can be used to make tea. This is quite good, but should probably be used in moderation. Oil from the seed has been used for flavoring gin and various liqueurs.

Medicine: The American and European species have similar medicinal properties. Angelica tea is carminative, its antiseptic oil inhibits flatulence and aids digestion.

This tea is also a diaphoretic, tonic, expectorant and stomachic. It was once drunk in the belief it could counteract the effect of various poisons, and give protection from diseases such as bubonic plague and malaria. At this point we pass from medicine to magic, as the plants were considered to be a panacea, useful for practically everything.

The Chinese *Angelica sinensis*, known as Dong Quai, is used to treat female complaints such as menstrual problems, and is considered so effective it is sometimes called Women's Ginseng.

The leaves have been used externally as a poultice for wounds, blood poisoning, rheumatism, skin sores and aching muscles. Use caution as they can be irritating if left on the skin for too long.

Other Uses: The aromatic dried leaves have been smoked with other herbs. Leaves and roots are a nice addition to potpourri. Angelica oil is used in perfumes.

Cultivation: Angelica may reach eight feet or more in height when flowering and makes a very striking specimen plant for the garden. Unfortunately it is a biennial and dies after flowering. It is easily grown from seed, though this is very short lived and must be planted as soon as it's ripe.

The plant likes rich, moist, woodland soil, with part shade. It self-seeds prolifically. I planted a single plant from a nursery in my garden in Connecticut and soon had more Angelica seedlings than I had room for. For all I know it's descendants are probably still there.

Related Species: Native Americans ate the spring shoots of a number of western species, but they are hard to identify at this stage, and resemble a number of toxic plants. Unless you can positively identify then they should be avoided.

A. lucida - Wild Celery
As the name suggests this species resembles Celery more than Angelica. The shoots, leaves and peeled young stems were eaten raw or cooked by the Aleuts.

A. tomentosa - California Angelica
A. genuaflexa - Bentleaf Angelica
Use as above.

Apios americana / Groundnut
Syn *A. tuberosa*
East   *Fabaceae*
The unobtrusive Groundnut vine is easily overlooked by the forager, yet its shallow rooted tubers are one of the best wild foods. The tubers measure from 1/2 – 3 inches in diameter and grow in long strings. I first found them accidentally, late one fall while clearing land for a garden. Though I had never seen them before, I immediately recognized them from a description I had once read, saying they resembled a string of pearls.

Groundnut is a close relative of the Soybean (*Glycine*), and was once included in the same genus. Like that plant it is very nutritious, the tubers contain up to 13% protein, as well as large amounts of carbohydrate and minerals. They were one of the wild foods that helped the Pilgrim Fathers (and Mothers) survive their first winter in the New World. They were taught how to use them by Native people, a kindness they repaid in 1654 by passing a law forbidding Native Americans from gathering the roots on "English" land, under penalty of flogging.

Gathering: The tubers are best while dormant from late fall to spring. They are easily located at this time by the masses of pale stringy dead stems that twine around nearby vegetation.

Preparation: The mild flavored tubers are good simply boiled and eaten hot, but can also be baked, roasted or added to soups. They are not good raw, as they leave an unpleasant taste in the mouth. Some people remove the skins (easiest after cooking), but it's not necessary.

Groundnut tubers were a staple food of Native Americans, and large quantities were cooked, peeled and dried for winter use.

Cultivation: Like most members of the *Fabaceae* the Groundnut is able to fix nitrogen by means of bacteria in nodules on the roots, and so enriches the soil it grows in. It can be grown from seed or individual tubers, in rich moist soil. A vigorous climber, it needs support of some kind, even if just nearby woody plants. It can be trained on to trellis as a deciduous screen.

Crop Use. Groundnut has been planted as a food crop, but never achieved any importance because it needs two or three years to produce tubers of useful size and humans are usually in a hurry. It has also been grown for its sweetly scented brown flowers. There has been renewed interest in its cultivation of late, and it could certainly be of value in the semi-wild vegetable garden. Apparently some improved cultivars exist, though they are hard to find.

Related Species:
A. priceana - **Price's Groundnut**
This species produces a single large edible tuber up to six inches in diameter. It is too rare for use as food from the wild, but has potential as a cultivated food crop.

Apium graveolens / **Wild Celery**
Throughout   *Apiaceae*
Yet another Wild Celery, but in this case the name is appropriate, as this is Garden Celery, escaped from cultivation and reverted to its wild ancestral form.

Caution: The familiar Celery smell helps in identification, but be very careful as the *Apiaceae* family contains many poisonous plants. Actually Wild Celery itself is often thought to be poisonous, but it is normally safe for use as flavoring. It may become toxic when growing in heavily fertilized soil, as it can accumulate nitrates from the soil. This is the reason the green tops are rarely eaten (except sparingly).

Flavoring: The stems and leaves are useful in small amounts for flavoring soups, sauces and tea. They are too tough and strongly flavored to be used in salads, unless you have an even tougher palate. Celery seed is often ground to powder for use as a condiment.

Medicine: The plant has been used as a carminative, and as a diuretic to treat kidney ailments.

Cultivation: Wild Celery is cultivated in China for use as flavoring. It is treated like garden Celery, grown from seed in moist soil and part shade.

Apocynum species / **Dogbane, Indian Hemp**
Throughout   *Apocynaceae*
Caution: These species are not edible, as they contain a poisonous cardiac glycoside called apocynamarin. They are included here because they were among the most important fiber plants of Native Americans.

The spring shoots somewhat resemble those of Milkweeds and have caused human poisoning, but this is rare because they taste horrible.

Medicine: Herbalists have used very small amounts of Indian Hemp as a heart stimulant and diuretic. Larger amounts can be lethal however, so it should be left alone.

Fiber: Native Americans gathered the plants for fiber after frost had killed the tops. They stripped the useful bark from the stems, and twisted the tough fibers into cord. This was used for cordage, bowstrings, fishing nets and lines. Finer material can be obtained by treating the bark fibers like those of Flax (*Linum*).

Cultivation: This species can be grown from seed or division. Once established it spreads vegetatively and can become a pest.

Arabis species / **Rock Cress**
North   *Brassicaceae*
The Rock Cresses occur naturally in cool northern and mountain areas. Several species are widely cultivated in gardens and may be found as escapes in unexpected places.

Greens: In cool weather the young plants can be used like Watercress (*Nasturtium*), as a tangy addition to salads, or as a potherb. They are rich in vitamin C. Like most members of the *Brassicaceae* they turn bitter in hot weather.

Perfume: The fragrant flowers of some species have been used in perfumes.

Animal Food: The flowers are a good nectar source for bees and other insects.

Propagation: The Rock Cresses often find their way into rock gardens for their pretty flowers. Propagate by cutting, division or seed, in well-drained soil.

Related Species: No species is poisonous, so any bearing palatable leaves can be used. The best include:
A. alpina
A. lyrata

Aralia species / **Spikenard**
East   *Araliaceae*
These species are closely related to the fabled Ginseng (*Panax*), which was once included in this genus.

Greens: The spring shoots of the Japanese species (*A. cordata*) are a popular vegetable in their native land, and are widely cultivated under the name Udo. They are blanched and used as a potherb, or added to soups and stir-fries. Spikenard can be used in the same ways.

Other Foods: The roots can be used for flavoring food.

Drinks: These species are mostly of interest for their aromatic creeping roots. Their flavor resembles that of Sarsaparilla (*Smilax officinalis*), though they aren't closely related. The chopped root can be steeped in boiling water for 30 minutes to make tea. It was once widely used for making root beer.

Medicine: Root beer was originally a medicinal preparation, taken as a spring tonic to "cleanse the blood", or for rheumatism and gout. It has also been drunk in the belief it would counteract the effects of some types of poisoning, and by pregnant women in the belief they would make delivery easier. It is interesting to compare the modern "root beers'", with their artificial sweeteners and other dubious additives, to the originals. These were a nutritious and tasty mix of various roots including Sassafras, Black Birch, Dandelion, Red Clover and Spikenard.

Native Americans used the root as a poultice for skin diseases, wounds, bone fractures and blood poisoning.

Cultivation: These plants prefer moist, rich, slightly acid, woodland soil with some shade. They can be grown from seed (it helps to scarify this with acid prior to planting), or root cuttings (plant immediately or root over winter in peat moss). Established plants spread vegetatively.

Useful species include:
A. hispida - **Bristly Sarsaparilla**
A. nudicaulis - **Wild Sarsaparilla**
A. racemosa - **Spikenard**
These species can all be used to make root beer.

Aralia spinosa / Devils Walking Stick

This southeastern species reaches to 25 feet in height, and is the only *Aralia* species that grows large enough to be considered a Tree (though it isn't really). Like many plants named after the devil it is covered in spines.

Greens: The spring leaves and shoots can be used as a potherb while young and tender. If the spines are too tough strip them off.

Fruit: Berries are sometimes produced abundantly. These have been cooked and eaten, but some people consider them poisonous, so they are best left alone. They are not very good anyway.

Medicine: The roots have been used medicinally like those of the Spikenard above. Native Americans used it externally and internally for snakebite.

Animal Food: Many birds eat the fruits and consequently bird-sown seedlings are common.

Cultivation: This plant is also known as Angelica Tree, because it produces a single large cluster of flowers at its apex, which rather resembles that of the herb Angelica. It is an unusual and attractive plant when in flower, but its ornamental value is somewhat limited by a menacing armament of sharp spines, and the fact that it isn't very hardy (its hardier Japanese cousin is often found in gardens as an ornamental).

Devils Walking Stick grows best in rich, moist soil and is usually propagated from root cuttings or division. It self sows readily.

Related species:
A. elata - **Japanese Angelica Tree**
This hardy Asian species is planted in gardens in the northeast (and occasionally elsewhere) and often escapes locally. It can be used as above.

Arctium lappa, A. minus / Burdocks

Throughout   Asteraceae
These pioneer species have followed Europeans all around the world, and are well distributed throughout most of North America. They are highly mobile because of their efficient seed dispersal mechanism, hooked seed capsules (burs) that cling to anything that passes by, whether furred, feathered or clothed. The burrs and the Dock-like leaves are responsible for the common name.

Food: Though often despised as weeds, the Burdocks are exceptional wild food plants. They provide a variety of nutritious and tasty foods, are rugged and hardy, can be used without guilt (they are persistent weeds) and don't resemble any dangerous plants.

Root gathering: The most important food from the Burdock is the root. In Japan these are so highly regarded that they are commonly cultivated as a crop. The plants are biennial, and only roots from first year plants are useful for food. These are quite easy to find, simply search for old dead plants that have flowered and then look nearby for the new rosettes. The roots are best gathered in mid summer, when they first reach a useful size (perhaps a foot long and a half inch in diameter). They grow much larger than this (3 - 4 feet), but these are often too woody to be palatable. The interior of older roots can still be useful, but aren't as good.

Collecting Burdock root isn't easy, as they are very well anchored. You can't just pull on the top to uproot it, as it will simply break off. You have to dig carefully and deeply to get unbroken roots.

Root preparation: The root is usually prepared by scraping off the tough outer skin, then chopping crosswise into very thin discs. It can then be eaten raw in salads, baked or boiled. If the flavor is too strong, boil for 10 minutes with baking soda, then change the cooking water and boil a further 10 minutes. In an emergency you can simply split the root lengthwise and eat the interior raw.

In Europe the roots were mixed with Dandelion root and other herbs to make a kind of root beer. They were also roasted as a coffee substitute.

Leaves: The very first spring leaves can be used as a salad, or potherb, as long as they are tender, but they aren't very good. I sometimes add a few of the smaller leaves to a green blender drink (See *Symphytum*).

Flower Stalk: Perhaps the best food produced by the Burdock is the immature flower stalk. The bitter skin is peeled off, and the tender interior is eaten raw in salads, or cooked as a vegetable.

Seed: Apparently the seed can be removed from the ripe burrs and sprouted like Alfalfa.

Medicine: Burdock root has a long history of medicinal use, and was mentioned in the first modern English herbal, "The Leach book of Bald", which was written by Bald the monk in the 10th century. He recommended a poultice of the leaves for gout, rheumatism, sore joints, old wounds and leprosy. Consistently enough the plant is still used for these ailments, though the root is generally preferred.

The plant is most highly valued as a blood purifier, but can also be used as a diuretic, diaphoretic and laxative. The leaves, stems and roots can be blended in water as a drink, which can reduce blood sugar levels if taken regularly.

A poultice or lotion of leaves or roots can be used on burns, sprains, wounds and skin complaints such as ringworm and acne.

Hair Treatment: A strong decoction of the leaves was thought to be beneficial for the hair and scalp.

Garden Uses: Burdock is a beneficial plant for the soil, as its deeply penetrating roots aerate and break up compacted ground, and extract nutrients from the subsoil. It is sometimes accused of depleting the soil of minerals, but such a statement is of dubious logic - obviously if left alone it will die and release those minerals back into the same soil in an easily useable form. It is the person who removes the plant that robs the soil.

Cultivation: In Japan there are a number of cultivated varieties of *A. lappa*, with large, mild flavored roots, yet

which retain much of their wild vigor. They are easily grown from seed, soaked overnight and planted in rich sunny soil. Once established they are little bothered by pests, and are pretty much independent of the gardener, especially if mulched to conserve moisture. Their only drawback is that they take up a lot of space for a long time. For this reason they are best grown in a semi-wild state, away from intensive vegetable or ornamental gardens (forest gardens or orchards are ideal).

Arctostaphylos uva ursi / **Bearberry**
North and Mountains   Ericaceae
This low mat-like shrub is a common sight in cool forests all around the temperate Northern Hemisphere.

Fruit: The abundant, dry, red berries stay on the plants well into winter, and Native Americans often ate them when other food was short. They are rich in carbohydrates and vitamin C, but are also rather astringent, and not particularly tasty when raw. The berries get sweeter when cooked, and are probably best mixed with tastier fruit, or boiled with a little milk (to reduce their astringency) and honey (to add sweetness). They can be used in pies and preserves and even fried.

Drink: The fruits can be boiled briefly for tea, or made into a drink like Manzanita cider (see Manzanita below). The leaves have occasionally been used for tea, but have strong medicinal properties so should be used in moderation.

Medicine: Bearberry leaves contain arbutin, the same chemical that gives the Cranberry (*Vaccinium*) its medicinal properties. Arbutin (also called ursin) passes through the kidneys unchanged, and reacts with the urine to form a potent antiseptic (as a side effect it may turn the urine green). It is also diuretic, so Bearberry leaf tea is a useful treatment for urinary infections such as cystitis. They were once in the USP as an astringent and diuretic. Other chemicals in Bearberry tea may cause nausea, and central nervous system depression, so use in moderation. The berries have been used to treat scurvy.

Fuel: The dry woody stems were commonly used as fuel in the arctic, where trees are scarce.

Cultivation: Bearberry can be grown from seed, but this is rather slow, so layering or cuttings (rooted over winter in damp sand) are usually used. It prefers acid soils, and sun or part shade.

Smoking

Native Americans so frequently smoked Bearberry leaves (alone or with other herbs such as Osier Dogwood - *Cornus*), that the plant became known as Kinnick-Kinnick, which translates as "that which is smoked".

For smoking the leaves are best gathered in summer, but they can be gathered year round in an 'emergency' (I can't imagine what that might be, but then I don't smoke). They are stripped of their woody stems and sun dried before use. Native Americans sometimes leached them in water to reduce their bitterness before drying. It has been said that retaining the smoke for a few seconds can bring about intoxication, as can smoking Bearberry and drinking alcohol at the same time. Probably neither of these practices is a good idea, as the plant is known to cause central nervous system depression.

Garden Uses: Bearberry is sometimes grown as an evergreen groundcover, or to attract birds, bees and other wildlife. Established plants form a thick dense mat that is good for preventing erosion.

Related species include:
A. Alpina - **Alpine Bearberry**.
Use as above. Its fruits are juicier and better flavored, but cooking still improves them.

A. Rubra - **Alpine Red Bearberry**
Use as above

Arctostaphylos species / Manzanita
West   *Ericaceae*

These western cousins of the Bearberries may grow as small trees, shrubs or prostrate groundcovers (some even hybridize with Bearberry). The name Manzanita means little Apple in Spanish, though they resemble tiny Apples in appearance only, not in taste.

Fruit: Manzanita berries ripen in late summer and hang on to the shrubs well into winter. They are dry and not particularly tasty, but were widely eaten by Native Americans because they are often abundant and are somewhat nutritious (they contain up to 20% sugar). In some cases they were important enough that each family of a tribe had their own grove of plants. They ground the dried berries to meal, for cooking into gruel, or to mix with flour for baking. The berries can be cooked like Bearberries in pies and preserves.

Drinks: While backpacking I will sometimes add the berries to water I am boiling for purification. When no water is available at all, you can suck the berries to keep your mouth moist. The green berries have been used for tea.

Medicine: A wash, or poultice, of the leaves has been used for Poison Oak rash.

Manzanita Cider

The best-known use of Manzanita berries is to prepare "Manzanita cider". This lemonade-like drink is made by simmering the cleaned berries for 15 minutes in an equal volume of water. The cooked fruit is then crushed (or put in a blender) and the brew left to steep for 24 hours (or until it reaches the desired strength). This is then strained and served.

An even better drink is made from the berry pulp with the seeds removed, though this takes a lot more work.

Smoking: The leaves were occasionally smoked like those of Bearberry.

Wood: Manzanita wood is so hard that nails can't easily be driven into it, and in fact it has been used to make wooden nails. It is finely grained and polishes well, so is prized by cabinetmakers, turners and carvers. It is of little commercial importance however, because the plants are rarely of sufficient size. Most wood goes for tourist trinkets or firewood (it's excellent for this).

Animal Food: The berries provide food for many forms of wildlife. The flowers are among the first to appear in late winter, and are an important source of food for bees (the shrubs are often alive with bees at this time).

Cultivation: Manzanita is an attractive ornamental shrub, though it can be a fire hazard in dry areas. Watching it burn can be quite awesome, as it explodes into flame and burns with black oily smoke. This is an adaptation to its fire prone habitat, and ensures the above ground parts burn away quickly, before sufficient heat is generated to damage the roots. The roots bind the soil and prevent erosion after bush fires have stripped off all surface vegetation. Fire is actually beneficial to the plants, and rejuvenates them by forcing them to sprout vigorous new growth. It also aids in the germination of the seed and reduces competition from trees, which would otherwise shade them out.

Manzanita can be propagated from seed or cuttings, but neither method is easy. The seed should be scarified with acid or boiling water, or you might try covering them with a layer of Pine needles, and setting them on fire, to simulate a bush fire.

Useful species include:
A. columbiana – **Columbia Manzanita**
A. glauca - **Great Berried Manzanita** (probably the best flavored species).

A. nevadensis - **Dwarf Manzanita**
A. patula - **Green Leaved Manzanita**
A. tomentosa - **Shaggy Bark Manzanita**

Arisaema triphyllum / Jack-In-The-Pulpit

East   *Araceae*

Caution: All parts of Jack-In-The-Pulpit are intensely acrid, due to tiny sharp crystals called raphides. These cause irritation and swelling of mucous membranes, and if eaten in sufficient quantity they could block the throat and cause death by asphyxiation.

Preparation: Though dangerously acrid when raw, the swollen starchy roots can be eaten if carefully prepared. Unlike many common toxins, the raphides are unaffected by heat so simply cooking them doesn't make them edible. It is sometimes said that Native Americans made the root edible by baking for several days in a fire pit, but this is incorrect. The roots can only be rendered edible by prolonged drying, which is done by slicing them thinly (like Potato chips) and leaving in a warm dry place for about six months. After this time they should be edible and very palatable. If they are still acrid after this time, leave even longer.

Uses: The dried sliced roots can be eaten as a snack like potato chips. They can also be ground to flour and mixed with an equal amount of wheat flour for use in baking.

Other Uses: The roots of a closely related European species were once cultivated as a commercial source of laundry starch. However it was very irritating to the skin and so this use was eventually abandoned.

Cultivation: This handsome plant is one of the most popular ornamentals for wild gardens in the east. It is easily grown from seed or cormlets (detach from the main plant), planted in a shady woodland soil, that is rich in humus, moist and slightly acid. Once established it self-sows readily, and was practically a weed in my garden in Connecticut.

Armoracia rusticana / Horseradish

Throughout   *Brassicaceae*

The Horseradish plant resembles a Broadleaf Dock (*Rumex*) in appearance, but is easily identified by the unmistakable pungency of its root. Though not native to North America it is widely cultivated, and is often found in waste places as an escape or relic of cultivation. The wild plant is essentially identical to the cultivated kind.

Interestingly an intact Horseradish root has no pungency at all, the acrid oil that gives it its characteristic flavor only appears when the root is damaged. Damage (such as grating) ruptures the cell walls, allowing an enzyme to react with a glycoside to form Mustard oil (allyl isothiocyanate). Put simply this means this bland root quickly develops enough pungency to take your breath away (literally). Like most plants that produce mustard oil, Horseradish irritates the kidneys and mucous membranes, and is toxic to some degree. However it is hard to eat enough to have any serious deleterious effect.

Gathering: The roots can be dug almost any time of year, though they are at their best while dormant, from late fall until new growth appears in early spring. In loose soil the roots of older plants may grow three feet in length, though smaller roots are of better quality for food. They should be dug from the ground carefully as they are brittle and break easily. This is especially important if you are trying to eradicate the plant, as any fragments remaining in the ground will sprout and form new plants. The tiniest rootlets left a foot deep, upside down, have a way of turning into new plants so you can easily end up with ten plants instead of one.

In mild areas the roots may be gathered as needed through the winter. Where the ground freezes you should dig all you need in late fall, and store over the winter in wet sand.

Uses: Horseradish is an acquired taste. A bite of the raw root may be the hottest thing you have ever experienced and this extreme pungency limits its use as food. It is far from insignificant however, as it is used to make the famous Horseradish sauce, as well as salad dressings. Try making "Horseradish Bread" instead of garlic bread.

If you dislike the pungency of the raw root, try cooking it. This destroys the acrid oil, leaving a relatively bland root vegetable. This is a nice addition to soup.

Leaves: The tender, new spring leaves can be added to salads, or cooked with other greens as a potherb. These are so good that the roots have actually been forced indoors like Chicory (*Cicorium*) to provide winter greens.

Horseradish Sauce

The easiest way to make Horseradish sauce is to puree the root in a blender with enough wine vinegar to form a paste. You can grate the root by hand, but you will probably have to do it outside to minimize fume inhalation. Season the grated root with salt and sugar. It will store for up to a month in the refrigerator. For a more elaborate recipe add cream, yogurt, mustard, pepper and / or lemon juice.

Medicine: The whole plant is said to contain an antibiotic. The grated root has been used as a rubefacient, poultice to treat frostbite, rheumatism and muscle pain. Care must be taken however, as the acrid root can irritate the skin if left on for too long. Keep the poultice on the skin only until it starts to feel hot, and then remove it.

A simple treatment to eliminate mucous in coughs and catarrh is to grate the root into a bowl, mix with honey and let it stand overnight. The following day drain off the syrup from the bottom of the bowl and take one teaspoon three times daily. Alternatively you can soak the grated root in honey for a few hours and then eat it.

The root is said to aid indigestion, and this is probably how Horseradish sauce originated.

Tooth Cleaner: I have read that the roots were once chewed to clean the teeth, though I have yet to meet anyone who could actually chew it for that long.

Cultivation: Horseradish doesn't usually set seed, so it is propagated vegetatively. This is very easy, as any fragment of root will grow into a new plant. Usually when a field is dug, small roots are trimmed from the large roots and re-planted, while the large roots are sold. It will grow under almost any conditions, but prefers a deep, rich, moist soil with full sun and a fairly cool climate. Mulching is helpful to keep down weeds and hold in moisture, but the plant hardly needs any encouragement.

The biggest problem with Horseradish is that it is very persistent once established, and not easy to remove. It isn't an invasive plant, but any fragment of root spread around inadvertently will grow, so it often pops up in unexpected places. The simplest solution to this problem is to plant it in a remote place where it can be left to do as it will. You can also confine it in some kind of container. The latter also makes harvesting easy, simply dig up the container and dump it out on the ground.

Horticultural Use: Horseradish is supposed to be a traditional garden companion for Potato (it is said to deter the Potato blister beetle, and benefit from the presence of Potato). However planting them together doesn't seem like a very good idea, as in digging up the potatoes you would inevitably chop up the roots and spread them around.

Aronia species / Chokeberries
Syn *Pyrus* spp
East *Rosaceae*

Chokeberries are sometimes confused with the Juneberries (*Amelanchier*), but can be distinguished by the tiny hair-like glands on top of their leaf midribs. The various species hybridize readily, so precise identification may be difficult.

Caution: The fruits of some *Aronia* species may not be edible raw, as they contain cyanogenic glycosides.

Fruit: The berries are available for quite a long time in summer. The common name comes from trying to eat them raw, in which case they are not usually very good. They are much better when cooked and sweetened in pies and sauces (add a little milk to reduce their astringency). They are rich in pectin (and vitamin C) and are good for preserves, alone or with other fruit. Native Americans prepared a snack by toasting the berries over hot coals.

Drink: The juice of the Black Chokeberry is now available commercially as an alternative to Cranberry juice. The berries can also be used to prepare a drink like Manzanita cider (see *Arctostaphylos*).

Horticultural Uses: With their flowers, berries and colorful fall foliage, the Chokeberries are attractive ornamentals for natural landscaping.

Cultivation: The Black Chokeberry is nutritious, self-fertile and extremely productive. It has been widely cultivated in Eastern Europe and a number of superior cultivars have been developed. It is now grown in North America as well, both commercially and as a home garden fruit.

Propagate these shrubs from seed (stratify for three months at 35 degrees and it should germinate promptly), division, semi ripe cuttings or suckers (detach with a piece of root and transplant). They like moist woodland soil, will grow in part shade, and once established spread vegetatively to form dense colonies.

Best species include:
A. arbutifolia - **Red Chokeberry**
*A. melanoc**arpa** - **Black Chokeberry**
A. floribunda - **Purple Chokeberry** (this may be a hybrid of the other two).

Artemisia tridentata / **Big Sagebrush**
West   *Asteraceae*
Sagebrush is very common in the west, and after rainstorms the desert is often scented with its characteristic sweet perfume. This is one of the largest of the Sage species, and in ideal conditions may reach 15 feet in height.

In recent years Sagebrush has proliferated on overgrazed rangeland, as it is bitter and unpalatable to most domestic livestock, so is ignored while more palatable competing plants are eliminated. We blame the plants of course and poison them with herbicides, or rip them out with tractors, rather than controlling our livestock and our greed. Sagebrush was a vital plant to Native Americans, and supplied them with many of the necessities of life.

Food: These plants have the characteristic bitter aromatic flavor of the *Artemisia* genus, but have occasionally been used as culinary herbs. The dried plants are sometimes burned on barbecues to add flavor.

They have also been used to flavor tea, beer and other alcoholic drinks. Native Americans made gruel from the seed of several species, notably the Sweet Sage (*A. dracunculoides*).

Medicine: Sagebrush leaf tea is said to aid digestion and relieve flatulence. The leaves of the California Sagebrush (*A. californica*) were used by Native American women to promote menstruation, and to aid in childbirth.

Native Americans used the leaves as a poultice or antiseptic wash, for wounds, insect bites and sore muscles. The dried dead leaves that cling to the plants were crushed and used as baby powder. This was also used for skin rashes in adults.

Repellants: Native Americans stored the aromatic leaves with food to repel insects, and burned them in campfires for the same purpose. They also occasionally smoked them.

Other Uses: The whole plants were used for thatch and to build the walls of temporary shelters. The stems are useful as fuel, and burn well even when green.

Toiletries: The leaves were used as toilet paper, menstrual pads and deodorants.

Incense
The aromatic leaves were burned in sweat lodges, and as purifying incense on ceremonial occasions. They have recently enjoyed a resurgence in popularity, and bundles of dried plants are widely available in New Age stores.

Fiber: Sage bark was an important source of fiber for Native Americans. They peeled strips from the larger shrubs, rubbed off the woody parts, and used the soft fibers for bedding, insulation, mats, cordage, baskets, robes and sandals.

Animal Food: Sagebrush is eaten by numerous wild creatures, and provides shelter for many more.

Cultivation: The plant prefers deep, non-saline soil, so the first European settlers often planted vegetable gardens where the plants grew well. Their dense brush is useful for preventing erosion, though like Wormwood they may inhibit the growth of neighboring plants. They do this by exuding a volatile toxin which keeps neighboring plants away by as much as six feet (interestingly fire destroys this effect in the soil).

Sagebrush is grown from ripe seed, sown in moist soil, though it can be hard to get good germination. It is very drought tolerant.

Garden Uses: Native Americans used a tea of the leaves as a garden insect repellant. An alcohol extract from the plant has been found to deter Colorado Potato Beetles from feeding on Potatoes.

Related species:
A. californica - **California Sagebrush**
A. frigidus - **Mountain Sagebrush**
A. ludoviciana - **White Sage**
Use as above.

A. dracunculoides - **Sweet Sage**
This sweet scented species somewhat resembles the garden herb Tarragon (*A. dracunculus*), and can be used as flavoring in the same ways.

A. absinthium / Wormwood

Wormwood is native to Eurasia, but very widely naturalized in waste places across North America. It has been used as a culinary flavoring for over 4000 years, which is rather surprising when you consider that it has an intensely bitter taste, and contains a toxic oil called thujone (which has potent medicinal properties).

Medicine - As the common name suggests, Wormwood was once commonly used as a vermifuge, to rid the body of internal parasites, but it isn't very pleasant or safe, and shouldn't be taken internally in medicinal quantities. It has also been used as a diaphoretic, a stomachic and a bitter tonic to stimulate the appetite (liqueurs such as vermouth are intended as aperitifs).

French soldiers in Algeria drank Absinthe to prevent malaria, and it does actually have some beneficial effect. Interestingly a related Chinese species *A. annua* is the source of one of the most important new anti-malaria drugs.

It has been used externally as an antiseptic wash, or poultice, for wounds, burns, skin sores, sprains, insect bites and to kill parasites.

Absinthe

Wormwood was once used for flavoring the potent liqueur absinthe. This is made by macerating Wormwood leaves in alcohol, with Fennel, Angelica, Calamus and other herbs. It is said to have been invented in Switzerland by a Dr Pierre Ordinaire as a medicinal elixir for treating stomach ailments.

The ingenious doctor created a unique drink (the original pre-ban absinthe is said to be one of the most extraordinary alcoholic beverages ever created) and it soon became popular as a recreational drink. Unlike most alcoholic drinks, which dull the mind, good absinthe is said to leave the mind clear and alert. Perhaps this is why it was so beloved by bohemian artists and poets, such as Rimbaud, Baudelaire, Picasso and Van Gogh.

Absinthe eventually gained the kind of notoriety today associated with drugs like heroin or cocaine. It was once called "madness in a bottle" and was accused of causing mental deterioration, hallucinations, convulsions, brain damage and moral depravity. Thujone from the Wormwood was said to be the problem, and it was eventually banned in most countries. In reality the amount of thujone in absinthe is very small, and is not a problem in any way. Absinthe is actually no more toxic than other drinks with a high alcohol content.

Due to changes in E.U. regulations absinthe is no longer illegal in Europe, and is being made there once again (though not as well as it was). It is still banned in the United States.

Other Uses - A strong decoction of the tops and leaves has been used as a hair rinse, a disinfectant, in herbal baths, and as an insecticidal wash to kill fleas on animals. The dried plant is used in potpourri, sweat lodges, as a strewing herb. It was once stored with food and clothing to repel insects (and evil spirits).

Cultivation - Wormwood is grown from root division or seed. It thrives in poor soils, and secretes absinthin which inhibits the growth of some neighboring plants. Gardeners have used a tea of the tops as a repellant for Carrot flies, slugs, aphids, cabbage worms and flies. It is sometimes planted as a border around the garden, though it should be confined to prevent it wandering.

A. vulgaris / Mugwort

This species lacks the toxic oil found in Wormwood, but is still very bitter. It is slightly better as flavoring than Wormwood and is more commonly used, but it could hardly be described as good. It has been used in soups, sauces and egg dishes. It was once a popular flavoring for beer, which is why it received the name Mugwort.

Mugwort is important to Chinese herbalists, as it is used in moxibustion, a therapy related to acupuncture.

A. douglasiana – Western Mugwort
This native western species can be used like Mugwort.

Arundinaria gigantea ssp. gigantea / Giant Cane

Southeast   Poaceae

This fast growing grass (divided into two sub-species) is the only native North American Bamboo. It is found in moist, fertile soils, usually near water, and in ideal conditions may grow up to 30 feet in height. It used to form large colonies known as canebrakes, which often covered thousands of acres and were a unique wildlife habitat. These have largely disappeared, as settlers considered them to be an indicator of fertile soil.

Though largely ignored in this country the Bamboos have many potential uses, as their importance in Asia shows. Bamboos have been called nature's greatest gift to uncivilized humans, and they can be useful to civilized ones as well.

Shoots: The young spring shoots of Large Cane are quite palatable, but are only available for a short time in spring. They are gathered just before they break through the earth's surface, as exposure to light makes them tough and unpleasant. In Asia experienced gatherers often walk barefoot in the groves and feel for the bumps caused by the shoots. Judicious harvesting doesn't harm the plants, and crowded stands may actually benefit from thinning.

The raw shoots contain hydrocyanic acid so are not edible, but this is easily removed by cooking the peeled and sliced shoots in a change of water. The cooked shoots can be added to stir fries and soups.

Seed: Like most Bamboos, Giant Cane doesn't set seed regularly, but every so often all of the plants in an area will flower, set seed, and then die. The plants will be replaced by new seedlings, but the process takes a few years. This seed is edible and nutritious, and can be prepared and used like Wild-Rice (*Zizania*).

Paper: Bamboo can be used to make paper in the same way as wood and is equally good. This is a very efficient way to produce paper, as the fast growing grasses produce up to six times as much cellulose per acre as trees. They have also been used to make wallboard and rayon (see *Picea*).

Bamboo Canes

In Asia these are a major source of raw materials, and almost every prosperous farm or village has it's own grove. The strong, light culms (stems) have been used for almost all of the essentials of life: building materials, water pipes, ladders, rafts, curtains, scaffolding, bridges, roof trusses, roofing tiles, furniture, fenceposts, musical instruments, food containers, weapons, screens, tent poles, supports of various kinds, pipes, fishing poles, nails, pins, concrete reinforcement, mats and anything requiring a long, straight pole. I have even seen a bicycle with a bamboo frame. The split strands can be twisted into strong ropes and cables of indefinite length. Native American Bamboos could be used for many of these same purposes.

Baskets: The split culms can be used for weaving baskets, mats, panels and fences.

Ply-Bamboo: The culms are split, flattened and glued together in alternating layers to form strong panels for use in construction and cabinetmaking. They have even been used experimentally for aircraft construction.

In recent years laminated Bamboo flooring has become widely accepted, as an attractive and ecologically sound, flooring material.

Animal food: In this country Large Cane is most often used as animal forage, and is said to be as good as other grasses. This is a very unimaginative use however, rather like using Black Walnut burl for firewood. The grazing of livestock was one of the main factors in reducing the acreage covered by these plants to a fraction of what it once was.

Gathering: Canes which die naturally are brittle and of little use for most purposes. The culms must be harvested when fully mature, but not old, three to four year old culms are usually best. They are cut at ground level, stripped of their thin branches and leaves (these can be fed to animals) and left to dry for about six months. Recent research has found that if the leaves are left on during this period, nutrients will drain from the culms, making them less attractive to insects and rot causing fungi. Leaching in water for several weeks has the same effect of making them more durable.

Horticultural uses: Even if Bamboos had no practical applications at all, they would be well worth planting for their uniquely exotic appearance. When you consider their multitude of uses, it becomes obvious that anyone planting an attractive and productive landscape should include some species (a number of exotic species are hardy enough for northern states).

Living Bamboos make an excellent screen or windbreak, and can help to prevent erosion on steep slopes and stream banks. Some species spread vigorously by means of creeping roots and are often considered a serious pest. Their uncontrolled spread can be prevented by planting inside a barrier, eating the shoots, stomping on the new shoots as they appear, or by repeated mowing around the grove. Of course the canes are an invaluable aid to gardeners as material for trellises and stakes. Bamboo fences of whole or split Bamboo are a fixture in many Japanese gardens, and their creation is a unique vernacular art form.

The foliage can be used as a mulch or compost material.

Cultivation: Bamboos are propagated vegetatively, by division or root cuttings. They are rarely grown from seed, as the plants don't produce it very often. For fastest growth they need rich, moist, well-drained soil and sunny stream banks are a favorite habitat. For maximum production you should fertilize regularly, especially if you cut a lot of shoots and canes. A healthy stand of Cane is very vigorous and even if all culms are cut at one time they will quickly regenerate. For a more sustained harvest a quarter or a fifth of the culms should be cut on an annual rotation.

Related species:

A. gigantea ssp. *tecta* - **Small Cane**
This species is a more reliable seed producer than the above, and bears regularly every 3 - 5 years. It is used in many of the same ways as above, though it is much smaller, only growing to about 6 feet. A number of other Bamboos may be found as escapes from cultivation. These may be used in the same ways.

Arundo donax / Giant Reed

South & west   *Poaceae*
Also known as Carrizo, this large grass was introduced to North America as an ornamental, and is now widely naturalized in warmer areas.

Shoots: Use the new spring shoots like those of the Giant cane (*Arundinaria*).

Seed: The tasty seeds are nutritious, but aren't produced regularly. Prepare and use like that of Wild-Rice (*Zizania*).

Root: It is said that the root is edible raw or cooked, but I haven't tried it.

Other Uses: This close relative of Reed (*Phragmites*) can be used like that plant for fiber, construction, baskets, mats, boats, fences, paper and wallboard.

Horticultural Uses: Growing up to 20 feet in height, the Giant Reed is a very imposing landscape plant. It is an excellent garden screen and windbreak, provides food and shelter for wildlife, and can be used to control erosion along waterways. The long canes can be used as supports for other plants. A potential problem in dry areas is that it can be a fire hazard.

Cultivation: Propagate from seed or division. It prefers moist soils, such as ditches and stream banks.

Asarum canadense / Wild Ginger

East   *Aristolachiaceae*
Wild Ginger is common in many areas, but low growing and inconspicuous. It is not closely related to culinary Ginger (*Zingiber officinale*), but its roots have a similar warm, aromatic flavor. This is due to an aromatic oil called asarone, which is toxic if consumed in quantity (see *Acorus*), so the plant should be used with caution. Digging the root kills the plant, so it shouldn't be used unless very common. You could try to take some root, without uprooting the whole plant.

Flavoring: The crisp, spicy roots can be used as a Ginger substitute, for baking, sauces, confectionery and tea. They are best gathered when dormant, but can be used year round. The related evergreen species are even easy to find in winter. They may be dried for later use.

Wild Ginger Tea
Simmer a 3 – 5 inch piece of cleaned chopped root in a cup of water for 10 minutes. Add sugar and lemon to taste.

Medicine: Wild Ginger has been used for heart, tooth and ear pains. More recently it was in the USP as a stomachic, carminative and tonic. Native Americans used the root of some *Asarum* species as a contraceptive, and to promote menstruation.

Tooth Care: The dried root was once added to commercial tooth powders.

Perfume: Oil from the plant is used in perfumes. The dried roots have been used to scent bedding.

Cultivation: This plant is easily grown from seed, or root division, in rich woodland soil with part shade. It is an attractive addition to wild gardens. It spreads by means of creeping rhizomes and can form a dense groundcover.

Related species: Some *Asarum* species are so rare they are protected by law and must never be used. Useful common species include:

A. arifolium
A. caudatum - Long Tailed Wild Ginger
A. hartwegii - Hartweg's Wild Ginger
A. lemmonii - Lemmon's Wild Ginger
Use as above.

Asclepias syriaca / Milkweed

East   *Asclepiadaceae*

This familiar weed of waste places, fields and urban areas, contains a milky juice that is responsible for the common name Milkweed. It is also responsible for the bitter flavor that pervades all parts of the plant. This can be removed by careful preparation, and then the plant is considered to be among the very best wild foods.

Caution: All Milkweeds contain toxins, and some species have actually poisoned livestock. In the case of this species, cooking eliminates the toxins, and the plant provides a number of useful foods. However you should be quite sure of your identification before eating any *Asclepias* species and cook it thoroughly (never eat any part raw). Also don't confuse them with the somewhat similar, but poisonous, Dogbanes (*Apocynum*).

Preparation: All parts of the plant are bitter, and must be cooked in at least one change of water to make them palatable. The usual method is to drop them in boiling water and simmer for a couple of minutes, drain, add fresh boiling water and again simmer for a minute or two. Then drain again, add more boiling water and simmer for 15 minutes until cooked. Most of the bitter principle remains in the first two lots of water. Never put Milkweed in cold water and bring to the boil, as this fixes the bitterness in the plant.

Never add any Milkweed parts to a recipe without first treating them in this way, otherwise they will impart a bitterness that will make it unusable.

Shoots: The tender spring shoots are used when 4 – 8 inches high. They have few identifying features at this time, so one must be careful not to confuse them with inedible, or toxic, plants (such as Dogbane - *Apocynum*). Gathering a single crop of shoots doesn't harm the plants, as they will simply produce more.

The cooked shoots may be used like Asparagus, added to soup or fried in tempura batter.

Leaves: The young leaves can be gathered from the top of the plant until the flowers appear and prepared as above. They contain asclepsin, an enzyme that tenderizes protein in the same manner as papain.

Flowers: The unopened flower buds are quite good when cooked as above.

Milkweed Pods

The immature seedpods are probably the best Milkweed food. They are gathered when firm, and only a couple of inches long, and cooked as described above. They are mucilaginous (slimy) like Okra pods, and can be used in much the same ways; as a vegetable, in tempura and to thicken soups and sauces.

Medicine: Milkweed roots contain a glycoside called asclepiadine, which has an effect on the heart similar to that of Digitalis. This is too dangerous for amateur use however, and should only be used with expert guidance. The root is actually quite toxic, and was used by Native Americans to induce temporary sterility. They chewed the stems of some species as an emetic (e.g. *A. subulata*).

The milky juice was said to be antiseptic and was used as a wound dressing by Native Americans. They also used it to remove warts.

Rubber: The milky white latex found in the Milkweeds is actually a kind of rubber. During World War Two they were investigated as a potential commercial rubber source, though they were never developed.

Down: In World War Two some Milkweed species were actually cultivated for their downy seeds (about 50 plants produce a pound), which was used as a substitute for Kapok to stuff lifejackets. Milkweed down is said to be more water resistant than down, and have 25% more insulating properties, so has been used in insulated clothing. comforters and pillows. Attempts have been made to commercialize Milkweed down, by mixing it with 40% goose down, so far with mixed results. It has also been used experimentally in disposable diapers, and has been mixed with cotton for making cloth.

Native Americans used the dry down as tinder for starting fires.

Fiber: Native Americans used the fiber from the stems for cordage, rope and nets. It is extracted and prepared in the same way as Flax (*Linum*), and is almost as good. A Milkweed variety was bred specifically for use as a fiber producer, but it didn't catch on. The fiber has also been used for making paper.

Animal Food: The nectar-rich flowers are an important source of food for hummingbirds, bees and insects. The leaves are repugnant and poisonous to most insects, with the notable exception of the larvae of the Monarch Butterfly. This insect feeds almost exclusively on Milkweed, and accumulates the plant toxins in its body. These cause the caterpillar to taste so unpleasant that most predators won't touch it.

Fuel / New crop: It has been proposed that some Milkweed species (notably *A. speciosa*) be cultivated as renewable sources of energy. Its been estimated that an acre of the plants could give 170 gallons of oil (see *Brassica napus* for more on converting this into biodiesel), 250 gallons of ethanol and 400 gallons of methanol, along with waxes and resins. After these chemicals are removed the remains are edible to livestock, and are apparently equal to Alfalfa in nutritional value.

Cultivation: A number of species (notably Butterflyweed - *A. tuberosa*) are grown as ornamentals, and several improved cultivars exist. They are worth growing for their beauty and the beneficial and beautiful insects they attract to the garden. They are easily grown from seed or root division in any good garden soil. Native Americans encouraged edible Milkweeds by scattering the seed on suitable sites.

Related species:
A. exaltata - **Tall Milkweed**
A. incarnata - **Swamp Milkweed**
A. speciosa - **Showy Milkweed**
These species are all good for food.

Caution:
A. eriocarpa - **Indian Milkweed**
A. latifolia - **Broad leaved Milkweed**
A. subverticillata - **Poison Milkweed**
A. tuberosa - **Butterflyweed**
These species (and others) are poisonous to varying degrees.

Asimina triloba / Pawpaw
East   *Annonaceae*

Most members of the *Annonaceae* live in the tropics, but this hardy little tree can survive temperatures of 30 degrees Fahrenheit below zero. It can be found throughout much of the east, growing as an understory shrub along watercourses, but it is never very common. In parts of the southeast foraging for Pawpaws was once a traditional fall activity.

Nutrients: The nutritious fruits contain 5% protein (which is quite high for a fruit), 15% carbohydrate and 1% fat, along with vitamins A and C.

Fruit: The 3 - 5 inch fruits often fall while still green and ripen on the ground into late fall. This is a useful trait for the forager as they can be gathered in this state, or picked from tree while green, and allowed to ripen indoors in a dark place. The green fruits slowly soften and wrinkle, turning dark brown and sweet in the process. Their flavor varies a lot from tree to tree, some are delicious, other are quite unpleasant, so sample any you find.

The cooked fruit can be made into preserves, or added to bread, pies and cakes to sweeten them. You can dry the pulp to make Pawpaw leather, or freeze it for later use.

Medicine: Pawpaw contains medicinal compounds called acetogenins, which promise to be useful in treating a range of disorders from cancer to malaria

Fish Poison: The seeds contain an alkaloid that stupefies fish, so Native Americans used them in the same way as Buckeye seed (*Aesculus*).

Fiber: Native Americans used the inner bark fibers to make clothing.

Insecticide: One of the most important potential uses of Pawpaw is as an insecticide. The leaves can be used in powdered form, or as an infusion, and are effective against aphids, mosquito larvae and caterpillars. The tree might soon be grown commercially for this purpose.

New crop: Pawpaw has great potential as a new fruit crop. A number of improved varieties are already available, and more are appearing. A tree might produce a bushel of fruit in a good year.

Pawpaw might also be grown as a source of insecticide or medicinal compounds. It coppices well, so can be cut regularly and will quickly regenerate itself.

Cultivation: With its unusually large leaves and abundance of edible fruit, the Pawpaw has great potential as a useful edible / ornamental garden tree. Young trees prefer to grow in the shade of larger trees, but the mature trees fruit better in full sun.

The Pawpaw likes rich, moist, woodland soil, and is easily grown from the seed, stratified at 40 degrees Fahrenheit for three to four months. The large seed should be sown in-situ, or in peat pots or tubes, as the plant has brittle roots and doesn't like to be transplanted. It may also be propagated by layering, or by root or hardwood cuttings. The young plants grow quickly, but need some shade for protection from the sun. I used to wonder why the first leaves to appear on my plants in spring would wither and die. I finally found out that it is because the young plants dislike strong sunlight.

Established plants need little care, and often sucker to form dense thickets. They are sometimes considered a weed. Seedling trees produce variable fruits, so they are often grafted with improved varieties. Pollination is improved by planting several individuals or varieties together.

Related species:
A. grandiflora – **Florida Pawpaw**
A. parviflora - **Dwarf Pawpaw**
The fruits are used as above, but usually aren't as good.

Asparagus officinalis / Wild Asparagus
Throughout   *Liliaceae*

Asparagus has been cultivated for food for over 3000 years, and has been taken from its original home in the Mediterranean to all parts of the world. It is widely cultivated in North America, and bird-sown plants can be found almost anywhere in the country. Wild seedlings are not usually as succulent as their pampered cousins, but are still good food.

Nutrients: Asparagus is rich in minerals including copper, iron, magnesium, phosphorus and sulfur.

Gathering: The best time to locate Asparagus is in summer, when the large feathery ferns are highly visible. Return the following spring and harvest by cutting the shoots off at ground level with a sharp knife. They are best cooked as soon as possible after cutting.

Uses: The tender shoots can be eaten raw in salads and are quite good. However the raw plant has been known to cause dermatitis in a few individuals, so be cautious about eating it raw. Most often the shoots are steamed for a few minutes and eaten with olive oil, butter or various sauces. They can also be used in soups and pies.

Medicine: Asparagus has long had a reputation as a diuretic. The raw plant is most potent in this regard, though the cooked plant can also be used. It has been used to treat water retention, though it shouldn't be eaten if there is any inflammation of the urinary tract, as it is mildly irritating. It may also give the urine a strange smell. Asparagus is also a good source of fiber to alleviate constipation.

Animal Food: In parts of Russia Asparagus is so common in the wild it has been used as animal forage.

Ornament: The feathery stems are great for use in fresh or dried floral arrangements.

Cultivation: With its delicate feathery leaves, and bright red berries, Asparagus is a very attractive plant, and isn't out of place in the ornamental garden. It likes full sun and lots of space to spread its roots (these may travel six feet in all directions). Don't plant it too near to trees or other plants. Asparagus is usually grown from 1 - 2 year old roots, and these are available in garden centers every spring. These are planted in an 18-inch deep hole, in deep rich soil. This hole is slowly filled up over the following weeks, as the plant grows. It can also be grown from seed quite easily, but this is slower. It is very drought tolerant

An Asparagus bed should be carefully dug and fertilized, as the plants will remain there for many years. They like a year round mulch, and a feed of manure once or twice a year. Once established it self-seeds enthusiastically with the aid of birds.

Atriplex species / Saltbush, Orach

Throughout   *Chenopodiaceae*

These species are often common on saline soils, along both coasts and in the alkaline deserts of the west. They are well adapted to dry climates and salty soils, and actually excrete excess salt through their leaves. This can turn them almost white, and earns them the name of Saltbush.

Caution: The plants are close cousins of Lambs Quarters (*Chenopodium album*) and like them contain mildly poisonous oxalic acid. They may also accumulate toxic nitrates or selenium from the soil, so should be eaten in moderation.

Greens: The young plants and growing shoots can be eaten raw or cooked any time they are available. They are very salty, so wash them before use. In some cases this will not be enough and you will need to change the cooking water at some point, to make them palatable. They can also be added to foods as a source of salt.

Seed: *Atriplex* seed contains about 12% protein and was gathered and used like that of Amaranth (see *Amaranthus*). The seeds of several species were important to Native Americans, and were gathered in large amounts for winter use.

Baking Powder: Native Americans used the ashes of *A. canescens* as baking powder.

Soap: The leaves and roots of some species (*A. californica, A. lentiformis*) contain so much saponin they can be used as soap like Soapwort (*Saponaria*).

Animal Food: Saltbush foliage is rich in protein (dried plants contain from 12 - 20% protein) and other nutrients. In parts of the west they are important forage plants, for both wild and domestic animals (*A. polycarpa* is known as Cattle Spinach). They are adapted to grow well in summer heat with little water, and do well on saline soils where few other forage plants can grow. *A. canescens* is cultivated as a desert forage crop in Israel.

Cultivation: At least one species (*A. hortensis*) has been cultivated for use as human food, while others are grown to feed livestock. It has been suggested they be interplanted with native grasses on dry rangeland to increase its productivity. They have been planted around buildings as a fire retardant groundcover.

These tough plants can be grown from seed, cuttings or division. Generally they prefer rich soils, but can also grow in very salty ones, and some have been investigated as possible crops for irrigation with seawater. They may also have a possible use to desalinate over-irrigated soil (they would be harvested repeatedly during the growing season, taking much salt with them). They are also tolerant of insect pests, overgrazing, heat and drought. Some species can survive on as little as three inches of rain per year.

The plants are sometimes discouraged in agricultural areas, as they are an alternate host for the Sugar Beet Leafhopper.

Best species include:
A. confertifolia - **Shadscale**
A. lentiformis - **Quailbrush**
A. powelli
Native Americans valued these three species for their edible seeds.

Avena fatua / Wild Oats

Throughout   *Poaceae*

Probably the Spaniards originally introduced this species into North America as a food crop. It is very widely naturalized in many places, and is a hated weed as it competes very successfully with cultivated and native plants. It is particularly abundant in California, where it grows through the mild winters and dies off in summer, coloring the hills their characteristic straw color. On the positive side, it is now important for preventing soil erosion in many places, and provides food for wild creatures.

The Uses Of Wild Plants

The specific name fatua means useless, presumably because it isn't as useful as the cultivated Oats (*A. sativa*). It is equally nutritious however.

Seed: Oats are among the most nutritious of all cereal grains. They contain about 14% protein, 7% fat, 60% carbohydrates and large amounts of vitamins and minerals, including iron, phosphorus, potassium and magnesium. It is possible to use the grain for porridge, pancakes and baking. Prepare it in the same way as Wild Rice (*Zizania*).

Drink: Tea has probably been made out of almost every imaginable plant material over the years, but Oat straw tea sounds particularly unappetizing. Actually it is surprisingly pleasant and quite nutritious. Prepare it by simmering the straw for a few minutes, then strain and serve with lemon and honey. It is said to be a useful detoxifying drink.

Medicine: Oats have been used as a soothing poultice for insect bites, chicken pox and Poison oak / Ivy rash. Cooked oatmeal is of considerable medicinal value as a source of fiber to relieve constipation. It has been used as a nutritive tonic, and is even said to be an aphrodisiac. Oat bran became very fashionable for a while, for its ability to reduce blood cholesterol levels.

Other Uses: Oatmeal has been used as a dry "shampoo" to remove grease from the hair and skin. The straw has been used for packing material and wallboard.

Cultivation: Oats prefer cool, moist, growing conditions, and are commonly grown in areas too cold for wheat. The seed is planted in early spring, and matures in about 90 days. The tough seed can survive temperatures of 240 degrees Fahrenheit, which helps it to thrive in California despite frequent grass fires.

Related species:
A. barbata - **Bearded Oats**
A. sativa - **Cultivated Oat**

Balsamorhiza species / Balsamroot

West   *Asteraceae*

In spring the large Sunflower-like flowers are sometimes so abundant they color fields yellow. Almost all parts of the Balsamroot are edible, and it was an important food source for some Native American tribes. It provides food almost year-round.

Buds: In late winter or early spring, buds develop on the rootstock. These are edible, and can be added to salads, cooked as a vegetable, or added to soups. To find them you need to locate the remains of last year's plants and dig.

Greens: The tender young spring shoots and leaves can be eaten raw or cooked. Older greens can also be eaten, after boiling in at least one change of water.

Stems: The stems and flower buds are eaten in spring, when only a few inches high. They are peeled and eaten raw, or cooked like Asparagus.

Seed: In early summer these plants produce an abundance of nutritious oily seed, which can be used like that of the related Sunflower (*Helianthus*). This is too small to shell, so is usually eaten whole as a snack, or ground to flour for breads, mush or thickening soup. Oil could be extracted from them.

The Paiutes pounded the whole seeds to meal, and mixed them with sweet Juniper berries (*Juniperus*) to make a kind of dessert.

Roots: These have a strong resinous flavor, which gives them their the common name, and makes them unpalatable to most people. Fortunately this is mostly concentrated in the skin, which can be peeled off prior to eating or cooking. The roots are tender and quite good when young, but get tough and woody with age. Like most edible roots they are best while dormant, from fall to early spring. Their quality varies considerably according to species and growing conditions, and you must experiment to find the most palatable.

The roots have been eaten raw, but are better boiled or baked (40 minutes at 350 degrees Fahrenheit). Native Americans wrapped them in their own leaves and baked them in a fire pit as for Camas (*Camassia*), as this makes them sweeter. They can also be roasted like Chicory (*Cicorium*) as a coffee substitute.

Animal Food: The plants provide food for Elk, Bighorn Sheep and many birds.

Cultivation: With its large Sunflower-like flowers, Balsamroot is an attractive ornamental perennial for dry areas. It is usually grown from seed, in well-drained soil and prefers light shade. It resents transplanting except when very young.

The best species include:
B. deltoidea - **Deltoid Balsamroot**
B. hookerii - **Hookers Balsamroot**
B. sagittata - **Arrow Leaved Balsamroot**

Barbarea vulgaris / **Wintercress**
Throughout   *Brassicaceae*

This European native is cultivated as a cool weather salad plant and is widely naturalized near human habitation. It gets its common name because it is very hardy, and in milder areas it often remains green throughout the winter. It is rich in vitamins and other nutrients.

Greens: Wintercress tastes very much like Watercress (*Nasturtium*), and can be used in the same ways, in salads, soups and sandwiches. It turns bitter and pungent when it flowers, or in warm weather, which limits its value to the cool weather of spring and fall. It is a fine potherb, though it may be necessary to change the cooking water at least once, to reduce its bitterness to a palatable level. It is sometimes mixed with bland potherbs to add flavor. The leaves shrink a lot in cooking, so you need more than you think.

Flower Buds: The unopened flower buds, gathered while still tightly furled, can be eaten raw, or cooked like miniature Broccoli. Again it may be necessary to change the cooking water once or twice to reduce their strong flavor.

Animal Food: The seeds are important food for many wild birds, and are sometimes added to wild birdseed mixtures.

Cultivation: This biennial is easily raised from seed, in average garden soil. It self-sows readily, and can become a weed if not kept under control. I consider it an essential winter salad garden plant.

Related species include:
B. verna - **Early Wintercress**
B. orthoceras - **American Wintercress**
Use as above. The latter species is native to North America.

Berberis vulgaris / **Common Barberry**
East   *Berberidaceae*

This European species is widely planted as an ornamental in North America, and is now naturalized in some areas. The Barberries are closely related to the Oregon Grapes (*Mahonia*), which are sometimes included in this genus.

Fruit: The sour red berries somewhat resemble Cranberries (*Vaccinium*), and can be used in the same ways, in sauces, preserves and pickles. It is best to remove the hard seeds before use. They are rich in pectin and are often added to fruit jellies to help them set. Their juice can be used as a substitute for lemon juice. A few berries are a nice addition to salads. Native Americans crushed the berries of related species into cakes, and dried them for winter use.

Drink: The berries make a pleasantly sour tea, which is traditionally sweetened with orange juice and honey.

Greens: The tender spring growth was eaten as a snack. Older leaves have been used for tea.

Medicine: Barberry bark contains berberine (also found in the unrelated Goldenseal - *Hydrastis canadensis*), which stimulates the liver. It was once widely used in medicine to treat jaundice, diarrhea, menstrual pains, digestive problems, to reduce blood pressure and as an antiseptic. For medicinal use the bark is gathered while the plants are dormant.

Cosmetics: A tea of the bark was used as an eyewash, skin lotion, and a beautifying hair rinse (especially for blonde hair).

Cultivation: Barberries have been cultivated as a fruit crop. They can be propagated from cuttings, suckers or seed (plant the ripe whole berries) and prefer well-drained soil with full sun or part shade. They may grow to ten feet in height, and with their formidable spines and vigorous growth, they can be a useful hedge plant.

Related species:
Most Barberries produce edible fruit. The best include:

B. canadensis - **American Barberry**
B. pinnata - **California Mahonia (Syn** *Mahonia pinnata*)
Used as above.

Betula lenta / Black Birch

Northeast   *Betulaceae*
At first glance the smooth bark resembles that of the Cherry, but Black Birch is easily identified by its pronounced odor and flavor of Wintergreen. The only other tree with a similar smell is the equally edible Yellow Birch (*B. alleghaniensis*).

This characteristic flavor is due to an oil, composed mainly of methyl salicylate, which is also found in the unrelated Wintergreens (*Gaultheria*). This can be extracted from the twigs by steam distillation, and was once widely used for food and medicinal purposes. Extensive commercial gathering once caused considerable damage, as it takes 400 small trees to produce a gallon of the oil. Fortunately the oil is now produced synthetically from salicylic acid and methanol.

Inner Bark: Obviously you should never strip bark off a tree for food, unless it to be cut down anyway. You can get it from the twigs and small branches though.

In late winter the inner bark is full of simple sugars, and has a sweet Wintergreen flavor. This has been eaten raw, cooked, or dried and ground to flour for baking.

Shoots: The leaf buds and tiny catkins can be added to salads. They may also be chewed to alleviate pangs of thirst when out hiking.

Tea: Make tea by steeping the buds, chopped twigs or inner bark in boiling water until cold, then reheat and drink (never boil). If you don't like the taste it is also said to be good for the hair.

Beer: The twigs and sap are used to make root beer. One recipe calls for boiling four gallons of Birch sap and a gallon of honey for ten minutes, and then mixing with four quarts of chopped twigs. This is left to cool, strained, and a cake of yeast is added. The resulting liquid is left to ferment for about a week, until it starts to clear and is then bottled. Chill and drink carefully as it can be pretty strong. I think there is a commercial opportunity for some enterprising microbrewers here.

Syrup: Birch sap can be made into syrup in the same way as the Maples (see *Acer*). It only contains about half as much sugar as Maple sap, so it takes twice as much to make an equal quantity of syrup (up to 100 gallons of sap to make a gallon of syrup). The sap itself was once considered to be a healthy and beneficial drink.

Medicine: Methyl salicylate is chemically similar to the common drug aspirin, and Birch tea has been used like that drug for rheumatism, headaches and inflammation. If you are allergic to aspirin you should be careful about using any part of the plant.

Birch oil has been used externally as an analgesic to relieve muscle pain, arthritis and rheumatism. It is easily absorbed through the skin, but can cause irritation if too concentrated. Birch tea is antiseptic, and can be used externally as a wash for wounds and burns. The strong flavor of the oil has been used to mask the flavor of less palatable medicines. Native Americans used tubes of the bark as splints for binding broken limbs.

Chewing sticks: Native Americans used the frayed twigs as chewing sticks to clean their teeth. We tend to think of chewing sticks as very inferior "poor mans" toothbrushes, but it now appears we are wrong. The plants commonly used as chewing sticks contain antiseptic agents that promote gum health as well as cleaning the teeth

Flavoring: Wintergreen is an important flavoring for a wide range of products, including perfumes, toothpaste, chewing gum and soft drinks.

Brooms: In Europe tightly bound bundles of springy Birch twigs are still used to make brooms (the trees are coppiced every 2 - 4 years for broom making). Very small bundles were once used to make kitchen whisks.

Wood: The wood is strong and nicely grained, but hard to season except by kiln drying. This is an important commercial lumber species, as it is used for turning, cabinetmaking, veneer and plywood.

Firewood: The wood is pretty good fuel, giving about 25 million Btu per cord. It also makes good charcoal. The Birches coppice easily and could be grown for firewood on a 10 - 20 year rotation.

The branches and twigs are good kindling. The bark is good tinder for fire starting, as it is full of inflammable oil, and burns even after being immersed in water. Native Americans made torches from bundles of the bark.

Cultivation: Black Birch is a fast growing pioneer tree, but fairly short-lived, reaching maturity in about one hundred years. It likes rich, moist soils and is propagated from seed. This is sown when ripe in late summer, or stratified at forty degrees for two months (it needs light to germinate). It is possible to transplant seedlings from around mature trees, where they would probably otherwise die. Trees with especially valuable characteristics, such as high sugar or oil content, can be propagated from cuttings.

Horticultural Uses: Birch leaves are a good addition to compost piles and these are said to work better if placed under the trees.

Fertilizer: *Betula* species live in association with nitrogen fixing actinomycete bacteria, and an acre of trees may fix over 200 pounds of nitrogen annually. This makes them an important component in maintaining forest soil fertility.

Wildlife: The Birches are important sources of food for moose, beaver, hare, grouse and porcupine,

Related species:
It is probable that any *Betula* species could be tapped for sap. The most useful include:

B. alleghaniensis* - Yellow Birch Syn *B. lutea
This species has the same Wintergreen flavor as Black Birch, so can be used in the same ways. It is the most important lumber producing Birch.

***B. nigra* – River Birch**
***B. populifolia* – Gray Birch**
***B. papyrifera* - Paper Birch**
These species don't have any Wintergreen flavor, but their shoots can be used as above, and they can also be tapped for sap.

Birch Bark
The bark of the Paper Birch (and to a lesser extent that of some others) was a very important resource for Native Americans of the northern forests. It is anti-bacterial, tough, waterproof, very durable and available in large sheets. Its best-known use was in making the famous Birch bark canoes, but it was also used for a wide variety of other articles. These included food containers (notably for storing Maple sugar), burden baskets, hats, wigwams, cups, writing paper, mats, snow goggles, moose calls, clothing and boxes. It was usually peeled from the trees in late winter, when the sap is running.

Brassica nigra / Black Mustard
Throughout   *Brassicaceae*
This relatively small and uninteresting looking plant has an impressive number of uses.

Caution: The pungency of Black Mustard (and other plants of the *Brassicaceae*) is due to acrid mustard oil, which may irritate the kidneys if taken in quantity. For this reason condiments such as mustard and Horseradish should be used in moderation. This is how most people prefer them anyway.

Prepared Mustard
The condiment known as mustard is easy to make. Start by browning a quantity of wheat flour in an oven or pan and then mix it with an equal amount of ground Mustard seed (mustard flour). This is then moistened with a little wine or vinegar, and made into a paste. Sweeten with honey if desired. Many other herbs and spices can also be added. The really macho might want to use Jack Daniels whiskey instead of vinegar, and maybe add a few Chiletepine peppers for a little extra bite.

Seed Gathering: Cut the whole plants as the first seeds ripen, pile them on paper (or put in a clean paper grocery sack) and leave to dry. When the pods are thoroughly dry, crush them to release their seed and then winnow to clean away the chaff.

Seed Uses: Grind the dry seeds to a fine powder in a food mill, food chopper or pestle and mortar. This can be used in soups, sauces and salad dressings, or in any recipe calling for mustard flour.

The seed can be sprouted like Alfalfa (See *Medicago*) or Peppergrass (See *Lepidium*). These wholesome sprouts are good in salads and sandwiches.

Greens: The leaves, and unopened flower buds, can be used in much the same ways as those of Wintercress (see *Barbarea*), and like them are only palatable in cool weather. The youngest leaves are good in salads, but older leaves need cooking, and you may have to change the cooking water to reduce their strong flavor. The yellow flowers have been added to salads for their color and pungent taste.

Cultivation: Because of its value as a condiment, Black Mustard is a minor crop plant. It is easily grown from seed, and does well in most soil types. Though *Brassica* species are toxic to most insects, several butterfly species have become resistant to mustard oil, and are actually attracted by it. These creatures live almost solely on plants of this family, and are serious pests for growers.

The Uses Of Wild Plants

Mustard as medicine

Mustard was once considered something of a wonder drug, and has been used for many different ailments. Its most important use is as a rubefacient poultice for sore muscles, rheumatism, bronchitis and colds. It is said to work by increasing the flow of blood to the affected area, thereby loosening muscles and removing toxins. As with the similar Horseradish poultice it must be used carefully as the oil is very irritating, and can actually raise blisters (you don't want to remove skin along with the toxins). For this reason the poultice is often made with egg white, flaxseed or other soothing materials. The ground seed has also been steeped in alcohol and used as a liniment for the same ailments.

Small amounts of mustard taken internally are said to aid digestion, and improve the appetite. This is probably the reason it was used as a condiment in the first place.

The glucosinolates in this (and other *Brassica*) species are potent detoxifying agents, and may help to prevent cancer.

Poison gas: The actively pungent ingredient in mustard (allyl isothiocyanate) was produced synthetically in World War One for use as a weapon. Known as mustard gas, it produces intense blistering, both externally and internally. It was used many times during that war, and was responsible for thousands of horrible deaths.

Green manure: The Mustards are great green manure plants. Hardy and fast growing, they accumulate calcium, iron and sulfur, and produce large amounts of organic matter in a short time. Dig them into the soil before they set seed, otherwise they can become weeds (they are often a pest to farmers). The plants also provide nectar for bees, attract predatory insects, and may act as a trap crop, diverting pests away from crop Brassicas.

The main drawback to using any member of the Cabbage family as green manure is that they can't be used in rotation with any of the Brassica crops (Kale, Broccoli, Cabbage or Cauliflower). This is because they are susceptible to the same pests and diseases.

Pollution Control: A novel potential use of the plant is to remove selenium from the soil. The plant (and some other *Brassica* species) has an affinity for selenium, which is chemically quite similar to sulfur. An acre of Mustard may remove up to five pounds of selenium from the soil in a year (if cut repeatedly).

Related Species:
Many *Brassica* species can be used as above, including:

***B. hirta* – White Mustard** Syn *B. alba* or *Sinapis alba*
The seeds of this species are also used to make the condiment we call mustard (use as above). This is milder than that made from the seeds of Black or Brown Mustard. It is commonly grown as a green manure plant, and can be found as an escape from cultivation.

***B. juncacea* - Indian Mustard**
This species is cultivated for Mustard greens, and for its pungent seeds (known as Brown Mustard when prepared as described above). It is now found wild in many areas.

B. napus / Rape
This European species is also found as an escape from cultivation. It is grown for animal feed, and as a source of the cooking oil known as Canola oil.

Oil: Rape may produce 900 pounds of oil per acre in cool climates, which is more than any other common temperate zone crop. This oil is generally used for food, but it also has other uses.

Diesel fuel: Rapeseed oil can be used as diesel fuel, though it is more valuable for food use than as a fuel. Sometimes it can be used for both purposes though, as quite a few people run their vehicles on used cooking oil from restaurants.

Rudolf Diesel designed his engine to run on vegetable oil, but this doesn't work in modern engines because it is too viscous. It will work if the oil is heated to reduce its viscosity, but this means modifying the engine. The modifications basically consist of installing a second fuel tank, and a system for heating the oil (using heat from the engine). Such a system works well, but the car must be started on conventional diesel fuel (or biodiesel) and idled for a while before stopping, to keep the fuel system clean.

You can use vegetable oil without modifying the engine, by thinning it with kerosene in the proportion of 1 part kerosene to 3 parts oil.

Biodiesel: Probably the best way to run an engine on vegetable oil is by turning it into biodiesel, which modifies the oil instead of the engine. Most vegetable oils are triglycerides, which consist of a glycerine molecule, with three esters attached. Making biodiesel consists of replacing the glycerine with alcohol, by a process called transesterification. This is simpler than it sounds, and I will describe it here, but can be quite dangerous (sodium and potassium hydroxides are very caustic), and there are several possible variations in the process. For these reasons I don't recommend that you try it without further study (unless of course you are reading this after the collapse of civilization as we knew it, in which case good luck!)

The alcohol can be methanol or ethanol, and is used in the proportion of 1 part alcohol to 4 parts oil. Sodium hydroxide (lye) or potassium hydroxide is used as a catalyst to initiate the chemical reaction. Any future Mad Max might be interested to know that the alcohol could be made by fermenting almost any sugar or starch. The sodium hydroxide could be made from wood ashes.

Making biodiesel

The first step is to thoroughly mix the sodium hydroxide with the methanol (use 3.5 grams per liter) to make sodium methoxide. The next step is to mix the sodium methoxide with the vegetable oil, in the proportion of 1 liter of sodium methoxide to 5 liters of oil. This is stirred for 15 minutes, and then left to sit for a minimum of 8 hours. During this period the glycerine produced will settle to the bottom of the container. After this time there will be an obvious difference between the layer of biodiesel on top and the layer of glycerine on the bottom. The two must be separated very carefully, or they will mix again. The simplest way to do this is to make it in a container with a stopcock at the bottom (this allows you to simply drain off the glycerine). Finally the biodiesel is filtered to remove any particles.

Obviously the growing of vegetable oil for motor fuel is an idea with limited potential. To run the average family car for its 10 - 12000 mile yearly average would take 4 - 5 acres of land (the average Hummer might take 20 acres). Perhaps we take gasoline too much for granted.

Home heating oil: Biodiesel isn't only useful as fuel for cars. It can also be used like Number 2 fuel oil in oil fired home heating furnaces. Probably the simplest way to do this is to mix up to 25% biodiesel with the conventional fuel oil, but it is possible to use 100% biodiesel. In some ways this is actually a better way to use this fuel, as a furnace is a simpler device than a modern diesel engine, and there are less problems with coking, clogging and corrosion of rubber parts.

Soap: The glycerine produced making biodiesel can be used to make soap, if impurities are removed.

Industrial chemicals: Rapeseed is also rich in erucic acid, an important industrial chemical that is used for making plastics. It is also added to lubricants to improve their efficiency under high pressure and heat.

Brodiaea species / Brodiaea Lilies
Syn *Hookera* **spp**
West   *Amaryllidaceae*

These plants are close relatives of the *Alliums*, but have none of their pungent flavor. They are endemic to grasslands of western North America.

Bulbs: All species produce small edible bulbs (actually corms) the size of marbles, with a sweet nutty flavor. These are considered to be some of the best flavored of all edible wild bulbs, but are too pretty for casual use, except when very abundant and overcrowded. They were a staple food for the Nez Perce and other western tribes.

Gathering: The best time to gather the bulbs is in early summer, when they start to die down and go dormant, but while the tops are still visible to aid in locating and identifying them. You can't simply uproot the bulbs, as they may be six inches deep, you have to dig.

Preparation: The bulbs aren't bad to eat raw, but they are a little slimy. They are better if cooked like potatoes. Frying the boiled roots reduces their sliminess. You might try cooking them in aluminum foil in a 350-degree oven for 45 minutes.

Native Americans baked large quantities of the bulbs in fire pits, and dried them for later use. This is probably the best way to use them, as the extended baking turns their starch into sugar and makes them quite sweet. See *Camassia* for more on this method of cooking.

Seeds: The immature seedpods can be eaten like green beans. The ripe seeds have been eaten in mixed seed mush or flour. However they are probably best left to produce more plants.

The Uses Of Wild Plants

Cultivation: A number of *Brodiaea* species are popular ornamentals, especially for wild or rock gardens. They can be grown from seed (slow), cormlets or purchased bulbs. They prefer well-drained soils, with full sun.

Cakile edentula / **Sea Rocket**
Coasts, Great Lakes   *Brassicaceae*
This native species is found along beaches, sand dunes and lakeshores in North America. It isn't uncommon, but should be used sparingly unless very abundant.

Leaves: The succulent mustard flavored young plants are a nice addition to salads, though some people consider them too strongly flavored. The seedlings are even better. The tender growing tips of older plants can be used in salads, while tougher parts may be cooked as a potherb, added to soups, or even pickled. If their flavor is too strong, change the cooking water, or mix them with other greens. The flowers and immature seedpods can be used in the same ways.

Cultivation: This annual can be grown from seed, in well-drained soils. A wide spreading root network makes it useful for stabilizing sand dunes and loose soil. It also enriches the soil with humus.

Related species:
C. maritima - **Horned Sea Rocket**
C. lanceolata - **Sea Rocket**
These naturalized European species are used as above.

Calandrinia ciliata / **Red Maids**
Syn *C. menziesii, C. caulescens*.
West   *Portulacaceae*
Greens: The fleshy leaves and stems can be eaten as a salad or potherb.

Seed: The tasty seed was prized by Native Americans and was gathered in surprising quantities for such a small plant. This was possible because they carefully managed the land around them to encourage the plants that were useful to them. They created large, almost pure, stands of Red Maids (and other species) by burning the land after the harvest. This prevented encroachment by other plants and created an ideal seedbed for the plants. They would also sow the seed if necessary.

Native Americans were able to efficiently harvest the large stands they created by the use of the seed beater. This is a simple shallow basket with a long handle, and was used to brush the seeds from the dry seed heads, into a larger basket held underneath. Some of the seeds would be missed and fall to the ground. This was good because they would grow into new plants for the following year.

There isn't an easy way to recreate the large stands of plants, but there is a simple way to collect the seeds. The fleshy plants contain enough moisture to flower and set seed even when uprooted. Uprooting may actually stimulate the plant to produce seed. All you have to do is store the plants in a warm place until they are thoroughly dry, thresh them, and collect the loose seed.

Native Americans used the seed for bread, gruel and pinole. Pinole, made by most California tribes, was a coarse meal made from various kinds of toasted seeds. It was usually moistened and shaped into balls, but was also eaten dry, added to soups, or boiled to form a gruel.

Cultivation: This attractive little annual has been planted as an ornamental. It is grown from seed in light soil.

Related species:
C. ambigua - **Desert Calandrinia**
Use as above.

Callirhoe involucrata / **Purple Poppy Mallow**
West   *Malvaceae*
Roots: The fleshy edible root should only be used when very common, as digging it kills the plant. These are quite good when young (old roots are woody) and it is surprising that this species isn't better known as a wild food plant. They were an important food for the Osage and other tribes. They were dug in late summer and fall, and stored in large numbers for winter use. They can be eaten raw, boiled or roasted. The roasted roots have a sweet flavor, and were often said to be superior to those of the better known Indian Breadroot (*Psoreala*).

Greens: The leaves can be used like their cousins the Mallows (*Malva*), as salad or potherbs.

Cultivation: The fragrant purple flowers make Poppy Mallow worth growing as an edible ornamental. Propagate from seed or softwood cuttings, in well-drained soil. It is drought tolerant and self-seeds readily.

Related species:
C. digitata - **Fringed Poppy Mallow**
C. pedata
Use as above.

Calochortus species / **Mariposa Lilies**
West   *Liliaceae*
Roots: The nutritious bulbs contain 25% sugar, 15% starch and 10% protein. They were a staple food for some Native American tribes (notably the Utes). They were also important for the first Mormon settlers in Utah, and helped them to survive after crickets destroyed their

crops in 1848. It is really too pretty for casual use, and should probably be left alone (I wouldn't normally use it)

The bulbs are dug after the flowers produce seed. They can often be gathered in quantity, as the plants frequently grow in densely packed beds. Take the larger bulbs, and replant the smaller ones so they can continue growing. Gather them as you need them, as they don't store well. Use in the same way as Camas (*Camassia*).

Greens: The tops and flowers are also edible and have been used in salads or as a potherb. However they are not substantial enough to be very useful, especially as the plants are so beautiful.

Cultivation: These perennial Lilies are very attractive and make a good edible ornamental. However they are not easy to grow unless given ideal conditions. They can be propagated from seed, bulbs or bulblets, in rich soil with light shade.

Caltha palustris / Marsh Marigold
East   *Helleboraceae*

Caution: Like many members of the Buttercup family, the Marsh marigold contains an acrid substance called protoanemonin, which makes it toxic when raw. Heat destroys this acridity however, and the plant can be used as a potherb if thoroughly cooked.

This attractive spring flower is getting scarcer in many places, and shouldn't be used unless it is abundant.

Potherb: This was a favorite potherb of wild food guru Euell Gibbons. Gather the young spring shoots, and change the cooking water at least twice to reduce their strong flavor. You might also mix the cooked potherb with blander greens such as Nettles (*Urtica*).

Warts: The caustic juice has been used to remove warts.

Cultivation: This beautiful plant is occasionally planted as an ornamental in wet soils. It can be propagated from seed or division and prefers poorly drained shady soil.

Related Species:
C. howellii - **White Marsh Marigold**
C. leptosepalus - **Heart Leaved Marsh Marigold**
C. natans - **Floating Marsh Marigold**
These poisonous western species have been used as above, but are not usually as good.

Camassia species / Camas
Throughout   *Liliaceae*
In some areas Camas is so abundant in early summer it colors fields blue, and many places have been named

after it, such as Camas Prairie and Camas Hot Springs. The common name is of Native American origin and means sweet, which aptly describes the flavor of the baked bulbs. Camas was one of the most important Native American food bulbs, and was a staple of some intermountain tribes.

Caution: Be careful when gathering Camas bulbs, as those of the poisonous Death Camas (*Zygadenus* species) look quite similar and grow in the same places. This plant can cause serious poisoning and even death, if sufficient quantities are ingested. A fatal dose of the most poisonous species is only one half pound per hundred pounds of bodyweight.

Because *Camassia* and *Zygadenus* bulbs look so much alike, they are most safely dug while the plants still have their blue flowers to aid in identification (Death Camas flowers are white). If the flowers are not present, examine the leaves; those of *Zygadenus* are folded into a keel and rough, while those of Camas are flat and smooth. Death Camas bulbs are bitter and not very good.

Gathering: Native Americans gathered the bulbs year round, but the main harvest was in fall, when the plants begin to die down, but are still identifiable. The autumn harvest was something of a celebration or festival. In a few weeks they obtained one of their staple winter foods. and a good harvest was something to celebrate.

The size of the bulb varies considerably with species and growing conditions, but all are edible. It is a good idea to re-plant any very small bulbs you find in a suitable location, to help perpetuate the species. Native American women and children dug the bulbs with digging sticks, and this is probably still the best way.

Nutrients: The bulbs contain about 10% protein and 35% carbohydrate, and are said to be more nutritious than potatoes. Most of the carbohydrate is in the form of inulin, which is not easily digested by humans, but can be converted to more digestible sugars by prolonged baking. If eaten in very large quantities the bulbs can cause gas, diarrhea and vomiting.

Preparation: Camas bulbs can be eaten raw, but aren't very good. The classic way to prepare them is baked in a fire pit, as this reduces their mucilaginous quality and turns the starchy inulin into sugar. This makes them taste very sweet, in fact too sweet for some palates.

Native Americans sliced the baked bulbs into discs and ate them alone or with other foods. They also mashed them into cakes and dried them in the sun for winter use. These were ground to flour for making gruel, or for baking bread. This is why the first European settlers sometimes referred to them as Biscuitroot. A delicacy was prepared by mixing the baked bulbs with mashed Grasshoppers or Ants.

Fire pit cooking
Native Americans built a fire pit by digging a hole three feet in diameter and one foot deep and lining it with stones (for the big fall harvest they dug huge pits up to thirty feet in diameter. A fire was lit in the pit to heat up the stones, and when these were sufficiently hot the ashes were scraped out and alternating layers of damp grass and bulbs put in. A layer of earth was placed on top of the final layer of grass, and the bulbs were left to bake for 24 - 72 hours. The heat retained by the stones slowly baked the bulbs, leaving them sweet and brown.

A simpler way to cook the bulbs is by baking them in a 375-degree oven for 45 minutes, or they can be baked in aluminum foil in the ashes of a campfire. They can also be boiled like potatoes for 15 - 30 minutes, but this gives then an unpleasant gummy texture. European settlers prepared a Pumpkin-like Pie from the boiled roots.

Syrup: Syrup has been made from the baked bulbs.

Animal Food: European settlers most often used the plants as hog feed, simply leaving the animals in the meadows to dig the bulbs for themselves. Understandably Native Americans resented this, as it deprived them of a staple food, and destroyed their carefully tended ancestral Camas gathering grounds.

Cultivation: These species are often quite beautiful and at least one species (*Camassia leichtlinii*) is widely planted as an ornamental. Grow from offsets, bulbs (move when dormant), or seed sown in fall. All species like sun or part shade, and a rich soil that is moist in winter and dry in summer. They are hardy and independent perennials, and once established will multiply vegetatively to form colonies. They may even self-seed and naturalize.

Individual Native American families often held gathering rights to specific patches of Camas plants and practiced a kind of semi-cultivation. When harvesting they would replant the smaller bulbs, which could grow to maturity quickly without competition from larger plants. They also planted any seeds they found. The stands were sometimes burned to reduce encroachment by woody plants. They were also weeded to eliminate the Death Camas, and reduce competition from other plants.

The famous plant breeder Luther Burbank thought *Camassia* species could become important as both ornamentals and food crops. They are indeed an ideal edible ornamental, and this is a good way to get Camas bulbs in their prime, without having to worry about potential poisoning.

The best species include:
Most species are found in the west, with the important exception of the eastern Wild Hyacinth (*C. scilloides*).

C. leichtlinii - **Leichtlin's Camas**
C. quamash - **Common Camas**
C. scilloides - **Wild Hyacinth**

Cannabis sativa / Indian Hemp
Eurasia   *Moraceae*
For longer than recorded history Indian Hemp has been a camp follower of humans. The plant loved the nitrogen rich dump heaps found around primitive villages and it has stayed near the works of humans ever since. The inhabitants of those villages no doubt encouraged the plant to grow nearby, as it is a valuable source of fiber and has potent medicinal and euphoriant properties. At times it has even been considered sacred.

This species has gained notoriety in the west as the source of the drugs marijuana and hashish and cultivation or possession of the plant is generally illegal. This is unfortunate, as Hemp is one of the most useful of all plants, which is why it was once one of the most important crops worldwide. Despite years of persecution, from both sides of the law, it is still occasionally found wild in waste places.

History: Hemp was originally introduced into North America in the 1600's, as a fiber plant to supply rope for the British navy. Cultivation for fiber continued after independence, right up until this century when it was declared an illegal plant. Quite a few places are named after Hemp, such as Hempstead.

When Hemp became a popular recreational drug in the 1960's cultivation began again, this time illicitly for the production of marijuana. Despite serious penalties cultivation proved so lucrative that clandestine Marijuana farming flourished, and it is now a major cash crops in some states. It is probably only a matter of time before someone genetically engineers a yeast or bactera to produce THC, or transplants the THC producing genes into an Oak tree (or into Kudzu or Water Hyacinth).

Constituents: The powerful euphoriant and narcotic effects of *Cannabis* are due to a resin that contains cannabidiolic acid. When dried or burned this is converted into delta tetrahydrocannabinol (THC), a potent central nervous system stimulant. Marijuana and hashish have been used around the world for thousands of years, but only quite recently have they become popular in the west.

There is much controversy concerning the health effects of THC, and despite the best efforts of many to prove otherwise, it still appears to be largely non-addictive and-non toxic even when consumed in large quantities over a long period of time. Few, if any, deaths have ever been directly attributed to it, though it is perhaps the mostly intensively studied drug ever. This is not an endorsement of the drug, as deliberately inhaling smoke is not a good idea and though it isn't addictive it can certainly be habit forming (like any pleasant activity).

Greens: The tender seedlings have been used as a potherb, though the plants contain a number of toxins.

Seed: The parched seeds have been ground to meal for baking bread. They have also been boiled to mush and then fried in batter. They are very rich in high quality protein, and a number of commercial hemp seed food products are now appearing.

Medical marijuana

Marijuana is a valuable anti-nausea drug for reducing some of the side effects of chemotherapy in cancer patients. It can also increase the appetite, which can be very helpful in fighting some of these life-threatening diseases. It is also of value in treating glaucoma, Alzheimer's disease, and multiple sclerosis and in some cases the relief it has brought has been called miraculous. Of course it can also make being alive more pleasant than it might otherwise be if you are dying.

These benefits have inspired a medical Marijuana lobby, working to make it legally available to those who could benefit from it. In my opinion the whole idea of making a plant illegal is absurd. There is no valid reason why this amazing plant should not be available to anyone who might benefit from it.

Medicine: The leaves and flowers of Hemp (or the extracted resin) were once highly esteemed as a medicinal herb. As close to a panacea as you could find, they were used as a sedative hypnotic (for insomnia), relaxant, analgesic (for migraine, rheumatism, labor pains, menstrual cramps) and appetite stimulant. They have also been smoked to relieve asthma and bronchitis.

The leaves have been used externally for insect bites and wounds, and may contain an antibiotic. The seeds are a laxative, tonic, diuretic and vermifuge.

Fiber

Hemp provides one of the best of all plant fibers for making rope, cord, twine, oakum and fabrics of all kinds. Hemp fiber has also been used to make paper, cardboard and wallboard for building.

Hemp has great potential as a fiber source for the future, as it produces up to four times as much cellulose per acre as trees. It could essentially replace wood as the source of most of our paper. This would also reduce the pollution associated with papermaking, as it needs less processing. In some places Hemp is still used for making high quality paper, such as that used for making cigarettes.

Sacrament: Some people consider Hemp to be a gift from god, a sacred herb and a bringer of visions.

Oil: Oil from the seed dries quickly when exposed to air, and was once widely used in the manufacture of paints and varnish, as well as lamp oil. It may produce 280 pounds of oil per acre.

Fuel: These fast growing plants could be cultivated as a source of biomass for producing alcohol or methane, or they could simply be dried and burned. Oil from the seeds could be used to produce biodiesel (see *Brassica*).

Cultivation: This annual is very easy to grow from seed and often self-seeds readily. It can even become a nuisance. It prefers rich soil with a high nitrogen content, such as garbage heaps and cultivated ground.

Growing Hemp for fiber is very different from growing it for drug use. For maximum fiber production male plants are preferred, and the varieties grown naturally contain little THC These are harvested prior to flowering. For drug use the flowering female plants are desired, and varieties with a very high THC content are used

Horticultural Uses: Hemp is attractive as well as useful. In ideal conditions it grows rapidly to twelve feet or more in height, and makes a fine temporary screen or windbreak. It is useful as a green manure crop, as it is one of the best accumulators of phosphorus. It is also an excellent smother crop, to clear fields of weeds. Hemp is said to repel many insect pests, and is a good companion plant.

Capsella bursa pastoris / Shepherds Purse
Throughout   *Brassicaceae*

This opportunistic little annual is naturalized all around the world, though rarely far from the work of humans. It has been so successful because it sets seed abundantly (it pollinates its flowers before they even open) and its seed may remain viable for up to thirty years. It is also very hardy, and can survive temperatures as low as ten degrees Fahrenheit. The common name was given because the pods were said to resemble the purses once carried by shepherds (as you might have guessed).

Greens: Unlike many members of the *Brassicaceae*, the leaves don't really get very pungent or bitter, so can be used any time they are available. They are probably at their best before the flowers appear. Their only drawback is that the leaves are small even when fully grown. The plants are actually cultivated for sale in Taiwan and China.

The leaves can be used in salads, or cooked for a few minutes as a potherb. They are good sautéed with onion.

Seed: The seed can be ground to meal and used as a condiment like Mustard. It has also been sprouted like Alfalfa (*Medicago*).

Medicinal Uses: Shepherds Purse leaves have long been an important wound herb, and were used as a battlefield dressing by soldiers as late as World War One. It may be used as a poultice (see *Plantago*) or wash. A tea of the leaves has been used to stop internal bleeding.

The plant has also been used to treat diarrhea, to regulate blood pressure, as a liver stimulant, a blood purifier and to stimulate uterine contractions.

Cultivation: This plant is easily grown from seed, and will grow in almost any soil, though it gets bigger and more succulent in rich moist soil.

Related species:
C. gracilis
C. rubella
Use as above.

Capsicum annuum var *aviculare* / Chiltepine, Bird Pepper Syn *C. baccatum*
Southwest & south Florida   *Solanaceae*

This tropical species only just makes it as far north as the United States, growing in Arizona, New Mexico, Texas and Florida. It is a subspecies of the familiar Chili Pepper, though its round red berry-like pods are of even greater pungency. Habitual Chiltepine eaters consider hot peppers such as Jalapenos to be "cool and refreshing".

Constituents: The active ingredient in all chilies is capsaicin, a fiery substance detectable in concentrations as low as one part in 15 million. It is most concentrated in the placental tissue around the seeds.

Caution: This species is becoming less common in the wild due to development of its desert habitat and commercial over-harvesting of the pods. As a consequence you should only gather the fruits if they are abundant and take care not to damage the plants.
You should also take care not to get any of the juice from the pods in your eyes, or on sensitive areas of skin, as it really burns.

Spice: The round pods are gathered in late summer and dried for later use. They are used like the other hot peppers, fresh or dried, as a condiment for soups, beans and sauces.

The popularity of peppers as a spice in hot climates (India, Mexico, Thailand) probably has something to do with the fact that they actually prevent the oxidation that makes food go bad. This means that these highly spiced foods actually keep fresh longer. They also promote sweating, which helps to cool the body.

Medicine: A very effective use of Peppers is to stop bleeding. It would seem downright masochistic to sprinkle such a pungent substance onto an open wound, yet the dried powdered pods (I've only used Cayenne pepper) stop bleeding very quickly, and don't really sting as much as you might expect.

Hot Peppers have been used in cases of bronchitis and emphysema to clean out the lungs. They are sometimes said to help protect against stroke, blood clots and heart disease. Herbalists generally consider them to be a carminative, stomachic, general tonic and detoxifier. Native Americans used them as a prophylactic against ailments of all kinds, even witchcraft. Capsaicin has been found to have the ability to kill off prostate cancer cells.

Animal Repellant: The pungency of capsaicin finds a practical use in dog repellant sprays for letter carriers and others. It has also been investigated as a relatively harmless bear repellant for wilderness hikers. Not surprisingly most animals dislike a face full of the fiery liquid, and it will even deter a charging animal. It also discourages human animals, and pepper spray is commonly sold as a substitute for Mace.

Foot Warmers: Apparently powdered peppers can be sprinkled into the socks to keep the feet warm in cold weather. The irritation causes increased blood flow and so keeps the feet warmer.

Cultivation: The Chiltepine has a promising future as a cultivated crop for arid areas. It can be grown from seed in much the same way as its domesticated cousins,

though germination is usually poor. This might be improved by scarification, to mimic a journey through a bird's digestive system. This is the way the plants are distributed in the wild, and is the origin of the common name Bird Pepper. It can also be grown from cuttings and this is much faster. The plants are more resistant to drought, cold and disease than garden peppers. The young plants like shade, and in the wild they are often found growing under Hackberry trees, the seeds having been dropped there by roosting birds.

Garden Uses: Hot pepper powder has been sprinkled on other plants to deter pests from eating them.

Cardamine species / Spring Cress
Throughout   *Brassicaceae*
The name Cress is of Anglo-Saxon origin, and was once applied to any member of the *Brassicaceae*.

Greens: The Spring Cresses are good raw in salads in spring when the weather is cool. Their young leaves and flower buds can be used as a potherb in the same way as Wintercress (*Barbarea*).

Cultivation: Most species prefer rich moist soil and are propagated by seed or division.

Species Include:
C. bulbosa - **Bulbous Spring Cress**
C. pulcherrima - **Large Flowered Bittercress**
These perennial species produce a palatable root, as well as tasty greens. Use them like those of the related Toothworts (*Dentaria*).

C. Pratensis - **Cuckoo Flower**
This cosmopolitan species is found all around the Northern Hemisphere. It is probably the best food species and is occasionally cultivated.

C. pennsylvanica - **Pennsylvania Bittercress**
C. hirsuta - **Hairy Bittercress**
C. oligosperma - **Little Western Bittercress**
C. rotundifolia - **Mountain Watercress**
All of these species provide tasty spring greens.

Carya species / Hickories
East   *Juglandaceae*
The Hickories are closely related to the Walnuts (*Juglans*). The most notable difference being that the husks of Hickory nuts split apart and fall off when ripe, while those of the Walnut hold together. There are only 15 *Carya* species worldwide, of which 11 are found in eastern North America. They are familiar trees in the warm southeastern states, though precise identification is sometimes difficult, as they hybridize readily. Exact

identification isn't important, as any with tasty nuts can be eaten. Their quality varies even within a species, so the only way to tell how good they are is to taste them.

Nutrients: Hickory nuts are very nutritious, containing up to 15% protein, 15% carbohydrate and 70% fat, which adds up to over 200 calories per ounce.

Nuts: The nuts were a staple food of some Native American tribes, and individual families often owned gathering rights to certain groves of trees. Like most wild nuts they don't bear dependably every year, producing heavy crops one year, and fewer nuts for the next couple of years. A mature tree might give about 100 pounds of nuts in a good year, though some have been known to yield twice that much. Trees in clearings bear more heavily than those in deep forest.

The best known Hickory species is the Pecan (*C. illinoensis*), which is an important commercial nut crop. Other species could be equally valuable if more breeding work is done. Gathering the wild nuts for sale was once a minor cottage industry in some areas.

Gathering: Gather the nuts as soon as they fall to the ground or forest animals will. Remove the husks with your foot as you go, otherwise you will be carrying more weight and bulk in husk than in nut. Allow the nuts to dry for several days, before storing in a cool, dry place. They store well and may stay wholesome for up to two years. They taste better after a short period of storage.

Shelling: Some Hickories naturally have thin shells and are opened as easily as the cultivated Pecan. Others need the attention of a hammer or heavy-duty nutcracker in the same way as Black Walnut (See *Juglans*). Even after cracking the shell, it isn't always easy to remove the

meat from the convoluted kernels. You may well end up with more small fragments than whole kernels.

Leaching: A few species produce bitter tasting nuts, notably the appropriately named Bitternut Hickory (*C. cordiformis*). These can be made palatable by burying them in the ground over the winter, to leach out the bitter substance. Native Americans apparently did this a lot.

Uses: Though getting the kernels from their shells can be difficult, using them is easy. The best are as good as the cultivated Pecan, and can be used in the same ways.

Oil: Hickory nuts were probably most important to Native Americans as a source of oil. The Creeks called this Hickory milk and used it like butter in much of their cooking. It is very good when fresh, but doesn't keep well. It can be extracted by pressing the kernels mechanically, though Native Americans usually obtained it by crushing and boiling them in water. It doesn't matter if bits of shell are boiled with them, as these are heavy and sink. The oil and nutmeats rise to the surface, where they can be skimmed off and separated, or mashed to make a kind of nut butter (you can use a blender).

Wood: Over 80% of all Hickory wood cut goes for making tool handles, as it has an unequalled combination of strength and resilience (weight for weight it is stronger than steel). It is also prized for wagon wheels, ladders and other purposes where shock resistance and toughness count. Some wood is used for cabinetmaking and paneling, though it shrinks a lot in drying. A traditional use of the wood is in making moonshine whiskey.

Firewood: Hickory is unexcelled as firewood, giving from 23 - 28 million Btu per cord. It is also used for making charcoal, and is considered among the best woods for smoking food.

Animal Food: The nuts are eaten by deer, bears and many rodents and birds. After you have finished shelling the nuts, leave out the broken shell fragments for wild birds to pick out the last fragments of kernel.

Other uses: The wood splits easily along its growth rings and making Hickory baskets and split brooms was once an important cottage industry. The inner bark was peeled from the trees in spring, and used for making rope and woven chair seats.

Oil: Hickory nut oil was once used in lamps.

Cultivation: The Hickories are long lived, climax forest species and eventually succeed almost all other trees (their seedlings grow well in the shade). They make handsome and productive shade trees for any large garden. They are grown from ripe nuts, planted immediately, or stratified for two months at 35 degrees Fahrenheit. It is vital that the seeds and seedlings are protected from rodents, or they will disappear without fail. Generally the trees like rich, deep, well-drained soil, and don't transplant well once established.

Young trees benefit from mulch. Regular feeding (such as sewage sludge) will increase growth and bring earlier bearing. For nut production a number of named varieties are available as grafted trees. These produce better nuts than wild trees and bear several years earlier.

Coppicing: If a Hickory tree is cut down it doesn't die, but rather sends up a number of shoots, any of which could grow into a new tree. This of course is the principle of coppicing, once widely practiced in Europe and the Hickory could be a valuable species for this in the future. A coppice of Hickory could be a very efficient way to obtain fuel wood for a homestead. See Hazel (*Corylus*) for more on coppicing.

Useful species include:
C. illinoensis - **Pecan**
The Pecan is the largest *Carya* species, sometimes reaching 200 feet in height. It has always been an important tree to humans and was actually considered sacred by some Native Americans tribes (they increased its range by planting it further north). The first European settlers often spared Pecan trees when clearing the forest and used the nuts for human and animal feed. The wild nuts are easier to shell than most *Carya* species. Today this is easily the most valuable cultivated native nut tree, yielding up to 1400 pounds per acre, and with many cultivars available. The wood is occasionally used for cabinetmaking and flooring.

C. ovata - **Shagbark Hickory**
C. laciniosa - **Big Shellbark Hickory (Kingnut)**
These species can be identified by their characteristic shaggy bark (it has been suggested this may have evolved to deter nut-loving squirrels from climbing them and eating the unripe nuts). Both species produce fine flavored nuts and are occasionally cultivated in northern areas. They are sometimes crossed with the Pecan to produce hardy hybrids. The Shagbark Hickory has the best wood for tool handles.

C. glabra - **Pignut Hickory**
C. pallida - **Sand Hickory**
C. tomentosa - **Mockernut Hickory**
These species usually produce tasty nuts.

Castanea dentata / American Chestnut
East & locally elsewhere   *Fagaceae*
Once there were billions of Chestnut trees in the eastern hardwood forest, this single species making up almost a

quarter of all the trees, yet most people in the east today have never even seen a mature American Chestnut tree. This is because they simply no longer exist over most of their former range. Some time around 1904 the fungus disease Chestnut Blight or *Cryphonectria* (formerly *Endothia) parasitica* was introduced on imported Asian Chestnuts. The native trees had no resistance to this hitherto unknown disease, and in the 1920's and 30's it infected almost all of the trees in its range.

The trees don't always die from the disease, many roots survive to this day, sending up suckers that grow vigorously to a height of 20 feet and a diameter of four inches or so, but eventually the disease kills the tops (some trees even produce a few fruits before succumbing). The persistent roots then start all over again, by sending up new shoots.

Though mature trees are rare in its native range, the plant is in no way endangered. Not only do roots persist, but trees planted on the West Coast live on, and a few groves even survive in the east. Recent developments even bring hope that the disease may be overcome and the trees will return.

Ever since the Blight first came to North America people have been searching for naturally resistant American Chestnuts, and have also crossed them with blight resistant Asian Chestnuts. There have been many false hopes raised in the past, but disease resistant strains may now finally be appearing.

Perhaps of even greater significance are reports that the fungus itself is being attacked by a virus which weakens it to the point where it no longer kills the tree, which then recovers from the infection. This happened in Europe and helped save the commercially important Chestnut forests there. Injections of this weakened fungus have been used experimentally in this country and have apparently helped trees to survive.

Its many uses once made the American Chestnut the single most important and useful tree species in North America. Hopefully in the near future it may once again take its place in the eastern hardwood forest

Nutrients: Chestnuts have been a staple food for people in Asia, Europe, North America and North Africa. Unlike most common nuts they don't have much protein or fat, but contain about 40% carbohydrate, which gives them a food value of about 1000 calories per pound. They are also rich in iron, phosphorus and potassium.

Food: Mature trees fruit abundantly almost every year, and are said to produce more food than an equivalent area of wheat. A fairly small (12 inch diameter) tree in my garden produced about 80 pounds of nuts this year.

The Uses Of Wild Plants

The trees were a very important source of food for Native Americans and the first European settlers.

Gathering: There are few mature American Chestnuts to be found in the east, but there are the Chinkapins and the introduced Asian species. American Chestnuts have been planted on the west coast, and these continue to thrive, happily out of the range of the disease.

Remove the spiny husks from the nuts as you collect them, by rolling them under your feet. Before the Blight the main problem for Chestnut gatherers and growers was the Chestnut Weevil. The larvae of this insect destroy the kernels of mature nuts, so the nuts must be gathered as soon as they are ripe, and frozen or heat-treated to kill the eggs (a microwave oven does this effectively). The nuts can then be dried or frozen (best) for later use.

Preparation: Chestnuts can be eaten raw, but they aren't very good and frequently cause gas. They are excellent when baked or roasted, as this turns some of the starch into sugar and gives them a sweet flavor. Traditionally they are roasted in the hot ashes of a fire. You puncture the leathery skins of all but one nut and put them in the ashes to bake. In theory the unpunctured nut is supposed to burst when they are all cooked, though this doesn't always work, so sample one occasionally until they are cooked. You can also boil them, or bake in an oven at 400 degrees for 20 minutes (puncture them).

In Europe Chestnuts were commonly made into flour for baking bread and cakes (these were often wrapped in Chestnut leaves for baking). They were also used for making a kind of porridge, usually mixed half-and-half with wheat or corn meal. They have even been roasted as a coffee substitute.

Wood: In colonial times the trees were very important for their attractive and rot resistant wood. This splits easily along the grain to make wide planks, which was a significant consideration before power saws. It is soft enough to be worked with quite simple tools, and was available in very large pieces. It is also very durable when in contact with water. Fallen trunks are sometimes still sound after lying on the ground for forty years.

Chestnut was considered as good as Oak (*Quercus*) for building construction, split rail fences, shingles, shakes, telephone poles, railroad ties, fence posts, bridge timbers and pilings. It is a little too soft to be really prized for cabinetmaking, though it was often used.

In Europe the Chestnut is frequently coppiced to provide the small diameter poles so useful for peasant farming. It was also widely used for split basket weaving. The bark was used for tanning leather.

Fences: In Britain coppiced Chestnut poles were commonly used for making pale fencing or palings, in fact this was the intended purpose of most plantings. The poles were harvested when about 5 - 6 inches in diameter and cut into sections the height of the fence required. They were split lengthwise into pales, which are cloven strips of wood about 2 X 1 inches in thickness. These were bound tightly into bundles to keep them straight and left to season. The seasoned pales were made up into fencing on a simple apparatus consisting of three pairs of galvanized wires. The pales were laid individually between the pairs of wires, which were then twisted (changing direction after each pale) to hold the wood securely. This fencing was made where the trees grew. It is light, durable, rolls up easily and is strong enough to resist animals and humans (many English children will tell you that it is awkward to climb over).

This fencing was once commonly made in Appalachia for use as snow fencing, to hold back snow and prevent it drifting. This craft could be a valuable source of income for homesteaders with Chestnut trees, as it needs little equipment and is fairly easy to learn.

Firewood: Chestnut wood is also good firewood, though rarely available in quantity today. The thrifty Europeans bound waste wood and prunings into faggots for fuel. Chestnut coppice is a good way to grow firewood (see *Populus* for more on fuel wood coppice). In colonial America Chestnut was converted into charcoal for the fledgling steel industry.

Animal Food. Chestnuts were very important food for wildlife and livestock.

Crop Use: In Southern Europe a peasant economy grew up around the indigenous Chestnut forests, and created a symbiotic relationship between humans and trees that lasted for over a thousand years. The finely tuned, self sustaining forest agriculture that developed was a model of agro-forestry, and could teach us a lot about ecologically sustainable agriculture. Sadly it has declined in the twentieth century.

The European forest farmers gradually replaced the wild Chestnut trees with grafted varieties, creating large forests of select cultivars. To replace a tree that was past its prime they would plant a young grafted sapling nearby. When the sapling was well established they would fell the old tree while the wood was still useful, leaving the sapling room to mature. The nuts were a staple human food, while livestock foraged for the nuts overlooked by human harvesters. The animals also kept the forest open and more accessible by eating low growing vegetation. Chestnut weevils were kept in check by chickens foraging under the trees. The wood of mature trees was used as lumber, while smaller branches were bound into faggots for fuel. Dead leaves were used as bedding for humans, and litter for livestock (their high tannin content makes them toxic to most insects). The soiled litter was used as fertilizer for vegetable gardens.

Propagation: These trees are easily grown from ripe seed, planted two inches deep in autumn. They must be kept moist to preserve viability and must be protected from rodents (which will eat them). The seedlings are planted out in a nursery bed after a year and into their permanent home three years later (they have a deep taproot so take care when moving them). Under ideal growing conditions they grow very rapidly, often adding an inch to their diameter annually, and producing useful lumber in only 50 years. Mature Chestnut trees may grow to 100 feet in height and four feet in diameter. They start bearing fruit in 7 - 10 years, or even earlier with some improved cultivars.

Wild nuts are usually fairly good, but cultivated trees are grafted for improved yield, quality and earlier bearing. Over the centuries many cultivars of Chestnut have been bred (especially in Europe), with special varieties for animal feed, desserts and flour.

Coppice: Coppiced Chestnut can be grown by itself, or as a productive understory beneath larger fruit or lumber producing trees (known in England as Coppice with standards). It is possible to grow Chestnuts as coppice even with the blight still around. See Hazel (*Corylus*) for more on coppicing.

Related Species: After the near total loss of the American Chestnut, a number of exotic relatives have been widely planted in the east, including:

C. crenata - **Japanese Chestnut**
C. molissima - **Chinese Chestnut**
These blight resistant species don't grow wild in North America, but are often planted for their excellent nuts. The Japanese species is very precocious, sometimes bearing fruit when only five years old.

Castanea pumila / Allegheny Chinkapin
Southeast   *Fagaceae*
Apparently the name Chinkapin is derived from the Algonkian word for Chestnut - chechinkamin. This shrubby relative of the Chestnut is also attacked by the Chestnut Blight, but it isn't seriously affected (it simply produces new stems) and often fruits abundantly. It has been suggested that the Chinkapin was once a large tree, which at some time in the past was affected by a similar disease, which reduced it to shrub size. Essentially this is what has happened to the American Chestnut, which no longer matures into a tree, but survives as a shrub.

Nuts: Chinkapin nuts are smaller than American Chestnuts, but can be used in the same ways (and sometimes find their way into markets). They are rich in vitamin C, phosphorus, iron and carbohydrate and give about 200 calories per 100 grams.

Wood: The wood is similar to Chestnut, though it doesn't get big enough to be an important timber species. It can be split and used like Chestnut for fencing.

Cultivation: This species has been suggested as a potential new nut crop. It is cultivated like the related Chestnut (see above), and in suitably rich, dry soil may attain a height of 45 feet. A number of improved varieties are available.

Related species:
C. alnifolia - **Dwarf Chinkapin** Syn *C. nana*
C. ozarkensis - **Ozark Chinkapin**
Use as above.

Castanopsis species / Chinkapins
Syn *Chrysolepis* species
West   *Fagaceae*
The western Chinkapins vary greatly in size, from small shrubs to large forest trees. They are unreliable nut producers from a consumer standpoint, taking two years to produce useful nuts, and often failing to do so. These are smaller than American Chestnuts, but equally tasty, and may be used in the same ways.

Species include:
C. chrysophylla - **Giant Chinkapin**
C. sempervirens - **Sierra Chinkapin**
The first species is a large tree, the latter is a shrub.

Ceanothus americana / **New Jersey Tea**

East   *Rhamnaceae*

Tea: New Jersey Tea has been called one of the best wild substitutes for oriental Tea. The leaves were quite widely used for tea in earlier times, notably when colonists boycotted oriental tea during the revolution. The great wild food forager Euell Gibbons found that the best tea was made by fermenting the leaves (rather like oriental tea is processed). He immersed them in boiling water, rolled them to break open their cells, and then left them to ferment for 24 hours. They can then be used immediately, or dried for later use.

Medicine: The tannin rich leaves have been used as an astringent. They also contain a substance that lowers blood pressure.

Soap: The flowers and fruits of a number of *Ceanothus* species are so rich in saponins they can be used as soap (see *Saponaria*).

Animal Food: The foliage is important browse for deer and other wildlife.

Smoke: Native Americans smoked the leaves of some species.

Cultivation: This attractive shrub is often cultivated as an ornamental. Propagate by root cuttings, semi-ripe cuttings or seed (sow when ripe, or stratify for 2 - 3 months at 35 degrees). This is a pioneer species of dry open woods, and often appears after disturbance such as forest fire. It is also a valuable soil builder, as it contains nitrogen fixing bacteria in root nodules.

Related Species: There are a large number of *Ceanothus* species in the west. None are poisonous and you can use the leaves and flowers of any of them for tea. Some are much better than others however. The best include:

C. integerrimus - **Deer Brush**
C. sanguineus - **Oregon Tea Tree**
C. velutinus - **Leather-Leaf Ceanothus**
These species all make good tea.

Celtis occidentalis / **American Hackberry**

Throughout   *Ulmaceae*

The Hackberry resembles its cousin the Elm, though in late summer it is easily distinguishable by its berries. The fallen fruit often makes a mess under the trees, which can help in finding them.

Fruit. The quality and abundance of the fruit varies according to growing conditions. In warmer climates they may be sweeter, in moist soils they are much fleshier, while in dry areas they may be very scarce or absent altogether. The berries have a thin sweet edible pulp covering a large seed. Don't bother removing the seed, just eat the whole berry.

Hackberries were commonly eaten by Native Americans and were an important food for some tribes. They sometimes ate them fresh, but more often they pounded them into a sticky mass and dried them into cakes. These were used to sweeten other foods, such as preserves, pies, breads and sauces.

Wood: The light, handsome wood resembles its cousin the Elm (*Ulmus*). It has occasionally been used for cabinetmaking, but more often it is used for low-grade uses such as packing cases and fence-posts. Native Americans used it for bows.

Firewood: Hackberry is good firewood, giving about 20 million Btu per cord.

Fiber: Native Americans used the fibrous bark for cordage, and to make sandals.

Animal Food: The trees are important to wildlife for food and shelter.

Cultivation: Hackberry can be propagated from seed, sown when ripe, or stratified at forty degrees for 3 - 4 months. Even with stratification the seed may take two or more years to germinate. A faster way to get plants is to transplant overcrowded seedlings from under mature trees, as these transplant well. It likes moist, well-drained soil, with a steady water supply from surface or underground water. Hackberry aggressively seeks out water, and its roots have a tendency to penetrate pipe joints and clog them. For this reason it should never be planted near drainage or water pipes.

Few pests bother the trees, though they are often attacked by the harmless, but disfiguring, witches' brooms. They are sometimes planted on stream banks to prevent erosion. Some desert species are important nurse trees.

Useful Species: All *Celtis* species can be used as above, the best include:

C. pallida - **Desert Hackberry**
C. reticulata - **Netleaf Hackberry   Syn *C. douglasii***

Cercidium microphyllum / **Yellow Paloverde**
Syn *Parkinsonia* spp

Southwest   *Fabaceae*

The name translates as "green stick" in Spanish, because that's exactly what the plant looks like for most of the year. It only bears leaves during the rainy season, and drops them in time of drought to conserve water. It photosynthesizes through its green bark for the rest of the year (about 40% of photosynthesis occurs in this way).

Seed: The Paloverde was an important source of food for the Pima and neighboring tribes. The immature 2 - 3 inch seedpods, and seeds, were cooked and eaten. The ripe seeds contain 25 - 50% protein and taste pretty good. They were parched and ground to flour for baking bread, or boiled to mush.

Animal Food: The foliage and seeds provide food for many desert animals. The nectar rich flowers attract many insects.

Cultivation: This species has been suggested as a potential food crop for arid areas. It is often planted as an ornamental in hot climates, as it is quite spectacular when in bloom in spring. Some people don't like it because the fallen leaves make a mess on the ground. It is very hardy, drought resistant and may live forty years or more. The trees are beneficial to the soil, as they help prevent erosion, add leaf litter and probably also contain nitrogen fixing bacteria in root nodules. They are important nurse trees, providing shade and enriched soil for many desert plants.

The tree is usually grown from seed. Before planting nick the hard seed coat with a file and soak in water overnight. It needs well-drained soil.

Related species:
C. floridum - **Blue Paloverde**
Used for food as above, though not as good. It is a better ornamental however.

Cereus giganteus / **Saguaro**
Syn *Carnegia gigantea*
Southwest   *Cactaceae*
The Saguaro (pronounced Sah-waro) is probably the most familiar symbol of the American desert. It is the largest and most impressive member of the Cactus family, often attaining tree-like proportions. Like most cacti it is slow growing, and in the inhospitable desert environment may take fifteen years to reach a height of six inches. They can eventually grow to 70 feet tall, and can live up to 250 years.

Cactus Adaptation: In a hot dry environment most plants rapidly lose water through their stomata (pores) as they respire and if this isn't replaced they die. They can close the stomata to prevent water loss, but not for too long, as this also shuts down respiration and photosynthesis. Cacti have solved this problem by developing a process called Crassulacean acid metabolism (CAM). They close their stomata in the day to avoid excessive water loss, and open them at night to

absorb carbon dioxide. Of course the plants can't photosynthesize in the dark, so they convert the carbon dioxide into malic acid and store it overnight. The following day the stomata close, and the malic acid is broken down to release carbon dioxide, which is used for photosynthesis.

The Cacti have simple flowers, but very advanced and well-adapted vegetative parts. Their leaves are absent to conserve water and the branches are reduced to spines to give protection from herbivores. The swollen stem stores water and carries on photosynthesis. The stem of the Saguaro is fluted and can expand to store a large quantity of water. In wet weather a mature plant may consist of 98% water and weigh as much as fifteen tons. With this reservoir of water it can survive droughts of several years' duration. The root system is shallow but very extensive, spreading up to 50 feet all around, so it can absorb rainfall quickly before it evaporates.

Experienced desert campers avoid making camp too near dead or damaged plants, as fifteen tons of falling spines can be quite disconcerting. In 1982 a man was killed while using a Saguaro for target practice (a stupid idea as the bullet holes can allow fatal infections to enter the plant). The damage he inflicted caused the plant to collapse on top of him.

Threats: In the United States the Saguaro is growing at its northernmost boundary, so is vulnerable to climactic change and other factors. These magnificent plants are still quite common in parts of the southwest, but they may start to disappear in the near future, as human activities are destroying large numbers of young plants.

The overgrazing of desert land by cattle doesn't damage the Saguaros directly, as they are too well armed to be eaten. It does affect them indirectly though, as it has eliminated many other important wildlife food plants. As a consequence the fruit and seeds of this plant have become more important as food for wildlife, so few of the thousands of seeds produced ever get to grow. Obviously is this continues the species will eventually vanish, as older generations die without leaving younger ones to replace them. Cows also kill young plants directly by trampling them.

Anther threat to the plants comes from "cactus rustlers", who dig the smaller specimens of Saguaro (and many other cactus species) and sell them to homeowners and collectors. This illegal activity is a lucrative international business, with collectors in America, Europe and Japan willing to pay handsomely for fine specimens. The recent popularity of cacti as interior decorations has also increased the demand. It is difficult to meet this demand by cultivation, as it may take 20 - 30 years for a Saguaro seedling to reach three feet in height

The Uses Of Wild Plants

and anyway it is much more profitable to simply gather from the wild. It is illegal to transplant or sell a Saguaro without a tag from the Department of Agriculture. This is a felony punishable by up to 5 years in prison and a fine of up to $250,000, but plants continue to be stolen.

Another serious threat to the plants comes from the retirement communities, golf courses and strip malls that are rapidly gobbling up the desert.

Fruit Gathering: Saguaro fruits are commonly known as *pitahayas* and were a staple food of some desert dwelling Native American tribes. They contain a lot of sugar and vitamins and are pretty good. The Saguaro harvesting moon of July was an important event in their calendar, and gathering the tasty fruit for food and drink was a time for celebration and feasting.

The fruits were gathered with long hooked poles, made by tying two or three ribs of Saguaro together, with a hooked branch on the end. If you try this, make sure you catch the fruits as they fall, as they may burst if they hit the ground. Also make sure you don't damage the plants with the sticks.

Fruit Use: The ripe fruits split open to reveal dark red flesh and black seeds. This can be scraped from the skins and eaten fresh, but it ferments and spoils quickly in the desert heat. The sweet flesh was used to make preserves and syrup. The best way to preserve the fruits is to dry them, though you must cook them first to kill the insect eggs that will almost certainly be in them. The seeds in the fruits are edible, but rather indigestible unless thoroughly chewed, so Native Americans often ate them separately (see below).

> ### Wine
> In the warm desert climate the expressed juice of the fruit ferments quickly and can easily be made into wine. This was (and still is) one of the most important Native American uses of the fruits. It was drunk for ceremonial purposes and for pleasure (often both at the same time; in pleasurable ceremonies).

Syrup: A sweet syrup can be made by boiling the chopped fruits in water, straining off the pulp and seeds and then boiling the remaining liquid to syrup. This stores quite well.

Seeds: The fruits were mashed in water, and then strained to separate the seeds from the flesh. Another way to get clean seed is to dry the fruit, pound it to meal and then winnow out the seed. See *Lemairocereus* for an unusual way to obtain clean seed. The cleaned seed can be dried for storage, or used immediately.

Native Americans usually ground the seed to meal and boiled it to make porridge, or baked it with an equal amount of wheat or corn meal for bread. The seeds contain 20% protein and about 30% oil, and were sometimes ground to make a kind of nut butter.

Wood: Native Americans used the long woody ribs of Saguaro skeletons for shelters, fencing, fuel and poles. European settlers used them for furniture.

Animal Food: Saguaros are very important to desert wildlife. The fruits are eaten by almost every animal that can get to them. The flowers provide nectar for insects, bats and hummingbirds.

Older plants provide valuable shelter for birds, notably the Gila Woodpecker which excavates a hole in the stem for its nest. After the Woodpeckers vacate these holes they are quickly taken over by other birds. Sometimes this happens even before they are vacated, bird squatters move in and simply refuse to move out. The hollowed-out interior is an ideal nesting site, secure from snakes and other predators and much cooler than the desert outside. The plant seals off the hole with a hard coating, and they seem to do little permanent damage. This coating actually makes the hole more durable than the rest of the plant, and holes from old dead plants, known as Apache boots, can sometimes be found on the desert floor. Native Americans used them for containers and drinking cups.

Cultivation: If you live in its native area, you should consider growing some Saguaros from seed. This isn't difficult, but it is slow. It is also possible to get the arms to take root and become new plants. One can buy young plants in many nurseries, but remember they must have a tag from the agriculture dept. The plant often doesn't transplant well from the wild and may die if not planted with its original orientation to the sun, as the side facing the sun has thicker skin for protection. Saguaro is very heat and drought resistant, but frost tender (at least as tender as citrus). In cultivation it is most often killed by over- watering.

In the wild the plants are commonly found growing near Mesquite, Paloverde and other trees, because birds roosting in the trees excrete the seeds in their droppings. The young seedlings thrive in the nitrogen enriched soil and shade found underneath the trees.

Cereus greggii / Night Blooming Cereus
Syn *Peniocereus greggii*
Southwest   *Cactaceae*

This inconspicuous smaller relative of the Saguaro reaches only about five feet in height and for most of the year it resembles a dried up Creosote Bush among the desert scrub. For a few days in June it's showy white flowers open from late evening to early morning. These give off a delicious scent that gives away the plants location, and earn it the alternate common name Queen-Of-The-Night. These flowers have made Night Blooming Cereus a popular garden ornamental, and so many wild plants have been dug up for sale that it is now rare in many areas.

Root: Like many cactus this species produces tasty edible fruit, though it is too uncommon to use in most places. Unlike most cacti it also produces a large tuberous root, which it uses to store water. This root is edible when cooked, which explains yet another common name for the plant, Sweet Potato Cactus. It is said to be quite good when baked in the ashes of a fire like Camas (see *Camassia*). Unfortunately digging the root kills the plant, which isn't very responsible, necessary or legal.

Cultivation: This species is often grown as an ornamental in warm climates. It is quite easy to propagate from stem cuttings, if you allow them to heal over for a couple of weeks, before planting out. Like its cousin the Saguaro it is worth propagating, especially as it is getting less common in the wild.

Cetraria islandica / Iceland Moss
North   Lichenes

Iceland moss is not a moss, but a lichen, which is actually two separate plants, a fungus and an algae, growing symbiotically. The algae photosynthesizes food for both plants, while the fungus provides a physical structure and protection from the elements. Lichens are incredibly tough little plants; able to thrive in places so inhospitable no other plants could even survive. They are resistant to cold, drought and heat and can survive temperatures of up to 250 degrees Fahrenheit.

Lichens are often the dominant plants in extremely cold areas, because they are just about the only species capable of surviving there. This species can be a valuable food source if properly prepared, and has kept people alive when there was nothing else to eat. It is rich in carbohydrate in the form of lichenin and isolichenin, and also contains a little protein, fat and vitamin C. The carbohydrates are chemically similar to those found in seaweeds, and like them are not easily digested by humans.

This is the most useful food lichen and is harvested commercially in Scandinavia.

Caution: Lichens contain cathartic acids that must be leached out before they are edible. Even the leached plants have been known to cause stomach problems, when used in quantity for prolonged periods.

Gathering: Lichens grow very slowly, and should only be used for food in emergencies, or when very abundant. Gather them by cutting, rather than uprooting, so they will be able to regenerate more easily.

Preparation: The irritant acids can be leached out by soaking overnight in several changes of water. Adding a little wood ashes or baking soda to the water will help neutralize the acids. You can also boil the moss in a couple of changes of water, with some wood ashes. After leaching, dry the moss and grind to powder.

Use: The leached moss contains a lot of mucilage and can be boiled, strained and sweetened to make a kind of jelly. Citrus peel and wild berries can be added for extra flavor and milk used instead of water. One part of lichen flour has been mixed with four parts wheat or corn flour (Native Americans sometimes used Elm bark flour) and baked into bread. In Scandinavia ships biscuits were sometimes baked with a proportion of lichen flour, as it was said to deter weevils. The flour has also been used to thicken soup, and has been made into a passable dessert. The latter was made by mixing the flour with water and leaving overnight to form a jelly. Fruit and sweetener were then added.

Drink: Lichen tea is made by steeping a teaspoon of the flour in a cup of boiling water, then flavoring with citrus peel, herbs and sweetening to taste. In Scandinavia the moss has been fermented to make "Danish Brandy".

Medicine: Iceland Moss contains a potent antibiotic which has been used for medicinal purposes and as a food preservative. The jelly was used by herbalists to treat pulmonary complaints, and it has recently been found to inhibit the growth of tuberculosis bacteria.

Alcohol: In the Soviet Union during World War Two this species (and other Lichens) was used to produce alcohol. They were first treated with hydrochloric acid to convert their starch into glucose, and then fermented and distilled in the usual way. Apparently sixteen pounds of moss would yield a gallon of alcohol.

Cultivation: Though lichens grow very slowly, they can do so where few other plants can grow at all, and so have been suggested as possible crop plants for the far north. They are easily propagated vegetatively, simply scatter small fragments of plant onto moist rocks and keep moist. They grow faster if given an organic fertilizer such as urine, cow dung or skimmed milk.

Lichens are sensitive to airborne pollutants because they obtain some of their nutrients from the air. If this is too dirty they simply cannot establish themselves, though they may survive if already established. This fact has been used to date early pollution, by looking on dated gravestones; one can see when the air became to dirty for lichens to get established.

Related species:
C. nivalis
Use as above.

Chenopodium album / Lambs Quarters

Throughout   *Chenopodiaceae*
Lambs Quarters is a perfect example of a pioneer species, and has managed to spread itself around the world in the footsteps of European colonists. Its success is due in large part to its amazing fecundity, typically a single plant will produce about 4000 seeds, though in ideal conditions they have been known to produce up to 100,000. Some seeds are able to germinate immediately, others must lie dormant for several years. This spreads out the germination over a few years, and helps to reduce the competition amongst all those seeds.

Nutrients: A close relative of Spinach, Lambs Quarters has been used as a salad or potherb for thousands of years. It contains large amounts of vitamins A, C and several B's, as well as calcium, iron and phosphorus.

Caution: The plant contains mildly toxic oxalic acid and so shouldn't be used in large quantities for long periods (see *Oxalis*). It may also accumulate nitrates on certain soils, notably those where lots of chemical fertilizers have been used. Nitrates are toxic to humans because they tie up oxygen in the blood. Having said that, I must add that the plant is no more toxic than spinach.

Lambs Quarter Fritters

2 lb greens
1 onion
1 ½ cups all-purpose flour
Salt and pepper
1 tsp baking powder
1 ½ - 2 cups water
1 beaten egg
Vegetable oil

    This dish is traditional in parts of Northern Europe. Chop the washed greens and onions, add seasoning and cook in the water that clings to them for 3 minutes. Make a batter of flour, egg and water. add the greens, mix thoroughly and fry like pancakes.

Greens: The young spring growth is good in salads, or as a potherb.

The tender flowering tips of older plants (gathered up until the flowers fade), can be boiled or steamed for 5 - 10 minutes. They shrink a lot in cooking so gather plenty. In Mexico those of Huazontle (*C. berlandierii var nuttaliae*) are boiled for 5 minutes, squeezed into bunches, dipped in eggs and fried.

The leaves are a useful addition to green drinks.

Seed: The seeds were widely eaten by hunter-gatherers around the world, and several species have been cultivated as seed crops. The most important of these is the South American Quinoa (*C. quinoa*), which was a staple grain crop for the Incas. Quinoa seed contains about 10 - 20% protein and up to 25% fat.

Gathering: Obtaining a quantity of cleaned seed is relatively easy. When the first seeds ripen, gather the whole head and leave it to dry in a paper bag in a warm place. Thresh the dried seed heads to free the seed, winnow out the chaff and it's ready to use. The flavor is improved by toasting in a frying pan like Pigweed

(*Amaranthus*), or by roasting for 45 minutes in a 350-degree oven.

Use: The dark gray flour is usually mixed with an equal amount of wheat flour, for making bread, pancakes and porridge. You can make porridge by simply boiling the whole seed to mush.

Medicine: The vitamin rich greens have been eaten to cure scurvy.

Animal Food: The seeds are relished by many kinds of birds and are an important wildlife food. The plant was once considered very good for domestic poultry, and was intentionally sown to provide them with food. This is the reason it is also known as Fat Hen.

Cultivation: This annual is easily grown from seed and thrives on sunny disturbed sites. It improves the soil by adding humus and bringing up minerals from the subsoil, and is a good green manure crop (it must be dug in before it sets seed). It is sometimes sown on bare ground as a quick cover to prevent erosion and subsequent nutrient loss. It is also a persistent weed, and I have spent quite a few hours hoeing down row after row after row.

Native Americans often encouraged the plants by scattering the seed in suitable locations, which is about all you really need to do for it. There is now at least one improved cultivar available. You might also try growing *C. quinoa*, as the seed is now quite widely available.

Related species:
C. berlandieri - **Berlandiers Lambs Quarters**
This species was domesticated in eastern North America about 4000 years ago (much as Quinoa was in South America), and improved cultivars were developed. It was cultivated up until the eighteenth century, but disappeared along with the Native American way of life.

C. californicum - **California Soap Plant**
This species is not edible, but its root and leaves contain so much saponin they are sometimes used as a soap substitute.

C. capitatum - **Strawberry Blite**
The young shoots and leaves can be eaten like the above. The attractive, red berry-like fruits can be used to add color to salads, but they don't really add much flavor. This plant is most often used in the far north where there are few green foods available. Native Americans used the fruits to dye skin, clothes and basket material. It is sometimes cultivated as an ornamental or salad plant.

C. fremontii - **Fremont's Goosefoot**
This species grows up to six feet in height and produces seed in abundance. Native American legend tells of it being cultivated as a seed crop, prior to the introduction of Corn from Mexico (just like *C. berlandierii*).

C. murale - **Nettle Leaved Goosefoot**
C. leptophyllum - **Narrow Leaved Goosefoot**
These species are both good food producers.

C. ambrosoides / Epazote
Syn *Teloxys ambrosoides*
This species differs from most of the *Chenopodium* genus in being very aromatic and quite poisonous. It is too toxic to be used as a potherb, and only safe to use as flavoring in small quantities. Its unique aroma and flavor is instantly identifiable, and the plant is an important culinary herb in Mexico. A few leaves are used to flavor bean dishes, chili and stews. It is said to prevent the gas associated with such dishes. You don't need much; a teaspoon of dry leaves, or six fresh leaves is enough for a large pot of beans. Use any more and the beans become unpleasantly bitter.

Medicine: A tea made from a teaspoon of fresh leaves in a cup of hot water, has been used as a remedy for flatulence. The plant was also used to eliminate intestinal worms, and is sometimes known as Wormseed because of this. Wormseed oil is distilled from a particularly potent variety of the plant (*C. ambrosoides* var *anthelminticum*). It is rarely used to treat humans today, but is still used by veterinarians.

Related species: *C. botrys* - **Jerusalem Oak**
Use like Epazote.

Chlorogalum pomeridianum / Soap Plant, Amole

West coast   *Liliaceae*

This rather inconspicuous perennial of woods and dry mountains opens its small flowers only on evenings and cloudy days.

Caution: The large bulbous root contains a lot of saponins and is quite toxic raw. These substances are destroyed by heat, so the cooked bulb is edible.

Root: Native Americans boiled the bulbs, peeled off the fibrous skin and ate the interior. The texture is somewhat mucilaginous, but the flavor isn't bad. They also roasted them in a fire pit as for Camas bulbs (see *Camassia*).

Greens: The young spring leaf shoots have occasionally been eaten as a potherb.

Medicine: The soapy juice of the bulb was used to clean wounds, and treat Poison Oak rash.

Soap: The plant gets its common name because the saponin rich bulbs can be used as soap. Simply strip off the hairy skin, and use the flesh as you would soap, making sure to rinse well afterward. This is an excellent dandruff shampoo, and an extract is sometimes found in expensive herbal shampoos. The saponins will poison fish in the same way as the Buckeye (*Aesculus*).

Brushes: Native Americans made brushes from the bristly fibers that cover the bulb. These fibers were glued together with the cooked mashed root, which hardens as it cools.

Glue: The juice of the root has been used as glue.

Cultivation: This perennial can be grown from bulbs or seed in dry sunny soil.

Related species:
C. angustifolium
C. parviflorum - **Small Flowered Amole**
Use as above.

Chondrus crispus / Irish Moss

North Atlantic   *Rhodophyta*

Irish moss contains carragheenan, an important commercial food additive. This is widely used by food processors, to add body, and as a stabilizer. This has probably been eaten by almost everyone in America at some time. There is a ready market for the wild plants, and gathering the moss ("Mossing") is a minor cottage industry on parts of the North Atlantic coast. See Kelp (*Macrocystis*) for more on the properties of alginates.

Caution: Carragheenan has been linked to some forms of cancer, and is suspected of having both teratogenic and mutagenic effects. It is still legally used as a food additive, but is on the FDA list as needing further study.

Carragheenan has little food value to humans, as we aren't able to digest it very well. Digestibility apparently improves with habitual consumption however. Like most seaweeds the plant is a useful source of vitamins and minerals.

Gathering: Irish Moss can be gathered any time you can get it, but is at its best in spring and early summer. Commercial moss gatherers (mossers) gather storm tossed moss year round, or rake it from the shallow water of the lower shore.

Wash the plants in fresh water to remove salt and sand and then spread them out in the sun to dry. If you leave it long enough it will be bleached white. Commercial mossers spread out a thin 2-inch layer, to be washed by the rain and dried in the sun. They usually have to turn it once or twice before it is thoroughly crisp and dry. They also have to leave it long enough to be bleached by the sun, as this is preferred by buyers.

Gelatin Substitute

The plant was used like agar or gelatin in puddings. Soak a quarter cup of dried weed for 15 minutes, and then boil in 2 1/2 cups of fresh water or milk for about 30 minutes until it almost dissolves. Stir carefully to prevent sticking or use a double boiler. The solids are then strained out, and the liquid is allowed to cool and set. Various fruits or vegetables can be added for flavoring. It has also been used to thicken soups and sauces.

Medicine: Irish Moss was used for its demulcent properties, to soothe mucous membranes and for respiratory problems. During World War One it was used to treat victims of poison gas.

Sewage Treatment: Irish Moss has been used experimentally in biological sewage treatment plants, in the final stage of the purification process.

Fertilizer: Like most seaweeds it is an excellent garden fertilizer. See *Macrocystis* for more on the uses of Seaweed in the garden.

Chrysanthemum leucanthemum / Ox-Eye Daisy

Northeast & elsewhere   *Asteraceae*

This European plant is quite common in North America, but is usually overlooked as a food plant. I like it a lot and use the leaves up until they flower. Some people complain it gets bitter and unpleasant with age.

Greens: The sweet and mildly aromatic leaves are a nice addition to salads. I have never used Ox-Eye Daisy as a potherb, but it is so used. A similar flavored Asian species, the annual Garland Chrysanthemum (*C. coronarium*) is widely cultivated in Japan as a food crop.

Medicine: The leaves can be used as a wound poultice and as a mild diuretic.

Insecticide: This species is a close relative of Pyrethrum Daisy (*C. coccineum*) and its dried powdered flower heads can be used as a mild insecticide or insect repellant. The active ingredient is apparently scabrin and not the more potent pyrethrins.

Cultivation: The perennial Ox-Eye Daisy is attractive enough to have been used as an ornamental, but it self-sows readily and can become a weed if not controlled. It is easily grown from seed in most soil types, and is worth planting in any wild or waste spot. It is also good for cut flowers.

Cichorium intybus / Chicory

Throughout   *Asteraceae*

Chicory has a history of cultivation dating back to the ancient Egyptians. It was introduced into North America as a food plant by early European settlers, and is now widely naturalized.

Nutrients: Chicory leaves are as bitter as those of Dandelion and almost as nutritious. They contain lots of vitamin A and C and many minerals including iron, potassium, calcium and phosphorus.

Food: Chicory is cultivated for three quite different foods, greens, roots (for coffee) and shoots (known as chicons) and specific varieties have been bred for each. Wild plants can be used in all of these ways, but are smaller and more bitter.

Greens: The tender new spring leaves can be used in the same ways as the related Dandelion (See *Taraxacum*), as salad greens, or as a potherb. As the plant matures they become impossibly bitter. Blanching reduces their bitterness considerably and this probably led to the forcing of the roots. It is cultivated in Italy for greens.

Shoots: Cultivated Chicory roots are forced indoors to provide tasty white shoots called *chicons*. This has become a major industry in Belgium and they are sometimes available in supermarkets under the name Belgian Endive.

Coffee

Chicory is perhaps best known for its use as a coffee substitute or extender. It was once so widely used as a coffee adulterant that its use was made illegal. However many people say Chicory actually improves the flavor of coffee, and it may reduce its harmful effect on the liver.

To make Chicory "coffee" the cleaned roots are dried thoroughly, until they are so brittle they snap easily. They are then ground to a powder and roasted in an oven until uniformly brown. The drink is prepared by mixing a teaspoon of the roasted powder with a cup of boiling water. You can also add roasted sprouted Barley, Carob, Cinnamon, or other goodies. It is often mixed with an equal amount of coffee.

Forcing: In cold climates the roots are sometimes dug in late fall and forced indoors over the winter. They are planted in a box of sand and stored in a cool dark place until required. To start them growing they are watered and moved to a warmer place. The pale shoots are harvested as needed. The roots will continue to produce more shoots until they are exhausted.

Root: The roots have been cooked like Salsify (*Tragopogon*), though they are bitter unless the cooking water is changed two or three times.

Medicine: The Roman physician Galen called Chicory the friend of the liver, and herbalists have long used it for urinary, kidney and liver problems. It is also used as a

digestive tonic, to neutralize hyperacidity and to eliminate mucus. It can be taken as food, in green drinks or as extracted juice, though the latter is extremely bitter unless mixed with other juices. The roots and leaves have been used externally for skin problems.
The juice has apparently been mixed with honey and applied to women's' breasts to make them firm. Maybe this use has something to do with the plants influence by the planet Venus, and its use in love potions.

Animal Food: Chicory has been used for animal forage.

Cultivation: The perennial Chicory is one of the easiest vegetables to grow. Even the cultivated varieties have retained some of their wild vigor, and need little care once established. It is easily propagated from seed, and thrives in most soil types (for the largest roots, and easier harvesting, a loose, rich, moist soil is best). It self-sows readily, and might be considered a weed if it weren't so useful.

Chicory has a generally beneficial effect on the garden. Its bright blue flowers are pretty and attract a variety of beneficial insects.

Cirsium species / Thistles

Throughout   *Asteraceae*

Though we don't generally think of Thistles as food, they were a favorite food of Native Americans, and in Japan a number of species are cultivated for their roots. They have all the attributes that make a good wild food plant. They are easily identified, have no poisonous look-alikes, are available year round, are quite nutritious and taste pretty good, even when raw. All parts have been eaten and no species is poisonous, though some may accumulate toxic nitrates when growing on heavily chemically fertilized fields. The many species vary a great deal in habit and edibility, so one must experiment with them to find the best.

Greens: The young spring leaves can be eaten as a salad plant. Just trim off the spines and chop well. Older leaves can be cooked as a potherb for fifteen minutes, though you might have to change the cooking water once or twice to reduce their bitterness.

Flower Stem: The stems are gathered before the flowers open, peeled of their tough skin, and eaten raw or cooked (they are good in soup). For a quick snack, split the stems lengthwise and eat the succulent interior.

Flowers: The larger flower buds can be cooked and eaten like Artichokes (a close relative). The dried flowers of all species have been used to curdle milk for making cheese. Use five teaspoons of dried flowers to a gallon of milk.

Roots: The roots can be eaten year round but are best while dormant in winter. Locate them at this time by the rosette of leaves. I have dug roots in midsummer and found them tasty straight from the ground, however some species are bitter unless cooked in a change of water. They can be boiled (preferably then sliced and fried), added to soup, or baked like Camas (see *Camassia*) in a fire pit. The slow baked roots were a favorite of Native Americans. They become very sweet when baked, as their starches turn to sugar. You might try baking them in aluminum foil in the ashes of a fire, or in a 350-degree oven for 30 minutes. Native Americans dried and ground the baked roots to flour, and added it to bread.

Coffee: The roasted roots can be used as a coffee substitute, like those of the related Chicory (see *Cicorium*).

Down: The downy seed have been used like those of Milkweed (*Asclepias*), for stuffing clothing and pillows. It was once commonly used as tinder to catch sparks for starting fires.

Animal Food: Though the fresh plant is inedible to most animals (except goats and donkeys), the cut and dried plants are nutritious feed for livestock. The flowers are a rich source of nectar for bees and other insects, and the seeds provide food for many birds.

Weed: Thistles are a typical sign of over grazed land, where livestock has eaten everything palatable, leaving only the plants which bite back. Without competition these can multiply freely. These plants are perfectly adapted for this niche, they are covered in spines, produce huge numbers of long-lived airborne seeds and have creeping perennial roots (which enable a single plant to cover twenty square feet in a single season). We blame the plants (*C. arvense* has been called the worst weed in the country), but they are really filling an ecological vacuum created by poor land management.

Thistles have also been called nature's last line of defense against soil degradation, which gives you a different way of looking at them.

They can be eradicated by repeated cutting, by digging and eating the roots, or by goats and donkeys.

Horticultural Uses: These deep-rooted plants improve the soil by breaking up compacted subsoil, and bringing minerals to the surface. The flowers and seeds attract beneficial insects and birds to the garden.

Biodynamic gardeners consider Thistles so beneficial they use a tea of the plant as a compost inoculant. Steep the foliage in water for several days as for Comfrey – (*Symphytum*).

Species Include:
All young Thistles are edible. The best include:

C. brevistylum - **Indian Thistle**
C. edule - **Edible Thistle**
C. foliosum - **Elk Thistle**
C. horridulum - **Yellow Thistle**
C. undulatum - **Wavy Leaved Thistle**
C. vulgare - **Bull Thistle**

Cladonia impexa / Reindeer Moss
Syn *Cladina* spp

North & mountains   Lichenes

Food: Reindeer Moss gets its common name because it is an important food for those animals. It can also be used as human food if prepared in the same way as Iceland Moss (*Cetraria*). Here we are entering the realm of the "survival food", as the resulting dish has been likened (forgive the pun) to snail slime.

Greens: Lichen, eaten while still warm from a Caribou's stomach, was an Inuit delicacy. For a special treat this was mixed with blood, and allowed to ferment in the smoke of a fire for a few days. White men with the courage to taste such an unconventional dish said it was actually very good.

Medicine: *Cladonia* species contain antibiotics and have been used in commercial burn preparations. They should be used with caution, as they occasionally cause dermatitis similar to that of Poison Ivy / Oak.

Alcohol: The plants could be used like Iceland Moss to make alcohol.

Model making: This lichen is used by model railroaders and others to make model trees. It is soaked in glycerine before use to stop it drying out.

Animal Food: These Lichens are very important food for arctic animals such as Musk Oxen and Caribou. They have also been fed to cattle when other forage plants are scarce.

Cultivation: Same as Iceland Moss.

Related Species:
C. rangiferina
C. stellaris
Use as above.

Claytonia species / Spring Beauties
Throughout   *Portulacaceae*

As the name suggests these beautiful flowers appear in spring and disappear by midsummer. Some species produce starchy corms up to two inches in diameter, others have edible taproots. Unfortunately (as with most root crops) taking them kills the plants, so is only permissible if the plants are very abundant. In such cases thinning could be beneficial, especially if you replant some of the smaller bulbs in a suitable location.

Roots and Corms: These are best gathered as the plants start to die down in summer, though they are good right until growth starts the following spring. They are not always easy to dig in quantity, as the corm may be six inches deep, so look for places where the plants are crowded together and dig systematically. You should be aware that a single corm might produce a number of stems, so the plants often appear more numerous than they really are.

They can be eaten raw or baked, but are best boiled whole, like tiny potatoes, for 15 - 30 minutes. If you want to peel them, do so after cooking.

Greens: These species are closely related to Miners Lettuce (*Montia*) and their succulent leaves have been used in the same ways, in salads or as a potherb. However they should only be used when abundant.

Cultivation: The Spring Beauties are a welcome sight in spring, so are often planted in wild gardens. They prefer rich woodland soil with some shade, and can be propagated from seed (slow), offsets or tubers.

Once established they spread vegetatively to form colonies and self-seed readily. They are tough little plants, and I have even found them growing on shady neglected lawns.

Best species Include:
C. caroliniana - **Carolina Spring Beauty**
C. lanceolata - **Western Spring Beauty**
C. megarhiza - **Alpine Spring Beauty**
C. virginica - **Spring Beauty**

Cleome species / Bee Weeds
West   *Capparidaceae*
The Bee Weeds were important food plants for the Navajo, Pueblo and other Native American tribes, and were encouraged to grow near their dwellings. The Anasazi cultivated them along with their corn, beans and squash, and their presence in certain areas is an indicator to archaeologists of possible ancient settlements.

Greens: The young leaves and stems can be used as a potherb until the flowers appear in July, though the cooking water must be changed at least once to remove their strange odor. Flower buds and green seedpods were be used in the same way.

Seed: Native Americans, and the first European settlers, ground the seed to flour for making bread and gruel.

Animal food: As the common name suggests, these plants are very attractive to bees as a nectar source. The seeds are eaten by many birds.

Cultivation: Several of these beautiful annuals have been grown as ornamentals. Propagate from seed in light soil with full sun.

Cnidoscolus stimulosus / Spurge Nettle
Southeast   *Euphorbiaceae*
Caution: The aboveground parts of Spurge Nettle are covered in the most potent stinging hairs of any North American plant. These can cause a severe allergic reaction in a few people, so use caution around the plants. You should wear thick gloves when gathering from them.

Roots: The tuberous roots of the Spurge Nettle are a valuable wild food, if you can find them at the end of the long roots. The underground parts have no sting; so can be gathered safely if you are careful. They are prepared in the same ways as Potatoes.

Related species:
C. texanus - **Bull Nettle**
This species produces edible seeds as well as a virulent sting. Wear gloves to protect the hands while gathering the pods. Dry them thoroughly, then thresh and winnow out the seeds. These can be eaten raw, roasted or ground to flour.

Cochlearia officinalis / Scurvy Grass
Northern Coasts   *Brassicaceae*
This northerly growing plant gets its common name because it is rich in vitamin C and was once used to treat scurvy (which is an old name for vitamin C deficiency). It was so effective it was dried and carried on sailing ships as a preventive. It is also rich in vitamin A.

Greens: Like many members of the *Brassicaceae*, Scurvy Grass is only palatable in cool weather, and becomes bitter and pungent in summer heat. The very young leaves of first year plants can be used in salads, and sandwiches, and are quite good. If they are too bitter to eat raw, then cook in at least one change of water.

Drink: Scurvy Grass was used to flavor beer, before the introduction of Hops.

Cultivation: This biennial or perennial plant is easily grown from seed, and is tolerant of saline soils. It is occasionally cultivated as a potherb in the far north.

Corylus species / Hazelnuts
Throughout   *Betulaceae*
The Hazels are widespread and common understory shrubs throughout much of North America. They are easily identified by the hanging brown catkins and the nuts. The European Hazel was once an important resource in Northern Europe, as it was coppiced to provide small diameter poles for farm and home use.

Nutrients: The nuts contain about 10% protein, 60% fat and large amounts of calcium, iron and magnesium. They are said to be more digestible than most nuts.

Gathering: Hazelnuts are often produced abundantly, but they are a favorite food of birds, mice, squirrels and many other wild creatures. A single squirrel may eat as many as eighty nuts in one day. With so many predators the ripe nuts don't stay around very long, so they must be gathered as soon as their papery husks start to turn brown in late summer. Plants that are isolated from woods, and associated rodents, often hold their nuts much longer.

Native Americans often took the nuts from rodent caches, but were usually careful to leave some other food in exchange. When gathering the Beaked Hazelnut (*C. cornuta*) wear gloves, as tiny sharp hairs on the husks can pierce and irritate the skin, rather like glass fibers.

Preparation: Dry the nuts in the sun, or in a warm room, for a few days (protected from animals of course) and then store them in a cool place. A traditional European storage method is to pack the nuts into jars until almost full, put salt in the top inch or so and seal tightly.

Uses: You may be familiar with the uses of Hazelnuts. They are good whole, or chopped, in cereals such as muesli and granola, and can be baked in bread and cakes. An interesting variation is to grind them to meal, and mix with wheat flour for baking. Immature nuts are edible, but don't store well.

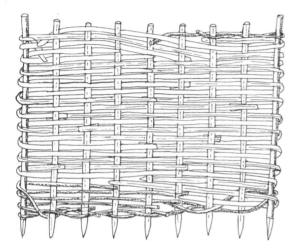

Greens: The newly opened spring leaves of some species have been eaten as a salad or potherb.

Oil: Hazelnut oil is one of the finest cooking and salad oils. It can be obtained by pressing, or by boiling as for Hickory (see *Carya* for more on this).

Firewood: The Hazels produce good firewood and the plants could be coppiced solely for this. See Poplar (*Populus*) for more on fuel wood coppicing.

Cordage: Native Americans used the bark fibers for cordage.

Animal food: Hazelnuts are important wildlife plants, providing food for nut eaters and herbivores. In densely populated Britain the areas of Hazel coppice (known as copses) were important refuges for wildlife.

Wood Polish: The oily kernels can be used as furniture polish, simply rub them on the wood and then polish with a cloth.

Wattle hurdles: One of the main uses of Hazel coppice in Britain was for making the portable fences known as wattle hurdles. These were originally used to temporarily enclose sheep in a field, but have also been used to shelter gardens from wind, to stabilize sand dunes, and for many other purposes.

The poles were cut when about 1 inch in diameter, split lengthwise, and woven around a line of poles set in a frame. The end result was a panel of solid woven fence about 5 - 6 feet long and 3 - 5 feet high. These sections were joined together as required to form any shaped enclosure that was needed.

These panels are as ornamental as they are effective and now find widespread use in gardens as rustic screens, gates and fencing. Making them provides a livelihood for some enterprising people in Britain, and could do the same in this country.

Hazel Coppice

Hazel was once a very important plant in Britain and other parts of Europe. It was coppiced to provide small diameter poles for a variety of uses (almost like Bamboo in Asia). These include, tool handles, garden supports, walking sticks, fishing poles, etc. They were split lengthwise for weaving baskets and wattle hurdles, and for use as barrel hoops.

Coppicing makes use of the fact that when you cut down a Hazel shrub it doesn't die, but sends up a number of new shoots. As these are growing from established roots, with plenty of light reaching the whole plant, growth is very rapid and vigorous. This is the most efficient way to grow small diameter wood, and was widely practiced in Europe up until relatively recently. This process doesn't harm the plants at all, and can actually prolong their life span considerably.

The production of coppice wood was an intensive kind of forestry, and many villages had communal woods to provide for local needs. It was also grown on large estates ,and auctioned off to craftsmen who would use it for a variety of purposes. This provided a steady income for landowners, so coppice land was highly prized. The coppiced woods were also used for raising pheasants for shooting, and so provided another, much prized, resource.

Walls: Woven wattle panels were once used in durable wattle and daub house construction. The panels were used to fill the spaces between Oak timber framing and were covered with a mixture of clay and straw. This was then covered in a more durable coat of plaster. Some houses built in this way have lasted 500 years or more.

Other uses for coppice: In the past all parts of the coppiced plants were used. The smallest twigs were sold to gardeners as pea and bean supports, thinner poles were sold as supports for a variety of plants, and any leftover wood was bound into faggots and sold for firewood.

Cultivation: In northern Europe the Hazel is the most reliable nut producing plant, and many varieties have been bred during its centuries of cultivation. The plants start bearing when quite young, and may reliably produce 500 pounds per acre annually (if you don't have a large squirrel population). They can be planted along with other nut trees, and will give a valuable yield for years before the larger trees start to bear. They are quite shade tolerant, and will grow underneath nut or fruit trees as a secondary productive layer They can also be planted in hedgerows and windbreaks to make them more productive. Some varieties are attractive as ornamentals.

Propagation: Hazels shrubs may live for 100 years, so give them a good site to grow on, with rich soil and full sun or light shade. Sow the ripe nuts in fall, or stratify for three months at forty degrees, and protect from rodents at all costs. They can also be propagated from suckers, layering or cuttings (taken in late autumn and rooted over winter). Some commercial cultivars begin to bear when about four years old, and reach maximum productivity in about 15 years. To ensure good pollination plant a number of varieties. In the eastern states Hazels may be attacked be a serious disease called Eastern Filbert Blight.

Coppicing: A coppice is established by planting the seedlings about 3 - 5 feet apart (as many as 800 to an acre). It takes 4 - 6 years to produce a vigorous root system. After that time the shrubs are cut down almost to ground level, leaving an angled stump (known as a stool) to ensure water drains off and doesn't cause rot. This causes the plant to send up vigorous new shoots. These are left for 3 - 12 years to grow to the required size and then cut again. This process may be repeated almost

indefinitely. If any plants die after being coppiced they can be replaced by layering from the next plant over.

Cutting was done on a rotation, with a section of the plantation being cut each year, so there was a sustained annual yield of poles. Most of this work was carried out in winter when there was little other farm work to be done.

Coppicing with standards was an old intensive farming practice, where larger timber trees were left to grow among the coppiced shrubs, and cut as needed. There must not be too many standards, as their shade will adversely affect coppice growth. King Henry VIII introduced a statute specifying no more than 12 standard trees to an acre of coppice.

Species include:
C. americana - **American Hazelnut**
 C. californica var *rostrata* - **California Hazelnut** Syn *C. rostrata*
C. cornuta - **Beaked Hazelnut**
All these species produce fine nuts.

Crataegus species / Hawthorns
Throughout   *Rosaceae*
Hawthorns are becoming increasingly common in some areas, as humans alter natural ecosystems and create new niches for these adaptable and rugged plants. Botanists have a hard time deciding how many species there are in this genus, as they hybridize readily and precise identification can be difficult. Fortunately you only need to identify it as a Hawthorn, as none are poisonous and any bearing palatable berries can be eaten.

Fruit: The fruits (haws) aren't the best tasting wild foods and their quality varies considerably, even within a species. Sample the fruit from each bush you find, some taste awful and even the best ones are nothing exceptional. However they are nutritious and common so you might want to experiment. Take care when gathering these spiny plants, they aren't called Haw-thorn for nothing. The fruits aren't usually eaten raw by themselves, but are usually mixed with tastier fruit, such as Cherries, Blackberries or Juneberries. All haws are improved by cooking. They are most often used to make a kind of preserve, with sugar and citrus peel for added flavor. They are rich in pectin and are sometimes added to other fruit preserves to supply this. They have also been fermented to make wine.

Native Americans ground the dried berries to meal, which they mixed with wheat or corn flour for baking.

Medicine: The European Hawthorn (*C. oxyacantha*) has an effect on the heart resembling that of digitalis. A tea of the bark, berries or flowers is used for most heart problems, to lower or raise blood pressure and to improve the circulation. Its action is slower than digitalis, with fewer side effects and it seems to have a generally beneficial effect. A number of commercial heart preparations based on Hawthorn are available in Europe. It isn't clear to what extent the native American Hawthorns have similar properties, though several species were used as cardiac tonics by Native Americans.

A tea of Hawthorn leaves is diuretic and was used to treat kidney stones and water retention. It is also a good astringent, and has been used as a gargle for sore throats, and to treat diarrhea.

Wood: Hawthorns rarely grow very large, so the use of their wood is limited to small items like walking sticks and wooden bowls. It burns well, and was once used for making charcoal, but its availability is limited.

Cordage: Native Americans used the bark fibers for cordage, and the thorns as awls.

Animal food: Hawthorns are important for wildlife. Small animals and birds relish the fruits and seeds, while the foliage is important browse for deer. The spiny thickets provide small animals with cover from predators.

Hedgerows: In Europe Hawthorns have long been the favorite plant for hedgerows, windbreaks and screens. The word hedge is derived from an Anglo-Saxon word for this plant. They are ideally suited to this use, as they are exceptionally hardy, well armed with thorns, fast growing, they don't mind being hacked, bent and manipulated, and they sucker vigorously. If carefully maintained they will form an impenetrable barrier. Any hole that appears in such a hedge can be temporarily closed with a few spiny branches. It is filled permanently by laying. This consists of cutting part way through a stem, bending it horizontally and pinning it to the

ground. During the next growing season it will send up vertical suckers along the stem and fill in the space. In densely populated Britain, Hawthorn hedgerows were very important to wildlife, as a source of both food and habitat. Indeed much of the wildlife in that country has disappeared in the past forty years, as hedgerows have been torn out to enlarge farm fields for mechanized farming. Another negative effect of their removal has been vastly increased soil erosion. Ironically the landowners once paid to tear them out, may now be paid to replant them.

Horticultural uses: Hawthorns have been planted as nurse trees, to protect tender seedlings from wind, cold and being eaten by herbivores. Their thorny branches are sometimes spread around newly planted seedlings to deter foraging herbivores (and cats). Some species are very ornamental in spring, when covered in white or pink blossom.

Cultivation: Hawthorns do well in most soil types, even poor ones. Propagate by layering or ripe seed (scarify in acid to remove the hard seed coat and plant out when at least six inches tall).

Hawthorns are affected by a number of diseases (Red Cedar / Hawthorn Rust is the worst) and pests (they are host for Apple Borers so are often discouraged near Apple orchards). Scions of cultivated Pear varieties have been grafted onto hardy Hawthorn rootstocks.

Species include:
C. coccinea - **Scarlet Hawthorn**
C. douglasii - **Black Hawthorn**
C. flava - **Summer Haw**
C. tomentosa - **Pear Haw**
C. oxyacantha - **European Hawthorn**
C. monogyna - **English Hawthorn**
The latter two species are locally naturalized from Europe.

C. aestivalis – **Mayhaw**
This southeastern species produces ripe fruit early in the year, hence the name. The juicy acid fruit has long been used in the southeast to make preserves, and is still quite popular. This may well be the best of the Hawthorn fruit, and it has been suggested as a possible new crop. A few superior cultivars exist, and are grown commercially on a small scale.

Cryptotaenia canadensis / **Wild Chervil**
East   *Apiaceae*
This aromatic species is not closely related to the familiar garden Chervil (*Anthriscus*), but is almost identical to another culinary herb, the Japanese Mitsuba (*C. japonica*). In fact it is sometimes considered merely a

geographic variation of that species. I must once again remind you to use caution when gathering and eating any wild member of the *Apiaceae*, as some are very poisonous.

Food: All parts of Wild Chervil are tasty and wholesome. The shoots, stems, flowers and seeds have been eaten raw in salads, used as a garnish, cooked as a potherb, added to soup and sauces, and used for tea.

Medicine: Native Americans used Wild Chervil as a wound herb. Mitsuba has been used to treat women's fertility problems.

Cultivation: This biennial species is grown from seed in moist soil, and prefers some shade. Imaginative gardeners have used it in the flower garden.

Cucurbita foetidissima / **Buffalo Gourd**

Southwest   *Cucurbitaceae*

This distinctive trailing vine is a close relative of the Squashes and Pumpkins (as you might guess from the gourd-like fruit). Like many of its cousins, it is a very vigorous species, the stems of a large plant may exceed 600 feet in total length (one individual measured over 7000 feet in total). Considering the area of foliage available for photosynthesis its not too surprising that the perennial root may grow to weigh 70 pounds in only three years. A plant may live for 40 years, and the roots have been known to grow to weigh several hundred pounds. Some Native Americans considered the plant to be sacred and never touched it; others performed special rites before harvesting.

Food: The whole plant is very bitter because it contains cucurbitacin, one of the bitterest substances known. As little as one part per billion is detectable to the taste. This limits its use as food.

Seed: The nutritious, oily seeds contain about 30% protein and 30% oil. A single plant can easily produce 100 small gourds, each containing 200 or more edible seeds. These are gathered as they ripen in September or October, dried in the sun to a uniform tan color, and then broken open to remove the seeds. These are washed thoroughly to remove any trace of bitterness, and then dried for storage. It is a good idea to wear gloves when handling the fruits, as they are covered in tiny hairs that can penetrate and irritate the skin.

Native Americans roasted the seed for 15 - 30 minutes to improve the flavor and to destroy digestive inhibitors. The seed coat can be eaten, so don't bother to shell them. They were often eaten as a snack like Pumpkin seeds. The ground seeds were used for baking bread, or to make a kind of porridge.

Oil: Wholesome oil can be extracted by boiling the seeds as for Hickory (*Carya*), or by mechanical or solvent, extraction.

Root: The starchy roots are bitter and toxic when raw, due to large amounts of saponins, but cooking makes them edible (if not particularly palatable).

Starch: This could probably be extracted from the root in the same way as for Kudzu (*Pueraria*).

Flowers: These have been used like Squash blossoms in tempura and salads.

Medicine: The root causes uterine contractions and was used by Indian women to aid in childbirth. It has also been used as a laxative, for hemorrhoids, headaches and various fevers and aches.

Animal food: The seed cake remaining after oil extraction is a valuable protein rich feed for animals.

Soap: The roots are rich in saponins and have been used as a shampoo or soap substitute. Simply chop the dried or fresh parts and agitate them in water. Be careful the first time you try this, as some people experience skin irritation from its use.

Fuel

Buffalo Gourd has potential as a source of renewable energy. The oil from the seeds can be used to make biodiesel (see *Brassica*) and it has been estimated that an acre of plants could produce 600 pounds of oil per acre annually.

If Buffalo Gourd is to become a viable energy crop more efficient production methods must be worked out (modern chemical farming is notoriously inefficient from an energy viewpoint). Breeding work is being done to increase the seed and oil yield, as this is very variable from plant to plant. As a bonus the starchy roots could be fermented to produce alcohol, which would be another significant energy source from the plant (and a component of biodiesel).

Gourds: Native Americans used the dried gourds as ornaments, rattles and containers.

Crop use: Buffalo Gourd is very tolerant of heat and drought, and could be a good crop for desert areas, where few crops can grow without extensive irrigation. In experiments it has yielded as much oil and protein as Soybean, but under far less hospitable conditions. Much higher yields are obtained if it is given some irrigation water.

One suggested method of cultivation is to plant rows of root cuttings. The first year the harvest would consist of the seeds in the gourds. The harvest in the second year would consist of seed and every other row of roots (these may weigh as much as 40 pounds). These rows would be immediately replanted with root cuttings. The harvest in the third year would consist of seed and alternate rows of three-year-old roots (these rows would then be replanted). This system could provide a sustained annual harvest of seed and starchy roots. It has been estimated that an acre of the plants grown in this way could yield 12000 pounds of starch, 1000 pounds of oil and 400 pounds of protein annually.

Cultivation: This perennial is easily grown from seed, or root cuttings (each with a piece of crown attached). Once established it may grow a foot per day, so should be given plenty of room. Don't plant it by your neighbor's fence.

The plants have occasionally been grown as trap crops, to lure Cucumber beetles and Corn Rootworms away from cultivated crops. It could also be useful as ground cover to prevent erosion.

Related species:
C. digitata - **Coyote Gourd**
C. palmata - **Coyote melon**
Use as above. The various species sometimes hybridize.

Cyperus esculentus / Chufa

Throughout   *Cyperaceae*
This cosmopolitan plant is found in Europe, Africa, Asia and North America. It closely resembles the Sedges (*Carex*) in that it has triangular stems, but unlike them it produces small edible tubers. These were cultivated for food by the Ancient Egyptians and are still popular in some countries. The name Chufa is of African origin.

Gathering: This species produces most abundantly in the warmer states, and in the cooler north yields are frequently too poor to bother with. The quantity and size of the tubers varies according to the growing conditions. The best crops come from wet sandy soils, and in such places the tubers can often be gathered by carefully pulling up the plants. Don't worry about destroying the plants, as some tubers invariably remain in the ground, and will grow to become new plants. Chufa is considered to be a serious pest in many areas anyway, and many landowners would be glad to be rid of it. The tubers are at their best in fall and winter. Use only the young tubers, and throw away the tough old ones (or replant).

Preparation: The first taste of a fresh tuber is quite a surprise, as their texture is unexpectedly soft and juicy, quite unlike most roots. The flavor somewhat resembles Coconut and Almond and they are in fact sometimes called Earth Almond. These nutritious and easily digested tubers can be eaten raw, cooked as a vegetable, or roasted like peanuts, and were a favorite food of Native Americans. The roasted tubers are a good trail snack.

The fresh tubers have a slightly resinous flavor, but drying eliminates this. The freshly gathered tubers are washed thoroughly and then dried for 4 - 5 days in a warm dry place. Native Americans stored the dried tubers for winter use, but it's easier to store them in the ground if possible.

Drink: The roasted tubers have been used as a coffee substitute.

Oil: Another unusual feature of the tubers is their high oil content (up to 30%). This is said to resemble Olive oil, and has been used for cooking and salads.

Flour: Flour can be obtained from the tubers, either by washing out the starch as for Kudzu (see *Pueraria*), or by drying and grinding the roots, then sifting the powder. This flour can be used with corn or wheat flour, for making bread, cookies and gruel.

Stems: In spring the base of the stem can be peeled and eaten, so long as it is still tender. Use like that of Sedge (*Carex*).

Horchata de Chufas

In Spain the tubers are used to make a drink called horchata de Chufas. This is prepared and sold fresh daily from roadside stands, and is still a popular drink, despite the introduction of more fashionable soft drinks.

The simplest way to make this drink is to soak a pound of clean tubers in water overnight, and then puree in a blender. Strain out any fibers, dilute with eight cups of water, sweeten to taste, and add the zest of a lemon. Chill for eight hours before serving. Native Americans made a similar drink, by mixing the flour with water, sugar and salt.

Medicine: The juice of the tubers is said to be a nutritive tonic for invalids.

Baskets: The fibrous stems and leaves have been used for basket weaving.

Fiber: Chufa is a relative of Papyrus (*Cyperus papyrus*), which was so important to the Ancient Egyptians for making paper. Chufa fibers have been used for cloth, rope, cordage, and for weaving mats, baskets and hats.

Animal food: The tubers are eaten by many wild animals and birds, and are planted to encourage wildfowl.

Crop use: The tubers have been cultivated for food in Spain, Egypt, Nigeria and elsewhere. They can be very productive, yielding up to three tons per acre, and grow on land where few crops do well without extensive drainage. Apparently cultivated varieties of Chufa were introduced into North America from Africa as food for slaves, and these became naturalized in the southeast. They bear larger tubers than the wild species, but are otherwise the same.

Despite its productivity and many uses, Chufa is usually thought of as a pernicious agricultural weed in this country, and is rarely planted for human food.

Cultivation: Chufa prefers light marshy soil, and can be grown by division, cuttings, or tubers planted in spring (best). These are soaked for 24 hours and then planted out 12 inches apart. You may have to protect the young plants from wildlife until they are well established. The first time I tried to grow them, every single tuber was eaten by birds or mice.

The plant matures in 3 - 4 months, and in warm climates can yield two crops a year. Once established it thrives without attention, and can be a productive perennial

crop. Enough tubers usually remain in the ground after harvesting to produce a crop the following year.

Some *Cyperus* species are pretty enough to be grown as ornamentals.

Related species: A number of other species produce edible tubers, but these are sometimes bitter and unpleasant. It is often hard to identify the exact species, but as none are poisonous this isn't a problem.

C. rotundus - **Nut-Grass**
C. strigosus - **Straw Colored Cyperus**
These also produce edible tubers. Use as above.

C. ferax - **Coarse Cyperus**
C. erythrorhizos - **Red Rooted Cyperus**
These species produce edible seed rather than tubers.

Daucus carota / Queen Anne's Lace

Throughout   *Apiaceae*

This common weed is also known as Wild Carrot, because it is the wild form of the garden Carrot. A native of Eurasia, but cultivated all across North America and now naturalized almost everywhere. Its kinship with the Carrot is not immediately obvious from the appearance of the thin white root, but the smell is instantly recognizable, as is the flavor.

Caution: Be careful when gathering any species that doesn't have flowers for positive identification, as some members of the *Apiaceae* are very poisonous. Some people warn that this species is poisonous. It isn't, but the finely divided leaves do resemble those of the highly dangerous Poison Hemlock (*Conium*), and could be confused with it. Don't gather this plant until you can positively identify that very poisonous species.

Root gathering: The roots of this biennial can be gathered for food from the end of their first year of growth, up until they start growing again the following spring. Plants at the right stage of growth are found by looking for mature plants with flowers, and then searching nearby for the feathery rosettes of leaves.

Root preparation: The roots can be used like garden carrots, eaten raw or cooked, but they aren't nearly as fleshy. They have a wiry core which is best removed. This is most easily done after they are cooked (cooking also makes them sweeter).

Drink: The roots have been used as a coffee substitute like Chicory (*Cicorium*).

Greens: The tender new spring foliage can be added to salads and soups.

Seed: The aromatic seeds are rather bitter, but have been used for tea and to flavor liqueurs. It has also been used like Caraway (*Carum*) for flavoring soups and sauces.

Flowers: The flowers have been fried in tempura batter.

Medicine: For medicinal purposes Wild Carrot is said to be stronger and more vital than the cultivated form. A poultice of the root has been used for skin infections and makes a good face pack for cosmetic purposes. A tea of the seed or leaves has been used as a diuretic, urinary antiseptic, carminative and digestive.

Reportedly a tea made from the seeds was once used as a "morning after pill", in the belief it could prevent pregnancy. I don't know how it was used, but presumably it worked to some extent, otherwise this would never have become an established use.

Domestic carrots are said to be beneficial to the liver, and have been used to treat jaundice. They are also said to build healthy blood, and even help to prevent cancer. Most of its health-building qualities are probably due to the very high carotene (vitamin A precursor) content, though this is lacking in the wild types.

Eradication: Wild Carrot is a common weed of waste ground, and spreads easily by means of its abundant seed. The best way to eliminate them is to dig the roots of first year plants and eat them, which of course prevents this biennial from ever flowering. You can also cut the flowering tops off second year plants (use them as cut flowers), before they set seed. If you do this for several years you will eventually eliminate the plant (you might even miss it).

Cultivation: The plant is so common in most areas there is little point in cultivating it, but if you wish to do so, treat it like garden carrot.

Related species:
D. pusillus - **American Carrot**
This native western species can be used as above. It was a favorite food of Native Americans, especially when roasted in a fire pit like Camas (*Camassia*).

Dentaria species / Toothworts
Throughout   *Brassicaceae*
These woodland herbs are closely related to the Bittercresses (*Cardamine*) and are sometimes included in that genus. The common and genus name refer to the tooth-like projections on the root.

Gathering: Though Toothworts are a palatable wild food, collecting the root can kill the plant, which is only

permissible when it is very abundant and overcrowded. Even then you should replant the crown when possible.

Preparation: The roots have a pleasant horseradish flavor, but aren't as pungent as true Horseradish. They are good raw in salads and sandwiches. They can also be cooked as a root vegetable, and add a nice flavor to vegetable soup.

Greens: The stems and young leaves can be used like those of *Cardamine*, as a potherb and salad.

Cultivation: These perennials prefer typical woodland soil, moist, acid and rich in humus. They can be grown from seed, but are more often propagated by root division. Once established they multiply quite rapidly, and have occasionally been used as a deciduous ground cover. In ideal conditions they will self-sow.

Best species include:
D. diphylla - **Two Leaved Toothwort**
D. laciniata - **Cut-leaf Toothwort**
D. tenella - **Slender Toothwort**

Dioscorea trifida / Wild Yam
East   *Dioscoreaceae*
Root: This plant produces edible tubers similar to those of the cultivated Yam, and is good enough to have been cultivated occasionally. These are inedible raw, but can be cooked and eaten like Yams.

Medicine: Some tropical Yam species are very important to the drug industry, because they contain chemicals that are used to produce the medically important hormones progesterone and cortisone. The value of the drugs produced from these plants is almost a billion dollars annually, and many species are now rare in the wild due to over-collecting.

Cultivation: Obtain shoots for planting by half burying the tuber in moist sand and keeping in a warm place. In a few weeks shoots should form, and when these are large enough they can be detached, and planted in rich, moist soil. It may also be grown from whole tubers, seed or cuttings. Yams are of tropical origin and need warm weather to be productive.

Related species:
D. batatas - **Chinese Yam**
This Asian species is found as an escape in parts of the southeast. Its edible tubers have an unusual flavor some people dislike, but it is cultivated for food in Asia. As the name suggests it is a popular food in China, and may sometimes be found for sale in Chinese markets in this country. It is also grown as an ornamental under the name Cinnamon Vine. This is the hardiest Yam species

and will survive the winter outside as far north as Pennsylvania. Use as above. Propagate from the small aerial tubers that are produced in the leaf axils.

D. bulbifera - Air Potato
This Asian species is found as an escape in the Gulf states. It bears edible tubers up to 6 inches long in the axils of its leaves. The plants climb vigorously, so the tubers are often high up in the air (hence the common name). Use as above.

Diospyros virginiana / Persimmon
East   *Ebenaceae*

Though Asian Persimmons are becoming familiar cultivated fruits in North America, the native American Persimmon is still hardly known. The reason for this neglect is that wild American Persimmons are incredibly astringent and unpleasant (you may still feel the effects the next day!), unless they are ripe almost to the point of decay. Even when soft and plump they can still be unpleasantly astringent, and a fully ripe American Persimmon is so soft it is impossible to ship to market. The quality of wild fruit varies considerably, some are never very good, while others are about as good as fruit gets (*Diospyros* means divine food). The flavor has been compared to Dates, though I think it is richer and better. The fruit are very sweet, because they contain about 30% sugar.

In Asia Persimmons (*D. kaki* and *D. lotus*) are as important as Apples are in America and over the years thousands of varieties have been bred, for dessert, drying and cooking. In this country Persimmon has been called one of the great weeds of the south.

Gathering: Persimmons often fruit abundantly; a single tree may produce more fruit than you know what to do with. In northern areas the fruit may not be fully ripe until mid-winter, which has led to the myth that frost is needed to eliminate their astringency. Frost actually has nothing to do with making them taste good, it's just that they take so long to ripen, they are almost always hit by frost. Some foragers lay sheets under the trees and shake the trunk to loosen ripe fruit. The ripest fruits are often already on the ground, simply pick up those sufficiently intact to use.

A nice feature of the Persimmon is that you can gather the fruit while still green and ripen them at home. Some people store them with a ripe apple, as this exudes ethylene gas, which hastens ripening. It is important that the fruit have good air circulation, otherwise they may go moldy before they ripen.

Preparation: The fruits usually contain a single hard seed, which should be removed from the pulp before drying or cooking, as it can spoil the flavor. Do this by pressing the pulp through a colander, which will also remove the skins and calyxes. The pulp can be frozen for later use.

The fully ripe fruits can be eaten out of hand as a delicious woods snack. The fresh pulp can be added to bread and cakes as a replacement for sugar.

Seed: Native Americans ground the seed to meal for baking and gruel.

Persimmon Leather

This was once a popular pioneer food and is still a great trail food for hikers. It is simply the cooked pulp dried to a leathery consistency. In China cultivated Persimmons are often dried and used like Prunes, and special drying varieties exist. Drying is probably the most practical and quickest way to introduce American persimmons to a wider market.

Drink: The leaves were made into tea by steeping in boiling water for ten minutes. The seeds have been roasted as a coffee substitute. The fruits were fermented to make Persimmon beer, a traditional southern drink.

Medicine: Native Americans used the astringent unripe fruit to stop bleeding and for diarrhea. The ripe fruit can be used as an astringent face pack for sore or tired skin.

Wood: Persimmon is a relative of Ebony and is occasionally used in cabinetmaking, though it is hard to season and work. It is very tough and has been used for golf clubs and mallet heads.

Animal food: J Russell Smith promoted American Persimmons as a source of feed for pigs and chickens. They have high food value, and are available over an extended period in winter, as they slowly fall from the trees (the animals can gather them directly). They are also important winter food for wildlife.

Cultivation: This vigorous tree is little bothered by pests, does well on poor, well drained soils and (unlike the tender Asian persimmons) is very hardy, surviving temperatures as low as minus 25 degrees Fahrenheit. It is usually grown from seed, planted when ripe or stratified for 2 - 3 months at forty degrees. Like most fruits it doesn't breed true, so for best flavor and maximum productivity the seedlings are usually grafted or budded with scions of improved varieties. Established trees spread by means of runners, and these can be used for propagating superior wild trees. Root cuttings can also be taken. Persimmon self-sows freely.

Quite a few improved cultivars exist, though they aren't easy to find. Most varieties are partly dioecious, which means that yields are increased by planting a male tree along with the females. Asian varieties have been grafted onto native roots to make them hardier. There are also hardy hybrids between the Asian and American species, and these are also worth investigating.

Aside from their value as food producers, Persimmons make fine shade trees, and have been planted purely for this. Ironically unfruitful male trees are usually preferred, as they don't drop messy fruit

Related species:
***D. texana* - Texas Persimmon**
The black fruits resemble Prunes in flavor, but like the American Persimmon are very astringent if not fully ripe. This is also an important tree for wildlife.

Dolichos lablab / Hyacinth Bean
Syn *Lablab purpureus*
Southeast   *Fabaceae*
The Hyacinth Bean is cultivated for its fragrant flowers, and edible beans, and may be found as an escape in the southeast. The young leaves, flowers, immature pods and ripe beans all contain cyanogenic glycosides and are toxic raw, but have been cooked and eaten. The seeds can be used in much the same ways as soybeans, as dry beans, sprouted and in tofu and tempeh

Cultivation: This species is perennial in the warm southeastern states, but it is treated as a tender annual in cooler areas and is started indoors in late winter. It likes well-drained soil, with full sun and is quite heat and drought resistant. Like most legumes its roots contain nitrogen fixing bacteria in root nodules. A number of improved cultivars are available.

Garden Uses: The plant has been used for green manure, as it quickly produces an abundance of plant material

(dig in when the flowers appear). It can also be used as a smother crop, fodder plant and ground cover.

Echinacea angustifolia / Purple Coneflower
East   *Asteraceae*
Medicine: Herbalists consider this species to be one of the most valuable blood cleansers of all plants. A tincture of the root is widely used to stimulate the immune system, and to help fight infectious diseases such as colds and influenza (it has significant anti-viral properties). Recent research indicates a scientific basis for this use, as it stimulates the production of white blood corpuscles and increases the production of interferon. If used regularly it should be taken in very small doses, as it becomes ineffective if consumed too frequently.

A root poultice has been used for infected sores (supposedly even gangrene), bites, inflamed gums, stings and muscle pains. Native Americans used it to treat snakebites, hence its other common name, Snakeroot. It has also been used as a douche for vaginal infections.

Cultivation: Because of its medicinal value this plant has been intensively gathered from the wild, and it is becoming much less common as a result. It is easy to grow from seed or division.

Related species:
***E. pallida* – Pale Purple Coneflower**
***E. purpurea* - Snakeroot**
Use as above.

Echinochloa species / Barnyard Grasses
Throughout   *Poaceae*
Some of these species are persistent and serious weeds in tropical countries, while others are cultivated on a small scale by peasant farmers.

Seed: Remove the seed from the husk by threshing and winnowing and it is ready to eat. Because they are common, and easy to work with, they were widely eaten by Native Americans. They often encouraged the growth of these plants near their settlements.

The seed can be parched and eaten as a snack, or ground to meal for gruel, baking and pancakes. It can also be boiled like rice and roasted as a coffee substitute.
The new green shoots have been cooked and eaten.

Cultivation: Grow this annual from seed in rich moist soil.

Useful species include:
E. colonum - **Jungle Rice**
E. crusgalli - **Barnyard Grass**
E. pungens
The latter two may be merely geographic variations of the same species.

Eichornia crassipes / **Water Hyacinth**

Southeast, California   *Pontederiaceae*
Water Hyacinth is native to tropical America, but is now naturalized in watercourses throughout the southeast and locally elsewhere. The plant is a classic example of the consequences of introducing a species into a habitat free of all its natural controls. It has become a serious problem in the waterways of tropical Africa, Asia and Australia. Its rampant growth prevents navigation, slows the free flow of water, and even reduces oxygen levels by shading underwater plants.

This is one of the fastest growing of all plants. Under ideal conditions it can double in volume every eight days, and theoretically the offspring of a single plant could cover all the water on the planet in two years.

Many attempts have been made to eradicate Water Hyacinth, by cutting, chemical poisons and biological methods. These are not always successful because it reproduces vegetatively from any small fragment, and unless an eradication program is 100% effective it will come back. Even if the plants are completely eliminated it may still float back in from elsewhere, or the long-lived seed may germinate

The plant is far from all bad however, and has many interesting potential uses. In the future we may even look upon it as a valuable resource.

Greens: The plant is not edible raw, but the mucilaginous young leaves and flower buds have been cooked and eaten. Older leaves are fibrous, mildly acrid and unpleasant. The inflated leaf bases and stolons have been fried or steamed.

Protein supplement: A leaf protein concentrate has been extracted from the juice of the leaves.

Salt: In its native Brazil the ashes of the leaves have been used as a salt substitute.

Pollution control: These fast growing plants may remove up to 90% of the nutrients suspended in the water they grow in. This ability could be put to use in recovering chemical fertilizer runoff and other nutrients, which would otherwise pollute watercourses. An acre of plants could recover as much as 3500 pounds of nitrogen and 800 pounds of phosphates annually. The plants might also be helpful in recovering dangerously toxic, but valuable, heavy metals like cadmium, lead, silver and mercury. It may also break down toxic compounds such as phenol, and absorb radioisotopes such as strontium 90.

Sewage treatment: Water Hyacinth has been used experimentally to purify wastewater in biological sewage treatment plants. It is estimated that an acre of the plants growing in a sewage lagoon could purify the waste of 300 people daily. A number of innovative experiments are underway to reduce the scale of such treatment plants, to the point where a street or even individual house may be able to process its own waste. It has already proven itself practical for purifying domestic greywater.

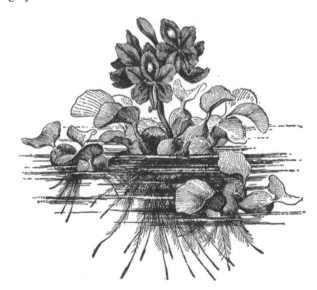

Uses for the foliage: To ensure maximum growth and nutrient intake the plants must be cut regularly. In large-scale ventures this would produce enormous quantities of green material; an acre of plants growing on sewage may produce a half-ton of foliage daily. Fortunately this green matter has numerous potential uses.

Fuel: The biomass could be digested anaerobically to produce methane, a half ton of foliage generating as much as 5000 cubic feet of methane. This would also produce a lot of fertilizer, containing all of the nutrients absorbed by the plants.

Energy could also be obtained by fermenting the plants to produce alcohol, and again valuable fertilizer is also produced. This potential as an energy source has even led some to suggest growing the plant as a biological solar collector. In parts of Asia the dried plants are used as fuel directly.

Paper: The plant fibers can be used to make high quality paper, newsprint, cardboard and even wallboard. The paper has been soaked in cement to make corrugated roofing sheets.

Animal food: The dried plants have been used as feed for livestock. They contain about 18% protein and 35% carbohydrate, along with many minerals and vitamins. Dried plants have been used as a feed for fish farming.

Cultivation: Water Hyacinth is a pretty plant, and was originally introduced into this country in 1884 as an ornamental. It is still a popular ornamental for ponds, but shouldn't be planted anywhere it can escape to wild water. In cold areas it doesn't survive the winter, but in mild climates it can become a problem. It propagates itself vegetatively from offsets without any help.

Fertilizer: In some tropical areas Water Hyacinth is an important fertilizer for home gardens, and it is actually cultivated for this in special ponds.

If wild plants are abundant you can use them for mulch, compost or green manure. They are rich in nitrogen, phosphorus, potassium and calcium.

Growth stimulant: Apparently the roots contain a growth hormone similar to giberellin.

Eleagnus commutata / Silverberry
North   *Oleaceae*
The silvery fruits are sweet but somewhat dry and mealy. Native Americans used them for soup and pemmican. The first European settlers made them into preserves.

Animal food: Birds eat the fruits and the flowers provide nectar for bees.

Cultivation: This very hardy plant is sometimes planted as an ornamental, or shelterbelt plant. It grows best in well-drained, somewhat alkaline, soil with full sun, and has the ability to fix nitrogen and so improve the soil. Propagate from seed, by sowing the whole ripe berry, or stratify for two months at forty degrees. It can also be

grown from semi-ripe cuttings, root cuttings or layering. Established plants spread by means of suckers.

Related species:
***E. angustifolia* - Russian Olive**
The fruit can be used as above and are actually sold in markets in parts of Asia. Several improved food varieties are available.

As the common name suggests, this species is not native, but is widely planted as an ornamental hedge and windbreak. It is tolerant of cold, wind, drought and air pollution, is good for urban areas, and is attractive to wildlife. It is quite invasive however, and is considered a pest in some areas. Propagate like the Silverberry.

***E. multiflora* - Goumi**
***E. umbellata* – Autumn Olive**
These species may be found as escapes. Goumi is sometimes cultivated for its fruit, and a number of improved cultivars are available. Use as above.

Elymus arenarius / Lyme Grass
Syn *Leymus arenarius*
Circumboreal   *Poaceae*
Many wild grasses produce edible seed, but very few produce large seeds in sufficient quantity to be useful for human food. This coastal species is an important exception, and has been used for food wherever it is found. It is prepared and used in much the same way as Wild-Rice (*Zizania*).

Native Americans sometimes chewed the young stems for their sweet juice.

Caution: Be careful when gathering this, or any other, grass seed to ensure that it is not parasitized with the poisonous Ergot fungus. This is fairly obvious when it occurs because large dark spurs replace some of the grains in the head.

This plant is protected in many areas, as it roots bind and hold sand dunes in place.

Roofing: The leaves and stems have been used for thatching roofs.

Arrows: The straight stems were used for arrows.

Cultivation: Lyme grass is a perennial relative of Rye, and has potential as a perennial grain crop. It thrives in harsh coastal climates, where few crops do well (it was once cultivated in Iceland). It is also quite ornamental and has been grown solely for this. Propagate from seed, or by division, in light sandy soils.

Related species:
All species can be used as above. The best include:

E. canadensis - **Canada Wild Rye**
E. condensatus -**Smooth Lyme Grass**
E. glaucus - **Western Rye Grass**
E. triticoides - **Alkali Rye Grass**
E. villosus

Ephedra species / Navajo Tea

Western deserts   *Gnetaceae*
The primitive *Ephedras* are native to the arid Southwest, and have adapted to this dry environment by discarding their leaves and photosynthesizing through their stems.

Drink: Native Americans used these species to make tea, by steeping the chopped stems (fresh or dried) in a cup of water for 20 minutes (sugar and lemon can be added if you wish). They can also be boiled for two minutes (it gets bitter if boiled for longer). This tea is pretty good, and later became popular with Mormon settlers. This is why it is also known as Mormon Tea.

The bitter seed was parched and used for "coffee" by the Shoshones. They also baked the seeds in bread.

The stems were chewed by Native Americans to relieve symptoms of thirst while traveling.

Medicine: The plant was also used to treat wounds and sores. It was used as a wash, or the dried powdered stems were sprinkled on the affected area. The tea was drunk as a diuretic, blood purifier, tonic and to treat urinary problems.

The related Asian species Ma Huang (*E. vulgaris*) contains the potent alkaloid ephedrine, which has many medicinal uses, but this probably isn't present in any American species.

Cultivation: Some species have been used as low maintenance ground cover, or ornamentals, in dry desert areas. They prefer dry, rocky soil, and may be propagated from seed, suckers or layering.

The best species include:
E. nevadensis - **Mormon Tea**
E. viridis - **Mountain Joint Fir**
E. fasciculata
E. torreyana - **Brigham Young Tea**

Epilobium angustifolium / Fireweed

Syn *Chamaenerion angustifolium*
North   *Onagraceae*
In cool northern and mountain areas Fireweed is a common pioneer plant on disturbed or damaged soil. It is one of the first plants to appear after forest fires (hence the common name). The plant fulfils an important ecological niche as a pioneer. Its downy airborne seed enables it to colonize disturbed ground quickly, and is sometimes produced so thickly it appears to be snowing in midsummer. The seed is quite long lived and may lay dormant in the soil for years until some disturbance causes light to reach them. The plant quickly produces a thick mat of creeping roots, which bind bare soil and prevent erosion. It also enriches the soil with an abundance of organic matter.

Food: Fireweed isn't one of the tastiest foods, but it forms extensive pure stands, and is often abundant. The leaves and stems are rich in vitamins A and C.

Shoots: The young spring shoots are gathered by snapping them off at the base (if they don't snap easily they are too old and will be bitter). They can be cooked for a few minutes like Asparagus (it is sometimes called Wild Asparagus), or chopped in salads. Native Americans split the mature stems and ate the interior pith. This isn't bad raw, but is more often cooked in soups, or added to baking.

The flower buds and flowers can be added to salads.

Drink: The natives of Siberia brewed an alcoholic drink from the pith of the stems and the hallucinogenic Fly Agaric (*Amanita muscariai*) fungus. The result has been said to resemble a cross between gin and LSD. The older leaves can be dried and used to make a tea. Steep three tablespoons of dried leaves in a pot of boiling water for ten minutes.

Medicine: An astringent tea of leaf or root has been used to clean wounds, and to treat diarrhea. The spring greens were considered a purifying tonic.

Down: The downy seeds have been used like those of Milkweed (*Asclepias*) for stuffing clothes and pillows.

Cordage: Native Americans made cord and twine from the fibers that remained after eating the interiors of the stems.

Animal food: The foliage is important forage for deer and elk. The flowers are a source of pollen and nectar for bees and other insects. Many birds eat the seed.

Cultivation: Propagate Fireweed from seed, cuttings or root division in almost any soil.

Garden uses: This beautiful plant has a long blooming period in summer, as the flower spike is indeterminate. Unfortunately it is unsuitable for most flower gardens because of its size and vigor. It can quickly become a nuisance, as it spreads both by self-sown seed and creeping roots. The large volume of organic matter makes Fireweed useful as green manure, or as an addition to the compost pile (just make sure it doesn't contain seeds). It has been used as a pioneer plant, to stabilize sand dunes and other loose or eroded soils.

Related species include:
E. hirsutum - **Hairy Willow Herb**
E. latifolium - **River Beauty**
E. montanum
These species are all better food than the above.

Equisetum arvense / Horsetail

Throughout   *Equisetaceae*
History: The primitive Horsetails are an ancient group of plants, that reproduce by means of spores rather than seeds. They were the dominant species on earth about 300 million years ago, and are still doing well, though there are only about 25 species left in this one genus. They helped form the coal and oil deposits we use today, and are the only 300 million year old plants still of use.

Caution: Domesticated animals are quite frequently poisoned by eating the mature plants, as they contain thiaminase, an enzyme that destroys the essential B vitamin thiamine. Some people state categorically that Horsetails are poisonous, and no part should never be eaten. Others eat the shoots in spring. I would advise against eating any part of them.

Buds: In early spring the clusters of buds that would become the new shoots have been eaten. Dig under the old stalks to obtain them.

Shoots: The tender tips of the naked fertile shoots are gathered just after they emerge from the ground and peeled to remove the tough skin. The juicy interior may then be eaten raw. More often they are cooked in two or three changes of water for 20 minutes. The Hopi dried and ground these shoots to flour, for making gruel or bread. They also ate the interior of older stems.

Medicine: An astringent tea of the stems is antiseptic and styptic, and has been used externally for skin sores, Poison Ivy rash and wounds.

The mineral rich tea contains calcium, iron, silica, sulfur and selenium, and herbalists sometimes recommend it to treat anemia, speed the healing of broken bones, and for mineral deficiencies. It has also been used as a diuretic, though in excess it may irritate the kidneys.

Fertilizer
Horsetail is often considered to be a noxious weed, but don't be too hasty to eliminate it from your garden. The plant is prized by Biodynamic gardeners for its ability to concentrate minerals. It makes a fine fertilizer, either composted or used in liquid form (see *Symphytum*). A liquid feed of Horsetail has been used to treat fungus diseases. The abrasive stems are said to be repellant to slugs and snails.

Scouring: The abrasive stems contain silica, and have long been used for scouring and cleaning things. This is why they are also called Scouring Rush and Pewterwort. They are also used by campers to clean pots, though it is usually less destructive to just use sand (also silica).

The Uses Of Wild Plants

Native Americans used the stems to smooth arrows, and to sharpen metal knives. More recently they have been found to be ideal for shaping the reeds of clarinets.

Glass: Ash from the burned stems contains almost 80% silica and was once used for making glass.

Cultivation: The Horsetails can be persistent weeds of poor damp soils, and are not popular with most gardeners. The simplest way to eradicate them is to change the growing conditions to favor more vigorous plants, by fertilizing and draining the soil. More imaginative gardeners use them as ornamentals, as their unusual appearance is very striking. They are most easily propagated by root division, and grow best on poor wet soils with some shade.

Related species:
All *Equisetum* species can be used for non-food uses.

Erodium cicutarium / **Cranes Bill, Filaree**
Throughout   *Geraniaceae*
Greens: This little immigrant is often very common in the west, but is only locally abundant elsewhere. In mild climates it stays green and edible all through the winter, and is a valuable source of vitamins and minerals. It is at its best in spring, when the tender new growth can be eaten raw in salads (though it may be a bit fuzzy). Older, less succulent, foliage can be used as a potherb if cooked in a change of water for 20 minutes. The flowers can be used to add color to salads.

Medicine: The plant is s nutritious addition to green drinks.

Cultivation: Filaree is sometimes cultivated as a forage plant, and is an important winter range plant in parts of the west. It is easily grown from seed or cuttings, and does well in most soil types. It naturalizes so readily it can easily become a weed.

The mature fruit splits into five beautiful spiral seeds, which unwind when wet and can actually screw themselves into the ground. They aren't of any use (they are sharp and can be quite painful) but they are amazing.

Related species:
E. moschatum - **White-Stem Filaree**
E. texanum - **Desert Herons Bill**
Use as above.

Eruca sativa / **Rocket**
Locally   *Brassicaceae*
This cultivated salad plant is often found as an escape. Like many members of the *Brassicaceae* it is best in

spring, when young and tender, and gets unpleasantly pungent in hot weather. It has become quite fashionable as a salad plant of late, under its Italian name of Arugala, and is very common in prepared salad mixes. It's a plant people tend to either love or hate, I don't like it very much, but I know people who find it almost irresistible and crave it. If you don't like it raw, try it in soups or as a potherb, as cooking changes the flavor a lot.

Cultivation: Rocket is easily grown from seed in any good garden soil. It is definitely a cool weather crop. In hot weather it gets very pungent, and flowers almost as soon as it has produced a few leaves. It self sows readily, and can become a minor weed.

Erythronium species / **Dogs Tooth Violet**
Throughout   *Liliaceae*
These spring flowers are found over most of the country. They are quite lovely when in bloom, but are easily overlooked the rest of the time. After several years of looking for *E. americanum* I finally found it in Vermont, then the following spring I found it growing in the woods in my garden in Connecticut. (though not flowering). The plants get their common name because their roots resemble dogs canine teeth. Some species are called Trout Lilies because of their speckled leaves.

Roots: These lovely little plants produce tasty edible roots, but are too pretty for casual use as food, especially as they are slow growing, and may take seven years to produce their first flowers. They are also hard to gather, as the tops break off if you pull on them, you must dig carefully. They are sometimes abundant however, in which case digging a few roots would do no harm. They are good raw in salads, or cooked like Camas (*Camassia*) bulbs. They were quite important to a number of Native American tribes, and were dried in large quantities for winter use.

Medicine: The roots have been used as a poultice for skin diseases.

Cultivation: Some *Erythronium* species are commonly planted as ornamentals in gardens, and spread to form large colonies. They like deep, rich, moist soil, and can be grown from seed (slow), offsets or bulbs.

Best species include:
E. americanum - **Trout Lily**
This species is often abundant in the east.

E. grandiflorum - **Yellow Fawn Lily**

Caution: *E. oreganum* is sometimes said to be inedible or even poisonous. Other species may be laxative if eaten in quantity.

Euphorbia lathyrus / Gopher Weed

Naturalized from Europe   *Euphorbiaceae*

Caution: Gopher Weed is not edible. It contains a poisonous latex, and cases of livestock poisoning from it are well documented. This latex contains hydrocarbons similar to those found in crude oil, and has a number of potential uses. The plant makes hydrocarbons by removing oxygen atoms from some of the carbohydrates (molecules of carbon, hydrogen and oxygen) it produces by photosynthesis.

Seeds: After careful preparation the seeds have been pickled, and eaten like Capers, but they are somewhat bitter. This is why the plant is called Caper Spurge in Britain. However all parts have caused poisoning so this is probably inadvisable.

Fish poison: The seeds were once used to poison fish.

Hydrocarbons

Gopher plant as been investigated as a potential renewable source of hydrocarbons for use as fuel, and for making plastics and lubricants.

Hydrocarbons can be extracted from the plants by drying, crushing and boiling in a solvent such as heptane. This is evaporated to leave a crude oily residue, which can be distilled (like crude oil) to yield a wide range of useful products.

It has been estimated that an acre of the plants could yield up to 900 pounds of oil annually. Breeding for maximum hydrocarbon content could perhaps double this. An additional fuel could be obtained by fermenting the crushed stems to produce alcohol (though one must first convert the starch and cellulose into simple sugars), or simply pressing them into logs for firewood. This isn't economical at present while fossil hydrocarbons can be obtained for less than the price of some bottled water, but might it be significant in the future

---

Crop plant: When the price of oil increases dramatically these plants could become an important commercial crop. It was previously thought that they could be grown on marginal desert land, but they don't produce very well unless irrigated.

Cultivation: Gopher Weed is easily grown from seed in most soil types. It is very drought tolerant, and will grow on as little as twelve inches of rain a year. The harvest takes about seven months from seed.

Horticultural uses: The plant can reach ten feet in height and makes an interesting temporary deciduous screen.

A more controversial use of the plant is indicated by its common names; Gopher Plant in the U.S. and Mole Plant in Britain. It is said to be abhorrent to these creatures and if planted around a garden will supposedly keep them from coming near. Some people report it is useless (to the point where moles have actually pushed it out of the ground), while others say it works very well. They say the secret is to plant them close together so they form a continuous barrier. It is hard to judge when something like this actually works, without doing carefully controlled experiments (it is easier to know when it doesn't). I haven't done any so I can't really comment.

Related species:
E. antisyphilitica - Candelilla
In the Unites States this species is only found in southern Texas and New Mexico. In Mexico and Central America the leaves are gathered to obtain Candelilla wax. This valuable hard wax is used in floor waxes, candles, chewing gum, leather dressings, paper and fabric size, varnish, lacquer and dental molds. The Unites States imports about five million kilograms of the wax annually.

Wild plants contain about two percent wax, though breeding could perhaps increase this to five percent The plants can be gathered any time of year, and stored until required for processing. The wax is extracted from the stems by boiling them in water, or with solvents.

Like its relative the Gopher Plant, Candelilla has been suggested as a potential new crop for arid areas, as it can survive on as little as four inches of rain per year, and thrives on 20 inches. It prefers poor, well-drained soil, tolerates high salinity, and may be propagated from cuttings, division or seed.

Fagus grandifolia / American Beech
East   *Fagaceae*

Nuts: The Beech is hardier than most other nut bearing trees, and tends to be more valued in northern areas, where few other nuts are available. In my experience the wild harvest is often unsatisfactory. In inhospitable climates the shells are often empty as a result of incomplete fertilization, and the nuts are only produced in quantity every few years. Nevertheless Beechnuts have been called a great neglected delicacy, and in a good year the oily nutritious seeds are certainly worth attention.

The kernels are about the same size as Sunflower seeds, and can be eaten like them as a snack, or in breads and cereals. Native Americans dried and ground the kernels to flour, for baking and gruel. The germinating seeds taste pretty good, so you might try sprouting them.

Oil: Beechnut oil is considered as good as that from Olives, and like that oil it stays sweet for several years without refrigeration. Native Americans extracted it by boiling the crushed nuts, and skimming the oil off the surface as it rises, as they did with Hickory (*Carya*). In Europe the oil is extracted by pressing.

Other foods: In spring the newly opened leaves can be added to salads, or used as a potherb. The inner bark was used for making bread in times of famine (See *Ulmus*).

Drink: Beechnuts were once a common coffee substitute in Europe. A teaspoon of the roasted, ground seeds were steeped in a cup of boiling water for fifteen minutes.

Medicine: Native Americans used a poultice, or tea, of the leaves to treat wounds, skin sores and frostbite. They are said to be mildly antiseptic.

Beds: In Europe the newly fallen leaves were once used for stuffing mattresses, and were considered superior to straw. If you try this make sure they are completely dry, or you might end up sleeping on a compost pile.

Smoke: The same dried leaves were occasionally smoked like Tobacco, alone or with more aromatic

herbs. This would no doubt be convenient for those misguided individuals who persist in smoking in bed, as they could actually smoke the bed.

Wood: Beech wood is hard and shock resistant, but difficult to season without cracking. It is used for tool handles, clubs, mallets, wooden tools (such as plane blocks), clogs, kitchenware, cabinetmaking and parquet flooring.

In Britain itinerant craftsmen known as *bodgers* once lived out in the Beech woods, turning the green wood into components for chairs.

Firewood: The wood is good fuel, giving about 24 million Btu per cord. It was once widely used for making charcoal.

Oil: Inferior, old, or tainted Beechnut oil was used for paint and varnish, or burned in lamps.

Animal food: Beechnuts are important food for wildlife, most notably for the now extinct Passenger Pigeon. The disappearance of the huge primeval Beech forests was one of the reasons for that bird's extinction.

Cultivation: Propagate from ripe seed, sown in autumn or stratified for three months at forty degrees. It has a shallow root system and transplants easily, so you can often transplant seedlings from around mature trees. Superior cultivars can be whip grafted.

Horticultural uses: These beautiful trees are widely planted as ornamentals in large gardens and parks. A number of cultivars are available, the most notable of which is probably the lovely bronze colored European Copper Beech (*F. sylvatica*).

Beeches have been grown as hedges, and young plants (though deciduous) usually retain their dead leaves until spring. These species are almost never planted as nut producers, though the tree crop expert J Russell Smith thought that careful selection and breeding for larger nuts could make them as valuable as the Walnut.

Ferocactus species / Barrel cactus
Syn *Echinocactus* spp
Southwest   *Cactaceae*
The Barrel Cacti are superb examples of adaptation to an extreme environment, almost literally barrels of water in the desert. In very wet seasons they may absorb so much water they become top heavy and fall over. Like most Cacti they are covered in spines, which not only protect the plant from being eaten, but cast shade on the stem (they may actually reduce the amount of sunlight hitting the stem by 20 percent).

Caution: Never damage any of the slow growing Barrel Cacti (*Echinocactus, Echinocereus, Ferocactus* species) unless you are endangered personally. They already suffer enough from the depredations of four wheelers, developers, cactus rustlers and generally thoughtless people and should be left alone. A number of these species are already considered threatened or endangered. Taking a few fruit from the commonest types may be permissible, if they are abundant, otherwise leave them alone.

Moisture

In the popular imagination the Barrel Cacti are best known as an emergency source of water, though it is far from a cool refreshing drink. The taste has been said to resemble gritty aspirin dissolved in water, and it is usually slimy, but it beats dying of thirst.

Liquid is obtained by cutting off the top, scooping out the pulp, and squeezing it to release its moisture. The quality and quantity of this liquid varies a lot and is better just after rain than during drought, when it may be almost empty.

One sometimes finds a plant with an abnormal top growth. Such a plant has survived decapitation and regenerated itself.

Fruit: The fruit can be eaten like those of the Prickly Pear (*Opuntia*).

Flower buds: Native Americans commonly ate the flower buds of some species. They were carefully gathered with sticks, boiled in several changes of water to reduce their bitterness. and then eaten immediately, or dried for later use. They were also baked in a fire pit (see *Camassia*), or fried.

Seed: The seeds contain 18% protein and 17% oil. They were extracted from the fruits and ground to meal, for use in baking and gruel. See (*Lemairocereus)* for more on this use.

Candy: The green flesh has little flavor, but is boiled in sugar syrup to make cactus candy.

Compass: Barrel cacti are sometimes called Compass Plants because their northeastern side, shaded from the hottest sun grows faster than the rest, causing the plant to lean to the southwest.

Cooking pots: Native Americans sometimes used the hollowed-out stems as cooking pots. This could hardly be recommended nowadays, even if it were very practical.

Cultivation: These strikingly attractive plants are in demand by collectors, as ornamentals for arid areas and as interior decorations, so there is a thriving illicit trade in these species (see *Cereus* for more on cactus rustling). The plants must carry an agriculture department tag to be legally sold. I would never buy plants gathered from the wild, legal or not, it's another form of unnecessary environmental destruction.

Growing most cacti from seed is a slow business, but it is worthwhile if you live in a dry hot climate. They are an investment for the future, like Black Walnut trees. A cactus nursery could be a potentially profitable sideline for a small desert homestead.

Best species include:
***F. wislizenii* - Fish-hook Barrel Cactus**
Used as above. Native Americans used the hooked spines as fishhooks.

***F. acanthodes* - Red Barrel Cactus**
***F. viridescens* – Coast Barrel Cactus**
These species both produce tasty fruit.

Ficus carica / Fig
South   *Moraceae*
The Fig is a native of the Middle East, but is quite common in warmer areas of this country and is even considered a pest in some places. Look for it in gardens, as an escape and on abandoned orchard and home sites. It is easily recognized by its large lobed leaves and familiar fruit.

Fruit: If you find a Fig tree bearing ripe fruit you are in luck, as the plant is a source of one of the most nutritious of all fruit. Ripe fresh figs are a treat people in cool northern states rarely get to experience, as they don't travel well. Dried figs travel very well of course and have long been a staple food of nomadic people. They are also great for backpacking, eaten whole or used for making Food bars (see *Juglans* for a recipe). They are no doubt familiar to you. In mild areas these vigorous plants can produce two crops of fruit a year.

Clothes: The large leaves of the Fig were the very first human clothing.

Cultivation: Figs are easily grown from cuttings, suckers or layering. They are drought resistant and do well in poor soils. They dislike very cold winters, but can be grown in the north, if planted against a warm, south-facing wall, or given protection in winter. In ideal conditions a Fig tree may grow 30 feet high and 90 feet across.

Foeniculum vulgare / Fennel
West   *Apiaceae*
This Mediterranean species is found as an escape throughout the country, but is most common in the west, especially near the sea. It is quite invasive, forming dense colonies and crowding out native plants, so you need have no qualms about gathering it from the wild. It has the same distinctive Licorice-like flavor as Anise and this, along with its yellow flowers, makes it easy to identify. This is fortunate as it is a member of the *Apiaceae*, which contains a number of dangerously toxic species. All above ground parts are edible.

Greens: The tender spring shoots are rich in vitamins A and C, and can be eaten like Celery. Use in salads, as a cooked vegetable and in soups. The succulent leafy tips are an interesting and tasty addition to salads. As the plants mature they become rather tough, though the leaf stalks may still be palatable when 4 - 6 inches long. Simply strip them from the plant, remove the tough leaves and use like the spring shoots.

Seed: The flowers, leaves and seed are used for flavoring. Apparently they contain substances that can help prevent edible fats from oxidizing and turning rancid. They can also be used to make a sweet tea (steep for 5 - 10 minutes), and have been used as a flavoring for liqueurs

Medicine: Fennel seed is a carminative and stomachic, and is a traditional remedy for digestive ailments. It can be taken as a tea, or simply eaten after meals, to aid digestion and freshen the breath. It has also been used to promote menstruation and lactation and was once widely used as a diuretic (often with Juniper berries). The herbalist Sebastian Kneipp claimed that the tea was useful for eliminating toxins from the body, and also recommended adding it to bathwater for the same purpose. The same tea is a soothing wash for sore eyes.

This strongly flavored plant is useful for disguising the taste of less pleasant medicinal herbs.

It has been said that large doses of Fennel oil can cause hallucinations. Apparently the body converts it into a kind of amphetamine.

Strewing herb: The aromatic stems were used as a strewing herb in medieval homes and churches, and may have insect repellant properties.

Oil: Fennel seed oil is used in perfumes, and to flavor toothpaste and candy.

Cultivation: The plant grows well in most neutral, well-drained sunny soils, and is propagated from seed or division. It is very drought resistant and self-sows readily. In mild climates Fennel grows vigorously and needs little attention once established. It can get quite large, so is best planted away by itself in the wild garden, or confined by a barrier.

Horticultural uses: Fennel flowers attract beneficial predatory insects to the garden, and are sometimes planted solely for this purpose.

Fragaria species / Wild Strawberries
Throughout   *Rosaceae*
There are Wild Strawberries growing all over the Northern Hemisphere. Even if you have never seen a Wild Strawberry you will recognize them, because they are merely smaller versions of the familiar fruit.

Fruit: These are one of the best tasting wild fruits; the only drawback is their small size. I don't have the patience to gather more than a cup or so, but some foragers gather them by the quart. It is nice to sit in a sunny Strawberry patch and eat the fruit; it makes you feel like a bear.

Backpacking when strawberries are in season can be very slow going, as each succeeding patch seems to get better and better, and you have to take your pack off to gather properly.

Preparation: You surely don't need any advice on preparing these fruits. They are best eaten raw out of hand, though they can be eaten with a lot of things. They can be used to make delicious raw preserves, though the nearest I have got to this (or any recipe) is to simply crush them to make syrup for pancakes. It has been suggested that they be dried for later use, but freezing is better.

Greens: The leaves can be gathered before the flowers appear and used for tea. They are very rich in vitamin C, but don't have much flavor, so are usually mixed with tastier herbs.

Medicine: Strawberries themselves are of little importance as medicine, though they are a mild laxative, and have been used as a poultice to treat sunburn. Recent research has come up with an interesting property for Strawberries. Apparently the fruits are rich in ellagic acid a substance that helps protect body cells from cancer. If you ever need an excuse to eat Strawberries, this is it.

The vitamin-rich leaves are more important as medicine than the fruits, and even today are used in some commercial diarrhea remedies. The tea is a good gargle for sore throats.

Tooth cleaner: The fruits are said to help clean the teeth; just keep a berry on your teeth for 5 minutes to remove the stains, and then brush with baking soda.

Cultivation: If you want wild Strawberries in your garden I would advise you to get a variety of Alpine Strawberries. These are improved wild plants with larger fruits and a longer fruiting season (I have harvested fruits from my plants for eight months continuously). They like rich, slightly acid soil, and are easily grown from seed. If planted early enough they will fruit the same year. They are pretty enough to use as a border or ground cover, though they don't produce runners. They self-seed readily, and generally take care of themselves.

Garden companions: Strawberries grow well under Pines, and are often mulched with the needles.

Best species include:
F. chiloensis - **Beach Strawberry**
This West Coast species may produce fruit all summer. It is a parent of the garden strawberry.

Galium aparine / **Goosegrass**
East   *Rubiaceae*

All surfaces of this weak stemmed, clinging plant are covered in minute hooks (they are the closest thing to vegetable Velcro) that enable it to support itself by grabbing onto surrounding vegetation. The fruits are also hooked, and attach themselves to passing animals for dispersal. By this means it has spread from its native Europe to most countries of the world.

The dried plant has the distinctive smell of new mown hay, which is caused by a glycoside called coumarin (the same substance found in Sweet Clover). If Goosegrass hay becomes spoiled, the coumarin may be converted into the anticoagulant di-coumarol and become toxic. See (*Melilotus*) for more on this.

Greens: In spring the foliage can be used as a potherb until it starts to set fruit, alone or with other plants. It isn't good raw because of the aforementioned hooks. The dried plant can be used as a culinary herb, but should be dried quickly, or toxins may develop.

Drink: This plant is a distant relative of Coffee, and if you can gather enough seeds they can be used to make one of the best wild substitutes for that drink. They are gathered as they ripen in early summer, roasted at 300 degrees Fahrenheit for about an hour until dark brown, crushed or ground to powder and used like Coffee. The problem is gathering enough of the seeds.

Medicine: A poultice, or an astringent wash, of the leaves was used for wounds, bleeding, burns and skin sores. A tea of the leaves is rich in minerals, and was said to help hasten the healing of broken bones. The tea was also used as a liver tonic, blood purifier (especially for skin problems) and diuretic. It is also believed to be beneficial for the lymph system.

Dicoumarol has important medicinal uses, but should only be used under medical supervision.

Other uses: The leaf tea has been used as a hair rinse to cure dandruff , and to stimulate hair growth. The hooked stems were used as a crude sieve. The dried plants have been used in potpourri, and as a strewing herb.

Animal food: Birds relish Goosegrass seeds, and it has been planted, or encouraged, as feed for domestic poultry (hence the name). Many wild and domesticated animals eat the foliage.

Cultivation: Goosegrass thrives in almost any situation from deep shade to full sun. It is grown from seed, in any average soil.

Related species include:
G. verum – **Lady's Bedstraw**
Used as above. Supposedly this plant got its name because it was put into women's mattresses to help them get pregnant. It is a good groundcover plant.

G. boreale - **Northern Bedstraw**
G. odoratum - **Sweet Woodruff**
G. triflorum - **Fragrant Bedstraw**
These three species can be used as above. The latter was once used by Ponca women to perfume their clothing.

G. kamtschaticum - **Northern Wild Licorice**
The sweetish roots may be used for tea.

Gaultheria procumbens / **Wintergreen**
East   *Ericaceae*
This plant is the original source of the familiar Wintergreen flavoring, which is due to an oil that permeates all parts of the plant. This oil has numerous uses, and was once extracted from the plant by means of steam distillation. This oil is only present in small quantities in the fresh plant, but more is formed by enzyme action after the plant wilts and the cell walls start to break down. The plants were left to ferment for a day or so before being distilled, to allow more oil to form.

Caution: Wintergreen is a chemical relative of aspirin, and it's suggested that anyone who is allergic to that drug should probably avoid it.

Fruits: The bright red berries hang on the plants right through the winter if not eaten by animals, and repeated freezing may even improve their flavor. The sweet berries taste almost like candy, and can be eaten as a snack to keep the mouth moist and fresh. They are good in salads, breads, muffins, pancakes and make superb preserves.

Leaves: These can be chopped and added to salads, or used to flavor other foods.

Drink: The aromatic evergreen leaves can be used to make an excellent tea. This is so good the plant is sometimes known as Teaberry. Fresh leaves are the best, and are available year round, so it isn't really worth drying them. If you make tea in the usual way it will be quite weak. A better brew is made by soaking the leaves in water for a day or two, to allow the enzymes to create more oil. This is then heated and drunk. This liquid can also be used for making wine or beer. The berries can be used for tea in the same way.

Medicine: The plant contains methyl salicylate, and may be used as medicine in the same ways as Black Birch (See *Betula*).

Smoke: Native Americans smoked the leaves.

Animal food: The berries are eaten by many wild creatures, and are especially useful because they hang on to the plants well into the winter. Deer love the foliage and ate my plants every year until I fenced them out.

Cultivation: Wintergreen grows naturally in acid Oak or evergreen woodland (it likes a thick mulch of Pine needles), though it is also common on burned over or disturbed areas. Grow from seed, planted when ripe, or stratified for two months at forty degrees. They can also be propagated by division, layering, root offsets or cuttings. Established plants spread to form a dense mat, and are useful as groundcover.

Related species include:
G. hispidula - **Creeping Snowberry** Syn *Chiogenes hispidula*
G. ovatifolia – **Oregon Wintergreen**
G. myrsinites - **Western Wintergreen**
Use as above.

Gaultheria shallon / **Salal Berry**
Northwest
Berries: Salal is closely related to the Wintergreen, but lacks the aromatic oil found in that plant, so the flavor is quite different. The tasty blue-black berries are often produced in abundance, and were an important food for Native Americans (the common name is theirs). The famous botanical explorer David Douglas thought it had potential as a commercial fruit.

The fruit are good raw, or can be used like Blueberries in pies, syrup and preserves. Native Americans crushed them into cakes, and dried them for traveling and winter use. Their quality may vary from plant to plant, so sample any you find. The best fruit are excellent.

Drink: The berries can be made into a beverage like Manzanita cider (see *Arctostaphylos*).

Wreaths: The branches are collected and sold to florists, for use in wreaths and other floral decorations. Gathering them from the wild has become a significant commercial industry, and as a consequence plants are often illegally cut from public lands. They have even been taken from inside National Parks.

Cultivation: Douglas was right when he thought of cultivating Salal, as it could be a useful soft fruit crop. It likes a rich, moist soil with lots of organic matter, and is propagated from seed, layering or cuttings. It may grow up to eight feet in height so can also be useful in landscaping. It is quite tolerant of shade.

Related species:
G. humifusa - **Alpine Salal**
Use as above.

Gaylussacia species / Huckleberries
Throughout   *Ericaceae*
The modest Huckleberry is a contender for the title of oldest living thing on earth, and also as one of the largest. The vegetative offspring of a single shrubby plant has been found to cover over 100 acres and has been estimated to be 13,000 years old. Obviously no single part is that old (or even more than a few years old), but the same individual organism has been growing and renewing itself for that long (which is exactly what trees do).

Berries: These species are closely related to the Blueberries (*Vaccinium*), and the berries are frequently confused. It's easy to tell the difference though, as Huckleberries are shiny black and contain ten hard seeds, while Blueberries are powdery blue and contain relatively soft seeds. These differences are irrelevant for the gatherer, as the fruit taste similar, and are used in the same ways (sometimes even together). Any species bearing tasty fruit can be used.

Wreaths: The branches of some species have been gathered and sold to florists, for use in wreaths.

Animal food: The foliage and berries are important to wildlife.

Cultivation: The plants are grown in the same ways as Blueberries, and have similar garden uses. They spread vegetatively to form dense thickets, and make a useful productive groundcover for shady acid soil.

Glechoma hederacea / Ground Ivy
Throughout   *Lamiaceae*
This small creeping plant is a close relative of Catnip and is sometimes included in the *Nepeta* genus. A native of Europe, it has been very successful in North America, and is now widely naturalized in waste places and gardens.

Greens: Small quantities of the mildly aromatic leaves can be added to salads, while still young and tender. They are rich in vitamin C and minerals.

Tea: Ground Ivy is most often used for tea, though you need quite a lot to make a good drink. Try a quarter cup of chopped fresh leaves, or an eighth of a cup of dry leaves, to a cup of water. The plant was once known as Gill-Over-The-Ground, a reminder of the time it was widely used to flavor beer (Anglo- Saxon ale-houses were sometimes called Gill houses). Another name was Alehoof.

Medicine: Herbalists used the plant as an expectorant, to soothe mucus membranes and for pulmonary complaints, including tuberculosis, colds, coughs and bronchitis. The plant has long been considered a good blood purifier, and has a decided diuretic effect.

The tea or poultice of the leaves has been used externally to treat sunburn, chapped skin and wounds.

Animal food: Like many members of the *Lamiaceae* this is a favorite plant of bees.

Garden uses: Ground Ivy might be useful as a groundcover, if it can be kept in check so it doesn't become a weed. It might also be used in herbal lawns, as it will tolerate light mowing.

Cultivation: Propagate from seed or division. It thrives in sun or shade, in most soil types, and spreads rapidly once established (often too rapidly).

Gleditsia triacanthos / **Honey Locust**
East   *Fabaceae*

The branches and trunk of this tree are covered in pronged spines (the specific name triacanthos means 3 spined). These make it impossible to climb (even a squirrel might have difficulty), but help in identifying it.

Pods: The sweet immature pods can be eaten raw, or cooked as a vegetable. Just take care not to gather the poisonous pods of the Kentucky Coffee Tree (*Gymnocladus dioica*) by mistake.

The mature pods are leathery and inedible, though the sweet inner pulp can be eaten as a snack, or made into a drink. They have also been fermented to make beer. The dried pods keep well if stored in a cool dry place.

Sugar: The pods can grow to a foot or more in length and contain about 30% sugar. It has been suggested that the trees be grown as a source of sugar.

Seeds: The ripe seeds were soaked overnight and cooked like beans. They were also ground to flour for baking bread, in the proportion of one part Honey Locust flour to two parts cornmeal.

Medicine: The wood contains fisetin and fuscin, two potentially important anti-cancer agents. These substances also inhibit highly carcinogenic aflatoxins.

Wood: Honey Locust wood has been used for cabinetmaking, construction and fence-posts (it is avoided by termites), bows, spears and digging sticks.

Firewood: The wood is excellent fuel giving about 24 million Btu per cord, and could be coppiced as a source of firewood (see *Populus* for more on this).

Fuel: The sugar-rich pods could be fermented to produce alcohol. An acre of trees can reportedly produce up to two and a half tons of pods annually, so this could be a potentially profitable and low impact way to produce fuel alcohol. Fermentation would also give large quantities of valuable nitrogen rich fertilizer, or high protein animal feed.

Animal food: The pods are eaten by wild and domesticated animals, and the plant could be a highly productive forage crop. It can also be dried and ground

to meal and added to feed. The flowers produce an abundance of nectar and are important to bees.

Cultivation: The Honey Locust grows rapidly, thrives in most kinds of soil, and is resistant to drought, saline soil, insect pests and air pollution. It is propagated from seed or cuttings (hard, green or root), while scions of choice varieties can be whip grafted or budded. It is not easily transplanted however, as a year old seedling may have a root two to three feet long (long cardboard tubes are used for container growing). It is quite precocious, producing its first pods when as young as five years old, but not very long-lived (100 years on average). It is a member of the *Fabaceae*, but doesn't fix nitrogen.

New crop: Honey Locust was widely planted as a shelterbelt tree in the 1930's. It was also studied as a possible new farm crop as a source of livestock feed, and some improved cultivars still exist from that time, notably Calhoun and Milwood. It might well be worth investigating again as a source of food or fuel. The feathery leaves cast relatively light shade, enabling other plants to grow underneath it.

Garden uses: Honey Locust is used as an ornamental in urban areas, though the spines and messy pods have limited its use. A spineless variety is available (*G. triacantha var inermis*), but it bears few pods, so planting it is pretty pointless.

The vicious thorns make this tree a good barrier plant or addition to hedgerows. An established Honey Locust hedge is pretty much impenetrable. It coppices readily

Glyceria species / **Manna Grasses**
Throughout   *Poaceae*

Seed: The tasty seeds of these common floating aquatic grasses disperse quickly, so must be gathered as soon as they ripen from June to August. Native Americans gathered them from canoes.

The seed can be prepared and used in the same way as Wild-Rice (*Zizania*). This was sometimes ground to flour, and mixed with an equal amount of corn or wheat flour for baking bread.

Wastewater treatment: Reed Sweetgrass (*G. maxima*) can extract large amounts of nutrients from water and convert them into useful biomass. It has a potential use in the treatment of wastewater in temperate climates. See Water Hyacinth (*Eichornia)* for more on this.

Species include:
G. fluitans - Floating Manna Grass
The seed of this species was once highly esteemed in parts of Europe, and was sold in markets. Used as above.

Glycyrrhiza lepidota / **American Licorice**
West   *Fabaceae*

This plant is closely related to cultivated Licorice (*G. glabra*) but isn't as sweetly flavored. It contains the same sweet substance, glycyrrhizin, which is fifty times sweeter than sugar. The genus name *Glycyrrhiza* means sweet root. The roots contain about 30% starch.

Caution: Licorice is not quite the harmless children's candy we imagine it to be, but is actually quite toxic if eaten in quantity. The roots are suspected of containing carcinogens and large amounts may cause heart irregularities and raise blood pressure. A number of fatalities have been attributed to the excessive habitual consumption of Licorice. All of this is not to say that you should never eat Licorice at all, it is safe to eat in small quantities.

Roots: The flavor of the woody roots varies from plant to plant. Some are quite sweet, while others are bitter and unpleasant. All are at their best while dormant from fall to early spring. Native Americans often chewed the raw roots for their sweet flavor. They also roasted them in a fire pit. They pounded the cooked roots, to remove the wiry central core, before eating them.

Shoots: The young spring shoots were cooked and eaten by the Cheyenne.

Drink: The woody roots can be used to make tea, though it isn't usually as good as cultivated Licorice. It can be made in the usual way, by steeping root shavings in boiling water for a few minutes. A better tea is made by simmering the root for a few minutes. The best tea is prepared by steeping the chopped roots overnight in cold water, and then heating and straining. The root has also been used to make beer.

Medicine: Domesticated Licorice has a number of important medicinal uses. It has traditionally been used as a mild expectorant, as it contains saponins that break up mucus. It is still found in some commercial cough preparations. An added benefit is that it helps to disguise the flavor of other herbs. In China it has been used to treat duodenal ulcers, rheumatoid arthritis, Addisons disease, oral herpes and many other ailments.

Licorice contains deoxycorticosterone, a chemical relative of sex hormones, which might explain why it was once esteemed as an aphrodisiac (or maybe not).

Chewing sticks: The frayed chewed end of the root has been used as a toothbrush.

Tobacco: The main use of Licorice root in North America is not for candy as one might imagine, but for flavoring tobacco.

Cultivation: American Licorice can be propagated from seed, cuttings or root division, and prefers rich, deep, moist soil and full sun. Cultivated Licorice needs to grow for several years to develop its full flavor. It is an easy crop to grow, and enough fragments usually remain in the ground after harvesting for the plant to regenerate, so replanting is not required.

Related species:
G. missouriensis
G. glabra - **Cultivated Licorice**
Use as above. The latter species is occasionally found as an escape. It can be used to make one of the very best herbal teas, perfect for those who complain that such teas are tasteless and boring.

Hamamelis virginiana / **Witch Hazel**
East   *Hamamelidaceae*

A notable feature of this common shrub is that it flowers in autumn after shedding its leaves. The seedpods mature through the winter, slowly drying until they burst explosively, hurling their seeds up to forty feet.

Tea: Make a tea from the leaves or flowers, by steeping two teaspoons in a cup of boiling water for five minutes. This is much improved by adding sweetener, and milk to reduce its astringency.

Chewing sticks: Native Americans chewed the twigs to clean their teeth.

Witch Hazel Extract
Witch Hazel can still be found in many household medicine cabinets, in the form of an extract made from the chopped twigs, but most commercial preparations are pretty weak. It is prepared by distilling a strong decoction of the twigs, and then adding alcohol as a preservative.

The extract is used as an astringent lotion to cleanse the skin, as after-shave, as a liniment for sore muscles, and as a wash for insect bites, wounds, burns, hemorrhoids, sore eyes and Poison Ivy rash (sometimes mixed into a paste with baking soda). A poultice of the leaves can be used for many of the same purposes.

Divination: The twigs are the preferred wood for use by water diviners, for detecting underground water sources and metals.

Beds: In Appalachia beds were sometimes stuffed with shavings of Witch Hazel, I'm not quite sure why this plant in particular.

Cultivation: Witch Hazel is grown as an ornamental, and as a source of medicinal materials. It prefers rich, moist soil with nearby water, though it is pretty adaptable, and grows well in most situations.

The ripe seed can be planted immediately, or stratified at forty degrees over the winter, but may take two years to germinate. Slightly immature seed may sprout immediately, as it seems dormancy is the last thing the plant puts into the seed. Layering or cuttings can also be taken, though the latter often don't thrive and eventually die. Perhaps they lack some symbiotic fungi or bacteria. Established plants sucker abundantly, and even in the wild reproduction is often vegetative.

Hedeoma pulegoides / American Pennyroyal

East   *Lamiaceae*

Caution: Pennyroyal should not be consumed by pregnant women (see below).

Tea: This species is not the cultivated European Pennyroyal (*Mentha pulegium*), but it has the same powerful and distinctive mint odor when crushed. Like many members of the *Lamiaceae* it is good for tea. Steep the fresh or dried leaves for five minutes.

Medicine: This plant was once known as Squaw Mint, because of its value in treating women's ailments. Native Americans used it for menstrual cramps, to promote menstruation (it was once in the USP for this), as an abortifacient, for headaches, to prevent nausea and to promote sweating in fevers (diaphoretic).

The tea was used externally as a wash for skin sores, and insect bites.

Cultivation: This species grows naturally in dry, woodland soil with some shade. It is easily propagated from seed, and self-sows readily.

Related species include:
H. drummondii - **New Mexico Pennyroyal**
H. hispida - **Rough Pennyroyal**
These western species can be used as above.

Caution:
H. apiculatum
H. todsenii
These species are rare and shouldn't be used.

Hedysarum occidentale / Western Sweet Vetch

North and west   Fabaceae

Root: The large sweet root has been called the best wild plant food in Alaska. It was an important food for Native Americans, and was gathered in large numbers each fall. It is at its best while dormant from fall to spring, and is improved by frost. Of course at this time identification is difficult, unless you mark it the previous summer. It can be eaten raw, or cooked like Carrot.

Cultivation: Several *Hedysarum* species have been grown as ornamentals for their pea-like flowers. They do best in cooler areas, and prefer well-drained soil and full sun. Propagation is usually by seed, if you can find it (the pods are a favorite food of rodents).

Related species:
H. boreale - **Northern Sweet Broom**
H. hedysaroides - **Licorice Root**
H. sulphurescens
Used as above. Some other species are toxic.

Helianthus annuus / Sunflower

Throughout   *Asteraceae*

This is the wild form of the familiar garden Sunflower. The main difference is that it produces many small flower heads, rather than a one large one. The plant was sacred to many Native American tribes because the flowers represent the sun. It is of interest to us because it produces highly nutritious seeds.

The Sunflower is a native American plant, but first became an important commercial crop in Russia, when breeders produced varieties with unusually large, oil-rich, seeds (now sometimes called *H. annuus macrocarpus*). Their use spread throughout Eastern Europe, until they were the most popular oilseed crop grown there. It is now an important commercial crop in its native land, though even today most varieties are of Russian origin.

Seeds: Sunflower seeds are familiar to most people. The only difference between the wild and cultivated forms is their size, as the wild seeds are much smaller.

Gathering: Native Americans gathered the plump oily seeds by cutting the whole head, drying it in the sun and then beating it to release the seeds. Sometimes they simply scraped them directly into a basket.

Nutrients

Sunflower seeds are extremely nutritious, containing about 20% protein, 20% carbohydrate and 40% fat (which is very rich in essential fatty acids). They also contain vitamins A, several B's, D (unusual), E and an abundance of easily digested minerals. It is said that people who eat a lot of Sunflower seeds usually have good teeth and bones. They also contain a lot of fiber, which makes them somewhat indigestible. I sometimes puree them in a blender to increase their digestibility.

Preparation: The tough seed coat is removed before eating. Traditionally you put seeds in one side of your mouth, shell them with your teeth and spit out the shells from the other side, in a continuous stream. If you want them for baking you need a faster way to shell them. Euell Gibbons used to do this in a food grinder, by using a large enough plate so the seeds could almost pass through and so were cracked, rather than ground. You can also crush them manually, or put them in a blender with water for a few seconds. The shells and bad kernels float in water, while the good kernels sink (just like witches). The cleaned kernels can be eaten immediately, or dried for later use. If you want to store them, you should freeze them for a few days, to kill any insect eggs.

Uses: The kernels can be used like nuts, eaten out of hand (some people prefer them roasted), in baked goods, granola and muesli. Native Americans used the ground seeds for bread, gruel and thickening soups. The immature seeds taste pretty good, but can't be stored for any length of time.

Drinks: The seed can be pureed with water to make "Sunflower milk". It can also be mixed with fruit juice and various greens to make a blender drink (See *Symphytum*). I find this to be the best way to make the seed digestible. The whole seeds have been ground and roasted as a coffee substitute.

Sprouts: The whole seeds can be sprouted like Alfalfa (the shells eventually fall off), or grown on trays of soil for a week or two to produce "Sunflower lettuce". Native Americans often ate the wild seedlings in spring.

Oil: The seeds contain about 20% fat (domesticated varieties are up to 60% fat), which can be extracted with a press, or by boiling the kernels in water, and skimming off the edible oil. It stores well without going rancid.

Medicine: Sunflowers aren't much used medicinally, though they can help prevent sickness by providing good nutrition. The high fiber seeds are a natural laxative.

Oil: Sunflower oil has been used for a variety of things aside from food. It is a good massage oil (add a little perfume), which not only lubricates, but is also beneficial to the skin. It has been used for lubricating oil, paint (said to be as good as Linseed oil), hair and skin lotion, lamp oil and soap.

Fuel: Sunflower oil has been used to power diesel engines (see *Brassica* for more on biodiesel). It can also be used as home heating oil. It has been estimated that an acre of the plants could produce about 100 gallons of oil annually (which might meet the fuel needs of a small farm tractor), along with high protein seed cake. Of course the oil is much more valuable as a source of food rather than fuel. Perhaps a more practical source of fuel is to use the stems and waste hulls, which could be pressed into fuel logs.

Animal food: The seeds are important as food for wild animals and birds. The flowers are a good source of nectar. The seeds, are sometimes fed to chickens to help them lay eggs. You could plant Sunflowers for chickens. Just give them the seed heads, and the birds will do all the work of extracting the seeds.

Other uses: The pithy stems were dipped in oil and used for lighting, by Native Americans and the early settlers. The pith from the stems has been used as tinder, and is so light it has been used to stuff lifejackets. The stems have been used for wallboard and paper.

Propagation: Sunflowers are easily grown from seed, in rich, moist soil with full sun, and commonly self-sow. They need a lot of nutrients for good growth, so should be planted in rich soils with lots of organic fertilizers. They have a reputation for exhausting the soil if repeatedly grown on the same piece of land, so they should be heavily fertilized and rotated annually. They need regular watering for maximum production. The large cultivated plants can easily reach twelve feet in height so often need staking to prevent them falling over.

Horticultural uses: Their hunger for nutrients can be put to use, to remove an excess of nitrate fertilizer from the soil. Their thirst has been used to dry up mosquito breeding places. Their height (6 - 12 feet or more) makes them a useful quick temporary garden screen. One day I'll plant a Sunflower maze for my children.

Some people plant pole beans next to Sunflowers, as the beans replenish the soil with nitrogen, and use the sturdy Sunflowers for support.

Fertilizer: Sunflowers use four-carbon photosynthesis, which makes them more efficient when growing in high heat and light intensity. These fast-growing plants are ideal for producing an abundance of vegetable matter for green manure or compost. They are used just before the flowers appear and the plants turn woody. In a long growing season you can get several crops of organic matter in one summer. It is often said that the ash from the plants is a good fertilizer, but burning removes a lot of their nutrients, so composting is much better.

Smother crop: Their luxuriant and rapid growth also makes them useful as a smother crop to eradicate persistent weeds (See *H. tuberosus* below). This fits in nicely with their use as a source of organic matter. Plant as a smother crop and harvest as a compost crop.

Related species include:
The seeds of any *Helianthus* species can be used as above, though some are too small to bother with. The best include:

***H. petiolaris* - Prairie Sunflower**

Helianthus tuberosus / Jerusalem Artichoke
Throughout   *Asteraceae*
This species is a close relative of the Sunflower, the important difference being that it is a perennial and produces edible tubers rather than seed. Though originally native to the plains, this species was widely cultivated by Native Americans, and was carried across much of the country even before the first Europeans arrived. It is very persistent once established, and its presence in remote areas serves as a possible clue to archaeologists, searching for the sites of ancient native settlements.

Nutrients: Like most members of the *Asteraceae* Jerusalem Artichokes store their food in the form of inulin rather than starch. Unfortunately we can't digest inulin very well, so their calorific value to us is only about 75 calories per pound (a lot less than the Potato to which they are often compared). This is also the reason they cause flatulence. They do contain useful quantities of minerals however, and are quite a substantial food.

Gathering: The plants are easily located in early autumn by their conspicuous yellow flowers. After these die down the tubers are ready to dig. If you can learn to recognize the tall dead stems, you can gather the tubers all winter, so long as the ground isn't frozen. You can also mark the plants when flowering, and return later to gather. The distinctive tubers don't resemble anything poisonous. They are best gathered after a few hard frosts have increased their sugar content and improved their flavor. The harvest varies greatly according to soil, location and genetic factors, but you can usually obtain a lot of food in a short time.

Digging the tubers causes very little damage to the plants, as gathering merely thins them out. Any tuber left in the ground (some inevitably are) will become a new plant. It is actually hard to eradicate the plants intentionally, let alone accidentally.

Don't dig more tubers than you can use in a short time, as they don't store well out of the ground. If you must store them (e.g. where the ground freezes solid), then store like carrots in moist sand.

Uses: The tubers aren't bad raw in salads, but most people prefer them cooked. The best way to do this is by stir-frying, or by baking in a fire pit as for Camas (see *Camassia*). Baking converts much of the inulin into sugar and makes them much sweeter. They can also be boiled, but have a tendency to turn to mush if overcooked. The tubers have also been dried and ground to flour for baking, thickening soups and diet pasta. They have even been pickled.

There is no need to peel the tubers, so long as you clean out the many crevices carefully. Better yet cut off the knobby parts and re-plant them.

Sugar: Considerable research has been done with the *Helianthus* species, and one variety has apparently been grown as a sugar producer. The sugar rich stems are harvested and the tubers are left in the ground to re-grow. Sugar can also be produced from the tubers, as inulin can be converted into fructose, and they have occasionally been grown for this.

Alcohol

The tubers can be fermented to produce alcohol for fuel. Considering the very high yields that can be obtained (reportedly 20 tons per acre), the plant has considerable potential as a source of fuel.

Fiber: The stems have been used like those of the Sunflower (see above).

Smother crop: These fast growing perennial plants can smother almost any weeds, and have been used to clean fields of persistent weeds. The problem then becomes how to get rid of this plant. The best way to do this is with pigs. If you don't have these animals available, you can dig up the tubers when the spring shoots emerge from the soil and give away their location.

Animal feed: The tubers were once grown as pig feed, as they can digest them better than we do. These animals even do the work of harvesting. Pen them in the field and they will dig up the tubers much more effectively than we can. They also cultivate and manure the soil in the process.

Cultivation: This plant can be grown anywhere in North America that has some cool winter weather, but does best in the colder areas. Like its cousin the Sunflower, it is a hungry plant, needing rich, moist soil and full sun for best growth. It is a perennial and rarely produces viable seed, but this doesn't matter, as it's easily propagated vegetatively from the tubers (or fragments of tuber). You can buy tubers from a garden center, but it's usually cheaper to buy them in a produce market (sometimes labeled as Sunchokes). Normally it is only necessary to plant them once, as no matter how thoroughly you harvest, some tubers usually remain in the ground and sprout the following spring.

Because this plant is so persistent it is best planted on waste ground, where it can be allowed to run wild (this is how Native Americans grew it). Simply mulch, fertilize when you have some to spare, and water as necessary to stop them drying out.

This highly productive crop is rarely bothered by pests or disease, is resistant to heat and drought, and grows so vigorously it can smother almost any competitor. It is also very resilient. When I lived in Washington state the tubers in my garden were repeatedly eaten by slugs, every time they sent up new shoots. This happened for about two months, yet by the end of the summer the plants were about nine feet high.

Garden uses: This plant could be grown as an ever multiplying source of emergency food by those who worry about the future. It is actually quite ornamental when grown en masse, the yellow flowers resembling small Sunflowers (which indeed they are) and some varieties produce them very freely. They also make a useful deciduous screen (often needing support in windy areas) and a compost material crop.

Related species:
H. laetiflorus - **Showy Sunflower**
H. nuttallii – **Nuttall's Sunflower**
Used as above, but not as good.

H. giganteus - **Giant Sunflower**
H. maximillianii – **Maximillian's Sunflower**
These two species produce both edible roots and useful seed, which can be used like that of the Sunflower. They are sometimes planted to encourage wildlife. The latter species has been investigated as a drought resistant perennial seed crop. It self-sows readily.

Hemerocalis fulva / Day Lily
Northeast   *Liliaceae*
This beautiful Asian ornamental is widely naturalized in the northeast, and locally elsewhere. In midsummer it puts on a stunning display of tawny orange flowers. Each individual bloom only opens for a single day (hence the name), but the many buds on each plant give it a flowering period of several weeks.

This plant has all the attributes of the ideal wild food plant. It's easily identified, abundant, tasty, provides food at any time of year and isn't harmed by gathering. Even if it were harmed this wouldn't be a bad thing, as it is an alien species and sometimes crowds out native plants. There is no reason to feel guilty about gathering food from it, as there is with some plants. It may even benefit from thinning.

Caution: Very occasionally someone gets sick from eating this plant for some reason, so use care.

Tubers: The tasty tuberous roots can be eaten year round, so long as they are crisp and white, but are at their best when dormant. They can be eaten raw, but more often they are prepared like Potatoes. Some people remove the skins after cooking (it's a lot easier than before), but I usually just eat the whole thing. In Japan, starch has been prepared from the tubers.

Shoots: While still small (below eight inches in height) the spring shoots are edible as a salad or potherb. There are rumors of toxicity linked to over-consumption, so they should probably be used in moderation.

Flowers: The flowers are also edible, and you needn't worry about taking them because the plants usually multiply vegetatively. They can be used like Squash blossoms.

The flower buds are sometimes eaten raw, but I find them slightly acrid and not pleasant. They are much better steamed for a few minutes, cooked in soups, fried in tempura.

In Asia the dried flowers are used as flavoring in many dishes and are commonly found in markets. Even the faded, day old flowers can be added to soup and stir fries. Both buds and flowers can be dried for later use, just soak in water to reconstitute.

Medicine: The leaves and tubers have been used as a poultice for burns.

Garden Uses

Day Lily is a lazy gardeners dream plant. It's beautiful, produces a variety of food, grows in most soil types, thrives in sun or part shade, is very hardy, is rarely bothered by pests or disease, provides cover for the soil and multiplies rapidly. In many areas it is even free for the taking.

Propagation: Day Lilies can be grown from seed, but vegetative propagation is faster and easier. This is usually by division, when dormant from late fall to early spring.

Once the plants are growing well they can be left alone, except to feed, harvest, thin or multiply. In rich soil, with full sun they are a formidable competitor, forming a solid barrier of vegetation, both above and below ground.

Related species include:
H. flava - **Lemon Lily**
The Lemon Lily is another native of Asia that was introduced into North American as an ornamental. It is occasionally found as an escape, but isn't very common in the wild. It can be used as above.

Heracleum maximum / Cow Parsnip
Syn *H. lanatum*
North and mountains   *Apiaceae*
Cow Parsnip has the distinction of being the largest North American member of the *Apiaceae,* and may reach ten feet in height. The specific name is derived from Hercules and probably refers to this great size. The plant is often common and provides a number of palatable foods. It was widely used by Native Americans.

Caution: Mature Cow Parsnip plants are distinctive, but caution must be exercised when using immature plants for food, as they have been confused with such deadly relatives as Water Hemlock (*Cicuta*) and Poison Hemlock (*Conium*). These are so dangerous that you probably shouldn't use the plant, unless you are very familiar with it.

The skin of this species contains furocoumarins, which causes photodermatitis in some individuals. This occurs when juice from the plants gets on your skin, which is then exposed to sunlight.

Roots: The perennial root can be eaten while dormant in winter. You may be able to locate them by the dead flower stalks and foliage. You can also mark them in summer and return in winter to harvest. I can't stress enough that you must be absolutely sure of your identification when gathering at this stage. The root is usually boiled, in one or more changes of water, to reduce the strong flavor.

Greens: The spring shoots are good peeled and added to salads, or as a potherb. The leaf stalks have been cooked in a change of water, to reduce their strong flavor, and used as a vegetable. They are also good in soups.

Stems: The flower stem can be eaten up until the flowers appear, and is best just before the flower buds unfurl. It is peeled, cut into sections, and boiled in a change of water until tender. Some people enjoy it raw and use it like Celery in salads (use caution when eating it raw).

Salt: Native Americans used the ashes of the burned stems as a salt substitute. See Coltsfoot (*Tussilago*) for a method of preparation.

Medicine: A tea of the seeds has been used as a carminative, and to aid digestion. The root has been used externally for wounds and skin sores.

Cultivation: Cow Parsnip is easy to grow from seed, sown in fall. It likes shady, moist woodland soil, especially near water. It is a very handsome plant and has potential as an edible ornamental.

Hordeum species / Wild Barley
West   *Poaceae*
Food: The seed was gathered and eaten by Native Americans. These are among the best wild grains, because the seeds are so large. The ripe grains are dried in the sun, beaten to remove the loose chaff, and then held over a flame to singe, but not burn, the seed coats. This is usually done in either a pan or a sieve, and they must be shaken carefully to stop them burning The grain is then rubbed to loosen the seed coat, and finally winnowed to clean it. It is then ground into flour.

Barley Greens

The green juice expressed from the young leaves of cultivated Barley (*H. vulgare*) is said to contain almost all of the nutrients humans require and to have powerful healing properties. It is also said to help protect the body against harmful pollutants such as pesticides, radiation and free radicals. The dried juice is available in natural food stores at high prices, yet the superior fresh juice is easily produced.

To grow Barley for juice extraction, soak the seed overnight, and then spread it thinly on a tray of rich, moist soil. The seeds should touch one another so almost no soil is visible underneath them. This is put in a warm, dark place until it starts to germinate, and is then brought into the light and watered regularly. It is ready for juice extraction when 8 – 10 inches high. For maximum nutritional content drink the sweet juice immediately. Of course you can also use the juice of wild plants.

European Barley can be found as an escape in many areas and was occasionally cultivated by Native Americans. The flour is usually mixed with wheat flour for baking bread; the wheat makes the bread lighter, while barley adds a sweet flavor. In Asia Barley is fermented to make *miso*.

Malt: Malted Barley is one of the three essential ingredients for making beer. The malting process basically consists of soaking the grain, and leaving it in a warm place to germinate. This causes the seed to convert much of its starch into maltose, a type of sugar that can be used by the yeast in the fermentation process. When the seed has converted most of its starch, it is roasted to stop it growing, and to develop its flavor.

Malt extract is also used as a sweetener in baked goods and many commercial foods.

Drinks: In Europe Barley flour (or water in which the grain has been boiled) is mixed with lemonade to make a nourishing drink for children and invalids. Sprouted Barley can be roasted as a coffee substitutes. It can be used alone, but is usually mixed with other herbs.

Small beer: Beer was the traditional drink of Northern European peasants, and was drunk at almost every meal. You might wonder how they got any work done if they were permanently intoxicated from all that beer, but the beer they drank was commonly small beer. This is much lower in alcohol than ordinary beer and was the soda pop of its day. It is made by re-using the mash left over from brewing beer (waste not, want not) and adding more hops and yeast. If well made it tastes pretty good and probably has commercial potential as a low alcohol beer.

Cultivation: Barley is one of the most adaptable of cereal grains, and attractive enough to be grown as an ornamental. Grown from seed, it does well in most soil types, even those too dry or saline for other grain crops.

Horticultural uses: Barley makes an excellent green manure or cover crop. It provides a large amount of biomass in a short time, and in mild winter areas will grow through the winter. It is often sown with a legume to add extra nitrogen. *H. pusillum* may have been cultivated as a grain crop by Native Americans.

Best species include:
H. jubatum - Wild Barley
H. murinum - Foxtail Grass
H. pusillum - Little Wild Barley
H. vulgare - Common Barley

Humulus americana / American Hop
East, central   *Moraceae*
Greens: This species is essentially identical to the common Hop. The spring shoots are good when cooked like Asparagus, though they have a slightly bitter flavor. In Europe, they were once a common spring food in Hop growing areas, and they are still occasionally found in markets.

Baking powder: Apparently the ripe dried fruits have been ground and used as baking powder. You have to experiment to get the quantity right.

Flowers: The flower cones, gathered when they open in late summer, are full of fragrant yellow powder. They are usually dried for later use.

Tea: The flowers have been used to make a rather bitter tea, though this is drunk more for its sleep inducing properties than for its flavor. They are usually mixed with tastier herbs such as Mint, rather than drunk alone.

Beer

It is fitting that Hop should follow Barley in this book, as they are the indispensable ingredients (along with yeast) of real beer. The aromatic resins in the cone-like female flowers not only add their irresistibly delicious flavor and aroma (the essence of summer), but also act as a preservative, which was an important asset when refrigeration didn't exist.

Hops are used in two ways when making beer. They are most often boiled with the wort (the mix of Barley malt and water) for a long period to add bitterness. They may also be added for the last few minutes of boiling, to add aroma and flavor (these are known as finishing Hops). There are specific varieties for each of these purposes.

Medicine: Hop tea is calmative and soothing and was used to promote sleep. The flowers were sewn into bed pillows (known as dream pillows) for the same reason. The plant contains a substance called lupulin, which is one of the closest chemical relatives of THC (the psychoactive substance found in *Cannabis*) and may be a mild depressant.

Hop has been used to reduce stomach acidity, lower blood pressure, as a diuretic and to relieve toothache. It is a mild antibiotic, so is useful for cleaning wounds. This might explain how it helps to preserve beer.

Fiber: The plant is a close relative of Hemp (*Cannabis*), and apparently its stems have been used for cordage.

Cultivation: Hops can be grown from seed, suckers, division or root cuttings. It likes a deep, rich, moist soil, with full sun, and needs something to climb on. It is very independent and needs very little care once established. I have seen Hops still thriving in a ghost town that was abandoned in the 1930's.

A persistent rumor among Marijuana growers is that if scions of this plant are grafted onto Hemp rootstocks you get a plant with the psychoactive properties of Hemp, but that looks like a Hop (and so won't attract unwanted attention). There is no truth to this, so unfortunately there

will be no psychoactive beer (a potential best seller if ever there was one).

Garden uses: Spent Hops (the stuff remaining after brewing) are sometimes available free from breweries. These are an excellent nitrogen rich fertilizer, mulch, compost material or soil amendment. They have also been used as litter for Chickens, and the resulting nitrogen enriched litter is great fertilizer.

Hop is as attractive as it is vigorous, and with the right support makes a great deciduous screen. In winter it dies back to the ground and disappears completely.

Related species:
H. lupulus - **European Hop**
H. japonicus - **Japanese Hop**
These species are occasionally found wild as escapes and can be used as above. It is very hard to differentiate between these three kinds of Hop, and they may all be merely geographic varieties of the same species.

Hydrocotyle species / Pennyworts
Throughout   *Apiaceae*
Pennyworts are often common, but so inconspicuous you might not pay any attention to them, unless they become problem weeds. They get the name Pennywort because

of their round leaves. They are members of the *Apiaceae*, but this is not readily apparent unless you examine the small flowers (or taste the leaves - they somewhat resemble Parsley). No species is poisonous, so any that taste good can be eaten.

Caution: Gotu Kola is said to cause headaches, nausea and other symptoms of toxicity when used excessively. Native species are probably safe, but it might be wise to use all species in moderation.

Greens: In mild climates the leaves are available year round. They are a little tough, but can be chopped finely and added to salads and sandwiches. They can also be used as a potherb.

Drink: The dried or fresh leaves have been used as tea. I most often use the plant as a minor addition to a green blender drink (see *Symphytum*).

Medicine: The leaf of the Asian Gotu Kola (*H. asiatica*) is said to be very beneficial to the brain, improving memory and other functions. Whether native species have any of these properties I don't know. The leaves are also diuretic, and have been used to purify the blood and eliminate toxins.

Gotu kola is esteemed in India and China as a potent rejuvenating herb, and even an elixir of life. One of the more conservative claims concerning its powers was made by the Indian sage Nando Narian. He claimed it could slow aging and prevent disease, and apparently lived for 107 years, so perhaps there is a grain of truth to it. If you believe other claims about the plant, young Nando was a mere boy, other people are said to have lived over 300 years with its help.

The Pennyworts are used externally as a poultice, or wash, for skin problems.

Water purification: Fast growing *H. umbellata* has been used experimentally to purify wastewater in sewage treatment plants. It is used like the Water Hyacinth (see *Eichornia*), but tolerates cooler weather than that plant.

Cultivation: These plants spread by means of runners, and in mild climates are often considered weeds of lawns. They can also be a rugged and productive groundcover, or lawn substitute (it all depends upon your perspective).

These species are easily grown from seed, or runners, in moist soil with full sun. If given enough water they will take care of themselves, and even surviving repeated mowing. I one planted three small plants of Gotu Kola, and within three months they had formed a dense mat completely covering two square yards.

Ilex vomitoria / Yaupon
Southeast   *Aquifoliaceae*

Tea: The aromatic leaves have been called the best substitute for oriental tea to be found growing wild in North America. They even contain caffeine. Known as Black Drink, this was a popular drink among all Native American tribes living within its range, and was also traded with other tribes living beyond it. They even used to hold special "Black Drink Ceremonies" that often lasted for days. Yaupon was also drunk by European settlers, and was popular during the American Civil War. It may cause dizziness when drunk in large amounts, probably because of the caffeine.

The evergreen leaves can be gathered any time of year. They aren't very good if used fresh, so are usually dried first. This can be done in the sun, or in an oven at 200 degrees Fahrenheit. The leaves are steeped in boiling water in the usual way.

Medicine: The specific name vomitoria, refers to the Native American use of a decoction of the leaves as an emetic, to purify the body for spiritual purposes. Made in the regular way the tea is not emetic. This effect may have been caused by boiling the leaves for an extended period, or by drinking salt water along with the tea.

Animal food: Birds and small animals eat the berries.

Cultivation: This evergreen shrub grows best in moist, acid woodland soil and is propagated from semi-ripe cuttings, layering or seed (very slow).

Related species include:
I. glabra – Inkberry
I. cassine / Dahoon
These species can be used for tea as described above, but they aren't as good. They may contain caffeine.

I. verticilliata - **Black Alder**

The leaves of Black Alder don't contain caffeine, but they make a pretty good tea nevertheless. This species fixes nitrogen by means of bacteria in root nodules and so improves the soil.

I. opaca - **Holly**

This species isn't as good as the above, but was commonly used to make tea in the South during the civil war. It doesn't contain caffeine.

Impatiens biflora / **Jewelweed**

Syn *I. capensis*

East   *Geraniaceae*

This plant gets its name because raindrops sit in tiny jewel-like beads on the leaves. It is also known as Touch-Me-Not, because the ripe seed pods explode when touched, catapulting their contents several feet.

Greens: Jewelweed is sometimes called Lambs Quarters, a name given to several wild potherbs. The succulent young shoots have been gathered when less than six inches tall, and steamed for a few minutes. They contain toxic oxalic acid, and have been known to poison livestock, so probably shouldn't be eaten raw, or in quantity.

Poison Ivy treatment

Jewelweed is considered to be the best herbal treatment for Poison Ivy rash. A wash or poultice of the leaves is applied to the affected area as soon as possible after exposure. Some people claim it actually neutralizes the toxic resin. See *Toxicodendron* for more on Poison Ivy.

You can make a healing solution by putting equal amounts of water and plants in a pot, and boiling until the volume is reduced by half. This can be used immediately, or frozen in ice cube trays for later use. It can be added to bathwater, or used as a wash or poultice.

The leaves are also commonly used for insect bites, Stinging Nettle rash, athletes foot, and various skin problems. They contain a fungicide which may be of help in some of these cases.

Related species:

Several other species may be used in the same ways, including:

I. pallida - **Pale Touch-Me-Not**

Inula helenium / **Elecampane**

Northeast   *Asteraceae*

This species was once widely cultivated for food, medicinal purposes and as an ornamental. In the northeastern states it has long since escaped cultivation and is widely naturalized.

Roots: The aromatic roots of young plants have been gathered while dormant, and cooked like Carrots. They were once commonly candied by boiling in sugar syrup.

Drinks: The roots and seeds have been used for tea and for flavoring liqueurs, notably absinthe. I often add a couple of leaves to a green blender drink (see *Symphytum*).

Greens: In spring the rather bitter young leaves can be used as a salad, or potherb.

Medicine: The roots contain an antiseptic (possibly antibiotic) and fungicidal substance called helenin, which can kill bacteria in concentrations as low as 1 in 10,000. A tea of the roots can be used externally for cleaning wounds, skin infections and sores. It was once used as a disinfectant wash after surgery.

The root tea (and candied root) has been used internally as an expectorant and for pulmonary complaints such as asthma, bronchitis and tuberculosis. It is also a diuretic and has been used to purify the body, and eliminate kidney stones.

Cultivation: Elecampane may grow up to eight feet in height, and with its yellow flowers is an interesting ornamental. It is easily grown from seed or division, in deep, rich moist soil. Established plants self-seed readily by means of airborne seeds, I planted one plant several years ago, and soon had more seedlings than I wanted.

Ipomoea pandurata / Man Of The Earth
East   *Convolvolaceae*

This relative of the Sweet Potato (*I. batatas*) is not uncommon in the east. It produces large edible roots, up to twenty pounds in weight and three feet long. Smaller roots about three inches in diameter are more useful for food, as they are less woody and easier to dig.

Roots: The roots contain a purgative milky juice and must be cooked before they can be eaten. They are probably best when baked in the same way as their domesticated cousin. They can also be peeled, sliced and boiled until tender, though it may be necessary to change the cooking water at least once, to reduce their bitterness.

The roots were an important food for Native Americans, and were usually baked in a fire pit as for Camas (see *Camassia*). The cooked roots were often sliced and dried for later use.

Medicine: The roots were once in the USP as a purgative.

Visions: The seeds of some *Ipomoea* species contain lysergic acid, a close chemical relative of the potent hallucinogen LSD (lysergic acid diethylamide).

Alcohol: The large starchy roots could be fermented as a source of alcohol.

Cultivation: Man-Of-The-Earth is an attractive plant, that resembles its cultivated relative the Morning Glory. It could be used as a hardy, edible ornamental vine. It can be grown from seed, cuttings, root crown division or layering, and likes rich moist soil. The large root helps make it drought resistant.

Related species include:
I. leptophylla - Bush Morning Glory
This species was commonly used for food by the Plains tribes. The botanist and writer H.D. Harrington called this species "one of the best (food) plants we ever tried". Choose smaller roots up to 3 inches in diameter, peel and eat raw, or cook like the related Sweet Potato. It has potential as a perennial food crop.

Iva annua / Marsh Elder
Southeast   *Asteraceae*
Seed: The seeds ripen in late fall, and resemble small Sunflower seeds. They contain 40% fat and 30% protein giving about 2500 calories per pound. They are also rich in thiamine, niacin, calcium, iron and phosphorus. The raw seeds have a hard seed coat, and rather objectionable smell and flavor, so they are roasted, threshed and winnowed to prepare them for eating. The properly prepared seeds are quite good.

New crop: Though almost unheard of today, this was one of the first wild plants to be domesticated in North America. It was first grown 4000 years ago, long before the introduction of corn. Cultivars with seed was up to ten times larger than that of wild plants were produced. Unfortunately these no longer exist, so anyone wanting to grow it as a crop will have to start all over again.

Marsh Elder is a cousin of Ragweed (*Ambrosia*), and like that plant is a major source of allergenic pollen. This causes hay fever in some unfortunate individuals.

Related species:
I. xanthifolia - False Ragweed
This species can be used as above. Native Americans scattered the seed in suitable sites around their villages, to encourage its growth.

Juglans nigra / Black Walnut
East and center   *Juglandaceae*
Black Walnut has long been prized as one of best woods for making furniture and gunstocks and as a consequence fine old trees are quite scarce. Their increasing rarity means prime timber trees are now very valuable (more than $30,000 for a good veneer tree). This inevitably means that most landowners (or their heirs) eventually decide to part with these handsome trees. This great value has also led to increased timber rustling, the theft of trees from private or public land.

Most of the trees remaining on private land are either too small, or too distorted, to supply commercial lumber, though such trees can still supply nuts. Larger trees can be found in parks and public gardens.

Food: Throughout the history of humans in North America, the Walnut has been an important tree. The nuts were a prized food of Native Americans, and they often held gathering rights to individual trees in the forest. The nuts also helped the first English settlers in Jamestown to survive the winter of 1610 when faced with starvation. The wood was one of the first exports from the English colonies to Europe. Pioneers often spared Black Walnuts when clearing the forest, because of their value as human and livestock food. Walnut gathering parties were once a popular social diversion in rural areas, and in hard times their collection was a minor industry. Even today around 25 million pounds of wild nuts are gathered annually.

Nutrients: The tasty nuts are very nutritious; a pound of kernels providing about 3000 calories, with about 20% easily digested protein, 60% fat and 15% carbohydrate. They are also rich in minerals including calcium, iron, potassium, phosphorus and sulfur. The nuts also contain linolenic acid, an essential fatty acid that is important for healthy brain functioning, and ellagic acid which protects against cancer.

Gathering: The nuts must be gathered promptly after they fall to the ground, or wild creatures will take them. Unlike their relatives the Hickories (Carya), Walnut husks cling to the shells after they fall. These can be removed with your foot while gathering. It is sometimes possible to gather nuts from hard road surfaces, already husked by passing cars and dried in the sun.

Food Bars

Ground Walnuts can be used as a base for meal replacement bars. I don't really use a recipe for this, but simply gather together nuts (Walnuts, Beech, Hickory, Hazel), seeds (Sunflower, Chia, Evening Primrose), dried fruits (Figs, Rose Hips, Mulberries, Apricots) and any suitable food supplements (brewers yeast, Powdered Kelp, Bee pollen, lecithin) and grind them all in a food mill. I then mix everything together, press the sticky mixture into meal-sized bars, and wrap them individually in airtight plastic. I don't know how long the prepared bars will stay fresh and wholesome, though I have kept them for a week without refrigeration. They are a great hiking food.

Preparation: Native Americans dried the nuts in the sun before removing their husks. To separate out the bad kernels, they put them in water. Good nuts sink, while bad ones float. They then dried and stored the nuts for a while, as their flavor improves with storage.

The only drawback to these delicious nuts is their thick, hard shells. There are a number of ways to shell them, the simplest is to hit them repeatedly with a hammer, but this may well leave you with nut butter instead of nut meats. An easier way is to use a heavy vise (it won't pulverize them), or one of the nutcrackers specifically designed to deal with the tough nuts.

Uses: The nuts can be used in the same ways as commercial Persian Walnuts (*J. regia*) in cakes, cookies, bread, ice cream pancakes and salads.

Oil: Native Americans extracted oil from the kernels by boiling them as for Hickory (*Carya*). This is a good way to use the seemingly useless mixture of pulverized bits of meat and shells, you may end up with after shelling. In China, Walnut "milk", made from ground Walnuts and boiled water, has been fed to babies when human milk wasn't available. It was considered cleaner and more suitable for humans than cow milk.

Pickle: Immature walnuts are esteemed by gourmets, as one of the very best pickles. The whole green nuts (including the husk) are gathered when still soft enough to stick a pin through. They are boiled, their fuzz is removed, and they are pickled in vinegar.

Sap: The trees have been tapped like Maples (see *Acer*) to obtain syrup.

Medicine: The astringent bark and leaves have been used to treat wounds, diarrhea and sore throats. The Apaches used Walnut husk juice to clean maggots from wounds and to kill parasites of all kinds. An infusion of the leaves of Persian Walnut has been used to treat diabetes, by lowering blood sugar levels.

Shells: Broken shells are available in large quantities from commercial nut processing plants. These are very hard, and are ground to powder for use as an abrasive. They have been used for sand blasting jet engine parts and electronic components, as mud in oil-drilling, and as filler for dynamite and textured paints.

Cosmetics: Walnut leaves have long been esteemed as a hair rinse, and are still found in some expensive herbal shampoos. Native Americans used the brown husks to color graying hair, and oil from the nuts as hair oil.

Chewing sticks: Pencil-sized sticks can be chewed to fray the end, and used as a brush to clean the teeth and gums. They have antibacterial properties.

Fuel: Walnut is fair firewood, giving about 19 million Btu per cord, but cutting and burning any good size Walnut tree is quite literally burning money.

Wood

Walnut has been called the king (or queen) of woods. It is easily worked, durable in contact with water, ages to a beautiful rich brown color, and splits easily along the grain (an important quality when all work was done by hand). It was one of the most important woods of colonial times, and was widely used for cabinetmaking, construction, fenceposts, pilings and bridges. During the two world wars it was used in large amounts for propellers and gunstocks, and this further depleted the already dwindling supply of fine timber trees.

The days of Walnut fenceposts are long gone. Today it is rarely used in solid form, even for fine furniture; instead it is sliced into veneer (a sizeable tree may yield 80,000 square feet of veneer. Any piece of Walnut furniture is potentially valuable, and antique hunters looking for bargains often scrape away at painted furniture in the hope of finding the rich brown color of Walnut beneath. Some people have made money searching out old barns built with clear Walnut beams and dismantling them for resale.

Other uses: Native Americans used the inner bark fibers for cordage. The brown juice from the hulls can be mixed with vinegar and salt to make ink, or used as a dye for clothing. These properties made the husks an early export from the New World colonies to England. They have also been dried and used as an insect repellant. The oil has been used in lamps and paint.

Horticultural uses: The tree crop advocate J. Russel Smith urged the widespread planting of Walnut trees, calling them "veritable engines of food production" (they may produce up to four tons of nuts per acre). As mature trees disappear this is more important than ever, and anyone with sufficient space and climate should think about planting a few trees on a suitable site. There is a saying that you plant these long-lived and slow growing, trees for your grandchildren (they might even be planted as a college fund). In Germany it was once traditional for a young farmer to have to prove he had planted a certain number of Walnut trees before he could get married. Mature Walnuts are also attractive shade trees.

Walnut foliage allows sufficient light to pass through it for other plants to grow underneath them. Not all plants however, as the trees are notorious for inhibiting neighboring plants (they secrete an allelopathic substance called juglone). This directly inhibits Alfalfa, Blueberry, Apple, Tomato and Potato plants (among others). For this reason it is inadvisable to plant a fruit or vegetable garden near the trees (or vice versa). Some people even caution against using Walnut leaves for mulch or compost.

Cultivation: To grow Walnuts you need ripe seed that hasn't ever dried out (drying usually kills them). Ideally you should obtain your seed locally from the best specimen trees you can find. Plant them in rich, deep, moist, well-drained soil and protect from rodents. Walnuts resent transplanting because of their deep taproot, so sow directly, or into cardboard tubes. Germination isn't usually very good, so expect only about 50% survival.

You can also grow Walnuts from grafted trees, and a number of improved cultivars are available. These start bearing when as young as five years old.

The trees like to grow on sheltered flood plains, where the soil is rich and deep and grow naturally in small groves, forest clearings and edges. They don't like exposed sites, or shallow soils.

If a young walnut gets damaged or deformed in any way (such as from deer or rodents), cut it back to ground level and it will send up straight new shoots. The strongest and straightest of these can be allowed to grow into a new trunk, while the rest are removed.

Related species: A number of other *Juglans* species can be found in North America.

J. cinerea - Butternut
Butternut is hardier than the Black Walnut, and grows further north. The nuts are just as good however, and can be used in the same ways The wood is much less valuable, so it is correspondingly more common. It is also less useful as fuel, giving only about 14 million Btu per cord. The juice from the husks was once widely used as dye. A number of improved cultivars are available.

J. californica var *californica* - **Southern California Black Walnut**
J. californica var *hindsii* - **Northern California Black Walnut**

These western species produce tasty nuts and can be used as above. Natural stands of the northern variety are frequently found on the sites of old Native American dwelling places. These are a remnant of the times when Native Americans encouraged their growth.

The California Black Walnuts are also highly prized for lumber, and consequently large trees are getting scarcer. Their rootstocks are used for grafting the commercially important Persian Walnut (*J. regia*).

J. major - **Arizona Walnut**
J. microcarpa - **Texas Black Walnut. Syn** *J. rupestris*
Used as above.

Juniperus species / Junipers

North   *Cupressaceae*
The Junipers are conifers, but their fleshy cones look more like berries, and are usually thought of as such. These may take three years to ripen, so there are berries at different stages of ripeness on one plant.

Caution: The berries are rich in sugar, but also contain bitter aromatic oils that mask the sweet taste. If eaten in quantity they can cause irritation to the kidneys, digestive system and urinary tract. These oils can also cause abortion if consumed in quantity during the last few months of pregnancy. This is why Common Juniper (*J. communis*) once received the rather unflattering name of Kill-Bastard.

Flavoring: The berries of most Junipers have a bitter after-taste, and are unpleasant to eat in quantity. This is probably a good thing as they are somewhat toxic. They are safe when used sparingly for flavoring, and their taste resembles Bay leaf. The slightly immature fruits are the most aromatic, and are preferred for flavoring. A few berries are often added to cabbage, bean and pea dishes. They can also be chewed to freshen the breath.

Staple: Native Americans dried and ground the resinous berries of some western species to meal and ate them as a staple food. This is hard to imagine, as to modern palates they are too bitter and aromatic to be very pleasant. This meal was mixed with wheat flour for baking bread, and as a coating for fried food (like breadcrumbs). They were also boiled in salt water to make a kind of porridge (this is better with sugar and milk).

Drinks: The berries can be used fresh to make tea, or roasted as a coffee substitute. The green foliage has also been used for tea, and is often better than the fruits.

Gin

The most important commercial use of Juniper is as a flavoring for Gin. This was first invented by a Doctor Sylvius, of Leyden in the Netherlands, and was intended to be an inexpensive way to get the medicinal benefits of the Juniper berry. Called genever (French for Juniper), the drink was an immediate success, though more as a cheap way to get drunk than as a medicine. Ironically instead of improving health, gin became a health problem, causing alcoholism, poverty and further misery for the poor.

Yeast: The white bloom on the berries is actually yeast, and this has been used like commercial yeast for baking. See Oregon Grape (*Mahonia*) for more on using it.

Medicine: A wash, or poultice, of the mashed berries was used to treat skin diseases, wounds, insect bites and fungal infections. It has antiseptic and perhaps antibiotic properties. Juniper liniment was used to treat sore muscles and rheumatism. Steam from the boiling berries, or the smoke of burning twigs, was inhaled to clear the nose. The steam was also thought to disinfect sickrooms.

The tea is a powerful diuretic, and was used to eliminate excess water and toxins from the body. It was also used for urinary infections such as urethritis and cystitis. It is said to stimulate acid secretions in the stomach and so help digestion.

Wood: The oil in Juniper wood makes it very resistant to decay. A Juniper fencepost may last fifty years or more in the ground. Most species are too small to be of any commercial value as lumber however. The wood is excellent firewood.

Insect repellant: The oil in the wood repels moths and other insects. Shavings were sewn into sachets, and kept with clothing to repel moths.

Fiber: The inner bark was used for cordage by Native Americans (especially *J. osteosperma*). The bark fluffs up when pounded, and was used by Native Americans for skirts, and as diapers for babies. It is also good tinder for fire starting.

Incense: Native Americans used the smoldering boughs to purify the air. They were also used in sweat lodges for this. The ground berries were added to smoking mixtures.

Horticultural uses: Junipers are very commonly used in low maintenance landscaping, around offices and other public buildings. They are popular because they are very tolerant of neglect, and are available in a variety of sizes and shapes, for windbreaks, hedges and groundcovers.

Junipers are pioneer species and among the first plants to colonize abandoned, or neglected fields. Established plants are difficult to eradicate, so in many cases such land is eventually allowed to return to forest.

Cultivation: Junipers like well-drained, rich soil, with lots of sun. They can be grown from semi-ripe cuttings, layering or seed.

Species include:
There are thirteen species in North America, the most useful are:

J. deppeana - **Alligator Juniper**
Syn *J. pachyphloea*. This species is said to bear the best-flavored berries.

J. californica - **California Juniper**
The fruits are sweeter and less resinous than most and were an important food for the Cahuilla people.

J. scopulorum - **Rocky Mountain Juniper**
J. occidentalis - **Western Juniper**
J. osteosperma - **Utah Juniper** Syn *J. utahensis*
The berries of the above species were eaten in quantity by Native Americans, but aren't very pleasant.

J. communis - **Common Juniper**
J. horizontalis - **Creeping Juniper**
The berries are used for flavoring in small amounts.

Juniperus virginiana / **Eastern Red Cedar**
Flavoring: The fruits have been used for flavoring in the same ways as the related Junipers (see above).

Medicine: The leaves of this species contain podophyllotoxin, the same chemical found in the unrelated Mayapple (*Podophyllum*), and it has similar medicinal uses.

Wood: The Eastern Red Cedar was once an important lumber species. Its wood has distinctive reddish purple heartwood, almost white sapwood, and a very strong and distinctive "Cedar" odor that is repellant to clothes eating moths. It is also extremely durable and was widely used for fence-posts and other outdoor purposes. It is good firewood (for a conifer), giving about 18 million Btu per cord.

Pencils: Eastern Red Cedar was once the preferred wood for making pencils, but eventually the supply of trees became insufficient to meet demand. For a while pencil manufacturers went around buying barns made of Eastern Red cedar and turned them into pencils. When these were gone a new wood was found, the Western Incense Cedar (*Calocedrus decurrens)*.

Insect repellant: The moth repellant wood was used to line clothes chests, drawers and closets.

Caution: Red Cedar is generally discouraged near Apple orchards, as it is host to the Cedar Apple Rust Fungus (*Gymnosporangium Juniperus virginianae).*

Kochia scoparia / **Summer Cypress**
Locally naturalized   *Chenopodiaceae*
This species has escaped from cultivation and naturalized in some areas, particularly in the western states.

Greens: The young 2 – 3 inch tall plants can be used as a potherb or salad. The tender growing tips of older plants can also be used in the same ways.

Seed: The seed can be used like that of the related Pigweed (*Amaranthus*), and it has been cultivated as a seed crop in parts of Asia.

Firewood: These woody plants can be used as fuel, and might even be compressed into commercial fuel logs like the related Russian Thistle (see *Salsola*).

Brooms: The slender branches have been bound together to make brooms.

Animal food: Summer Cypress is rich in protein and has been favorably compared to Alfalfa as a forage plant. It has been suggested that it be cultivated for livestock food, though there are reports of livestock poisoning when large quantities are consumed. This is probably caused by oxalic acid.

Cultivation: This species is easily grown from fresh seed (this is very short lived), in most soil types.

Fertilizer: The plant has been grown as a source of green manure or compost material. This should be dug in, or cut, when the flowers appear.

Lactuca species / Wild Lettuce

Throughout   *Asteraceae*

A number of *Lactuca* species grow in North America, including the wild ancestor of garden Lettuce (*L. sativa*). Most of these are very bitter, and only really palatable when young. Garden Lettuces have been carefully bred over the years to reduce this bitterness, and even they get bitter in hot weather, or when flowering.

Greens: These species are only useful in spring, when their leaves are just a few inches high. They can be used like the related Dandelion (see *Taraxacum*). The leaves get increasingly bitter with age, and by the time the flower stalk appears they are inedible.

Stem: If it's not too bitter, the flower stalk can be peeled and eaten raw or cooked.

Medicine: Herbalists call the milky juice that exudes from wounds in the plant lactucarium. It somewhat resembles opium in appearance, and in the popular imagination it became imbued with the same properties as that powerful drug. It isn't really like opium at all, though it may contain some alkaloids, and be a very mild sedative. The juice was once collected in the same way as opium, by wounding the plants and scraping off the coagulated latex. It is still cultivated in some places to produce this latex for medicinal use.

> ### Compass
> When growing in full sun, the leaves of these plants tend to align themselves on a north south axis, hence the name Compass Plant.

The leaves have been made into tea, or smoked, for their mild sedative effect. The gum has been smoked like opium, by heating it and inhaling the smoke through a pipe. It has also been dissolved in alcohol and drunk. The latter method definitely has a sedative effect, though the alcohol no doubt has a lot to do with it.

Cultivation: Wild Lettuces are grown from seed in the same way as cultivated Lettuce, though they are usually so common in the wild that few people bother.

Useful species include:
L. canadensis - **Wild Lettuce**
L. serriola - **Prickly Lettuce**

L. tatarica - **Chicory Lettuce**
L. pulchella - **Blue Lettuce**
L. virosa - **Prickly Lettuce**

Laminaria digitata / Sea Tangle

Oceans   *Phaeophyta*

This common seaweed is one of the most advanced of the algae and one of the best edible ones.

Food: Prepare this tasty seaweed by slicing the fronds into thin strips across the grain and drying them. The dried fronds are soaked in water before use. They can be used for making jelly in the same way as Iceland Moss (*Chondrus*). In Japan the leaf blades of related species are used to make *kombu*. They are also fried in tempura, added to soup, cooked as a vegetable, dried and ground to powder.

Medicine: This plant is diuretic and has been used in detoxification programs.

Chemicals: The plant is an important source of alginates and iodine. It also contains mannitol, which has been used in making explosives, diet foods, laxatives and "sugar free" chewing gum. Ash from the burned plants was once used commercially as a source of soda ash for making glass and soap.

Animal food: The plant has been used as livestock forage in Europe.

Cultivation: The related *L. japonica* is cultivated on a large scale in China, for food and as a source of alginates and other chemicals. Annual production is around one and a half million tons annually. The intensively cultivated plants are grown on rafts, which keep the plants at an optimum depth at all times, and superior cultivars are used. These stands produce up to ten times as much biomass as natural forests of Giant Kelp.

Fertilizer: Like many seaweeds these plants make good garden fertilizer (see Giant Kelp - *Macrocystis*).

Related species:
L. farlowi
L. longicruris – **Oarweed**
L. saccharina - **Sweet Wrack**
These species are used as above. The latter is particularly rich in the sugars laminarin and mannitol, and has been fermented to produce alcohol.

Larrea tridentata / Creosote Bush

West   *Zygophyllaceae*

This rugged little shrub can survive on as little as three inches of water annually, and is a dominant species over many thousands of square miles of desert. It gets the name Creosote Bush because it gives off volatile aromatic oils, and often perfumes the desert air with its distinctive scent (particularly after rain).

Though rather nondescript in appearance, this is a rather astonishing plant. Some individuals are among the oldest living things, and colonies consisting of a single clone have been estimated to be from 9000 - 11000 years old.

Another unusual feature of the plant, and perhaps connected with its extreme longevity, is a phenolic compound called nordihydroguaiaretic acid (NDGA). This substance is an anti-oxidant, which captures destructive free radicals and inhibits oxidizing enzymes, and so may help slow the aging process. It has apparently extended the life of mice and insects, when given to young and actively growing animals. Unfortunately it doesn't help the mature creatures and can cause kidney damage in humans, so it isn't an elixir of youth. It is of value in studying the aging process however.

Food: The flower buds have been pickled and eaten like those of Broom (Cytisus). NDGA has been used as a preservative for oils and fats, but was banned from use in food because of its toxicity.

Medicine: The leaves are said to be one of best herbal antibiotics, for the urinary, respiratory and intestinal tracts. Native Americans used them to prevent infections, purify the body and treat skin parasites, wounds, bruises and dandruff. They used them as an antiseptic poultice, a wash, or dried as a powder. Native American women used it for menstrual problems, and as a contraceptive. A strong decoction is emetic.

The plants were burned in sweat lodges to purify the body during fasting, and to treat coughs, colds and other pulmonary complaints.

NDGA has been investigated for it's anti-tumor activity.

Chemicals: NDGA is used as an antioxidant in a number of industrial processes, to stabilize polymers, lubricants and synthetic rubber.

Glue: The resinous incrustations found on the branches are lac, a resin produced by the Lac insect - *Tarcardiella larreae*. This turns to liquid when heated, but solidifies upon cooling, so was used by Native Americans as glue, for making arrows and fixing broken pots.

Miscellaneous uses: Though the resins are repugnant to most animals, the plant material remaining after resin extraction is an excellent animal feed, almost as good as Alfalfa (*Medicago*). Native Americans used the plants for thatch and fuel.

Cultivation: This species is widely used for landscaping in the southwest. Like many desert species it exudes allelopathic substances that inhibit neighboring plants.

Related species include:
L. divaricata
L. mexicana
Use as above.

Lathyrus japonicus / Beach Pea
Syn *L. maritime*
Coasts & Great Lakes   *Fabaceae*
As the common name suggests, this species is found along beaches and sand dunes. It looks rather like the cultivated Garden pea, and can be used in the same ways. Though rarely eaten today, it was commonly eaten by Native Americans and European peasants.

Caution: Beach Pea is often considered poisonous, and it does contain some toxins, but the amount you would ingest from eating the seeds or pods is negligible and cooking removes a lot of the toxin. The toxin, B - aminopropionitrile (BAPN) is unusual in that it inhibits the cross linkage of protein and can cause irreversible paralysis. Fortunately this only occurs if the plant is eaten in quantity, as almost the only food, for long periods. Ironically this destructive substance is being studied for its potential to extend life, by reversing the aging process.

Seed: One need have no worry about occasionally eating moderate amounts of the tiny Peas. These are quite palatable if gathered while young, but many people make the mistake of gathering them when they are old and tough. Their main drawback is their small size; a lot are needed to make a substantial serving. One solution to this is to eat the young pods along with the peas. You can even gather the pods before the peas start to swell, and use them like Snow Peas.

The immature pods, or peas, can be boiled, stir-fried or steamed. The mature peas can be used like dried peas in soups, or ground to flour.

Greens: Native Americans ate the spring foliage when a few inches high. This may contain greater quantities of toxins, so is probably best left alone.

Cultivation: This species has occasionally been cultivated as a food crop and deserves more attention. It is a perennial Pea that grows well in poor soils, and is tolerant of saline soils.

Related species include:
Some other species are edible, but a few are toxic, so be very sure of your identification.

L. montanus - Bitter Vetch
This species bears edible tubers as well as seed. These can be eaten raw or cooked.

L. polyphyllus - Leafy Pea
L. polymorphus - Hoary Pea Vine
L. vestitus
Used as above.

Laurocerasus ilicifolia / Hollyleaf Cherry
Syn *Prunus ilicifolia*

West   *Rosaceae*

The fruits of this evergreen western species are valued for their large seeds, rather than the thin flesh. Like the related Cherries (*Prunus*), the pits are toxic raw, but Native Americans found they could make them safe to eat by leaching out the poisonous amygdalin. The leached seeds are a nutritious food, containing about 30% protein and 40% fat.

Preparation: The fruits were gathered in late summer and dried in the sun. They were then cracked open to obtain the kernels, which were leached like Acorns (*Quercus*) to remove the toxin.

Flour: The leached seeds were ground to meal and baked into bread, or boiled for gruel. It should probably be thoroughly cooked before use.

Fruit: The thin flesh of the fruits is pretty good when fully ripe. It has been eaten raw, or dried and ground to powder, for use in soups and sauces.

Related species:
L. lyoni - Catalina Cherry
Catalina Cherry is found on only a few islands off the coast of Southern California. It is closely related to the Hollyleaf Cherry and was used in the same ways. The flesh is better than the above.

Ledum species / Labrador Tea
North   *Ericaceae*

Caution: All Ledum species contain andromedotoxins and have poisoned livestock, so should be used with caution.

Flavoring: The leathery leaves have been used as a culinary flavoring, either dried and ground to powder, or boiled whole and removed before serving (like Bay leaves).

Tea: A tea of the dried leaves is bitter, aromatic and mildly stimulating, though it has never been really popular. This might not be such a bad thing as the plants contain a number of toxins. Steep the dried (not green) leaves for a few minutes, in the usual way. Never steep them for longer than fifteen minutes, or boil them, as this will release toxins. The leaves have been mixed with oriental tea, or other herbs.

Beer: In Germany the leaves were once used to flavor beer and the resulting brew was considered to be more intoxicating than that made with Hops. This is probably due to the andromedotoxins, as beer drinkers often consume large quantities.

Medicine: Labrador tea was once recommended for glandular problems, sore throats, mucus membrane inflammation and as a mild laxative. A strong decoction has been used externally to kill the parasites that cause scabies (and other body parasites). A wash or poultice has been used for wounds and burns.

Smoke: In Siberia the fumes of *L. decumbens* were inhaled for their narcotic effect. Native Americans burned them in sweat lodges.

Other uses: The leaves have been stored with clothes to repel moths. In Russia they have been used to tan leather.

Cultivation: These species can be grown from seed (slow), division, layering or semi-ripe cuttings and generally transplant easily. They prefer moist, light, acid woodland soil.

Species include:
Ledum species can be found all around the cooler areas of the Northern Hemisphere.

L. columbianum - Coastal Labrador Tea.
L. decumbens - Northern Labrador Tea Syn *L. palustre ssp decumbens*
L. groenlandicum - Labrador Tea *Syn L. palustre ssp groenlandicum*
L. glandulosum - Trappers tea
All of these species have been used for tea, but *L. groenlandicum* is considered the best.

Lepidium species / Peppergrass
Native or naturalized   *Brassicaceae*

Greens: All *Lepidium* species, native and exotic are edible and many are tasty and nutritious (up to 10,000 i.u. of vitamin A per 100 grams). Like most members of the Mustard family they are best in cool weather, and usually become bitter and unpalatable in summer.

The tender young plants are good in salads and some species have been cultivated for this. Older parts can be used raw if finely chopped. They can also be cooked as a potherb, though you may need to change the cooking water to reduce their strong flavor.

Seed sprouts

In Britain the seed is sprouted indoors for quick salad greens. Sprinkle a thin layer of seed on a wet paper towel, and leave in a warm dark place for several days to sprout. When most of the seed has germinated bring them out into the light to turn green and grow. They are ready to eat when 2 - 3 two inches tall (in about a week).

The seeds can be used as a condiment like the Mustards (*Brassica*).

Medicine: A tea of the leaves has been used as a wash for Poison Ivy.

Animal food: The seeds are valuable food for birds and are sometimes planted or encouraged as poultry feed.

Cultivation: *L. sativum* is cultivated as a dry land substitute for Watercress, and is known, appropriately enough, as Garden Cress. It is easily grown from seed, in almost any soil, so long as the weather is cool. It bolts quickly in hot weather.

Lewisia rediviva / Bitterroot
West   *Portulacaceae*

This genus is named after Meriweather Lewis, of the Lewis and Clark expedition. The specific name means revived or brought back to life, and was given for the plants amazing ability to survive adverse conditions. It's said that one specimen survived a dip in boiling water and then being dried for use as a herbarium specimen. When later planted it supposedly recovered and eventually flowered.

Food: Bitterroot is too beautiful to be killed for its edible root, especially as the root is bitter (surprise) and not that palatable. Apparently one can learn to like the flavor however, because they were a staple food of the Nez Perce and other northwestern tribes.

Gathering: The roots were usually dug when the tops start to die down in fall, but are still visible to help identify them. They can be eaten right through the winter if you can find them, but they are harder to locate and identify at this time.

Preparation: The starchy roots have been eaten raw in early spring, when their flavor is at its mildest. At other times they are usually very bitter unless cooked. Much of this bitterness is found in the skin, and peeling reduces it considerably. Removing the skin is easiest in early spring, or after soaking in water. Then you can simply roll the plants between the hands.

The peeled root can be boiled in a change of water to a jelly-like consistency. Native Americans baked them in fire pits in large quantities (you can bake them in an oven at 350 degrees for 45 minutes). They dried the cooked roots for winter use, and made flour from them.

Cultivation: This plant, so tenacious as it clings to windswept mountain peaks, usually withers and dies when transplanted and pampered in the sheltered garden (perhaps it misses the view). Initially it may seem to be doing fine, but is merely using up its stored food reserves and dies when these are exhausted. For this reason it shouldn't be transplanted from the wild. If you want to grow Bitterroot, propagate from seed, leaf cutting or division, in well-drained, dry, rocky soil. If you can't get them to grow in your garden, wild plants wouldn't either.

Related species: A number of other species are edible, though they are also too attractive for casual use (and some are quite rare).

***L. columbiana* - Columbia Lewisia**.
This species may be quite abundant at times.

Liatris punctata / Gayfeather
Liatris pycnostachya /Prairie Blazing Star
East   *Asteraceae*

Roots: The young roots are edible, but vary in palatability, so sample any you find growing in abundance (don't use them if they are scarce). They were an important food for Native Americans on the prairies, and were stored in large quantities for winter use. The roots are best while dormant, from fall until spring. They get sweeter with exposure to frost, as it turns their starch into sugar. Baking in a fire pit (see *Camassia*) also makes them sweeter, and the baked roots were a favorite food of the Kiowa people. They can also be baked in a 350-degree oven, or boiled. If eaten in quantity they may have a diuretic effect.

Cultivation: It is sometimes difficult to identify individual *Liatris* species, as they hybridize readily. They have been cultivated as ornamentals, especially for cut or dried flowers. They prefer rich soil with part shade and can be grow from seed, root cuttings or division. They are quite drought resistant and multiply rapidly.

Ligusticum scoticum / Scotch Lovage
Coasts   *Apiaceae*

Flavoring: This isn't the same species as cultivated Lovage (*Levisticum officinale*), but it is related, and can be used for flavoring in the same ways.

Stems: The young spring shoots can be peeled and eaten raw in salads, added to soups, or cooked like Asparagus (they may be quite strongly flavored). They are good until the flowers appear.

Drink: The flowers, leaves and seed can be used for tea, by steeping in boiling water for fifteen minutes.

Cultivation: Propagate from seed or root division in average garden soil. It needs little attention once established.

Related species:
L. filicinum - Lovage
L. hultenii - Sea Lovage
L. grayii - Grays Lovage
These species can be used in the same ways.

Lilium species / Lilies

Native   L*iliaceae*

Caution: Though all *Lilium* species produce edible bulbs, not all so called "Lilies" are members of this genus, so be cautious before you eat any Lily. Be especially careful not to confuse them with the poisonous Death Camas species (*Zigadenus*), as they are superficially quite similar when not in flower. Lily bulbs are covered in scales.

Bulbs: These beautiful plants are often uncommon and probably shouldn't be used for food except in extreme emergency, or when they are exceptionally abundant. Even then they should be used sparingly and any small bulbs or offsets should be re-planted.

It is a shame one can't eat Lily bulbs with a clear conscience, as they can be a good source of food. They were commonly eaten by Native Americans, most often baked like Camas (*Camassia*) bulbs, but also boiled.

Flowers: In Asia the flowers and flower buds are prized as food, and are widely cultivated as a food crop. They are used like those of Day Lily (*Hemerocalis*) in stir-fries, tempura and soups. Some species are bitter, and must be boiled in a change of water to make them palatable. The flowers are really too beautiful to gather from the wild, especially as they don't produce a very substantial food. It makes more sense to use the flowers of cultivated varieties.

Cultivation: Many *Lilium* species are prized as ornamentals, and an enormous number of varieties and hybrids have been produced. They also have potential as a food crop, and are ideally suited to the edible ornamental garden. Their only drawback is that you might find it hard to eat them when you see how beautiful they are.

Generally the Lilies prefer rich moist, neutral soil with part shade and are propagated from bulbs, bulblets, bulbils (small bulbs found in leaf axils), bulb scales, or seed. Once established they naturally form dense colonies.

Useful species: The only species that are common enough to use (sparingly) for food are:

L. canadense - Canada Lily
L. columbianum - Columbia Lily
L. superbum - Turks Cap Lily
These species were important food plants for Native Americans.

Caution:
L. parryi - Parry's Lily
This western species is very rare.

Limnanthes alba / Meadow Foam

California, Oregon.   *Limnanthaceae*

This species has recently received attention from the U.S. Department of Agriculture, because the oil in the seeds is very rich in long chain fatty acids, and resembles that found in Jojoba seed (see *Simmondsia*). This very stable oil has potentially important uses as a lubricant for high speed and high-pressure machinery and for precision instruments. It could also be used for manufacturing plastics, waxes and cosmetics.

Meadow Foam has been grown as an industrial oilseed crop on a small scale in Oregon. If breeding work is done to isolate high yielding cultivars, it has the potential to become an important crop.

Cultivation: Some members of this genus are popular ornamental annuals. Grow from seed in moist soil.

Lindera benzoin / Spicebush

East   *Lauraceae*

Spicebush is identifiable any time of year by the characteristic odor that permeates every part.

Tea: The twigs, flowers (best), leaves and red berries can be used to make a delicately flavored tea. Simply infuse the dried or fresh parts for a few minutes, then add honey and maybe lemon or orange peel for extra flavor.

Flavoring: Spicebush is also known as Wild Allspice because the leaf buds, flowers and berries (best) have been used as a substitute for that flavoring. They are best used fresh or frozen, and are not as good when dried.

Kindling: The bark and twigs contain inflammable oil and are good for kindling, even when green.

Animal food: Many species of animals and birds eat the foliage and fruits.

Cultivation: Plant the short-lived seed as soon as it is ripe, or stratify at forty degrees for four months. Cuttings and suckers can also be used for propagation. It grows naturally as an understory shrub in rich, moist woodland soil and is very tolerant of shade. However it fruits and grows better if given some sun.

Spicebush is occasionally planted as an ornamental, for its spring flowers and bright red fruit. It forms dense colonies and can become invasive, so should be planted where it can expand without encroaching on other plants.

Linum usitatissimum - Common Flax

West   *Linaceae*

This versatile plant is not native, but is often found as an escape from cultivation.

Caution: The cells of the Flax plant contain chemicals that combine to form cyanide when the plant is crushed or digested. Cyanide, as you probably know, is a deadly poison. It inactivates cellular respiratory enzymes and causes fatal oxygen starvation. This is why symptoms of poisoning include difficult and rapid breathing, faintness, flushed face, headaches, unsteadiness, coma and death.

Seed: The cooked seed is the only part of the flax plant that can be eaten. Cooking inactivates the enzyme needed to make cyanide and also improves the flavor. Native Americans used the seed of related species in quantity. They parched the seed by toasting it in a fire and then removed the seed coats by threshing and winnowing. The cleaned seed was ground to meal for baking or gruel. Some cultivated varieties of Flax have been bred specifically for food use.

Medicine: The mucilaginous seed has been used in the same ways as Slippery Elm bark (*Ulmus glabra*), as a poultice for burns, skin infections, wounds and insect bites. The poultice should be made and used quickly, otherwise irritating toxins may be produced.

Flaxseed oil is rich in essential fatty acids, including the omega 3 fatty acids, which can help control cholesterol in the body. They can also help the body to eliminate heavy metals and have other health benefits.

Linen

Flax has been an important source of fiber for several thousand years. Turning the plants into linen cloth is quite a labor intensive process. The stems are pulled (not cut) after the plants flower, and are soaked in water for several weeks, until the chemicals binding the tough outer layer of stem fibers begin to rot. This was usually done by building a dam of plants across a small stream. This process is called retting, and was once notorious for the stench created by the rotting plants. The stems were then dried and pounded to free the individual fibers, which were combed and spun into thread. The threads were used to make linen, string and rope.

Linseed oil: Flax seed oil is known commercially as linseed oil. and has numerous industrial uses. It is a drying oil (especially when heated to make boiled linseed oil), which means it absorbs oxygen and dries to form a protective waterproof coat. It is still used to make paint, wood preservatives, glaziers putty, printing ink and varnish, though oil based synthetics have replaced it in many cases. It is still a good treatment for wooden implements, such as tool handles and bats, as it protects them from drying out and splitting, or rotting.

The original linoleum floor covering was made from a filler of wood flour (dust), bound together with linseed oil and fabric. It is extremely durable, and with increasing interest in green building it is enjoying something of a revival. The oil is also used in the manufacture of some types of particleboard.

Cordage: The stems can be used as emergency twine with no preparation at all, and will even take a knot.

Thatch: In Flax growing areas, the long lasting stems have been used for thatching roofs.

Paper: Flax is still important in the manufacture of high quality paper, such as writing and cigarette papers.

Animal food: The plants are sometimes the cause of poisoning in livestock, especially in ruminants such as cattle. The seed cake left after oil extraction is a common animal feed.

Cultivation: Flax is easily grown from seed. It likes full sun and rich fertile soil.

Related species:
L. perenne / **Blue Flax**
This native species can be used in many of the same ways as the above.

L. lewisii - **Blue Flax**
Native Americans ate the seed of this perennial.

Lithocarpus densiflorus / Tanbark Oak
West coast   *Fagaceae*
Nuts: Tanbark Oak was once included in the *Quercus* genus. Its acorns are edible after leaching to remove their tannin (see *Quercus* for more on this). They are among the best tasting of all acorns, and were a staple food for some Native American tribes.

Other uses: As the common name suggests the bark has been used as a source of tannin for tanning leather. The wood is good firewood.

Cultivation: This species is occasionally grown as an ornamental in mild climates. Propagate as for Oaks.

Lomatium species / Biscuitroot
Syn *Peucadanum* or **Cogswellia** spp
West   Apiaceae
Many *Lomatium* species produce edible roots, and none are poisonous, so you might experiment with any you

find growing in abundance. However they do resemble a number of toxic species, so be absolutely sure of your identification.

Roots: The roots have a sweet, nutty, flavor somewhat like Celery or Carrot, and were commonly eaten by Native Americans. They are best while dormant from midsummer to early spring. The roots are peeled to reveal a whitish interior, which can be eaten raw or cooked. The boiled roots are not particularly tasty, but can be improved by frying.

Native Americans dried the peeled roots and ground them to a meal. This was mixed with water to make cakes (or they simply mashed the peeled roots into cakes), which were then baked, or dried in the sun. The resulting bread, or biscuit, was used in winter, and while traveling, and was actually a trade item among some tribes. This gave the plants their common name.

Greens: The young shoots, stems and leaves have been eaten raw or cooked as a vegetable. Any bitterness may be reduced by changing the cooking water.

Seed: The seed has been used for flavoring various foods, and for baking.

Tea: The leaves, stems, flowers and seed can be used to make a tasty tea.

Incense: Native Americans burned the plant to purify places and people.

Cultivation: Some species have been grown as ornamentals in wild gardens. They are grown from seed, in well-drained soil with full sun.

Best species include:
L. canbyi - **Canby's Desert Parsley**
L. eurycarpum
L. dissectum - **Toza** Syn *Leptotaenia multifida*
L. geyerii - **Geyer's Desert Parsley**
L. kous - **Cous**
L. macrocarpum - **Gray Desert Parsley**
L. montanum - **Mountain Lomatium**

Lonicera species / Honeysuckles
Throughout   *Caprifoliaceae*
Caution: Some *Lonicera* species bear edible fruit, but others are poisonous and may even have caused death. You should be very sure of your identification before using them.

Fruit: Several Honeysuckle species bear sweet, tasty fruits. These ripen in early summer and may hang on the bushes for several weeks. They can be used in the same ways as Blueberries (*Vaccinium*), raw, in pies preserves and muffins.

Medicine: I consider the delicious scent of the cultivated Honeysuckle to be its greatest medicinal property. On a more mundane level, the flowers and seeds have been used as a diuretic. The leaves of some species contain antibiotics and/or salicylic acid. These were used as a poultice for skin diseases.

Animal food: The berries and foliage are important food for wildlife. The nectar rich flowers are a food source for many insects.

Baskets: The long flexible vines are excellent material for making baskets. The bark fibers have been wound into rope and cordage.

Perfume: The sweetly scented flowers have been used in potpourri and perfumes.

Garden uses: Climbing Honeysuckles have been planted as ornamentals for their sweet flowers, and to cover screens and arbors. Some of the species mentioned below are good enough to be cultivated for their fruits, and are worth further investigation. Some Asian species have been grown as bush fruits, and a number of improved cultivars have been selected (unfortunately these are not readily available). Other native species are useful as ground cover, to prevent erosion, as wildlife cover and in hedgerows.

Cultivation: The plants generally prefer rich, moist soil, with full sun or part shade. They can be propagated from ripe seed sown immediately, or stratified for 2 - 3 months at forty degrees. Seed may remain viable for fifteen years. They can also be propagated by layering, semi-ripe cuttings, or division. The climbing species need support and control to stop them running wild. They can be controlled by burning, or repeated cutting or grazing.

Useful species include:
L. ciliosa - **Orange Honeysuckle**
L. morrowi – **Morrow's Honeysuckle**
L. utahensis - **Utah Honeysuckle**
L. villosa - **Blue Fly-Honeysuckle**
These species all produce edible fruits.

Lophophora williamsii / **Peyote**
Chihuahuan Desert   *Cactaceae*
This little cactus has gained considerable notoriety and attention, as the source of the hallucinogenic alkaloid mescaline, which is chemically related to the amphetamines. This was important to Native Americans as a bringer of visions, and was widely used by the drug

culture of the 1960's (especially after the publication of Aldous Huxleys book "The Doors of Perception").

Caution: Peyote is not edible, and is too rare to use anyway. It produces vivid hallucinations similar to those of LSD though it isn't as potent. It tastes very unpleasant and frequently causes nausea and vomiting (due to various other alkaloids). Despite these effects it is considered to be relatively safe to ingest. The usual dose is between 5 and 30 buttons. Native Americans sometimes took them for several days to completely detach themselves from everyday reality. They fasted and purified themselves before using Peyote, and this frequently reduces the unpleasant side-effects.

Though Peyote was only introduced to Native Americans in the north after the civil war (as they were pushed from their ancestral homelands) it quickly became an important sacrament, and very specific rituals developed. The white invaders tried to stop the use of this drug (as did the Spaniards in Mexico), as it symbolized traditional ways and was thought to be anti-Christian.

Like many cacti, Peyote is extremely slow growing, taking 12 - 13 years before it flowers for the first time. The plants have a very distinct spindle shape, with only the tip sticking out above the ground. As plants get larger they produce offshoots around the base. Older plants contain the most mescaline.

Native Americans would cut the tops, known as buttons, from the taproot, as this didn't kill it, but rather encouraged it to produce offshoots. Uprooting kills the plant. Intensive gathering in the 1960's and 70's has had a drastic effect on wild plant populations, and it is now rare in most areas. The buttons were dried and put on strings for sale, and were once commonly found in rural markets in Mexico.

Peyote is also notable for being one of the few cacti that doesn't have spines of any sort.

Lycium species / **Buckberry**
Throughout   *Solanaceae*
Fruits: The fruits of many *Lycium* species are edible, but their quality varies a lot, so it's best to taste any you find. The berries ripen in May or June, and stay on the plants for a long time (they are sometimes still available in winter). They are often produced abundantly, and were an important food source for some desert tribes. They may even have semi-domesticated it.

The fully ripe berries can be eaten raw, but are better cooked or dried. Native Americans dried them like raisins for winter storage, and then ground them to meal for baking and gruel. They also strained the cooked berries to remove the seeds, and used the remaining pulp in soups, puddings and to make syrup.

The Chinese Wolfberry (*L. barbarum*) is extremely high in antioxidants, vitamin A, amino acids and minerals. It is occasionally cultivated for its berries and they are sold in health food stores (they are also gathered from the wild for sale). I don't know whether the native species are as nutritious, but they are worth investigating.

Drink: A beverage similar to Manzanita cider can be made by crushing the berries and steeping them in hot water (See *Arctostaphylos*).

Greens: The young shoots were occasionally eaten by Native Americans, though they are members of the *Solanaceae*, so any green parts should be avoided.

Garden uses: These spiny plants have been used to make stock proof hedges. An African species (*L. ferocissimum*) has been recommended as the ultimate barrier plant. The spiny branches can be laid around tender tree seedlings to protect them from herbivores.

Cultivation: The Buckberries are propagated from suckers, cuttings, layering or seed. On rich soils they sucker freely and can become an invasive nuisance. For this reason they are best grown in poor soils, where they will be less vigorous.

Species include:
L. andersonii - **Anderson's Thornbush**
L. exsertum
L. fremontii - **Fremont's Thornbush**
L. halmifolium - **Matrimony Vine**
L. pallidum - **Box Thorn**
L. carolinianum - **Box Thorn**
The last two species may be found almost throughout the country.

Macrocystis pyrifera / Giant Kelp

West coast   *Phaeophyta*
This algae creates large Kelp forests off of the West Coast. It is one of the fastest growing plants in the world, sometimes growing fourteen inches in a single day..

Nutrients: Kelp has little calorific value for humans, as we can't easily digest the algin. However if it is eaten regularly our stomachs start to produce enzymes that help us to digest it. The plants are still useful as food though, as a rich source of minerals and vitamins.

Alginates: Giant Kelp is an important commercial source of alginates. These are widely used in the food processing industry, to prevent ice crystals forming in frozen foods and to make dairy foods (ice cream, milk-

shakes, salad dressings) smoother and thicker. It is also used to give a foamy head to some beers and soft drinks.

Food: You can cut the growing plants from a boat, but it is usually easier to gather fronds that have been recently washed ashore. Just make sure they are fairly fresh. They can be used to make jelly in the same way as Irish Moss (*Chondrus*). The dried, powdered fronds can be used as a mineral rich salt substitute.

Medicine: Algin forms a thick gel when mixed with water, and has been used as a bulk laxative. Because it is so little affected by stomach acids it has been used as a time-release coating for some drugs.

The indigestible gel also gives a feeling of fullness in the stomach, and has been used in diet pills to prevent the pangs of hunger experienced by people trying to lose weight.

Chemicals: Kelp has long been harvested for use as garden fertilizer, and as a source of potash and iodine, but only became commercially important as a source of alginates in the 1930's. Many Kelp beds are now cut regularly on a large scale, and cutting is controlled and managed for sustained yield.

Algin is found in a wide range of industrial products and processes. It is used as a suspending and emulsifying agent for paints, cosmetics, plastics, insecticides, adhesives, waterproofing, fabric size, inks and glazing. It can also be used for making synthetic fibers, in a process similar to that used for making rayon.

Fuel: The rapidly growing Kelp fronds could be used as a source of biomass for producing methane or alcohol fuels (along with various chemicals). It has been suggested that it could be grown on nets out beyond the continental shelf, using nutrients from the deep ocean (raised by wind power) as fertilizer. It has been estimated that four square kilometers could provide for the energy needs of 500 Americans (or perhaps many thousands of Africans).

Animal food: Kelp is occasionally used as livestock feed, and has nutritional qualities similar to Alfalfa (*Medicago*).

Preparation: Before the fronds can be used as fertilizer they should be washed in fresh water (or left to be washed by the rain) to remove excess salt. They can then be dug into the soil as green manure, added to compost piles or used as mulch. They can also be used as a liquid foliar feed. A number of commercial liquid seaweed fertilizers are available. It is possible to make your own, by allowing the plants to rot in water, as for Comfrey (see *Symphytum*). A less smelly alternative is to boil the fronds in water for a half-hour, and then dilute with 10 parts water to one part fertilizer. This liquid is also said to be useful for germinating hard to start seedlings and rooting cuttings.

Plants (like humans) can have too much of a good thing. Seaweed must be used in small quantities, as in excess it may actually be harmful to plant growth. A good foliar feed might be one part liquid fertilizer diluted with 100 parts water.

Fertilizer

Seaweeds are very rich in minerals because they grow in seawater, which contains an abundance of all the elements necessary for plant growth. An analysis of their mineral content reads like a list of essential plant nutrients; copper, magnesium, manganese, boron, zinc, phosphorus, potassium, sulfur, calcium, iron and molybdenum. They also contain other minerals not known to be essential for plant growth, but that are valuable to humans.

They also contain cytokinins, substances similar to growth hormones, that make plants larger, healthier and more resistant to stresses such as drought, heat, frost, insects and disease. The algin in seaweed is an excellent soil conditioner, and may make nutrients in the soil more readily available to plants. It is said that a number of garden pests (e.g. nematodes) avoid soil fertilized with seaweed.

Transplant aid: Another horticultural use of seaweeds is as an aid in tree planting. A solution of algin can be used to coat bare root trees, to help them survive transportation and transplant shock, and it definitely increases their chances of survival. Plants may also be watered with an algin solution before and after transplanting. It is said that some plants treated with algin have been transplanted while blooming without even wilting (I am somewhat skeptical about this).

Madia glomerata / Tarweed
West   *Asteraceae*
You might be familiar with Tarweed because its sticky tar-like secretions stick to clothing and make a mess.

Seed: The abundant oily seeds were an important food for some Native American tribes. They parched and ground them to make flour for baking and gruel, or crushed them to make a kind of peanut butter. They also extracted a sweet oil by boiling the seeds as for Hickory (see *Carya*).

Industrial oil: The oil has been used like that of Flax (*Linum*) in paints, varnish and lamps. It is also a good massage oil.

Cultivation: *Madia sativa* have been cultivated as an oilseed crop in Europe and South America. It is easily grown from seed, in well-drained soil, with full sun and may even become a weed. Yields are only about 600 pounds of oil per acre, so it has never been very widely grown.

Related species:
M. elegans - Common Madia
M. gracilis - Slender Tarweed
M. sativa - Chile Tarweed
These species may be used as above.

Mahonia species / Oregon Grape
Syn *Berberis* species
West   *Berberidaceae*
These species are close relatives of the Barberries (*Berberis*), and are often included in that genus. The important difference is that *Mahonia* species don't have spines, and their fruits are less sour. Any species with palatable fruit can be eaten.

Fruit: The fruits can be used for food in much the same ways as the Barberries, but are somewhat better. Their quality varies a lot with individuals and species, so you must taste any you find to locate the best. Some are good raw and can be added to fruit salads, but most are too sour. These are usually best cooked in pies or preserves. Some people advise moderation in the use of the fruits, because they contain berberine (see below), and say they should be avoided during pregnancy.

Flowers: These can be added to salads for their color.

Drink: A pleasant drink can be made by simmering the berries in water, or by crushing them and extracting the juice in the same way as for Grapes (*Vitis*). These drinks are improved by the addition of sugar, or by mixing them with sweeter juices.

Yeast: The white bloom covering the berries contains wild yeasts and can be used to bake bread. Culture it by soaking the berries in flour, sugar and warm water.

Medicine: The roots contain the alkaloid berberine, and have the same medicinal uses as the Barberries. They are used as a tonic for the kidneys, thyroid and liver, and as a blood purifier to treat rheumatism and skin diseases. A tea of the root is mildly antiseptic and has been used as a wash for wounds.

Animal food: All species are important for wildlife.

The Uses Of Wild Plants

Cultivation: Some species are widely planted for their pretty blossoms, berries and shiny Holly-like leaves. They generally prefer moist, rich soil, and are propagated from suckers, seed, layering or cuttings. The creeping *M. repens* has been used as a groundcover.

Useful species include:
M. aquifolium
M. nervosa
M. repens

Malus pumila / Wild Apples

Syn *Pyrus malus*

Throughout   *Rosaceae*

The Apples are closely related to the Pears (*Pyrus*) and are often included in that genus. This is the most important fruit of temperate regions, and is prized for its ease of cultivation, resistance to damage and deterioration, moderately high food value and fine flavor. There are several thousand named varieties in existence, adapted to widely differing climates and with many different qualities, though most are now rarely grown.

The domesticated Apple is not native to North America, but was introduced by the first European settlers and escaped soon after. It can now be found growing wild almost anywhere in the country.

Nutrients: Apples are a well-balanced food, containing about 14% carbohydrate, 85% water and small amounts of malic acid, pectin, enzymes, fiber, iron, magnesium, phosphorus and vitamins B1, C and E. Like many members of the *Rosaceae*, the seeds contain cyanogenic glycosides and are toxic if eaten in large amounts. There is a story of a man who ate a whole cupful of seeds and died of cyanide poisoning. This is a pretty unusual way to die, and in small amounts the seeds are quite harmless, maybe even beneficial.

Gathering: The best apple trees you are likely to find, are those in abandoned orchards or home-sites, still bearing fruit years after being abandoned. These tend to be superior to the truly wild types. Fruits from wild seedling trees are usually too sour to eat raw, but are good if cooked with sweetener.

Apple foraging can be a very rewarding activity, giving a lot of food in a very short time. Don't worry if there are bruises, blemishes or even wormholes in your apples, just use the good parts and discard the rest. If you want to keep them for a while, pick the fruits before they fall to the ground, because bruised Apples don't store well.

The season for gathering apples is a lot longer than you might think. You can start gathering immature fruit for applesauce in midsummer, while the fallen fruit may still

be edible in midwinter, even if frozen. When an apple is ripe the seeds are dark brown.

Storage: Apples will keep fresh for several months if stored correctly. Wrap the unblemished fruits individually in paper and store in a cool room. It is important that they be undamaged, as injured flesh exudes ethylene gas, causing the fruit to ripen and too much ripeness becomes decay. You have probably heard the saying "one rotten apple spoils the whole barrel", well this is why.

Apples are usually preserved in the form of cooked applesauce or apple butter. They can also be sliced into thin rings and dried in the sun. You can get a tool that will peel and make a single spiral out of a whole apple. The dried fruits are good in breakfast cereals and baked goods, and are a great backpacking food.

Uses: From a nutritional standpoint apples are best eaten raw. Some people eat them whole, skin, core seeds and all, and this may well be the best way. The skin contains five times as much vitamin C as the flesh, as well as many other nutrients, so don't peel them without good reason. Apples are also good stewed, baked, fried, made into pies, cakes, preserves and sauces. Very sour (or unripe) apples can be used for sauce or jelly.

Drink: Apple juice is familiar to everyone. It used to be made by grating the fruits, and then crushing the pulp in a cider press, or in a muslin bag by hand. Nowadays it is much easier to use an electric vegetable juicer.

If the juice is left in a warm place it will start to ferment, without the addition of yeast. After a couple of days it will develop a light carbonation, and tastes like apple soda. I found this semi-fermented juice to be one of the great pleasures of the New England fall. If fermentation is allowed to continue for a longer period, much of the sugar is converted into alcohol, and it becomes hard cider. This has an alcohol content that exceeds that of beer. Commercial cider is made by blending sweet and sour apples together in the right proportions. The wild yeasts are killed off (they can give it an off flavor) and special cultivated yeast strains are added.

In very cold climates hard cider can be made even stronger, by leaving it outdoors on freezing winter nights. A lot of the water in the cider will freeze (and can be removed), leaving the alcohol still liquid (alcohol freezes at about minus one hundred degrees Celsius).

Vinegar: If you leave the fermented juice long enough it eventually turns into apple cider vinegar. This can be used in salad dressings, as a condiment and for medicinal purposes.

Verjuice: The juice of sour apples is called verjuice and can be used as a substitute for vinegar, or lemon juice, in salad dressings.

Tea: It has been said that apple juice can kill some forms of bacteria. I wouldn't rely on this as a means of water purification, but I have added chopped apples, or just the peel, to my canteen to flavor the water. Apple peelings can also be used to make tea.

Medicine: Another apple saying is "an apple a day keeps the doctor away"(remember "garlic for vampires, apples for doctors"). This sounds ridiculous at face value, but contains an element of truth. It is a reference to the laxative properties of whole apples, as they provide fiber and pectin to aid in elimination. They also contain easily digested minerals, enzymes and acids, and are said to stimulate the digestion, liver and kidneys. Because of these properties apples are sometimes the basis for a "fruit fast", where one eats only apples for a number of days.

Paradoxically apples have been used both as a laxative and to treat diarrhea (their pectin and tannin content helps in this). Pectin has also been found to be useful in reducing the amount of heavy metals (notably strontium 90) absorbed by the body. Apparently pectin binds these elements so they are excreted rather than being absorbed into the bones. Prepared pectin is normally used as one would have to eat about fifteen apples daily to get the effect.

Apple cider vinegar has been used to treat athletes foot, skin itching, and as a douche for some types of vaginal infections.

Wood: Apple wood has a beautiful grain, but is too scarce to be of much commercial importance, as most trees are small and contorted. It is also very hard and quickly dulls woodworking tools. The wood is used in cabinetmaking, carving, turning, and for tool handles, mallets and golf clubs.

Fuel: Apple is very good firewood, giving about 24 million Btu per cord and a fine scent. It isn't often available though, unless an orchard is being destroyed.

Pectin: Pectin, derived from apple pomace (the residue left after juice making), is an important industrial chemical. Its binding properties make it of value for food processing, hairdressing, toothpaste, glues, medicines and even in steel manufacture (for tempering steel). Sour apples contain more pectin than sweet ones.

Cosmetics: Apple cider vinegar can be used as a hair wash. A face pack of mashed apples is said to improve the complexion.

Cultivation: Apple seed should be soaked for 24 hours, and then stratified at 32 degrees for three months. They are sometimes treated with the hormone giberellic acid to speed germination. Alternatively you might simply sow the seed in autumn, in a rodent free place, and keep your fingers crossed for a year or two. They like deep, rich, well-drained, moist soil and full sun. Apples don't come true from seed, and with a few exceptions most seedlings are inferior to their parents (you could try cross pollinating your preferred varieties). Select cultivars are propagated by grafting or budding.

Fertilizer: Apple pomace is an excellent garden fertilizer, though not widely available. It is usually mixed with leaves or hay to aerate it, and used as green manure, compost material or mulch.

Related species:
M. baccata- **Siberian Crab Apple**
M. sylvestris – **European Crab Apple**
These species can also be found as escapes from cultivation. Their fruits tend to be sour, but can be used as above.

M. angustifolia - **Southern Crab Apple**
M. coronaria - **Sweet Crab Apple**
M. fusca - **Oregon Crab Apple**
M. ioensis - **Prairie Crab Apple**
These are the native American Apple species. They grow as small trees, or understory shrubs, and bear small, sour fruits that can be used in sauce or jelly. Native Americans apparently made the fruit less acid by burying them in baskets in the ground over winter. They also crushed and dried them into cakes (often with other fruit) for later use.

These species have potential for breeding garden fruits, especially *M. coronaria*. The roots are sometimes used for grafting cultivated apples.

The Uses Of Wild Plants

Malva species / Mallows

Throughout   *Malvaceae*
Strictly speaking no wild member of the *Malva* genus is poisonous, and any species you find can be tried as food. However at least one species has poisoned cattle in Australia, probably as a result of concentrating nitrates from the soil. This proves the exception to the rule, and shows that you should always be cautious about what you put into your mouth.

Nutrients: The Mallows are among the richest plant sources of carotene (which the body converts into vitamin A), containing as much as 16,000 i.u. per ounce. They also contain a lot of vitamin C, and many minerals.

Greens: In mild climates these hardy plants may remain green all winter, which makes them especially valuable in such areas. The tender young leaves can be used in salads, but are best boiled as greens. Older leaves can be chopped and cooked as a potherb, though you might want to change the cooking water once or twice. This is not necessary to remove any unpleasant taste, but reduces their slimy, mucilaginous quality. The dried leaves have been used for tea.

Flowers: The flowers can be added to salads.

Seedpods: The green seedpods have been peeled and used like their relative Okra, to thicken soups, and as a cooked vegetable. Their unusual shape and texture makes them an interesting addition to salads.

Medicine: The name Mallow is derived from the Greek "to soften", and is a reference to their soothing properties. The whole plants can be used as an emollient in the same ways as Marshmallow (*Althaea*), though they aren't quite as effective.

A wash of the leaves, or a leaf poultice, is used for wounds and bee stings. The slimy liquid obtained by boiling the pods or roots has been used as a lotion for skin problems like eczema, or dry sore skin.

It has recently been found that foods that are rich in carotene can help prevent some kinds of cancer. That would make these plants a valuable addition to the diet. The leaves have been eaten to cure constipation.

Cultivation: Several Mallow species are grown as ornamentals for their lovely flowers (*M. moschata, M. alcea*), while others (*M. neglecta* and *M. rotundifolia*) are common weeds of gardens and fields. None of these are native, but the ornamental species may be found as escapes, while the weedy ones are widely naturalized.

Generally these species prefer moist soil and full sun. The annual and biennial types are grown from seed, while the perennials can be grown from seed, division or soft cuttings.

Best species include:
M. moschata - Musk Mallow
M. neglecta - Common Mallow (Syn *M. parviflora*)
M. rotundifolia - Low Mallow
M. sylvestris - High Mallow
M. verticillata - Curly Mallow (Syn *M. crispa*)

Marshallocereus thurberii / Organpipe Cactus

Syn *Lemairocereus thurberii* or *Stenocereus thurberii*
Southwest   *Cactaceae*
Fruit: This species is a close relative of the Saguaro and was once in the *Cereus* genus. Like that plant its fruit were an important food source to Native Americans in the southwest. They are among the best flavored of all Cactus fruit, and are still eaten where found in sufficient numbers. Gather and use like the Saguaro.

Drink: An important Native American use for the fruit was for making wine (see *Cereus*) and this is still widely consumed at ceremonial and social gatherings.

Seed: The hard seeds pass through the digestive system unharmed, which led Native Americans to use a rather unconventional way of separating the seeds from the pulp. They would eat the whole fruit and then defecate in a selected spot. The feces dried quickly in the dry desert air, and were then crushed and the seeds therein collected. These were washed thoroughly, parched and then ground to flour for baking.

Other uses: The ribs of these cactus have been used like those of Saguaro for building shelters and fences. The pulp of the plants has been used as waterproof caulk for boats and baskets.

Animal food: The Organpipe cactus has a symbiotic relationship with Bats, and they each depend on the other for survival. The bats pollinate the flowers and disperse the seeds. In return for these services, the Bats receive food in the form of nectar and fruit.

Cultivation: Organpipe Cactus is grown in the same way as Saguaro, though it is even less hardy. In Mexico it is sometimes planted as a spiny hedge.

Matteucia struthiopteris / Ostrich Fern

Syn *M. pennsylvanica, Pteretis pennsylvanica*
North   *Polypodiaceae*
Ostrich Fern is fairly easy to identify because it produces two distinct kinds of fronds; leafy ones in spring, and fertile reproductive ones in early summer.

This is probably the best edible fern species. Unlike the Bracken fern (*Pteridium*) it is not thought to contain any carcinogens, though it does contain thiaminase, an enzyme that destroys the nutrient thiamine. This is destroyed by cooking however.

Shoots: The curled fronds, known as fiddleheads, can be found underneath the dead foliage from the previous year. They are only good for about 2 - 3 weeks in spring, when they start to uncurl (mature ferns are not edible). Only gather them where the plants are abundant, and don't take too many shoots from a single plant, or you may damage or kill it. Collect the shoots when only 6 - 8 inches in height, as they become unpalatable as they get larger. It is best to go out gathering in the morning, as they open quickly in the course of a day. Break them off as low down as they snap easily.

Brush off the inedible brown fuzzy covering from the fiddleheads and wash carefully. They can then be steamed or boiled for 10 minutes. The cooked fiddleheads can be added to soup, stir fries and salads.

The fronds are so highly prized as food in Maine and the Canadian Maritime provinces, that they are gathered from the wild and canned commercially (eating them is a local spring tradition there). Commercial gathering is having an adverse impact in some areas, as repeated picking can exhaust and kill the plant.

Roots: The woody rhizomes contain a lot of starch and in Japan this is extracted and sold for use in the same way as Kudzu starch (see *Pueraria* for details of starch extraction). Some Native American tribes ate the roots, usually in time of famine.

The underground buds that will become next season's fronds, have been cooked and eaten in late winter. The Abenaki people ate the whole crown.

Fiddleheads have been obtained in winter, by forcing the roots indoors like Chicory (see *Cicorium*).

Cultivation: Ferns don't produce seed, so the easiest way to propagate them is by division. They naturally grow in shady, moist, acid, woodland soil.

This is one of the most attractive of all ferns and is widely used as an ornamental. It also has potential as a food crop, and annual yields of up to 2000 pounds per acre may be possible. It has been suggested that it be grown in conjunction with coppiced trees, which would give it the required shade. The fiddleheads would provide a steady annual income while the coppiced trees grew to marketable size. The coppice would be worked in winter without disturbing the ferns. Of course you would have to find a market for the fiddleheads.

Medeola virginiana / Indian Cucumber
East   *Liliaceae*

Root: The crisp root has a pleasant Cucumber-like flavor, and is edible year round. Unfortunately it isn't a very common plant and shouldn't be used casually for food, as digging the root will kill it. It is best eaten raw, in salads or sandwiches, and is very good. It can also be cooked as a vegetable, added to soup or even pickled. The inedible berries are mildly purgative.

Cultivation: This attractive little plant is often planted in wild gardens. Propagate from seed, or root division when dormant. It likes rich moist woodland soil, and once established will form small colonies.

Medicago sativa / Alfalfa
Naturalized   *Fabaceae*

Alfalfa is one of the most commercially important non-food legumes. It isn't native to North America, but is very widely planted as animal feed, and to improve soil fertility and is often found as an escape. Its deep penetrating roots make it one of the richest sources of minerals of all plants.

Alfalfa Sprouts

A few years ago Alfalfa was something you fed to rabbits or cows, not humans, but Alfalfa seed sprouts are now an everyday food and can be found in almost all supermarkets. They are easy to produce; all you need is seed, water and a warm place. Soak the seeds overnight to hydrate them, and then keep them moist (but not wet), by rinsing them 1 - 3 times daily. When the sprouts are about an inch long, expose them to sunlight so they turn green, as this makes them more nutritious. They are usually ready to eat in 7 - 10 days.

Greens: The tender young foliage has been used in small quantities as a salad or potherb (best mixed with other greens). Be cautious, as they can concentrate nitrates from chemical fertilizers in the soil, and become toxic. They may also contain other toxins.

The dried leaves have been ground to powder and made into "natural vitamin pills".

Seed: Native Americans ground the seed of related species to meal for baking and gruel.

Medicine: The fresh or dried (better) leaves can be made into a nutritious, mineral rich tea. It doesn't have much flavor, so is usually mixed with Mint or other strongly flavored herbs.

Animal food: Alfalfa has the highest protein content of all common livestock forage plants, and is used as animal feed in a variety of forms. Many wild birds eat the seeds.

Cultivation: Alfalfa is easily grown from seed, and prefers deep, well-drained, fairly neutral soils. Varieties are available for widely different growing conditions. If it is to be cut frequently the soil should be fairly rich. It fixes more nitrogen if inoculated with suitable bacteria.

Horticultural uses: This drought tolerant hardy perennial contain nitrogen fixing bacteria in nodules on its roots, and has been known to fix over 200 pounds of nitrogen per acre annually. It is sometimes planted as a cover crop, or green manure, to improve impoverished soils. The plant is often allowed to grow for several years to improve the soil. During which time the land will produce hay, seed (potentially valuable) and nectar (it pays to have beehives nearby).

Fertilizer: The fresh or dried leaves can be used as garden fertilizer and compost activator. They are useful not only for their high content of nitrogen and other nutrients, but also because they contain a growth stimulant called triacontanol. Alfalfa hay has been composted, shredded and dried for use as a peat substitute for starting seeds.

Related species.
M. lupulina - **Black Medick**
M. hispida - **Bur Clover**
Used as above. Native Americans boiled the seed of the latter species to make mush.

Melilotus officinalis, M. alba / **Sweet Clovers**
Throughout   *Fabaceae*
These nitrogen-fixing legumes were introduced into North America as forage crops, and are now widely naturalized.

Caution: The protein rich leaves are commonly used for hay, but they can become toxic if improperly cured. Shortly after the plant was introduced into North Dakota in the 1920's, cattle were found to be bleeding to death from the slightest injury, their blood having lost the ability to clot. Spoiled Sweet Clover hay was found to be the cause, as the spoilage converts a relatively harmless substance in the plant called coumarin into a harmful one called dicoumarol. This substance reduces the ability of the blood to clot, to the point where any injury can cause fatal hemorrhaging.

Coumarin gives the dried plants their characteristic new mown hay scent, and dried Sweet Clover has long been used as a culinary flavoring. It was banned from use in the food processing industry in 1954 because it is toxic to the liver.

Flavoring: The dried leaves of these two species have a new mown hay scent and flavor, and have been used for flavoring cheese, soup and wine.

Greens: The tender new leaves have occasionally been used in salads. They leaves have also been used for tea, but may be emetic if drunk in quantity. If you dry the plants for anything make sure it is done quickly, as it could (conceivably) spoil and become toxic.

Seed: The seeds have been sprouted like Alfalfa (*Medicago*).

Medicine: The leaves are useful as a wash or poultice for wounds and may contain an antibiotic. A tea has been used externally for sore muscles and as an eyewash. The tea has been used internally as a carminative and digestive. The anticoagulant properties of dicoumarol have found a place in traditional medicine, to treat thrombosis and phlebitis, though it is too dangerous to use without expert supervision.

Animal food: These plants are very important to bees and other insects as a source of nectar. They are also valuable forage for cattle and deer.

Rat poison: Dicoumarol, and related anticoagulant chemicals, have been used as rodenticides. They are particularly effective because they kill indirectly by causing hemorrhaging, and so don't arouse the suspicion of these intelligent creatures, as a poison might.

Fertilizer
Sweet Clover has been called the aristocrat of weeds, as the six-foot tall plants are unsurpassed at accumulating nutrients and restoring fertility to damaged land. Their penetrating roots reach deep into the soil, to loosen it and bring minerals to the surface. They are said to produce greater amounts of organic matter than any other common green manure plants. Their root nodules contain nitrogen-fixing bacteria

The plants should be incorporated into the soil at the end of their first year, or in the second year as they reach full size, but before they flower and turn woody.

Perfume: The dried plants have been widely used in potpourri and sachets. These were sometimes kept with clothes in the belief that their scent would repel moths.

Smoke: The leaves were added to herbal smoking mixes.

Cultivation: These biennials are grown from seed, and do well in most soil types. I've seen it thriving in the cracks in the sidewalk in the middle of Seattle.

Melissa officinalis / Lemon Balm

Locally naturalized   *Lamiaceae*

This creeping perennial is locally naturalized across the country. It is fairly easy to identify by its pronounced Lemon odor and flavor.

Flavoring: The leaves are best gathered just before the flowers open, by nipping off the growing tips. If you don't take too much it will re-sprout quickly and grow even bushier. Add the tender leaves to salads, fruit dishes and cooked foods.

Drink: The fresh or dried leaves can be used to make a pleasant lemon flavored tea. Use alone or with other herbs.

Medicine: The tea was drunk to alleviate fevers, flu and especially for menstrual cramps. It is a diaphoretic carminative, antispasmodic, calmative, stomachic and mild sedative (it is a good bedtime drink).

The leaves have been used externally to treat insect bites, and their scent may actually prevent some insects from biting. It has been added to bath water to aid relaxation.

Insect repellant: Lemon Balm has been used to repel mosquitoes and blackflies. Unlike some insect repellants this one doesn't repel humans as well.

Other uses: The dried leaves are used in potpourri and sachets and are sometimes stored with clothing to repel moths. The oil is used in perfumes. The leaves have been chewed to freshen the breath. It was once used as a strewing herb, thrown on earthen floors to disguise bad smells.

Cultivation: Lemon Balm prefers full sun, but will also grow in part shade. It is easily grown from seed or root division and does well in most garden soils. Like its cousins, the Mints, it spreads by means of creeping roots, and can become a pest unless confined. It also self-sows readily. When I moved house it came with me without any help, hitching a ride in the pots of other plants.

Mentha species / Mints

Throughout   *Lamiaceae*

Mint is undoubtedly the most well known of all herbal flavorings, even if some people don't know the flavor is from a green plant rather than a chemical one. The best known and most commonly used, species are Spearmint (*M. spicata*) and Peppermint (*M. piperita*), both of which are now naturalized in North America. There are numerous other species also, both native and introduced. The nutritious leaves contain vitamins A, C, D, E and K.

Gathering: All of the Mint species are edible, though their palatability varies enormously, according to climate, moisture, the time of year and genetic factors. Some wild types are delicious; others have so little flavor they are not worth gathering. All are easily identified by their scent, and none are poisonous, so you can sample any you find. The leaves are best gathered before the flowers appear. Ideally you should harvest in early morning, as the essential oil content is highest at this time. Dry the leaves quickly, in a warm dry place.

Flavoring: I prefer peppermint for tea and Spearmint for culinary purposes. The tender young leaves are good for flavoring salads, mint sauce and jelly. They have occasionally been used as a potherb. My son wraps a couple of mint leaves around a sweet Stevia leaf to make a completely natural mint candy.

Tea: Mint tea is probably the most popular herbal tea of all. Use the fresh or dried leaves, and steep in boiling water for a few minutes, to the strength you desire. Never boil the leaves, as this may ruin the flavor. Mint tea can be drunk as a warming bedtime drink, or with ice as a cooling summer one. It also makes particularly good sun tea. I sometimes add the leaves to my canteen while hiking to improve the flavor of the water. I also use it as flavoring if I have to boil water to purify it.

Medicine: The oil in Mint leaves is antiseptic, so they are useful for treating wounds, and as a carminative. The tea is used to allay nausea and promote sleep.

Oil: Mints are cultivated on a large scale for their oil, which is distilled to satisfy the demands of the food processing industry.

Perfume: The plants were once popular as strewing herbs, and in potpourri. It was a custom in some places to rub dining tables with mint before eating, to clean and deodorize them. This isn't a bad idea, as the oil is antiseptic as well as sweet smelling.

Smoke: The leaves have been smoked, alone or with other herbs. Mint oil is added to tobacco to make menthol cigarettes

Tooth cleaner: Rub Mint leaves on your teeth to freshen them, or chew a few leaves as a quick breath freshener.

Cosmetics: The leaves have been used in skin lotions, and as a face pack to cleanse the skin.

The Uses Of Wild Plants

Cultivation: These vigorous plants are easily propagated by root cuttings, division or soft cuttings. If you are buying, or transplanting, any Mint always smell and taste it first to make sure you are getting a good variety. This varies greatly with individuals, and you don't want to have your garden overrun by some inferior type. Mint can also be grown from seed, but seedling quality is quite variable. They grow in any moist soil and like part shade.

Be cautious where you plant Mint, it may well become a pest if the creeping roots aren't confined. To prevent this you can plant them in a container sunk into the ground to confine them. You might also grow it in a semi-wild state, well away from the intensively cultivated garden. Mints are generally beneficial in the garden, because they attract pollinating and predatory insects.

Useful species include:
Mentha species hybridize quite readily, so you will often find crosses between them.

M. spicata - **Spearmint**
M. piperita - **Peppermint**
M. aquatica - **Water Mint**
It is no accident that these three naturalized species are some of the best tasting Mints. That is the reason they were introduced from Europe. The easiest way to tell the difference between Peppermint and Spearmint is the smell. Also the former have stalked leaves, while the latter leaves are sessile (stalkless).

M. arvensis - **Field Mint, Tule Mint**
This strongly flavored native species is often very good.

M. pulegium - **Pennyroyal**.
This pungently flavored European herb is naturalized in North America, and is quite abundant in some areas. The leaves can be used for tea in moderation, but are toxic if consumed in quantity. They have been used medicinally as an abortifacient, diuretic, diaphoretic and for menstrual cramps. Their odor is said to repel insects.

Mesembryanthemum crystallinum / Ice Plant

Coastal California and Florida   *Aizoaceae*
This succulent South African native is covered in little water-filled beads that resemble ice crystals, hence the common and specific names. It is grown as an ornamental in California, and is now thoroughly naturalized in many areas. Ice Plant, and its relative the Hottentot Fig (below), can be quite invasive and are considered pests for their tendency to crowd out native vegetation.

Greens: The leaves have been used as a salad, potherb and pickle, and have been fermented like sauerkraut.

Fruit: The fruits ripen in late summer, and have been eaten raw, cooked, dried and pickled. They have also been fermented to make an alcoholic drink.

Chemicals: Ice plant was once dried and burned as a source of soda ash (see Glasswort - *Salicornia*).

Cultivation: Because of its attractive flowers and drought resistance the Ice Plant is an important ornamental for hot dry areas with mild winters (it doesn't like frost). Propagate from cuttings, division, leaf cuttings or seed. It will grow in most soil types (even saline ones), with either full sun or part shade. It has also been planted as a fire-retardant groundcover.

Related species:
M. chilense - **Sea Fig**
The native Sea Fig can be found on sand dunes and beaches along the bottom half of the west coast. The succulent fruits are quite good, if a little salty (wash well). The leaves can also be eaten, but aren't very good.

M. edule - **Hottentot Fig (Syn *Carpobrutus edule*)**.
This native of South Africa has naturalized on the West Coast. It gets it unusual name because the Hottentots of South Africa ate the sweetish fruits. These can be eaten as above. They are an important food for wildlife, especially Ground Squirrels. The foliage is reported to be edible, but tastes pretty unpleasant.

This drought resistant, low maintenance plant is frequently planted along highways and in public places in California. It has also been used to stabilize sand dunes and prevent erosion. It is very succulent and may help reduce the potential for fire. In some areas it has become a pest for its habit of choking out native plants.

Monarda didyma / Bee Balm
East   *Lamiaceae*

Flavoring: The whole plant has a Bergamot-like scent. The young leaves can be added to salads, or used to flavor fruit preserves, fruit salads and cheese.

Drink: This plant is also known as Oswego Tea, because the Oswego people taught the first European settlers to use it for tea. The deliciously scented leaves are gathered as the flowers open, and used fresh or dried, just steep for 5 - 10 minutes. They are good alone or with other herbs. Some people add them to oriental tea to make a kind of substitute Earl Grey (this is usually flavored with true Bergamot *Citrus bergamia*). Unlike most herbal teas you can simmer the leaves for a few minutes (not too long) to bring out the flavor.

Medicine: The plant contains the antiseptic thymol, and may be used as a wash or poultice for wounds. It has been taken internally as a carminative, a mild sedative, and to relieve nausea.

Perfume: The powdered leaves have been burned as incense, and added to candles to scent them. They have also been used as insect repellant.

Animal food: The flowers are a favorite nectar source for hummingbirds, bees and other insects.

Cultivation: Bee Balm is a popular ornamental, and there are varieties with white, pink, red or purple flowers. It is a vigorous plant, and needs little care once established. The only drawback is its aggressiveness, as like many of its cousins in the *Lamiaceae* it spreads rapidly by means of creeping roots. Because of this it should be confined in a sunken container, or planted away in a corner of the garden where it can run free.

It is easily grown from seed or division, and prefers rich moist soil, though it will grow in most soil types. It also likes full sun, and in the shade it may get leggy.

Garden uses: The plants creeping habit can be put to good use in controlling erosion on stream banks. Native Americans occasionally cultivated Horsemint.

Related species:
All species can be used as above, the best include:

M. fistulosa - **Wild Bergamot**
M. citriodora - **Lemon Bee Balm**
M. punctata - **Horsemint**

Montia perfoliata / Miners Lettuce
West   *Portulacaceae*

Miners Lettuce is a close relative of the Spring Beauties, but doesn't bear tuberous roots. It is still a very useful food plant however, as the foliage is both tender and tasty. The plant got its common name because gold miners commonly ate it during the 1849 California gold rush. Before that event it was known as Indian Lettuce or Spanish Lettuce for obvious reasons.

> **Leafy greens**
> The mildly flavored leaves are a great base for a wild spring salad. They can also be used as a potherb, by steaming or boiling for 2 - 5 minutes.

Cultivation: Miners Lettuce is only considered to be a weed by people who don't eat it. It is good enough to have been cultivated as a salad plant in European kitchen gardens. It prefers cool moist weather and dies off in hot summers (it is a winter/spring annual in most of California). It is easily grown from seed, in rich garden soil and thrives in full sun or part shade. It is usually only necessary to plant it once, as it self-sows freely and perpetuates itself.

Related species:
All *Montia* species are edible. The best include:

M. cordifolia - **Broad Leaved Montia**
M. parviflora - **Little Leaf Montia**
M. sibirica - **Siberian Miners Lettuce**

Morus species / Mulberries
Throughout   *Moraceae*

In North America Mulberries are usually considered a nuisance, and gardeners are solemnly warned not to plant them. This is because they fruit so abundantly, the soft mushy berries fall from the trees in large numbers. These mess up the ground underneath them, attract vermin and even damage the paint of cars parked underneath them (either directly, or when transformed into bird droppings). Another problem is that bird-sown seedlings may sprout up abundantly as weeds. I think these are minor drawbacks when you consider the virtues of the plants (I like trees more than cars anyway).

The fruits somewhat resemble small Blackberries in appearance, though they differ in being multiple fruits, formed from a number of flowers.

Nutrients: In parts of Asia it was said that no one goes hungry during Mulberry ripening time. The food value of the dried fruit is similar to that of Figs; with about 70% fruit sugar, 3% protein and many vitamins and minerals.

The Uses Of Wild Plants

Gathering: The mess made by the fruits is an advantage for the forager, as it makes them easier to find. One can hardly miss the purple stained mess of squashed fruits underneath the trees. The fruiting period lasts for several weeks, though in some places birds will strip off the fruit as it ripens, so you would hardly know it was there.

The flavor of individual trees varies considerably, so taste any ripe fruit you find, and use the best. Some people collect the berries by spreading sheets under the trees, and then shaking the trunks to bring down the loose ripe fruit. In this way it is possible to gather large quantities of fruit with minimal effort. They must be dried if you don't want to use them immediately, as they deteriorate quickly.

Uses: Fresh Mulberries can be used like Blackberries, eaten raw out of hand, in salads, frozen, dried, or cooked in preserves, pies and pancakes. In parts of the Middle East and Afghanistan dried Mulberries are a staple food. These are a great backpacking food, with good flavor, light weight and high nutritional content.

Drink: A sweet juice may be extracted from the fruit, in the same way as from Grapes (*Vitis*).

Greens: Apparently young spring growth has been eaten as a potherb, though it is sometimes said that one shouldn't eat the leaves, or green fruits, and that they can cause hallucinations.

Medicine: Mulberries are not important medicinally, though their high fiber content makes them useful as a mild laxative.

Fiber: Native Americans used the inner bark for rope and cordage.

Wood: The wood of these small trees isn't of much commercial value, though Red Mulberry (*M. rubra*) is occasionally used by cabinetmakers. It is quite resistant to decay, so is most often used for fence-posts. It is also good firewood.

Animal food: The leaves of the White Mulberry (*M. alba*) are the chief food of Silkworms, and that species was originally introduced into this country in an attempt to start a domestic silk industry. This failed because the silk producing process is very labor intensive and labor costs were too high.

Mulberries are very attractive to birds and many wild animals. They have also been promoted as feed for pigs, but make more sense as feed for humans.

Cultivation: These trees are easy to grow (they are often considered weeds) and can be very productive in terms of yield for effort expended. They are also quite long lived, and may last 100 years or more.

Generally Mulberries prefer rich, deep, moist soil, though they will grow in much worse. Insect pests do not seriously bother them, though they are often bothered by feathered pests, as the fruits are a favorite food of many birds. They have even been planted as decoys to keep birds from cultivated fruit trees. However the trees often bear so abundantly that there is plenty for all, and the birds often stay around to eat garden pests.

Propagation: Mulberries can be propagated vegetatively by means of hardwood cuttings. This is supposed to be very easy, but I haven't found it so. They are also grown from ripe seed, sown immediately, or stratified for 3 - 4 months at forty degrees. It is also possible to transplant self-sown seedlings. The disadvantage of growing from seed is that they are dioecious, and you won't know whether you have a male or female until they flower in several years time. Another problem is that fruit quality will be variable. With vegetative propagation you know both the sex and the quality of the fruit. Special varieties can also be propagated by budding.

New Crop: Though an old crop in Asia, they are new in the west. The most likely commercial use for Mulberries is as dried fruit, preserves or juice. The fresh fruit is too perishable to transport any distance.

Improved *Morus* cultivars are available and they are well worth growing. I have only grown one Mulberry cultivar (a variety of *M. alba* from Pakistan), but I highly recommend the Asian varieties, as superior to any others I have seen. The fruits are larger, sweeter, and are produced in abundance (it is self-pollinated).

Species include:
M. rubra - **Red Mulberry** Native
M. nigra - **Black Mulberry** Naturalized from Europe

M. alba - **White Mulberry**
Native to Asia, but occasionally planted or naturalized in North America. This is the species that is eaten by silkworms, and is an important food source in Afghanistan. It is well adapted to hot summers and cold dry winters, and has been suggested as a drought resistant crop for parts of the high desert southwest. The fruits are often seedless.

M. microphylla - **Western Mulberry**
This drought resistant southwestern shrub is found along watercourses. It is edible, but not as sweet as the other species.

Myrica cerifera / **Bayberry**
East   *Myricaceae*
Flavoring: The aromatic, leathery leaves can be used as a culinary herb like those of Bay, added during cooking, but removed before serving. The dried and powdered leaves, or leaf buds, have been used as a condiment. The berries can be used as flavoring, after their waxy coating is removed.

Drink: A tea can be made by steeping the evergreen leaves in boiling water for a few minutes. Don't boil as this may release toxins.

Beer: The leaves of the Sweet Gale (*M. gale)* have been used in brewing beer, and to flavor mead and various liqueurs. With the current popularity of micro-breweries and high quality beers, it might be an opportune time to re-introduce unusual herb beers such as this. I think there is a market for them.

Medicine: A strong tea of the leaves was used as an astringent to treat diarrhea (as a drink or enema), sore throats and wounds. It was also used as a wash to kill skin parasites. A very strong decoction has been used as an emetic to treat poisoning.

Insect repellant: Insects seem to dislike the odor of the plant, so the dried leaves have been sewed into sachets, to repel moths from clothing. They also impart a pleasant scent.

Perfume: The leaves and berries have been used in potpourri, and their distilled oil in perfumes.

Wax
Bayberry is also known as Wax Myrtle or Candleberry, as the waxy coating on the berries was once used like beeswax to make aromatic candles and soap. A quarter of the weight of the fruits is wax, which can be removed by boiling them in water and skimming off the floating wax. These candles were highly prized, as they give of a delicious Bayberry scent as they burn. Needless to say, most present day commercial Bayberry candles are fake. The berries may be found on the bushes all year round.

Cultivation: These species can be propagated from cleaned ripe seed. Sow immediately in moist acid soil, or stratify at 35 degrees Fahrenheit for three months. Layering, division, semi-ripe cuttings or suckers can also be used. They are able to grow on very poor soils, because they fix nitrogen by means of bacteria in root nodules. Some species are popular drought resistant ornamentals. They are dioecious, so male and female plants are needed to produce fruit.

Related species: Almost all *Myrica* species yield useful wax, though the quantity and quality varies according to species.

M. inodora - **Odorless Bayberry**
For obvious reasons this species is no good for perfume, though the wax can be used for (odorless) candles.

M. californica - **California Wax Myrtle**
M. heterophylla
M. gale - **Sweet Gale**
M. pennsylvanica - **Northern Bayberry**
M. pumila - **Dwarf Candleberry**
Use as above.

Nasturtium officinale / **Watercress**
Syn *Rorippa nasturtium aquaticum*
Throughout   *Brassicaceae*
This prolific plant is sometimes considered a weed for its habit of replacing native plants, but is a welcome sight for the forager. Wild Watercress is exactly the same as cultivated Watercress, and is a very valuable wild food plant. Euell Gibbons called it the "king of wild salad plants", but it is equally useful as a potherb.

Nutrients: Watercress has been regarded as a special food for several thousand years, and with good reason. As an aquatic plant it is continuously bathed in nutrients as they are washed from the soil, and consequently it is very rich in minerals, including iron, iodine (perhaps the richest source of any land plant), copper, manganese and sulfur. It is also a good source of vitamins A, C and E.

Caution: Sadly most streams and lakes are now polluted by bacteria and other contaminants (*E. coli, Giardia*), and the water is not safe to drink. By the same standard Watercress gathered from them shouldn't be eaten raw. It can safely be cooked and eaten though. If there is any possibility of chemical pollution it shouldn't be eaten at all.

In areas frequented by sheep and perhaps other livestock, the plants may also contain liver flukes and their eggs, from the droppings of those animals. These parasites can live quite happily inside humans, and are very dangerous. It has been suggested that using chlorine bleach or water purification tablets will kill the parasites, but this is by no means certain. Fortunately cooking kills these organisms, so the cooked plants can safely be eaten.

There is also the possibility of confusing Watercress with the poisonous Water Hemlock (*Cicuta*). This isn't likely if you use reasonable care in your identification, but it has happened.

Watercress contains the irritating mustard oil found in many members of the *Brassicaceae,* and can irritate the kidneys if eaten in excess. Use in moderation.

Gathering: Growing under the moderating influence of water, this hardy plant is less affected by hot or cold weather than most, and can often be gathered year round. Gather the plants by pinching off the growing tips, leaving the roots and lower leaves to continue growing. It is palatable at all times and stages of growth.

Uses: Raw Watercress is good in salads, sandwiches (a genteel delicacy) and salad dressing, just make sure it is safe. It is also good cooked as a potherb, and in sauces, soups and stir-fries.

Medicine: Watercress has been recommended to stimulate the glands, and as an expectorant, diuretic and wound herb.

Cultivation: Watercress cultivation is rather specialized because of specific habitat requirements, but it grows easily enough if given the right conditions. It does best in springs, ditches and shallow streams, but it will grow in any wet soil. In Europe it was once grown in special Watercress beds, created beside streams to take advantage of the slowly flowing water. The water must not be stagnant, or the plants will rot. It can be grown on dry land, but a lot of care must be taken to keep it moist, and it isn't as vigorous under these conditions.

The plant can be grown from seed, but it is faster and easier to get a bunch of fresh Watercress from a market, and simply root it in water. It also transplants well, so you might take some from the wild and re-domesticate it.

Crop use: Given a suitable site Watercress is a valuable, reliable, hardy and easily maintained perennial crop. Growing it yourself also ensures that it is safe for use raw in salads. The plant can also be a valuable part of a cultivated freshwater ecosystem, providing shelter and food for numerous organisms, which in turn provide food for fish, birds and small mammals.

Nelumbo lutea / American Lotus
East   Nymphaceae
This aquatic species is a close relative of the Asian Sacred Lotus (*N. nucifera*) of Asia, but a lot hardier. It was an important food plant for some Native American tribes. They often transported it to suitable new sites, and actively encouraged its growth.

Root gathering: The Lotus is quite common in some areas, but very beautiful, so you should only take the roots if they are abundant. They are gathered when the plant is dormant in late autumn and winter. Native American women used to dive for them, or wade and dig them with their toes, but the water is pretty chilly at this time of year. Present day gatherers use a potato hook or a hooked pole, and gather in rubber waders or from a boat.

Root preparation: The roots are acrid and unpleasant raw, but when peeled and cooked they somewhat resemble Sweet Potatoes. Sacred Lotus roots are a common food in China. They are peeled, cut into strips and added to soups and stir-fries. They are often dried for later use.

Seeds: The Lotus is also known as the Water Chinquapin because of its large nutritious seeds. The strange looking seedpods sometimes collect by the thousands in sheltered inlets, having been blown there by the wind. In such a case gathering a supply of seed is easy, nature having done the work of collecting them together.

The immature seeds can be cooked and eaten like green shell beans. The fully ripe seeds have a hard shell, which must be removed before use. The shelled seeds can be cooked in soup, roasted as a snack, or ground to flour for baking.

Greens: The young leaves are somewhat bitter, but while still tender they have been used as a potherb. They can also be added to soups.

Dried ornament: I first saw the unusual seedpods in a dried flower arrangement and wondered what they were. They are a clever seed dispersal mechanism. The pods break away from the plants when ripe and float away. Over time they absorb water and rot, eventually releasing their seeds in a new location.

Cultivation: The Lotus is beautiful when in bloom, and makes a fine ornamental for shallow (up to two feet deep), slow moving ponds and lakes with full sun. To propagate from seed, file through the tough seed coat to allow water to penetrate. It is probably easiest to start them indoors, where you can keep an eye on them. If you have a lot of seed you can sow them directly into the water, by rolling them in balls of mud so they sink. They can also be multiplied by root division, and this is the most reliable method. If they like the growing conditions they will spread rapidly.

Related species:
N. nucifera - **Sacred Lotus**
This species is occasionally naturalized in warmer areas, and can be used as above. It is widely cultivated for food in parts of Asia, and a number of cultivars are available.

Nepeta cataria / Catnip
Throughout   *Lamiaceae*
Food: The tender new spring shoots of Catnip can be added to salads.

Tea: Catnip tea has long been a popular beverage in Europe. Use about two tablespoons of dried leaves to a cup of boiling water. Like most members of the *Lamiaceae* it should never be boiled.

Medicine: Doctors recommended Catnip tea as a mild sedative, diaphoretic and carminative until relatively recently. It is still used to treat diarrhea, and in enemas for cleansing the colon.

Repellant: It is said that Catnip has a repellant effect on rats, and that a row of plants around a building will keep them away. Maybe the plant reminds them of cats, and makes them uncomfortable. It is also disliked by many insects, and is sometimes used as a repellant.

Cat bait
Catnip gets its name for its intoxicating effect on Cats. This is apparently due to a substance called nepetalactone and has four distinct phases. These are sniffing, licking and chewing, chin and cheek rubbing and finally head over rolling and body rubbing. Curiously the plant affects only about 60% of cats.

Because of its feline attraction, the plant has been used as bait to catch feral cats. The dried leaves are often added to commercial domestic cat toys to make cats pay attention to them.

Smoke: A belief among pot-less pot smokers of the 1960's was that if you smoked the dried leaves of Catnip, you would get high (as high as a cat). This is not true, but some people like to smoke them for their own virtues.

Cultivation: There is an old saying about growing Catnip "If you set it the cats will get it, if you sow it the cats won't know it." This probably means the disturbance during transplanting will release enough scent to let nearby cats know it is around. If you sow seed on the other hand, they won't know its there until it is well established. In my experience they will pretty soon find out, and come from all around to roll and chew the plants. Fortunately it is a pretty rugged plant and takes such abuse quite well.

Catnip will grow in most soil types, but prefers rich, moist soil with full sun. It is very hardy, and pretty much looks after itself. Individual plants are not long lived and often die after flowering, so keep dividing it, and cut off the flowers before they set seed. It self-sows vigorously.

Garden uses: Catnip is sometimes grown with vegetables to repel ants, spittlebugs and other pests. It is also made into a spray for this purpose.

Nuphar species / Pond Lilies
Throughout   *Nymphaceae*
The large underwater roots of these attractive aquatic plants are edible, and may be gathered from midsummer to early spring. However this is often easier said than done, as they are found underground and underwater. Gather them with a potato hook in the same way as for the American Lotus (*Nelumbo*).

The Uses Of Wild Plants

Root: The roots are acrid when raw, and must be peeled and cooked to make them edible. The best way to do this is to boil them for 15 minutes, peel off the skin and cook the starchy cores for a further 10 minutes. These can be eaten as they are, or then fried, baked or added to soups. Their flavor varies with species; some are tasty simply boiled, others are too bitter to be eaten at all. Supposedly one can eliminate any bitterness by cooking in at least one change of water, but this doesn't always happen. It is a good idea to eat a small amount of root before digging a lot, to make sure it is palatable.

Flour: Starch may be extracted from the roots in the same way as for Kudzu (*Pueraria*). This works very well because the water leaches out any bitterness. Starch can also be obtained by drying and grinding the cooked root.

Seed: The large seeds, called *Wokas*, were a staple food of some Native American tribes, and the annual seed harvest was an important social event. Entire tribes would move into the marshes to gather the pods as they ripen in mid to late summer (one marsh contained 10,000 acres of plants - a lot of food). They gathered the seed pods from canoes in large quantities, and dried (or fermented) them to free the seed.

The seed can be popped like popcorn, though it isn't as explosive, and eaten as a snack. It was also ground to meal for baking or gruel (simmer one part flour to one part water for an hour or so). It can also be boiled as a vegetable, but it may be bitter unless you change the cooking water at least once. Native Americans cooked and ate the immature seeds like shell beans.

Greens: The young leaves have been eaten raw, and used as a potherb.

Animal food: The roots are a staple food for muskrats, while various parts are important food for beaver, moose and ducks.

Cultivation: Same as for Lotus (*Nelumbo*).

Best species include:
N. advena - **Common Spatterdock**
N. polysepalum - **Indian Pond Lily**

Nymphaea species / Water Lilies
Throughout   *Nymphaceae*
Food: The roots, leaves and seeds of these lovely aquatic perennials are used for food in the same way as their cousins; the American Lotus (*Nelumbo*) and the Pond Lilies (*Nuphar*). The flower buds have also been cooked and eaten.

Medicine: An astringent decoction of the roots has been used as a gargle for sore throats, and as a wash for wounds.

Cultivation: Same as for Lotus (*Nelumbo*).

Oenanthe sarmentosa / Water Parsley
West   *Apiaceae*
Caution: I keep mentioning that no member of the *Apiaceae* should be eaten without positive identification (or any other family for that matter), because a number of species are very poisonous. This plant is a good example of why I keep repeating this caution. Water Parsley is actually a fine edible plant, but it is a close relative of a number of extremely dangerous plants. Its European cousin the Hemlock Water Dropwort - *O. crocata* may have killed more people in Britain than any other plant except Tobacco. To make matters worse it is best used for food while dormant, and the flowers aren't present to aid in identification at that time. Don't even sample a leaf or two of the plant without being absolutely certain of your identification. A single mouthful of the quite similar Water Hemlock (*Cicuta douglasii*) could kill you.

Roots: It is unfortunate that this plant isn't more distinctive, as its tuberous roots have a mild Parsley flavor and are very good. They were a popular food for Native Americans in Oregon.

Other foods: The tender young stems and leaves can be eaten raw or cooked, or used for flavoring.

Cultivation: Water Parsley might be worth cultivating as a root crop, as the hazards of gathering it from the wild prevent most people from using it. It is grown from seed, in moist soil or shallow water.

Oenothera species / Evening Primrose
Syn *Onagra* species

Throughout   *Onagraceae*

There are species of Evening Primrose to be found over most of North America. They are very useful wild plants, and provide a variety of tasty foods.

Roots: Several perennial and biennial species produce edible roots. These are gathered when dormant from fall to early spring. Locate them by finding the easily identifiable mature plants, and then search nearby for the leaf rosettes of young plants. They are easy to recognize once you are familiar with them.

The palatability of the roots varies with species, and stage of growth (generally younger plants are best). Some are good enough to eat raw; others must be cooked in a change of water to make them palatable (peeling helps). At least one species is good enough to have been cultivated occasionally.

Greens: The young leaves and crowns can be used like those of Dandelion (*Taraxacum*), and some species are even good raw. Older leaves are bitter, but can be eaten if treated like Dandelions, and boiled in a change of water for about twenty minutes.

Seed: The immature seedpods can be added to salads or cooked in soups. If they are bitter, change the cooking water at least once. The abundantly produced seeds are also edible, and given the special oil they contain (see below), it may be worth going out to look for them. Use them like Poppy seed in baking and granola.

Medicine: The leaves have been eaten for their beneficial effect on the liver and digestion. They have been used externally as a poultice for skin diseases.

Evening Primrose Oil

Recently oil from the seeds of Evening Primrose (*O. biennis*) has received attention from scientists (and health food promoters) because it contains gamma-linolenic acid. This essential fatty acid is used by the body to produce prostaglandins (the only other source is human milk), which help to control many body functions.

This oil is said to help in treating diabetes, cancer, schizophrenia, arthritis, hypertension, multiple sclerosis, obesity, acne and many other ailments. It may also lower blood cholesterol levels.

Cultivation: At least one species (*O. biennis*) has been cultivated as a biennial root vegetable (known as German Rampion). Others have been grown as ornamentals for their pretty flowers, and a few are considered weeds. They are ideal low maintenance plants; even the biennial species need little attention once established, and self-seed readily. Propagate from seed, division or soft cutting, they will grow in most soil types, though they prefer light sandy ones for maximum root growth. The flowers are pollinated by moths.

The best food species include:
O. biennis - Evening Primrose
O. brevipes - Desert Primrose
O. californica - California Evening Primrose
O. perennis
O. hookerii – Hooker's Evening Primrose

Caution: Some *Oenothera* species are endangered or threatened and should never be used. These include:
O. avita Ssp eurekensis
O. deltoides ssp howellii

Opuntia species / Prickly pears, Chollas

Almost throughout   *Cactaceae*

The *Opuntias* are the weeds of the Cactus family. Unlike most of their cousins, they are relatively fast growing, opportunistic and short-lived (though they may still live for twenty years). They are undoubtedly the most useful Cactus species for foragers, as they are widely distributed, common, rugged, easily recognized and provide a variety of foods. We usually think of cacti as being desert dwellers, but there are *Opuntia* species growing in almost all of the lower 48 states and even in parts of Canada. They are becoming increasingly common on overgrazed land in many areas, and are often considered to be problematic weeds.

History: These species are native to the Americas, but have traveled widely around the world. They are now naturalized around the Mediterranean, in Australia, Africa and elsewhere.

The story of their introduction to Australia is one, of the classic examples of a human ecological blunder. The first Prickly Pears were introduced into Australia in the 18th century, with others following in the 19th. Free of the predators that constrained them in their native land, they began to spread uncontrollably, and by 1925 they covered as much as 60 million acres of land. Much of which was well watered and potentially valuable for other purposes. On half of this land they were practically the only plants, and in some areas an acre might contain 800 tons of vegetable matter.

This situation was eventually brought under control by the introduction of the Argentine Moth borer (*Cactoblastis cactorum*). The larvae of this moth eats into the pads and almost totally destroys them. These and other Cactus eating insects, eventually reduced the densely packed stands by up to 95%. The plants are still common in Australia, but not out of control, so the story has a happy ending. This episode is often cited as an example of successful biological control of a serious plant pest.

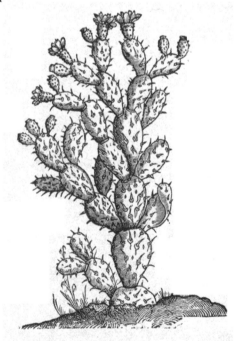

Caution: Like most Cacti, the *Opuntias* are well armed, often with both simple spines and the more insidious glochids. Glochids are tufts of tiny barbed bristles that embed themselves in anything they touch, causing irritation and pain. You don't even need to touch the

plant directly to be impaled, a shoe or bag brushed against the plant will become covered in these bristles, and when you touch the object they are transferred to you. The larger spines are easier to avoid, but can be pretty nasty. If left in the skin they may work themselves in deeper, like Porcupine quills, and can cause infection. Obviously humans can remove them fairly easily, but animals can be crippled, or even die from them.

If you get the glochids in your skin, scrape them off with a razor or knife; the small amounts remaining in your skin will go away on their own. The best way to remove the spines from your flesh is said to be pulling them out with pliers (ouch)! If a whole Cholla pad gets stuck to you, try inserting a comb between skin and joint to pull it off, or cut it off with scissors and pull out the spines.

Food: No *Opuntia* species is poisonous, though the quality of the food produced by these plants varies considerably, according to species, growing conditions and other factors. You must experiment to find the best. These plants were an important food source for some Native American tribes. They give a variety of foods over a long period, and start producing food in early spring, when few other green foods are available.

Gathering Pads: The young pads are best eaten when from 2 - 3 inches in diameter. They are known as *nopalitos* in Mexico, and are actually cultivated there. They are becoming increasingly common in food markets across this country, as people become more adventurous in their eating habits. Native Americans gathered the pods in early morning when still wet with dew, as this apparently made the glochids less troublesome. If you don't have any gloves, gather them (or the fruit) with tongs improvised from sticks.

One must disarm the pads before use, a task most easily accomplished by scraping or skinning them. Sometimes the glochids can be removed by brushing.

Using pads: The cleaned pads can be eaten raw in salads, boiled (this makes them easier to peel), pickled or dried. A simple cooking method is to put the whole pads on the coals of a fire for about twenty minutes (turn them over half way through). This burns off the spines and cooks them at the same time (trial and error is needed to cook them just right). When prepared in the ways mentioned above, the pads tend to be rather slimy and not to everyone's taste. If you find them too slimy, try cutting the peeled pads into strips, and frying them with Garlic or Onion, in breadcrumbs or batter.

Flower buds: Native Americans removed the spines by stirring them in baskets with stones (its simpler to use a stiff brush). The cleaned buds can be boiled for about 15 minutes and eaten as a vegetable. Often they are added to greens such as Saltbush (*Atriplex*). They sometimes baked the cleaned flower buds, pads and fruits in a fire pit overnight. They also dried and ground them to flour for gruel, baking or storage.

Preparing fruit: The succulent fruits, known as tunas, are commonly eaten, though their quality varies a lot with species. It is best to brush the glochids from the fruit when gathering, and disarm them later, in the same way as the pads (some types are almost spineless). Skinning is usually the easiest method, simply impale the fruit on a fork, slice off the top and bottom, make a slit from top to bottom and roll off the skin. Make sure no glochids are stuck to the skinned flesh (immersion in boiling water makes skinning easier).

Using fruit: These are often good raw, but contain a lot of hard seeds. These can be removed by cutting the fruit in half, and scooping them out. You can also eat them whole and spit out the seed. The cleaned flesh can be used to make preserves, syrup, juice, wine and candy. Native Americans baked the fruit in a fire pit and dried it for later use. They said that eating too many of the fruits could make a person sick, so use in moderation.

Seeds: Native Americans ground the seeds to meal for baking and gruel. See Saguaro (*Cereus*) for more on the uses of Cactus seed.

Drink: As with other Cacti, the fruit and pads have been used as a source of water (or more properly moisture), by desperate people in time of need. The fruits have also been fermented like those of the Saguaro to make wine.

Medicine: The split pads were used as a poultice for wounds. The fruits are laxative and diuretic, and may occasionally color the urine red (an apparently harmless, if somewhat alarming phenomenon).

Animal food: The juicy pads are very attractive to thirsty herbivores, which is why they have spines of course. The pads of some species have been used as livestock feed in time of drought, after their spines were singed off. I have read that animals have relied on such plants as their sole source of food and drink for months at a time. I am somewhat dubious however, as it would seem difficult to remove all the spines.

The fruit is often eaten by desert animals, and the seeds are dispersed in their droppings.

Alcohol: Some *Opuntia* varieties are extremely productive sources of fruit, producing up to 30 tons per acre. These contain about 15% sugar and could be fermented to produce alcohol. The pads might also be used in the same way. This could make the plant a useful source of fuel alcohol.

Mucilage: Native Americans soaked the pads in water, and used the mucilaginous juice as size for painting (or they simply rubbed a cut pad onto the paint).

Waterproofing: In Mexico this juice has been used for making whitewash, paint and waterproofing, especially for adobe walls. It is now being used experimentally to coat cob (earth) walls, as it appears to allow them to breathe while at the same time shedding rainwater.

Paper: Old woody pads and stems have been used to make high quality paper.

Tattoos: Native Americans used the larger spines for tattooing, with charcoal as the pigment.

Horticultural uses: *Opuntias* have beautiful flowers and fruits, an attractive and striking form, and are extremely heat and drought resistant. These features make them popular ornamentals in desert areas. Hardier species can be used to add an exotic touch to northern gardens.

Some species are grown as a crop for pads, fresh or dried fruit, or for making preserves.

The *Opuntias* are very independent, and need little attention once established. They are sometimes planted as barriers to keep out animals (both human and non-human), and their spines are a very effective deterrent. They have also been planted as windbreaks or fire retardant ground cover, as the fleshy pads don't burn readily.

Cultivation: These species have almost magical powers of vegetative propagation. Break off a pad, throw it on the ground, and it is able to take root. You can quickly get as many plants as you need by rooting them in light sandy soil. They can also be grown from seed (nick with a file, or scarify, to penetrate the tough seed coat), though as with all Cacti this is quite slow. They may take 3 - 5 years to bear fruit from seed.

New crops: Luther Burbank apparently spent 15 years growing several million *Opuntia* seedlings, in a quest for spineless plants with perfectly smooth pads. He said this was the most difficult and painful (literally) project he ever undertook. He claimed an acre of his fast growing spineless hybrids could produce up to 300 tons of vegetable matter within three years, and 30 tons of fruit annually. He intended this spineless plant to be used as a perennial livestock food for arid areas, as they grow vigorously where few other plants can survive. He also proposed that such plants be cultivated in areas subject to periodic famine, as a reserve of food for emergencies. He was very enthusiastic in his promotion of the plant, but it never became very popular. One reason was that the plants have low value as feed for livestock. Another problem was that seedlings from the plants aren't spineless, and have the potential to become a pest.

Useful species include:
Opuntia species hybridize readily, which can complicate identification. This isn't important as no species is poisonous, and any with palatable parts can be eaten. The genus is divided into two distinct types, the Prickly Pears with flat pads, and the Chollas with cylindrical ones.

Prickly Pears:
O. basilaris -**Beavertail Cactus**
O. phaeacantha - **Prickly Pear Cactus**
O. ficus indica - **Indian Fig**
O. leptocaulis - **Desert Christmas Cactus**
These species all produce good fruit. The last two species have been cultivated as fruit crops.

Chollas:
These species are now usually given their own genus *Cylindropuntia*, but I am including them here for convenience sake. Generally they are less useful as food, though they provide edible flower buds and fruits (sometimes the pads were eaten in times of scarcity).

O. acanthocarpa - **Buckthorn Cholla**
O. bigelovii - **Teddy Bear Cholla**
The flower buds of these two species were particularly prized by Native Americans.

O. arbuscula
O. echinocarpa - **Staghorn Cholla**
O. versicolor
O. whippleii
These species often produce good fruit.

Origanum vulgare / Wild Marjoram
Northeast   *Lamiaceae*
Flavoring: This aromatic native of the Mediterranean is widely naturalized in the northeastern states. It is often said to be the culinary herb Oregano, but the wild types aren't as aromatic or tasty as the cultivated varieties. The flavor is similar enough to make a fair substitute though. Use it fresh, or dried, to flavor pizza, pasta, sauces and egg and cheese dishes. Young tender tips can be chopped and added to salads.

Drinks: The fresh or dried leaves have been used for tea, and to brew beer.

Medicine: The ancient Greeks considered this a powerful healing herb, and used it externally for treating wounds, preventing infections (it is antiseptic) and soothing aching muscles. The tea is also carminative and stomachic.

Smoke: The dried leaves have been mixed with other herbs and smoked. They are also used in potpourri.

Cultivation: Wild Marjoram is easily grown from seed, soft cuttings or division. It thrives in poor dry soils and once established needs little care. It can be invasive, so is best grown in a semi-wild state.

Oryzopsis species / Mountain-Rice
Throughout   *Poaceae*
These grasses often produce an abundance of hard black seeds, which were a staple food for Native Americans in the Great Basin. Unfortunately they are becoming scarcer in many places, eliminated by the overgrazing of livestock. For this reason they should only be used where abundant (or cultivated). The seed contains about 25% carbohydrate.

Gathering: Native American women gathered the seed heads in July, as soon as the seed is ripe, but before it falls from the plant. You must watch carefully as it falls readily when ripe. They also took the seed from rodent caches, but this isn't a good idea (apart from ethical considerations) because rodent nests in the southwest may contain fleas that carry bubonic plague (this disease is endemic to that area).

Preparation: Native Americans put the seed heads in small piles, and set them on fire. The idea is to free the seed from the husk, and burn off the hairy scales, without destroying it. To this end the burning seed was stirred with a stick, or it was dampened with a little water to reduce the intensity of the fire. It can also be prepared in the same way as Wild- Rice (*Zizania*). The seed was then cleaned by winnowing.

Use: The cleaned seed was ground to meal (used alone or with an equal amount of cornmeal), for gruel, baking and thickening soup.

Cultivation: Some species were cultivated by Native Americans as grain crops. They have also been planted to prevent erosion. It is easily grown from seed (cover with soil to hide it from birds).

Best species include:
O. asperifolia - **White Grained Mountain-Rice**
This eastern species produces large tasty seeds, and has been suggested as a possible perennial grain crop.

O. hymenoides - **Sand Grass**
So called because it can grow in almost pure sand. Sand Grass has been called the most important wild food grass of the southwest, and was a favorite of the Zuni people. It is a cool season grass, and ripens in early summer long before corn. It needs little water to produce seed, and

could be a useful food crop for arid land farmers (as it once was for Native Americans). It also has potential as a perennial grain crop.

Osmorrhiza species / Sweet Cicely

Throughout   *Apiaceae*

Roots: The roots of these species have a strong, sweet Anise/Fennel flavor. Their palatability varies with species and growing conditions. The best are fleshy and tasty even raw, others are too strongly flavored to eat, but can be used as flavoring or for tea. The roots are at their best when dormant, but one must always be cautious about gathering a plant of the *Apiaceae* when it isn't flowering, as there is always a danger of gathering a poisonous plant by mistake (the characteristic Anise odor helps in this case).

Seed: The immature seed can be eaten in salads. Ripe seed is good for flavoring.

Drink: All parts have been used for tea.

Medicine: Sweet Cicely tea has been used as a carminative and stomachic.

Horse bait: The Omaha and Ponca people are said to have used the aromatic roots to catch their untethered horses. Apparently their horses were so fond of it that a person would only have to walk upwind of the animals with a root, and they would come running.

Cultivation: Propagate from seed, or division, in rich moist soils.

Best species: All species can be used for food. The best include:

O. claytoni - **Sweet Cicely**
O. longistylis - **Anise Root**
Eastern species.

O. chilensis - **Mountain Sweet Cicely**
O. occidentalis - **Western Sweet Cicely**
Western species.

Oxalis species / Wood Sorrel

Throughout   *Oxalidaceae*

The Wood Sorrels produce two kinds of flowers, conventional showy ones, and inconspicuous self-fertilizing (cleistogamous) ones that produce an abundance of seed. The plant may throw this seed several feet to disperse it.

Caution: Wood Sorrel leaves have a strong sour taste, rather like grape skins or Sorrel leaves (*Rumex*), which

this is why they share the name Sorrel with those unrelated plants. The same flavor is due to the same chemical - oxalic acid, which is toxic in large amounts, as it inhibits calcium absorption and can damage the kidneys. The plants contain quite a lot of oxalic acid (*O. corniculata* contains up to 7% dry weight of oxalic acid), so shouldn't be eaten excessively.

Greens: The sour leaves are a pleasant minor addition to salads while tender. They have also been baked in pies, or boiled as a potherb. Boiling removes a lot of the oxalic acid, but they should still be used in moderation. They were a favorite of Native Americans, who ate them raw, cooked or fermented to make a kind of sauerkraut.

Seeds: The small seedpods can be added to salads for their sour flavor.

Drink: Add a few Sorrel leaves to herbal tea instead of lemon.

Roots: The small tuberous roots of the Violet Wood Sorrel (*O. violacea*) were eaten raw or cooked by the Ponca people. The larger roots of the South American Oca (*O. tuberosa*) are cultivated as a root vegetable in its native Andes.

Medicine: The leaves have been used as an antiseptic poultice, or wash, for wounds, burns and insect bites. They have also been eaten to purify the blood (their high vitamin C may explain this use).

Cultivation: Several *Oxalis* species are common and persistent farm or garden weeds. About the only good thing you can say about them is that they help alleviate thirst when weeding. They are easily grown from seed or division, in rich moist soil, not that you would really want to.

The Uses of Wild Plants

Oxyria digyna / **Mountain Sorrel**

North & mountains   *Polygonaceae*

Greens: This species has a flavor similar to the other Sorrels (see *Oxalis* and *Rumex),* because it contains the same toxic oxalic acid. This means it should be used in moderation. It also contains a lot of vitamins A and C, and was prized by Native Americans in the far north, living where green edible plants are scarce. They mashed and fermented it with other greens to make a kind of sauerkraut. Pinch off the growing tips any time they are available, and use in salads, or as a potherb.

Drink: The leaves can be steeped in water to make "lemonade".

Medicine: The plant was once known as Scurvy Grass, because of its antiscorbutic properties.

Panax quinquefolium / **American Ginseng**

East   *Araliaceae*

History: Ginseng is the most prized of all native North American herbs. This is because of its resemblance to the Asian Ginseng (*P. schinseng*), which has been an important part of Chinese folklore and mythology for thousands of years. For better or worse much of that lore has been passed on to its similar American cousin.

Both the Chinese and Native Americans considered their respective species to have magical properties, and to be a panacea for essentially all human ailments. This may have something to do with the fact that the roots often have a vaguely human shape, and so were thought to cure the whole body. The more human-like a root was shaped, the more potent it was thought to be. Roots that didn't fit this pattern were sometimes judiciously trimmed to a more human configuration.

The Chinese considered Asian Ginseng to be much more than a mere woodland herb; it was the root of emperors and the rich and powerful, even a link with the divine. Many folk tales surrounded the root, for example it was sometimes said that the plant could transform itself into human or animal form (especially the awesome tiger), and could help or harm a person as they deserved.

Wild roots have always been considered more potent than cultivated ones, and so were more valuable (they still sell for about twice as much). Wild Ginseng was essentially eradicated from most of China centuries ago, and has long been confined to the wildest and most inaccessible mountains. This has only increased its value, so that today wild Chinese roots are worth more than gold.

Because of this great value and scarcity, it was of major significance when, in 1716, a Jesuit missionary in

Canada found the almost identical American Ginseng growing wild in abundance. In the ensuing years Ginseng was to play an important role as a trade item in the European colonization of North America. This widely available root was more valuable than fur, and easier to obtain and ship. The colonists took the very profitable role of intermediary, between the Native Americans who were happy to gather it, and the wealthy Chinese who consumed it. In later years poorer settlers did the collecting, and it provided one of the few sources of cash income for many pioneers.

As with its Asian cousin, American Ginseng was ruthlessly exploited. At the peak of the Ginseng boom about 300 tons of dried roots were gathered from the forests annually. This continued until there were simply too few roots left to make it commercially viable, and gathering became more sporadic. This gave the plant a little time to recover.

Just when the plant was beginning to re-establish itself in many areas, another Ginseng boom began, this time for domestic consumption for the "health food market" Almost as much Ginseng is gathered today as in the peak of the last boom, yet the plants are not nearly so plentiful. In fact this once common plant is now close to extinction in some areas, and is protected as rare or endangered in a number of states. Greedy commercial gatherers will no doubt continue to take wild plants, until it again becomes so rare that gathering ceases to be profitable. One thing working against its total elimination is that the seeds may lay dormant for 2 - 3 years before germinating, and take several more to reach useful size.

Gathering: I will give details about gathering Ginseng here, though I trust you will not collect it from the wild. Digging in many areas is rightfully illegal anyway. The roots should be dug after the plant has produced its red berries (plant them nearby) and is going dormant. In Asia it was customary to say a prayer over a plant before digging. It was then removed by pouring water around the base, to soften and loosen the soil. It must be dug very carefully so as not to snap off any of the rootlets. It was then dried in a warm place until brittle and very dry. Any moisture remaining in the root will cause it to deteriorate in storage

Caution: The plants may be toxic if eaten in excess, so use cautiously. Chronic Ginseng users sometimes complain of diarrhea, nervousness and loss of appetite.

Food: The roots have been eaten as a cooked vegetable, though this is absurd considering their value. I saw one recipe calling for three pounds of roots. That would be an expensive meal, and probably also rather unhealthy.

Medicine

Western researchers consider Ginseng to be merely a demulcent, stomachic and appetite stimulant, but in China and Russia it is considered to be an important drug. In those countries they believe it helps the body to resist external stress, and give it to cosmonauts and athletes to improve performance. They say it stimulates the endocrine glands, the adrenal cortex, the central nervous system and the cardiovascular system. They also say it lowers blood pressure, increases work capacity, and helps animals and humans to resist psychological stress, extreme cold and even radiation. They say it can also increase mental acuity, and help one maintain concentration during prolonged and intense mental work (students often take it during exams). In China Ginseng has long been considered to be an aphrodisiac, rejuvenator, promoter of long life and a general panacea for men.

You might want to try using the root while doing hard physical or mental labor (backpacking or exams). Simply chew a sliver of the dried root until it dissolves; it even tastes pretty good.

Drink: The traditional use of Ginseng root is to make tea. This is prepared by shaving pieces of root into cold water, bringing to a boil and then simmering to the desired strength. It has a pleasant flavor and can become quite habit forming.

Cultivation: Ginseng is grown from stratified seed. This is often treated with giberellic acid, and then stored in damp moss over the winter. Untreated seed may remain dormant for several years. Perhaps the best way to get started in Ginseng growing, is to purchase a few 2 - 3 year old roots, and plant them in the best conditions you can provide. If they like their habitat they will bear fruit in a year or two, and the seed can be planted around its parents. In this way you will gradually accumulate experience before handling delicate seedlings. The plants take about five years to mature from seed.

The plant likes a rich, moist, deciduous woodland soil with lots of humus, and about 80% shade (if you don't have trees this can be provided by screens) and from 20 - 40 inches of rain per year. It grows naturally in the same conditions as Trillium (*Trillium*), Wild Ginger (*Asarum*), Jack- In-The-Pulpit (*Arisaema*) and Mayapple (*Podophyllum*), so plant it where these plants thrive.

To successfully grow Ginseng you must simulate its natural environment as closely as possible, and take care not to overcrowd the plants. They are very vulnerable to pests and disease when growing in less than ideal conditions. Commercial growers often grow them under deciduous trees, in long beds 2 - 4 feet wide.

New crop: Ginseng cultivation undeservedly received a bad reputation in the past, when it was unrealistically promoted as a get-rich-quick scheme and didn't pay off as promised. The problem is that the plant is not easy to grow, as it is very particular about soil and light conditions, and is vulnerable to a number of pests and diseases. Nevertheless it can be a profitable part time business for a skilled grower, and some people have been very successful at it. The annual American harvest of cultivated roots is about 200,000 pounds annually, so someone is doing it right.

Ginseng could be a useful crop for forest gardens, or could be grown to make private woodlots more productive. It grows in deep shade where most other plants don't do well, and could provide a useful supplemental income. Once a population was established, you could selectively harvest a proportion of the roots each year, after they have set seed. Such plants would be more wild than cultivated, and so could be of higher value.

Related species:
P. trifolium - **Dwarf Ginseng** Syn *Aralia trifolium*
Also known as Groundnut, this plant is smaller than the above and much more common. Unfortunately it has little, if any, of the medicinal properties of its larger relative (which is why it is more common of course). The small tuber may be eaten as a root vegetable, or used for tea.

The Uses of Wild Plants

Panicum species / Panic Grasses

Throughout   *Poaceae*

Seed: The seeds fall from the plant quickly once ripe, so are often gathered before they are quite mature. The husks were loosened from the seeds by parching (this also improves the flavor), or by them beating with sticks. They were then winnowed to remove the chaff. The cleaned seed was boiled like rice, or ground to meal for tortillas, gruel or baking. Native Americans dried little cakes in the sun.

Cultivation: Grow from seed in moist rich soil.

Best species: All species produce edible seed, but some are better than others, including:

P. capillare - Old Witch Grass
P. hirticaule
P. urvilleanum - Desert Panicum
The seed of these perennial species are as big as Millet, and they were important food plants for Native Americans.

P. sonorum
This species was cultivated by the Cocopa people on the mud flats of the Colorado delta. They planted it in spring, as water levels started to fall, and pretty much left it to its own devices until it was ripe. Their specially adapted cultivars grew up to seven feet tall and yielded a lot of seed. Cultivation ended after upstream dams destroyed the delta, and most varieties were lost. Fortunately at least one still exists.

Parthenium argentatum / Guayule

Texas and Mexico   *Asteraceae*

Guayule is not edible, but is included because it is the only native North American plant that has been used as a commercial source of rubber. It produces long chain hydrocarbon polymers very similar to those of the Rubber Tree (*Hevea brasiliensis*), unlike the other native rubber producers, which produce shorter polymers.

The latex was first used by the Aztecs to make rubber balls for games, and was extracted by chewing the leaves. The plant first became commercially important as a source of rubber early in this century, when factories were opened in Mexico to process the abundant wild plants. By 1910 Guayule was yielding over 50% of the rubber used in the United States, and almost 10% of the entire world supply. Factories in California were supplied by cultivated plants. Interest in the plant waned when cheap *Hevea* rubber became available from Asia, and all Guayule rubber producing activities stopped.

When Asian rubber supplies were cut off by world war two, Guayule again received the attention of rubber processors. Ambitious plans were laid to plant 400,000 acres in California with it, and 30,000 acres were actually planted. However total U.S. production of Guayule rubber during the war was only about 1400 tons, with a further 7000 tons produced by Mexican factories. It never fulfilled its promise because cheaper synthetic rubber (made from oil) became available, and displaced natural rubber for many uses. All plans for Guayule exploitation ended with the war.

Synthetic rubber has by no means totally replaced the natural product, as natural rubber is stronger, which is an important attribute in some applications. The most important present day use of the natural product is for tires. Auto tires contain up to 40% natural rubber, and truck and aircraft tires even more.

The National Academy of Sciences recently recommended that Guayule be developed as a domestic source of rubber. Mexico has plans to increase domestic production to as much as 30,000 tons per year. If conscientiously grown and processed this plant could become a non-polluting and renewable resource of hydrocarbons, and possibly an important crop for arid marginal lands.

Extraction: The latex was originally extracted from the plant stems by macerating them in water and skimming off the floating rubber. The raw latex contains up to 50% resins, (unlike *Hevea* rubber), which shortens the life span of the rubber if not removed. The latex is now extracted with solvents that also remove the resins (which have important uses in themselves).

Fiber: In addition to rubber and resins, a processing plant produces large amounts of crushed stems, which can be used to make paper or wallboard.

Wax: The leaves are a source of useful wax.

New crops: The commercial cultivation of Guayule is only really viable where water is very scarce (it can grow on as little as ten inches of rain annually). It has been suggested as a possible crop for Native American lands in the arid Southwest, and some arid third world areas. Wild plants contain about 6% latex, though breeding work may increase this to as much as 20%, which would make a big difference to the economic viability of the crop. Work has also been done to cross the plant with its larger cousin, *Parthenium tomentosum var stramonium*, in an attempt to increase both yields and insect resistance.

Cultivation: The plants are grown from seed or division on light, well-drained soil. They are quite hardy, but do best in mild climates. Like many desert shrubs Guayule is allelopathic, and secretes substances that inhibit the growth of neighboring plants, so it is not a good companion plant. These substances even inhibit other Guayule plants, which is why one rarely finds seedlings growing near a parent plant in the wild.

Passiflora incarnata / Passion-Flower, Maypop

South   *Passifloraceae*

Most of the Passionflowers are tropical plants, but this one has ventured north as far as the southern United States. It is the only native species.

Contrary to what you might imagine this species is not an aphrodisiac, the common name was given because the plant reminded some imaginative missionary of the crucifixion of Christ. The five stamens represented his wounds, the ten petals the ten disciples (yes I know there were twelve, but they didn't count Judas or Peter) and the fringe of the flowers represented the crown of thorns.

Caution: The only edible parts of the plant are the fruits, all other parts are poisonous. They contain hydrocyanic acid and a number of potent alkaloids, including harmine and harmaline. These two alkaloids are found in a number of hallucinogenic plants, and in South America they have been used to induce visions. Harmine was used experimentally as a "truth serum" in World War Two. These are not safe uses however.

Fruit: The succulent fruit are often palatable, and some species are cultivated commercially. Discard the skins and eat the pulp raw, or cooked in pies and preserves. The hard seeds are usually discarded, but they are also edible. Gathering the fruit was once a common summer pastime for children in parts of the southeast.

Drink: The fruit may be added to juice drinks, or used for sun tea.

Medicine: The potent alkaloids in the plant are of medicinal value, though too toxic for casual use. They have been used as sedatives.

Smoke: Apparently the leaves have been smoked like Marijuana, but they are too toxic to be safe. The line between intoxication and poisoning is very fine, and you cross it at your own risk.

Fiber: The fibrous stems have been used for cordage.

Crop use: Passionflowers are grown as ornamentals in mild climates, and some species have been grown as commercial fruit crops. In ideal conditions they can be very productive, a thirty-foot vine producing as much as thirty pounds of fruit annually. The vine may be trained along wires to make a deciduous screen.

Cultivation: Maypop can be grown from leaf bud cuttings, layering or seed (the latter may be tricky), in well-drained, rich soil and full sun. It is a very hardy plant, the top dying back to the ground in winter, and reappearing in spring (hence the common name Maypop). In ideal conditions they are very vigorous and in mild climates they can get out of hand and become a weedy nuisance. A number of superior cultivars of *P. edulis* are available, but these are not very frost tolerant.

Related species include:
P. caerulea - Granadilla
This species is commonly grown as an ornamental and may often be found as an escape from cultivation. The fruit are not usually very good.

P. lutea – Yellow Passionflower
Occasionally found as an escape in milder areas.

Pastinaca sativa / Wild Parsnip

Throughout   *Apiaceae*

This is the wild form of the garden Parsnip, escaped from vegetable gardens, and naturalized near human habitation all across the country.

Caution: This is a fine wild food plant, but it somewhat resembles the lethally poisonous Water Hemlock (*Cicuta douglasii*). It has been confused with that plant on a number of occasions, with fatal results. The problem is that it is eaten while the flowers are not present to aid in identification. You must be absolutely sure you have the right plant before using it. If you are not certain then leave it alone; *Cicuta douglasii* can kill in 15 minutes. It has also been confused with the Poison Hemlock (*Conium maculatum*).

Both wild and cultivated Parsnips contain chemicals called furocoumarins, which can cause photodermatitis (this resembles Poison Ivy rash). This happens when juice from the plant gets on skin, and it is then exposed to the ultra-violet rays in sunlight.

Gathering: Parsnip is a biennial, and the root is best from the end of its first year, until it starts growing again in its second year. It is found by locating the old dead plants that have gone to seed, and then looking around for the leaf rosettes of new plants. I already mentioned the danger of mistakenly gathering a poisonous relative, so be cautious when identifying them. Like the garden Parsnip, the root is sweetest after frost has turned its starch into sugar. The later in winter you gather the roots the sweeter they will be.

Preparation: The roots have the same flavor as garden Parsnips, but are less fleshy, and have a wiry central core. They are used in the much the same ways, boiled, baked, in pies and soups. It's easier to remove the cores after cooking, either individually, or by pureeing the cooked roots, and then removing the fibers.

Wine: In northern Europe cultivated Parsnips have been used to make a surprisingly palatable wine.

Cultivation: Parsnips are easily grown from fresh seed. They will grow in poor soils and part shade.

Perideridia gairdneri / Yampa
Syn *Carum gairdneri*
West   *Apiaceae*
Caution: The caution I just gave you about eating members of the *Apiaceae* applies here also, some are very poisonous. Be very careful about identification, especially when gathering a plant that isn't flowering (and dig up the root with the top attached).

Roots: The Yampa is a close relative of the culinary herb Caraway, and was once included in the *Carum* genus. The small tuberous roots were a staple of the Shoshone, Snake and other tribes, and they moved to the best gathering grounds every fall. The small tubers are at their best in loose, rich, moist soil, and are usually gathered as the tops go dormant in fall.

The roots have a nutty flavor, and are one of the best edible wild roots. They can be eaten raw, but are most often boiled for 10 - 30 minutes, or baked at 350 degrees for 30 minutes or so (probably best). Some people remove the thin skins before eating, but it's not really necessary. Native Americans split the tubers lengthwise and dried them for storage. These were then soaked in water and cooked, or ground to flour for baking, gruel or for thickening soup.

Seed: The seed has been used for flavoring.

Animal food: The roots are important food for wildlife, notably Grizzly Bears.

Crop use: It has been suggested that Yampa could become an important food crop, if breeding work was done to increase their size. They are grown from seed in rich, moist soil.

Related species:
All other *Perideridia* species may be eaten as above. The best include:

P. bolanderii - **Bolander's Yampa**
P. kelloggii - **Kellog's Yampa**
P. oregana - **Oregon Yampa**
P. pringlei - **Indian Carrot**
P. parishii - **Parish's Yampa** Syn *Eulophus parishii*

Phacelia ramosissima / Scorpionweed
West   Hydrophyllaceae
Food: The young leaves can be used as a potherb, but aren't very good.

Pest Control: Scorpionweed provides food for a parasite of Scale insects. It may be grown in, and around, orchards to encourage these parasites, which may help reduce the population of these pests.

Fertilizer: The related *P. tanacetifolia* grows very vigorously from seed, and is one of the best summer green manure crops. With its blue flowers it is an attractive annual and makes a good cut flower. The flowers also attract beneficial predatory insects to the garden, and are a good source of nectar for bees.

Phalaris species / Canary Grasses
Throughout   *Poaceae*
Caution: When collecting any grass seeds one should look for the dark colored spurs of the poisonous Ergot (*Claviceps*) fungi growing in place of the seeds. Discard any such spurs you find, or don't use the plants at all. The green parts have apparently poisoned livestock and should also be avoided.

Seed: These grasses are quite common on waste ground near human habitation. They produce large edible seed and have occasionally been cultivated as food crops.

Species include:
P. Canariensis – **Canary Grass**
This is one of the best edible species. The seed is a favorite of many birds, and is sometimes found in commercial birdseed mixes.

P. caroliniana - **Maygrass**
This species was cultivated as a seed crop by Native Americans in the Ozarks.

Phaseolus acutifolius / **Tepary bean**

Southwest   *Fabaceae*
This small bean grows wild throughout much of the southwest. It has been an important food crop for Native Americans for 5000 years, and is still grown by Pima and Papago farmers in remote areas. It is prized as a prolific producer of nutritious beans (they contain 20 - 30% protein), that is able to tolerate drier conditions than most other food crops. The name Tepary is of Native American origin. The plant is gaining in popularity as a crop for arid areas, and may soon be a commonly available food product.

Caution: A number of *Phaseolus* species (including several cultivated ones) contain hydrocyanic acid and their beans are poisonous in the raw state. This toxin is destroyed by heat so they are quite safe when cooked.

Gathering: Native Americans usually gathered the ripe seedpods in early morning, as the heat of the day dries out the pods, causing them to shatter when touched. The pods are then allowed to dry fully, and are beaten or walked on to release the beans. These are cleaned and used immediately, or further dried and stored. It is a good idea to freeze the dry beans for a few days, as this kills any insect eggs they may contain.

New crop

Tepary Bean has potential as a crop for desert areas around the world, where water is scarce or expensive. It is unusually heat and drought resistant (it will crop with only 8 - 12 inches of water), fixes nitrogen and may give crops of 700 pounds of beans per acre without irrigation (and as much as 1400 pounds with irrigation).

Uses: The Tepary Bean is related to the Kidney, Pole and Lima beans, and can be used in the same ways. The immature pods may be somewhat toxic raw, but can be cooked like green beans as a vegetable, or added to soups. The dry beans are soaked overnight and cooked like pinto beans. They are particularly good in soup and chili. They can also be dried and ground to flour.

Cultivation: This species is easily grown from seed, and likes deep moisture retentive alluvial soils. It should be watered sparingly, as too much water encourages the plant to produce leaves instead of seed. Like most desert annuals it is adapted to flower and set seed quickly,

before the available moisture runs out. It may mature in only 60 - 90 days. In the long desert growing season Native Americans often obtained two crops of beans in a year, the first planted in early spring, the second in mid-summer. The wild plant is a vigorous climber and may reach 10 feet in height. A few cultivars are still available, though most aren't such strong climbers

Related species:
A number of other *Phaseolus* species produce edible seeds, including:

P. polystachios - **Wild Bean**
P. filiformis
P. metcalfii
These species are used as above. The latter is a perennial, and has a long swollen taproot to help it survive drought.

Phragmites australis / **Common Reed**

Syn *P. communis*
Throughout   *Poaceae*
The aptly named Common Reed can be astonishingly abundant at times, growing in almost pure stands covering thousands of acres of marshland. This is a plant that has benefited from human activities, and it has become increasingly common where roads and other human structures prevent natural drainage, and so create marshy conditions. It also thrives in water that is polluted by sewage or fertilizer runoff.

The Reed is often considered a sign of useless land, which is too wet for farming, building, recreation, growing trees or other moneymaking activities. This is a rather shortsighted view, as this versatile plant has numerous potential uses. In fact land suitable for growing it could conceivably be quite valuable one day.

Flour: The perennial roots contain a lot of starch while dormant, and this can be extracted and used for food in the same way as that of Kudzu (*Pueraria*).

Roots: The dormant roots have been roasted and eaten like those of Cattail (*Typha*).

Shoots: The white shoots that appear on the roots in late winter can be broken off and eaten raw, cooked or pickled. As these elongate and appear above ground (or water), they can be peeled of their tough outer layers and cooked.

Sugar: The young growing stems are rich in sugar up until they flower, and a sweet flour can be obtained by drying, pounding and sifting them. This was an important sweetener for some Native American tribes, and was added to many foods to make them more palatable. They often mixed it with water to make balls, which swell when toasted like Marshmallows. It was also mixed with water as a drink.

Chewing gum: The gum that exudes from wounds in the stem was sometimes chewed by Native Americans.

Seed: Though the plants are not dependable seed producers, the seed is nutritious, and is occasionally produced in abundance. The seed hulls are hard to remove, so are usually left on when making flour.

Stems: The most widely utilized part of the Reed is the stem. Reed stems have been used for many things in the past; some of the commonest uses are listed below.

Boats: Boats were made by lashing the stems into long bundles, and then tying the bundles together to form the required shape. These were often an important means of transportation in areas where trees were scarce. They have been as simple as a one-man canoe, or large enough to carry a dozen people on a lengthy ocean voyage.

Houses: Houses have been built using the same technique of lashing reeds into bundles, and then tying the bundles together. The final form varies greatly, from simple huts to elaborate public buildings. Such houses might last 15 - 20 years, and are immune to earthquake damage (a significant property in some areas). In the marshes of southern Iraq, Reed houses were once sited on islands built out of Reeds and mud, and made accessible by reed boats. Chopped Reeds were used as reinforcement for mud bricks and walls, and have been mixed into the plaster used to cover such walls to make them more weather resistant. Compressed reeds have been used to make wallboard.

Paper: In Eastern Europe large quantities of Reeds are used for making paper. In the Danube delta 100,000 tons of Reed paper pulp is produced annually. This isn't used alone but is mixed with 80% wood pulp. Reeds could also be used as a source of cellulose for other products.

Thatch: In Europe the durable stems are considered to be the best material for thatched roofs. They are gathered in winter, after the leaves wither and drop. These are actually superior to modern composite roofing; as not only are they longer lasting (a good Reed roof should last up to 50 years). but they also provide insulation.

Other uses: Reed fibers have been used for nets, ropes, twine, baskets, mattresses, beehives and mats. The stems were dipped in oil or fat and burned as lights.

Native Americans used the stems for pipe stems, prayer sticks and lightweight arrows for hunting birds (these were tipped with a hard wood such as Mountain Mahogany (*Cercocarpus*).

Pollution cleanup: Reeds thrive in water polluted with sewage or fertilizer runoff, as they take the nutrients found in such water and convert them into plant material. They can actually be used to clean up contaminated water, and in Germany they have been used to purify water in biological sewage treatment plants. Reeds (and other aquatic plants) secrete substances that can kill pathogenic bacteria, and their roots supply oxygen to the bacteria that handle the sewage. They have also been used experimentally to treat some kinds of toxic chemical sludge (such as material dredged from polluted river bottoms), and can actually render it less harmful.

In this country artificial wetlands (not just of Reeds) are being created, as a final step in purifying the huge quantities of water coming out of sewage treatment plants. So far these projects have been very successful and the idea holds much promise for treating wastewater and creating wildlife habitat (natural wetlands are still disappearing in many areas). In the Netherlands Reeds have been used to dry out reclaimed land.

Greywater treatment: Domestic greywater can be purified by passing it through a bed of gravel in which Reeds are growing. It is fairly easy to make such a system for your own home

Fuel: The biomass produced when purifying water could be fermented to produce methane or alcohol (and fertilizer). The dried stems have been compressed into logs for fuel.

Animal food: The dense stands of plants are vital to aquatic birds and animals, for both shelter and food. Young plants have been used as animal feed in Europe.

Cultivation: Reeds are extremely productive plants and spread rapidly in suitable conditions. A single rhizome may grow up to twenty feet in a season, and send out shoots at every node. They are quite long lived, and unlike most plants can grow in dense pure stands (essentially monocultures) without suffering serious damage from insects or disease (a valuable asset for a new crop plant).

Propagate by root division or layering, in shallow water or mud. They can be used to control erosion, but will eventually choke shallow waterways unless controlled. It is a very graceful plant, and attractive enough to be planted as an ornamental in shallow water (though too invasive for small areas).

Fertilizer: If you live close to a source of reeds you can have an abundant source of free fertilizer for your garden. The green or dried foliage can be composted, or dug into the soil to add organic matter. In this way you will be reclaiming some of the nutrients recently washed from the land. If you have a suitable site it may even be worth growing your own Reeds (if they don't already grow there).

Physalis species / Ground Cherries

Throughout   *Solanaceae*
Various species of Ground Cherry can be found growing across the country, and are often considered weeds. A few have been cultivated, as ornamentals (notably the Chinese Lantern), or for their edible fruit (the Tomatillo and Cape Gooseberry).

Caution: The Ground Cherries are members of the *Solanaceae*, one of the most economically important plant families (it includes such important foods as the Potato, Tomato, Eggplant and Peppers). This family also contains a number of very poisonous species (even some important commercial crops often have poisonous parts). It is generally considered that all green parts of all *Solanaceous* species are poisonous to some degree, as they contain the alkaloid solanine (or even more dangerous poisons). Some people believe all parts of all species are unwholesome and best avoided. The ripe fruits of these species are edible and very good.

Gathering: Unripe Ground Cherries often fall from the plant with the papery calyx intact and ripen on the ground. This is a useful characteristic for the gardener or forager, as it means the fruit can be gathered while green and ripened at home in a protected place. It also means they keep longer than most fruits. Native Americans used to dry them in the calyx for winter use.

Preparation: These versatile fruits can often be found in abundance and are an important wild food. They can be used as a substitute for Tomatoes or wild berries in pies, preserves, chili and soups. The flavor of the fruit varies with species, some are sweet and delicious raw in desserts and salads, while others are best cooked. Native Americans often boiled them with Hot Peppers and onions to make a sauce.

Decoration: The dried plants, with their lantern-like husks, are often used in flower arrangements.

Cultivation: A number of species are cultivated for food or as ornamentals, but most are considered pests. In truth they are only a nuisance if you don't put them to good use. Native Americans sometimes cultivated them, or encouraged the volunteers that appeared in their fields. Most *Physalis* species are tender tropical plants, and like a long, hot growing season. For this reason they are usually grown as annuals in the north (like their cousin the Tomato), though many are actually perennial. They can be propagated from root cuttings in milder climates.

Useful species include:
All yellow flowered species produce edible fruit. The best include:

P. ixocarpa - **Tomatillo** (found as a garden escape in warmer areas)

P. lobata - **Purple Ground Cherry** Syn *Quincula lobata*.

Phytolacca americana / Pokeweed

East & locally elsewhere   *Phytolaccaceae*
Caution: The young spring shoots have been called the most widely used American wild green food. They are sometimes cultivated, and even canned, commercially. So it is somewhat surprising to hear botanists and pharmacologists sometimes warn that one should not even touch the raw plant with bare hands. Apparently the plants contain substances called mitogens, which may cause blood abnormalities if they come into contact with blood (such as through a cut).

The only parts of the plant that should ever be eaten are the new shoots (when less than eight inches tall), and these must be properly cooked to be edible. The root is extremely poisonous and has caused a number of fatalities. There are occasional reports of people getting sick after eating cooked Pokeweed, but I don't know any of the details.

Gathering: The spring shoots are cut as close to the ground as possible, when about 6 - 8 inches high. Harvesting a few of these does little harm to the vigorous plants, as they simply produce more. It might be a good idea to wear gloves while handling the raw plant as a precaution.

Forcing: The roots have been brought indoors in late autumn and forced like those of Chicory (*Cicorium*), to produce early spring greens.

Poke sallet

This isn't a salad by any modern definition, but that's what it's called. Prepare it by peeling off the outer leaves and cooking the shoots in boiling water for 1 minute. Drain, add new boiling water, boil for another minute and then drain again (this removes most of the water soluble toxins). Add fresh boiling water, cook for a further 15 minutes, then drain and discard the water. The cooked shoots can be eaten as they are, added to soups or fried in tempura.

The re-growth from plants already harvested has also been eaten, after preparing as just described. Seedlings have also been eaten, but they are not as good (and may not be as safe).

Medicine: Mitogens are substances that stimulate cell division, and have been used in the laboratory to study the immune response and certain diseases. An extract of the plant has been studied as a possible treatment for herpes, as it seems to inhibit the growth of the virus. Other chemicals in the plants have been studied as possible anti-cancer drugs.

The berries of a related African species; Endod (*P. dodecandra*) can kill the Snail that carries the deadly tropical disease schistosomiasis. They have potential value as a locally produced, low cost molluscicide for controlling this serious health threat. They could also be used to eradicate mosquitoes and other disease carrying insects. I don't know whether this species has any of those properties.

Animal food: The berries are a favorite food of birds and this explains the plants wide dispersal. It is said the seeds germinate better after going through the bird's digestive system (this is a form of scarification), and they may not germinate at all if they do not receive this treatment.

Other uses: The juice of the berries has been used as a fish poison, and as purple ink.

Horticultural uses: Though generally considered to be a weed, Poke is a truly spectacular plant. With its purple and green stems and shiny purple berries, it would probably be a prized ornamental if it were harder to grow (some things are just too easy). It is not a plant for small gardens though, as when growing in full sun and rich moist soil it may reach ten feet in height. It can also become a troublesome weed, as bird sown seedlings spring up everywhere. Another problem is that the plant may carry mosaic disease, which attacks a number of important garden vegetables. It has been cultivated as a potherb in several countries

Cultivation: Poke is usually grown from seed. This is soaked in sulfuric acid for 5 minutes to simulate the trip through a bird, or stratified for 6 - 12 weeks. It will grow in part shade, but prefers full sun.

Picea mariana / Black Spruce

North   *Pinaceae*

The Black Spruce is one of the most widely distributed, and successful, of all North American conifers. In some northern areas almost pure stands of Spruce cover many thousands of square miles.

Food: In times of scarcity the immature cones and tender candles (leaf buds) have been eaten.

Drink: A vitamin C rich tea can be made from Black Spruce boughs at any time of the year, but the best is made from the light green spring growth (add Citrus peel and honey). The same young tips can also be used to make very palatable Spruce beer

Medicine: A tea of the needles may be added to bathwater to soothe aching muscles. The needles were added to sweat lodges for the same purpose.

Spruce Gum

The resin that seeps from wounds in the tree is probably the best wild chewing gum, and once formed the basis of a minor industry. The lumps of resin were collected in winter when they are hard and brittle, by knocking them from the trees with a pole. They were melted, strained to remove dirt and debris, allowed to cool and then broken into bite size lumps. To chew Spruce gum you must first soften it by sucking, and then chew slowly. It takes a while to get used to this gum, but you can grow to like it. Unlike modern gums which lose their flavor in minutes, this one tastes better the longer it is chewed. Old time loggers said it tasted best after three days (I guess you had to make your own entertainment in the lumber camps).

Wood: Spruce wood is light, soft and strong. This species doesn't get big enough to be an important source of wood, but several others (notably Sitka Spruce) are important lumber producers. Cloven Spruce is prized by luthiers for its excellent acoustical properties and is used for making violins and guitars. Spruces are commonly used for making paper, though more because of their abundance than for any special quality.

They are poor firewood, averaging about 15 million Btu per cord, but are widely used because they are common.

Cellulose: Black Spruce is also used as a source of cellulose for making rayon and cellophane. The lignin that binds the cellulose fibers is removed with solvents, and the cellulose is dissolved and spun into long threads. This is used for weaving (rayon), or further treated to make cellophane and other plastics. Cellulose can be treated with nitric and sulfuric acids to make explosives.

Glue: The resin was also used for glue; most notably for gluing and caulking Birch bark canoes. The hard resin was heated to melt it, and then mixed with animal fat and powdered charcoal (to make it more flexible). This was applied while hot and hardens as it cools.

Rootlets

The supple rootlets may be a quarter of an inch in diameter, and twenty feet long, and can easily be pulled from the ground in long lengths. Native Americans considered them to be the best material for sewing Birch bark canoes and other items. For fine work the roots were split lengthwise, and boiled to make them supple. They can be used as emergency cord right out of the ground.

Beds: Green boughs from the tree were used to make browse beds (see *Abies*).

Cultivation: Spruces are grown from seed in much the same way as the Pines. Natural layering sometimes takes place when a branch touching the ground takes root and this could be tried as a propagation method for special varieties. This hardy climax species is able to grow in the shade of other trees and eventually replaces them.

Garden uses: Spruces grow in almost pure stands because their roots secrete allelopathic substances that inhibit other plants. This is why Spruce forests are not good places to forage for food plants, and why the trees are not good for soil improvement. Strawberries actually like spruces, and the needles make fine mulch for them.

Related species:
P. glauca - **White Spruce**
This is the most important Canadian timber tree and one of the commonest pulpwood species. It is not very good for gum or beer.

P. rubens - **Red Spruce**
This species is as good as the Black Spruce as a source of chewing gum, and for Spruce beer.

P. sitchensis - **Sitka Spruce**
This is the most important timber species in Alaska. It has the highest strength to weight ratio of any common

wood, as it is both light and very strong. It was once important for building airplanes, but is now most often used for construction, boatbuilding and pulpwood. In the mild maritime climate of southern Alaska, the young trees may grow two and a half feet per year, and reach 100 feet in height in only fifty years (they make a good windbreak). They may live as long as 700 years.

Pinus species / Pinon Pines
Southwest *Pinaceae*

These shrubby little trees are among the smallest members of the *Pinus* genus, but they are the most important food producing conifers. Their seeds were a staple food of most Native American tribes living within their range.

Threats: Wild Pinon seeds are gathered commercially, and there is concern that this is having an adverse effect on the plants in some places. Commercial gathering not only means that fewer seedling Pinons appear, but has an effect on every creature which eats the nuts. In turn this affects every plant these creatures turn to for food when the nuts are scarce. The only thing preventing greater and more organized commercial gathering, is the irregular nature of the harvest.

Nutrients: Pinon seeds contain about 15% protein, 60% fat and 17% carbohydrate, which gives them a fuel value of about 3000 calories per pound. They are also rich in phosphorus.

Gathering: The trees naturally bear irregularly. In some years they bear so abundantly one can practically sweep seed off the ground, and seed will still be available the following spring. In other years almost no seed is produced at all. Irregular bearing is common in many wild plants as a way of preventing too many predators relying on the seed for food.

The nuts ripen in the tightly closed green cones, high up in the branches, by the beginning of September. Native

Americans used long poles to get at the cones, and this is still the best way to reach them. Hook the branch and twist off the cone. They often had older children climb the trees and knock down the cones (adults are often too heavy for the trees). You could also use an orchard ladder. Don't break branches, or (it's been done) cut down the trees to get at the cones. It is a good idea to wear old clothes when gathering the cones, as they are covered in resin and can really mess up your clothing A hat isn't a bad idea either. Native Americans sometimes took caches of nuts from Packrat nests (there may be up to 30 pounds of seeds in a nest).

On National Forest land you will probably need a permit to gather the nuts. Ask at a ranger station, as they can also give you advice about when, and where, to forage.

Preparation: To loosen the seeds the cones must be dried (easier), or roasted in a fire pit (quicker). They are then beaten to release the seeds. Native Americans often left large piles of cones to dry out over winter, and gathered the seed in spring (if you try this watch out for rodents). Individual cones contain from 10 - 20 seeds, though light colored seed may be abortive, and empty. You can separate the seeds in water, good seeds will sink, while trash and empty seeds float. Store the seed in its coat in a dry place and shell just before use. Shelled seeds don't store well.

In some species the seed can be eaten whole, but in most cases the tough seed coat must be removed. This can be done with the fingers, teeth, a hammer, a rolling pin, or vice grip pliers (set so to a width which crushes the shell but not the kernel).

Uses: Pine nuts can be eaten raw, but usually taste better if roasted for 10 minutes at 450 degrees. Native Americans toasted them by shaking in a pan with hot coals. Roasting the nuts may also help to preserve them, and they are easier to shell when hot (simply walk on them). The roasted seed may be ground to meal for baking or gruel, or simply eaten whole. Pine nuts are a traditional ingredient of Basil pesto.

Baby food: Easily digested and nutritious, Pine nut gruel makes good baby food. Motherless Paiute babies were commonly fed on it.

Animal food: The nuts are a very important source of food for many wild creatures. The most notable of these are the various species of Jay, indeed it believed that the large seeded Pinon Pines exist as a result of selection by these birds. Jays have been gathering and storing Pine seed for over 25 million years, and this lengthy symbiotic selection process has resulted in the predominance of trees bearing large seeds that don't readily drop from the open cones.

Firewood: Pinon Pines are quite good firewood, and large areas were once almost totally deforested to make charcoal for smelting metal ores. Firewood gathering is once again becoming a problem for these slow growing trees. The forest service has actually encouraged their destruction in some areas, by issuing permits to cut live Pinon for firewood (even though some of these trees may be 200 years old).

Christmas trees: Pinon Pines are becoming increasingly popular as Christmas trees. Perhaps another reason to buy a living tree and plant it outside after Christmas. I bought two live Italian Stone Pines last Christmas. They are doing well and I hope to eventually get nuts from them.

New Crops: These species (and other nut bearing Pines from around the world) have potential as cultivated nut crops for arid areas. As yet very little selection work has been done to improve them.

Cultivation: Propagate from seed as for other Pines (see below). Generally they prefer light, well-drained soil.

Useful species: All of the useful American nut-bearing Pines are found in the Southwest. The Pinon Pines are:

P. edulis - Colorado Pinon
The Colorado Pinon has been called the most important American wild nut tree. It is certainly the most valuable nut bearing Pine.

P. cembroides - Mexican Pinon
P. quadrifolia - Parry Pinon

P. monophylla - Single Leaf Pinon
The Single Leaf Pinon is easily identifiable as the only Pine species with needles in bundles of one (actually a bundle of five fused into one).

The other native nut Pines are:
P. sabiniana - Digger Pine
This species occurs in the foothills of California, and is characterized by its open crown and relatively sparse foliage. The large spiny cones contain fat tasty seeds, but are often hard to reach. I have gathered good seeds from the ground in spring. The mottled brown seed coat is a hard shell and must be cracked individually, like other nuts.

The interior of the immature cone has been eaten, after roasting in the ashes of a fire for about 30 minutes.

P. albicaulis - Whitebark Pine
P. flexilis - Limber Pine
These closely related species are sometimes said to bear the best-flavored Pine nuts.

P. strobiformis - Southwestern White Pine
This species is a close relative of *P. flexilis*. The small, hard-shelled seeds are good.

P. torreyana - Torrey Pine
This species produces edible seeds, but isn't very useful because its range is limited to a very small area of Southern California.

P. lambertiana - Sugar Pine
The Sugar Pine is one of the giants of the Pine family, growing up to 200 feet tall (John Muir called it the Queen of the Sierra). Its edible seeds were prized by the Miwok people, but the huge cones (these may be 18 inches in length), are often 100 hundred feet off the ground (with a smooth fifty foot trunk before the branches start). If you get some ripe cones, remove the seed as Native Americans did, break the tip off the cone and split it lengthways into quarters, then peel off the scales to free the seed. These are shelled and eaten like the Pinons.

Sugar Pine gum was chewed like that of Black Spruce (*Picea*). John Muir is said to have used it for sweetening. The needles make a fair tea.

P. coulterii - Coulter Pine
Also known as the Bigcone Pine, for its huge cones up to 15 inches long (the heaviest of all Pine cones). The seeds were commonly eaten by Native Americans

Pinus species / Other Pines
The rest of the native Pines don't bear useful seed. All Pine seed is edible, but most is too small to be useful for food.

Inner bark: In late winter the inner bark (cambium) of the Pines is rich in sugars and quite sweet. In a few species it is almost palatable. Of course stripping the bark off a tree will probably kill it, which is unacceptable nowadays, but I suppose it is worth knowing they can supply food in an emergency. You can sometimes get bark from the stumps of logged trees. Many Native American tribes ate Pine bark almost regularly, when other foods became scarce. Most notably the people sometimes called the Adirondacks, which was actually a derogatory term meaning "tree eaters". The inner bark was boiled, or dried and ground to flour.

Drink: Tea can be made from the leaves of any Pine, but some are much better than others, so you have to experiment. Half fill a cup with chopped young needles (these have the best flavor) and then fill with boiling water. When this has cooled sufficiently, strain, sweeten to taste and add lemon.

Other foods: The unopened leaf buds (candles), and immature cones, of many species can be eaten raw or cooked. The resin has been chewed as gum. These wind-pollinated trees produce pollen in abundance, and apparently this was sometimes gathered and eaten by Native Americans.

Medicine: Pine needle tea is so rich in vitamin C that it has been used to cure scurvy. Native Americans sometimes underwent a spring purification fast, when they would consume only Pine tea for several days.

The tea has also been added to bathwater, or used as a liniment, to soothe sore muscles.

Wound dressing: Resin from the trunk is a natural antiseptic, and is used by the trees to protect their wounds from infection and to speed healing. The resin has the same effect on human wounds, and has been mixed with fat, or oil, for use as an ointment.

Wood: The Pines are among the most important commercial tree species and enormous numbers are cut annually for lumber. Generally lumbering is a large scale mechanized operation (the very word lumbering evokes bigness), yet converting trees into boards can easily be done on a small scale using a portable lumber mill. These relatively simple tool makes ecologically sound lumbering quite feasible, and could actually increase the employment opportunities in logging, while making it far less destructive. Rather than building roads and transporting the entire tree out of the forest, it becomes possible to just take out the finished boards.

Sawdust can be used as an inexpensive insulation (usually treated with fire retardant). It has also been mixed with concrete for making building blocks.

Fuel: Pine burns quickly and often throws sparks, but is widely used as firewood because it is often the most available wood. Fuel value ranges from a low of about 13 million Btu per cord (*P. strobus*) up to 18 million Btu (*P. palustris*). I like to have a mix of pine and hardwood, as they complement each other. Pine gets a blaze going fast, but doesn't last very long. Hardwoods are slow to start, but keep going for a long time.

The small twigs on the lower branches are good kindling for lighting fires. The resinous cones can be used to start fires in wet weather.

The Uses of Wild Plants

Beds: The green branches of the pines were used for thatching shelters, and making camp beds in the same way as Balsam Fir (*Abies*). A modern version of the Pine bed is to sweep loose dead needles into a pile about a foot deep, four feet wide and seven feet long. You throw a tarp over them and sleep on top; it is infinitely better than bare ground (or most backpacking mats).

Other uses: Native Americans used the rootlets like those of Spruce (*Picea*), for cord, and to sew Birch bark utensils. The resin was heated and used as glue or pitch like Spruce. Warriors used to spread the pitch on their skin and then stick feathers to it (presumably to make themselves look fierce and otherworldly).

Chemicals: In the age of sailing ships, pitch, creosote, and turpentine (obtained from the resin), were important commodities, and were known collectively as naval stores. Collecting and producing these was once a significant industry. Other useful chemicals can also be distilled from pine resin.

Garden use: The evergreen Pines look good in both winter and summer so are popular as garden ornamentals. They are also planted as lumber producers, Christmas trees, windbreaks and screens.

Cultivation: Pines are grown from ripe seed, sown immediately, or stratified for three months at 40 degrees. They should be sited carefully as they may secrete substances that inhibit neighboring plants. They may also increase soil acidity.

Pine Needles: The fallen needles are often an abundant, but overlooked, garden resource. They are a great mulch for acid-loving plants such as Strawberries and Blueberries (though in very dry weather they can become a fire hazard). They can also be used with other plants if a liming agent is added to neutralize their acidity. They can be dug into the soil to add organic matter (again with a little lime) and break down quickly when buried.

The needles and shredded bark are an excellent material for paths. They are attractive, available in quantity, free, natural looking and need very little maintenance (simply add more if they get dirty or thin). Their only drawback is that they can be slippery if used on sloping ground. The shredded branches have been incorporated into very poor soils to add organic matter.

Species include:
The native Pines are divided into three groups, according to the type of lumber they produce:

White Pines
P. strobus - Eastern White Pine
This was the most important lumber species in colonial times, when magnificent trees of 200 feet tall were quite common. It has been estimated that there were over 750 billion board feet of this wood in the forest when the first Europeans arrived, of which perhaps 15 billion remain (hardly a renewable resource as such). The wood is one of the finest of all softwoods, and it was used for almost everything; construction, cabinetmaking, millwork, paneling and even matchsticks. It was also an important export commodity, especially for the masts of wooden ships, and was a major source of income for the early colonies, second only to fur in importance. The disappearance of these trees from settled areas was one of the main incentives for westward settlement.

P. monticola - Western White Pine
P. lambertiana - Sugar Pine (see also page 147)
The wood of these western species is similar to *P. strobus* and they have pretty much replaced it as a source of high quality softwood. The reason for this is that there are still a few old growth trees left.

Southern Yellow Pines
P. echinata - Shortleaf Pine
P. elliottii - Slash Pine
P. palustris - Longleaf Pine
P. taeda - Loblolly Pine
These fast growing Southeastern species are very important producers of construction grade lumber and pulpwood.

Pinus rigida – Pitch Pine
This species produces copious amounts of resin, and was once tapped as a source of naval stores. A strip of the resinous wood can be burned like a candle.

Pitch Pine is unusual among the pines in that it will coppice (regenerate from the stump), sending up new shoots after it is cut down. This feature makes it potentially useful as a source of wood chips, pulpwood or biomass.

Western Yellow Pines
P. contorta - Lodgepole Pine
This species gets its common name because Native Americans prized the long straight saplings for tipi poles.

P. jeffreyi - Jeffrey Pine
P. ponderosa - Ponderosa Pine
P. radiata - Monterey Pine
Monterey Pine can't stand cold climates, and is native to a very restricted area of the California coast. It was actually trapped in a few coastal areas by climactic change sometime in the past, and doesn't do particularly well there. In an ideal mild, wet, climate it may grow very rapidly, up to 20 feet in five years. Though little used in its native land, it has become the most widely planted timber tree in the Southern Hemisphere.

P. aristata - **Bristlecone Pine**

This species deserves a mention as one of the world's longest living trees. It is known to live up to 5000 years, which would be about seventy human lifetimes. To put this in perspective, if the lifetime of a tree was seventy years, a human life would be about one year.

These trees have a couple of special uses. They enable meteorologists to study the climate for the life of the tree, the better the growing season the wider the annular ring. They are also useful to archaeologists who can date wooden artifacts by comparing their growth rings with those of the living Bristlecones.

Plantago major / **Great Plantain**

Throughout   *Plantaginaceae*

This species has followed European explorers and settlers all around the world. This fact was not unnoticed by indigenous people in several countries, who named the plant "White Mans Foot", "Englishman's Foot" or similar names.

Greens: In spring the tender, newly emerged leaves can be used in sandwiches and salads, or boiled as a potherb for 10 - 15 minutes. They are rich in vitamins A and C and quite nutritious.

Older leaves tend to be hairy and somewhat tough, but can be used as a potherb if you strip off the tough veins. They are better used in soups and stews (it may help to put them in blender for a few seconds). They can also be improved by covering them with an opaque container for a few days to blanch them.

Seed: Native Americans boiled the seed like Rice, added it to soup, or dried and ground it to meal for baking.

Emergency wound dressing

The leaves have long been used to treat wounds, Poison Ivy rash, insect bites, grazes and minor burns. It was sometimes called Rattlesnake Weed because of its use in treating Snakebite. Crush a handful of clean leaves to a pulp and bind them on to the affected areas. An even more effective method is to chew the leaves to a pulp, as human saliva has additional healing properties.

Medicine: The mucilaginous seed of the related Psyllium (*P. ovata*) is very widely used as a laxative. It is one of the commonest commercial bulk laxatives, and has even been added to commercial breakfast cereals for this. The seed of this species can be used in the same way though it is not as effective.

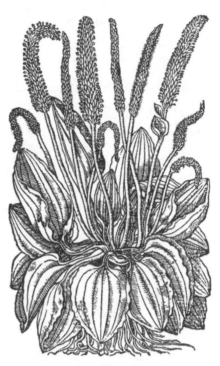

Animal food: The seeds are an important food for birds.

Cultivation: Plantain is such a common plant of disturbed soils that it seems absurd to even think about planting it (there are few places where it's completely absent). Nevertheless it can be grown from seed or division. If that is too difficult simply transplant some from the nearest lawn.

Garden uses: Despite its abundance I don't consider Plantain a bad weed, though people who absolutely must have a perfect lawn will probably disagree (it is one of the lawn lovers worst enemies). The plant even has its good points; it protects disturbed land from erosion, provides food for many forms of wildlife and attracts birds to the garden.

Related species: Many species are palatable in spring and none are poisonous, so you can experiment with any species you find. The best include:

P. fastigiata - **Indian Wheat**

This species gets its common name because it bears edible brown seed. This can be used as above.

P. maritima - **Sea Plantain**

As the names suggests, this is a coastal species, though it is also found elsewhere. Its fleshy grass-like leaves are a nice addition to salads, and can also be cooked. They have also been pickled.

P. macrocarpa - **Sea Plantain**

This northwestern species may be used as above.

***P. coronopus* - Buckhorn Plantain**
This species is a good enough salad plant to be cultivated commercially in parts of Italy.

Podophyllum peltatum / **Mayapple**
East   *Berberidaceae*

Caution: Mayapple is quite common in moist woodland in the east, and is easily identified by its distinctive umbrella shaped leaves. It has another more picturesque name American Mandrake, and like the true Mandrake of Europe (*Mandragora officinarum*) it is very poisonous (Native Americans sometimes used the root to commit suicide). A number of substances are responsible for its toxicity, including podophyllotoxin and alpha and beta peltatain, which are violently purgative and irritant. All green parts are dangerous, the only edible part is the ripe yellow fruits. Even the seeds are slightly poisonous and shouldn't be eaten in quantity. A few people are allergic to the fruits, so use caution the first few times you try them, and always eat in moderation (they are also mildly laxative).

Gathering: Plants with a single stem are immature and only those with a forked stem are actually old enough to bear fruit. By the time the fruit is fully ripe the plant is practically dead (it may be only a brown stalk), so you should locate the plants in advance. Gather the fruit as soon as it is ripe, as wild animals eat them and they disappear quickly. The immature green fruits have an unpleasant smell, while the ripe yellow fruits are very aromatic (they practically fall from the plant).

Uses: Many people enjoy the sweet, ripe fruit raw out of hand, and compare the flavor to Strawberries. Cut off the end and eat the soft pulp. The musky flavor of the raw fruit is too strong for some people. If you find this to be the case then try cooking them. Strain out the seeds after cooking, and use the pulp in preserves, pies and desserts.

Drink: The fruit pulp is good mixed with other fruit juices.

Medicine: Native Americans used the root as a purgative and tonic for the whole body, and especially the liver. Even today small amounts are sometimes found in commercial "liver tonics". Resin from the root has been used as paint for removing warts. Whatever it's medicinal virtues, the plant is too toxic for casual use, and there is no reason for anyone to use it.

Podophyllotoxin has been found to prevent cell division, so has been used to arrest the growth of some kinds of tumors. It is now used to make anti-cancer drugs for treating testicular, and other, cancers. Alpha and beta peltatain also show similar action.

Cultivation: Mayapple is a woodland plant, so is ideal for forest gardens. It is occasionally grown in gardens as an ornamental, and the colonies make a fine deciduous groundcover. It grows best in partly shady, moist conditions, and is propagated by root division (easy) or seed. Established plants spread by means of creeping rhizomes. It is very hardy

New crop: The politician and botanist De Witt Clinton suggested growing Mayapples as a commercial fruit on the banks of the Erie Canal. I don't know about the location, but the fruits definitely have potential as a cultivated crop.

Insecticide: The Menominee use a tea of the leaves as an insecticide.

Polygonatum **species** / **Solomon's Seal**
East   *Liliaceae*

Name: There are a number of theories as to how Solomon's Seal got its common name. It has been suggested that the round leaf scars on the rhizome resemble the seal of Solomon, others say if you cut a section of the root that resembles the seal. Another explanation is that if a flower is dipped in ink and printed onto paper, that outline resembles the Star of David. Finally others argue it has nothing to do with printed seals at all, but was named because the root has been used to treat (or seal) wounds.

Uses: The spring shoots can be peeled and cooked like Asparagus. Taking a couple of shoots from a plant in spring won't hurt it, as it will simply produce more, but taking more than one crop would.

Roots: The root is edible, but not really good enough to justify killing the plant. The tough skin must be peeled off before use. This is most easily done after an initial boiling has loosened it (Native Americans added wood ashes to the water to hasten this). The inner root is then boiled until thoroughly cooked (frying the cooked root is said to improve its flavor).

Flour can be extracted from the roots by washing and macerating in the same way as for Kudzu (*Pueraria*), or by grinding and sifting the dried roots. This starch can be used as a thickening agent.

Caution: The berries are not edible, as they contain purgative arthraquinone glycosides similar to those in Cascara Sagrada bark.

Medicine: The dried powdered root was sprinkled on wounds to stop bleeding, and hasten healing, and is probably an antiseptic. It was also used to treat skin diseases and Poison Ivy rash.

In China the roots of a Eurasian species (*P. multiflorum*) have been used to treat diabetes. They also have a reputation for promoting longevity, and acting as a general tonic to strengthen the body.

Cultivation: These pretty plants have been grown as ornamentals. They prefer rich woodland soil, and are grown from seed or root division (ensure each piece has at least one bud).

Polygonum cuspidatum / Japanese Knotweed   Syn *Reynoutria cuspidatum*

Northeast   *Polygonaceae*
This distinctive Japanese alien is becoming increasingly common as an urban weed in both Europe and North America. It is a good wild food, easy to identify and abundant enough to be a pest. It is also a very aggressive plant, which seems able to advance and colonize new ground inexorably.

Caution: The sour flavor is caused by oxalic acid, so use in moderation.

Shoots: The new shoots are gathered in early spring, up until they reach a foot in height, and used as a substitute for Rhubarb in pies, muffins and preserves (the taste is almost identical). Older stems can be eaten until they reach 2 - 3 feet in height, but you have to peel off the outer skin. This leaves a flimsy hollow tube of tender edible material.

Greens: The young leaves have been used as a potherb in Japan, after cooking in a change of water (or cook with milder-flavored greens).

Root: The rhizome is said to be edible when cooked, but not very palatable.

Medicine: All parts of the plant are mildly laxative when eaten, so use in moderation.

Animal food: The seeds are eaten by many birds. The dense stands of foliage provide cover for small animals.

Horticultural uses: Japanese Knotweed was originally introduced as an ornamental, and makes an attractive deciduous screen up to ten feet tall. It is especially handsome when in flower. Unfortunately it is also invasive and hard to eradicate. Prevent it spreading by mowing around it. Eliminate it by digging, or repeated cultivation to exhaust the roots.

If you have the room you could use this species to grow material for the compost pile. Scythe it down a few times each summer to encourage new growth (and slow it down).

Cultivation: Because of its imperialistic tendencies Japanese Knotweed should only be planted in large areas, where it can spread freely. It may be grown from seed, cutting or root division, in any reasonable soil. Be warned that this isn't a plant for the timid or lazy. If you plant it you might regret it.

Related species:
P. alaskanum - **Alaskan Knotweed**
P. alpinum - **Alpine Bistort**
P. sachalinense - **Giant Knotweed**
These species can be used as above.

Polygonum viviparum / Western Bistort
This inconspicuous plant is only really noticeable when flowering. It is often found in abundance in mountain meadows, and is a useful wild food plant.

Greens: The young leaves are quite palatable and may be used in salads, or as a potherb. They are rich in vitamin C.

Seeds: The seeds are edible, the challenge is to find enough to be worthwhile. They are related to Buckwheat and can be used in the same way.

Bulbils: The specific name *viviparum* means "bearing live young", and refers to the bulbils that are often the plants main means of propagation. These can be added to salads.

Roots: The roots were an important food for the Cheyenne, Blackfoot and other Native American tribes, and are pretty good if gathered while dormant. Young roots may be eaten raw, but older ones are better cooked. When baked they have a sweet, nutty flavor. They can also be boiled (frying the boiled roots improves their flavor), sautéed, stir fried or added to soups.

Related species:
P. bistortoides - **American Bistort**
The tuberous roots of this species are usually larger than the above, but can be used in the same ways.

P. hydropiper - **Water Pepper** Syn *Persicaria hydropiper*
Water Pepper is an important culinary herb in Japan, and is widely cultivated there. The seeds are sprouted in soil until a few inches high, like Peppergrass (see *Lepidium*) and used in salads and sushi. The young leaves have been used sparingly to spice up salads or potherbs, though they are quite acrid.

The seed has been used like that of Mustard as a condiment and seasoning.

P. album
P. aviculare - **Smartweed**
P. elliptica
P. persicaria - **Ladys Thumb** Syn *Persicaria vulgaris*
These species can be used like Water Pepper.

P. cilinode - **Fringed Bindweed**
P. convolvolus - **Black Bindweed**
P. scandens - **False Buckwheat**
The seeds of these plants can be ground to flour, and used like those of the related Buckwheat, in baking and pancakes. They are hard to gather in quantity however.

Populus species / Poplars, Aspens, Cottonwoods

Throughout   Populaceae
These fast growing, short-lived pioneer trees colonize open disturbed land. They fulfill an important ecological role in preventing erosion, enriching the soil, and providing shelter for the less hardy trees and shrubs that eventually replace them.

Populus species can be found growing throughout most of the country. The most notable species is probably the Quaking Aspen (*P. tremuloides*), which is the most widespread tree in North America. It grows in cool northern and mountainous areas from Alaska to Labrador to Mexico.

Inner bark: Native Americans ate the sugar-rich inner bark, when food was scarce in late winter and early spring. The bark was peeled from the tree in long strips, and the outer layer was removed to leave the edible inner cambium layer. This was chopped, boiled and eaten, or dried and ground to flour for baking or gruel.

Greens: The new shoots, young leaves and pistillate catkins have also been eaten, but aren't very good.

Medicine: The bark contains salicylic acid, and is used medicinally in the same ways as that of the related Willows (*Salix*).

The aromatic leaf buds of *P. candicans* have been used to make a salve for skin problems, burns and wounds.

Other uses: Native Americans used the long, supple shoots for wigwams and other shelters. Smaller shoots were woven into baskets. The inner bark was used for cordage. The downy seeds have been used for stuffing pillows.

Animal food: These species are important sources of food for many kinds of wildlife, including moose, bear, deer, birds, hare, porcupine and beaver (the inner bark is a favorite food of the latter). The inner bark has also been used to keep domestic livestock alive, when nothing else was available. Bees make propolis from these trees.

Wood: Generally the wood of these species is soft, weak, hard to season and splits easily. However it is often abundant (or all that remains after more valuable woods have been cut), so is used for plywood, crates, matchsticks and fence-posts. It is even used for constructing log cabins and pole buildings, mostly by owner builders who ignore building codes.

Wood Chips: The wood shreds well, so is commonly used for particleboard (perhaps its most important commercial use), wallboard, insulation and packing material. The use of wood chips has now spread beyond particleboard, to structural panels called oriented strand board, and even structural members such as floor joists. The day isn't far off when a whole house can be built using such products (if it isn't already here).

Using chips is a very efficient way to use wood, as the whole tree can be used and there is very little waste. We may soon see coppiced plantations of trees such as these, planted to grow wood chips for building construction.

Carbon sink: There could be another benefit of growing and coppicing trees for wood chips. They could (at least in theory) help to slow global warming caused by the burning of fossil fuels and subsequent buildup of carbon dioxide. Fast growing plantations of coppiced trees absorb a lot more carbon dioxide than mature forests.

Paper: The wood is also widely used as pulpwood for making paper, and some hybrid Poplar plantations are now being planted for paper production.

Chemicals: Distillation of the wood can produce fuel oil, charcoal, ammonia, methanol and many other valuable products. The wood could be fermented to produce alcohol or methane.

Phytoremediation: With their deeply penetrating roots some *Populus* species have the ability to tap into contaminated groundwater and extract it from the ground. In this way they may be of help in cleaning up polluted groundwater. This is a potentially significant future use.

New Crop

Some hybrids of these species are unusually vigorous and grow very rapidly. Some may add up to seven feet in height and three inches in diameter annually, and reach a trunk diameter of sixteen inches in only fourteen years. They are mostly crosses of *P. nigra, P. robusta, P. trichocarpa, P. deltoides* and *P. laevigiata.* These hybrids have a number of potential uses; as sources of wood chips, paper, renewable energy and industrial chemicals.

Coppice: When one of these trees is cut down, it sends up numerous suckers, which grow even faster than the original tree, because they are growing on established roots. This is known as coppicing (see Hazel - *Corylus* for more on this).

For firewood or pulpwood the stems are harvested when from 5 - 20 years old, depending on the rate of growth. Generally it is profitable to wait as long as possible before harvesting, as the trees put on more growth annually as they get larger, for at least the first 20 years or so.

Horticultural uses: The hardiness and rapid growth of these species makes them ideal windbreak and shelterbelt

trees. They have also been used for rejuvenating damaged or eroded soil, and as pioneers for rapid reforestation. Some *Populus* species are resistant to air pollution, but they don't make good street trees, because their roots penetrate and clog drains, and they may heave paved surfaces.

Cultivation: Female Poplars produce an abundance of downy seed, but this is short lived and often infertile, so vegetative propagation is important even in the wild. The plants are easily grown from hardwood cuttings, which are usually about 12 inches long and 1/2 inch thick, though larger ones are sometimes used. They are taken while the trees are dormant. When taking cuttings it is a good practice to make a flat cut on top, and an angle cut on the bottom, so you know which way is up. Planted six inches deep, they usually root in a few weeks.

You only need one cutting of a *Populus* species to become self-sufficient in plants. You can take cuttings from your cutting over the years, and build up a stock of plants of varying ages. The only drawback to this is that the plants will be genetically identical, not only in their vigor, but also in their resistance (or lack of) to disease and other stress.

The plants will tolerate most soils, but grow best on rich, deep, soil with lots of moisture. The hybrids must have good soil for really vigorous growth.

Rooting Hormone: Poplars can be used like the Willows (*Salix*) as a source of a natural "rooting hormone".

Porphyra umbilicalis / **Laver**

Oceans   *Rhodophyta*

Laver is a member of the most important edible seaweed genus. Various *Porphyra* species are cultivated around the globe (notably in Japan), and worldwide production is valued at over a billion dollars annually.

Food: Laver is so important because it is one of the tastiest seaweeds. Clean the fronds by soaking them in fresh water for a couple of hours. They can then be used immediately, or dried for later use (dried fronds turn black). The fronds can be boiled until tender, or added to soups and sauces. In coastal areas of the British Isles Laver was rolled in oatmeal and fried, as a breakfast dish called Laverbread. In Japan it is known as nori, and is very widely used in sushi, sauces, tempura and soups.

Cultivation: *Porphyra* species were traditionally cultivated in Japan by embedding net-covered Bamboo poles into the seabed, and leaving them until the young plants get established on them. They were then moved to less salty water in estuaries, as this produces more tender plants. They were grown in this rather haphazard fashion for centuries because no one knew how they reproduced. This mystery has now been solved, and what was previously thought to be a different species is now known to be the reproductive phase of this plant. Modern Nori growers can now seed their nets with spores, and so get larger crops faster.

These species might profitably be cultivated in this country, if the right locations could be found.

Related species:
P. laciniata
P. miniata – **Red Laver**
P. nereocystis - **Purple Laver**
P. perforata - **Purple Laver**
Used as above.

Portulaca oleracea / **Purslane**

Throughout   *Portulacaceae*

Purslane is native to the warmer parts of Eurasia, but has made itself at home in most countries of the world (including most of North America).

Caution: Purslane is rich in vitamins A and C and iron, and is one of the best plant sources of omega 3 fatty acids. It also contains oxalic acid, so shouldn't be used excessively.

Greens: Purslane is such a good food plant that it is cultivated in many countries. Gather the tender new growing tips by pinching them off the plant. This will encourage the plant to put out more of the same. You can take several harvests from a single plant in the course of a summer without harming it (though as a common weed you may want to harm it).

The slightly sour tips are good raw in sandwiches and salads, or can be boiled as a potherb. In China they are stir fried, added to soup and pickled. If you object to the mucilaginous quality of boiled Purslane, then try frying, or baking the tender tips with egg and breadcrumbs.

Seed: Purslane seed can be ground to flour and used alone, or mixed with equal amount of wheat or other flour, for gruel and baking, It can also be sprouted like Alfalfa. Though the individual seeds are small, a single plant may produce as many as 50,000 of them, so it is possible to accumulate a useful quantity.

There is a useful shortcut to gathering the seeds. The fleshy plants contain enough moisture to flower and set seed after being uprooted. In fact uprooting actually stimulates the plant to produce seed. All you have to do is put the plant tops in a paper bag, and leave them in a warm dry place until they are completely dry. You then simply crush the seed heads and collect the seed.

Medicine: The leaves have been used as a soothing poultice for burns, wounds and sore eyes. When eaten in quantity they are mildly laxative. Apparently they also contain a substance that kills dysentery bacteria.

Cultivation: Purslane has a long history of cultivation in its homeland, and improved varieties are available.

However in this country most gardeners are only interested in eradicating it, the idea of actually planting this vigorous weed sounds downright foolish. There is some justification for this, as it can be a bad weed if it gets out of hand. This is unfortunate though, because Purslane is also a good food crop. It grows well with pretty much no attention, and is as good as any food plant you are likely to buy. In my first garden it took several years of careful neglect before I had enough Purslane growing to satisfy my needs. In later gardens I have come to have a greater appreciation of its weed status.

If you have a vegetable garden and warm summer weather, there is a very good chance you already have Purslane growing as a weed, or soon will have. It appears in disturbed garden soil as if by magic, because the seed may lay dormant in the soil for up to forty years, waiting for suitable growing conditions.

The key to controlling Purslane is not to let it set seed, otherwise a huge bank of seeds will build up in the soil. You can only do this by regular and conscientious weeding. Don't leave the uprooted plants on the soil after weeding, as they will either re-root themselves or set seed (or both).

Purslane is easily grown from seed or cuttings, in full sun, and well-drained soil. The fleshy, moisture filled leaves enable it to thrive with very little water. It can't stand cold weather, and in cool northern areas doesn't even appear as a weed until midsummer.

New crop: Purslane has potential as a commercial food crop, once people find out how good it is. I have seen it for sale at Mexican vegetable stalls at our local flea market. The easiest way to use it would be in mixed salad greens.

Related species:
***P. retusa* - Western Purslane**
Used as above.

Potentilla anserina / Silverweed
North   *Rosaceae*
This attractive little plant gets its common name because the undersides of the leaves have a silver sheen.

Food: The starchy, nutritious roots can be eaten like Carrot, raw or cooked. These can be a substantial food and were important to Native Americans. They dried them in quantity for winter use, and the gathering season was an important event.

The best roots grow in loose sandy soil. Unlike most wild roots, the larger ones are usually better than small

ones, which are often too insubstantial to bother with. They can be used anytime of year, but are best when dormant in fall and winter.

Medicine: An astringent tea of the leaves was drunk to cure diarrhea.

Foot cooler: It is said that people used to line their shoes with the leaves to keep their feet cool.

Horticultural uses: This plant is tasty, nutritious and easily grown, and could be planted as a food crop. It spreads rapidly by means of runners (like Strawberries), and has potential as an edible groundcover.

Cultivation: Silverweed can be grown from seed, or runners, in moist, sandy soil. It prefers cool weather.

Related species:
P. glandulosa
***P. reptans* - Creeping Cinquefoil**
***P. fruticosa* - Shrubby Cinquefoil**
These species don't produce edible roots, though their leaves have been used for tea. The latter is such a favorite forage plant for deer, that it is an indicator of overgrazing (it is one of first plants to disappear on overcrowded range). It is sometimes grown as an ornamental.

P. egedei*- Pacific Cinquefoil**. Syn ***P. pacifica
The roots can be used like those of Silverweed. It is sometimes called Wild Sweet Potato because of the edible root. The plants were so prized by Native Americans for their sweetish flavor that they were sometimes given as gifts.

Proboscidea louisianica / **Unicorn plant**
Syn *Martynia* spp
Southwest   *Martyniaceae*

Pods: The distinctive horned seedpods of this sprawling plant earn it the name Unicorn plant. These are edible for a short time in early summer, when 1 - 2 inches long and still tender. Larger pods become bitter and unpleasant. The pods are washed, scrubbed to remove their hairs and cooked for about 15 minutes, changing the cooking water at least once. The cooked pods can be eaten whole, used to thicken soups, pickled or fried in tempura.

Seed: The nutritious seeds contain 25% protein and 35% oil, and can be eaten after the tough seed coat is removed. Native Americans ate the seed raw, roasted like Sunflower seed, or ground to flour for gruel or baking. The immature seed was eaten whole.

Oil: This can be extracted from the seeds by boiling as for Hickory (*Carya*). The problem is getting enough to make this worthwhile.

Ornament: The pods are frequently used in dried flower arrangements and are sometimes sold for this. Native Americans used the "claws" of the pods as decorations in basket weaving.

Cultivation: This frost tender species is cultivated in much the same way as the Tomato. In the north it is started indoors early and set out after all danger of frost. The first time I planted them they refused to germinate, until I peeled off the hard black seed coats. These had become soft from soaking in water. Filing through the hard dry coat would also work. Unicorn plant needs full sun, rich soil, plenty of water and lots of room to spread, as it can get quite large. It will self-seed if given suitable conditions.

If you ignore their unpleasant smell, the plants are quite attractive, and have been grown purely as ornamentals. Native Americans grew *P. parviflora* as a seed crop, and some of their cultivars are still available.

Related species:
P. annua
P. arenaria
P. parviflora
P. althaefolia - **Desert Unicorn Plant**
Used as above.

Prosopis juliflora / **Mesquite**
Southwest   *Mimosaceae*

The Mesquite was the most important food-producing plant of the lower Sonoran desert. The sweet, nutritious pods were a staple food of almost all Native Americans living in its range, and they often lived among the groves of trees for much of the year. The annual harvest was an important social occasion and a time of feasting. The pods were so important that each family would own gathering rights to their own groves of trees. Another indication of their value is that the Seri people had eight words to describe the pods in various stages of ripeness.

How things have changed, Mesquite is now considered a major pest by ranchers, and is frequently removed to "improve" rangeland. Despite efforts to eradicate it, Mesquite has greatly increased in abundance and range in the past century and now grows over large areas of the southwest. The main reason it has spread is because of cattle ranching. The plant is adapted to distribute its seed by means of large herbivores and cows fill the bill perfectly. These animals eat the sweet nutritious pods and excrete the rock hard seeds on new soil in fresh manure. The seeds actually germinate more readily after the trip through a cow, as it softens the hard seed coat. Overgrazing by livestock has also eliminated its more palatable (and less well-armed) competition, which also helps the Mesquite.

The plant is disliked when it gets too abundant, because it competes for nutrients, and takes large amounts of water from the soil. However it is a source of food and shelter for wildlife, and provides organic matter and nitrogen for the soil.

Mesquite needs a lot of water, which is somewhat surprising considering the dry climate in which it grows. It survives by growing near watercourses, or tapping in to underground sources of water. Its wide spreading root network may go down as much as two hundred feet to seek out water deep underground. In some areas the rapid extraction of groundwater for human development, has lowered the water table to the point where the trees can no longer survive.

Nutrients: The edible part of the Mesquite pod is the sweet middle layer (mesocarp) that makes up about 50% of the pod. This contains about 15% high quality protein, 35% sugar (mainly sucrose) and lots of calcium and iron.

Gathering: The pods ripen in summer and are harvested from July to September. In some years they are produced so abundantly they lie in deep piles under the trees. Their quality varies from tree to tree, so sample the pods from different trees before you gather in quantity. Native Americans were quite choosy, only taking pods from the best trees. The pods can be gathered in quantity quickly; a woman could collect up to 400 pounds of pods in a single day. The sweetest pods are those that have just fallen off the trees.

Sometimes most of the pods in an area will contain the larvae of Bruchid beetles, which didn't deter people in the past, but probably will deter you. If you don't look too closely until the pods are dried and ground to flour, you probably wouldn't know the difference. You can heat, microwave or freeze the pods soon after gathering to kill the insect eggs therein.

Uses: The Spanish name for the plant is Algaroba, the same one they have for the Carob (*Ceratonia siliqua*), because the flavor of their pods is quite similar. The tastiest pods can be chewed straight from the tree, but most types have a bitter aftertaste and aren't that good. Ripe pods can be dried for storage.

The immature pods can be gathered in midsummer while still green and made into a drink, cooked as a vegetable, or eaten raw while hiking to give energy.

Flour: The main use of the pods was to make flour. The ripe, whole pods (with no wormholes) were dried, ground to meal and sifted to remove the fibrous parts (these were soaked in water to extract any remaining sugar and make a tasty drink). Two women could make up to 80 pounds of flour in one day. This was then mixed with water, made into cakes and dried for storage The flour can be mixed with wheat flour for baking bread, muffins and pancakes. Mesquite bread was said to resemble cake or "nice corn bread". The Pima and Cahuilla people made gruel by boiling six parts of salt water, one part corn or wheat flour, and two parts of Mesquite flour. Simmer for 10 minutes.

Syrup: The pods contain so much sugar they can be used to make a palatable syrup with possible commercial potential. This was made by boiling the pods for two hours. The liquid was then strained to remove the fibrous parts and boiled down to syrup.

Seed: These have a very hard seed coat and have been likened to steel ball bearings. It has also been said that they are equally edible. If eaten whole they will pass straight through you practically untouched, though their germination capacity may be enhanced. They also contain digestion inhibitors so shouldn't be eaten raw anyway. The seeds are usually ground to flour and used for baking or gruel.

Flowers: The nectar rich flowers have been added to salads, or eaten as a snack.

Drink: Mesquite pods were used to make tasty drinks in several ways. The simplest way was to mix the flour with water. Another drink can be made by boiling the pods for 20 minutes. The green pods can also be used to make a drink. These beverages were sometimes fermented to make a kind of beer.

A pleasant drink can be made by steeping the ripe seed overnight in cold water, or steeping it in hot water for a few minutes.

Water: Mesquite trees are a pretty reliable indicator of underground water, and wells are sometimes drilled near them.

Medicine: Native Americans made an eyewash from the pods, to soothe eyes irritated by the desert dust, sun and wind.

Fiber: The inner bark was used to make rope, cordage, baskets and even cloth. The small rootlets were used for cordage.

Glue: Resin from the trees was used as glue.

Wood: Mesquite wood is of little commercial value because it is very hard, and the trees are usually small and gnarled. It is occasionally used in cabinetmaking and parquet flooring. It is very durable in the ground and is often used for fence-posts. Native Americans used it to build small log houses.

Firewood: Nowadays the main use of Mesquite wood is for firewood, as it burns very hot. It was widely used by Native Americans and the first European settlers and soldiers. A considerable proportion of the plant may be underground, so after the soldiers had taken the aboveground portion, they would rip the roots from the earth with oxen. The wood was also used in huge quantities for smelting silver and other metal ores.

All of this has its modern equivalent in the sale of small packages of Mesquite wood or charcoal for use on backyard barbecues. It apparently imparts a delicate flavor to the food (along with a healthy dose of smoke carcinogens). I can't help feeling there is something a little sad in little packages of such a wild western wood sitting on a shelf in the supermarket. If you live where the trees grow you can get the same mesquite flavor by throwing a few empty pods on to the barbeque.

Alcohol: The sugary pods could be fermented to produce alcohol, and might be potentially useful as a source of fuel (or intoxication for that matter).

Animal food: The flowers are an important nectar source for bees and the honey they make from them is excellent. The pods provide food for a wide range of animals, both wild and domesticated. They are useful forage for livestock in time of drought.

New crop: As a producer of food and fuel, it has been suggested that the Mesquite could become a valuable new crop for arid areas, especially in third world countries. It is able to fix atmospheric nitrogen by means of root nodules and adds humus, so improves the soil it grows in. Their root network prevents erosion along washes, where flash floods often tear away the banks.

Mesquite sprouts readily from the stump, and could be coppiced as a source of poles, fenceposts or firewood (see *Corylus*). Hedges of the plants have been used to protect cultivated fields from grazing animals.

Fertilizer: The dried ground pods left over from producing food or alcohol could be used as nitrogen rich fertilizer.

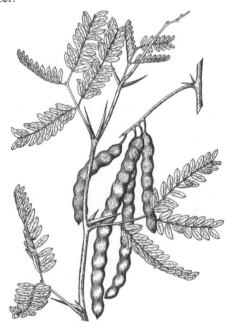

Cultivation: Mesquite seed should be scarified with acid, or nicked with a file, prior to planting, to allow water to penetrate through the tough seed coat and hasten germination. The trees grow in any well-drained soil, and once established they can be hard to eradicate.

In the wild Mesquite is an important nurse tree for Cacti and other desert plants.

Related species:
P. velutina - **Velvet Mesquite**
P. glandulosa - **Honey Mesquite**
These closely related species (sometimes considered merely subspecies of *P. juliflora*) are used in the same ways.

P. pubescens - **Screwbean**
Syn *Strombocarpa pubescens*
This species is less common than the Mesquite, but just as useful. The distinctive yellow spiral pods ripen in late summer, but hang on the trees well into autumn. These pods are even richer in sugar than those of Mesquite and often better flavored. They can be used in the same ways and are often good enough to eat straight from the tree.

Prunus species / Cherries
Throughout   *Rosaceae*
The *Prunus* species in North America can be roughly divided into the Cherries (with round pits) and the Plums (with flattened ones). The genus also includes the Almonds, Apricots and Peaches, but these are not often found growing wild in this country.

Caution: Only the fleshy part of the fruit is edible, the leaves, bark and seeds are quite poisonous. They contain a glycoside called amygdalin, which is converted into cyanide when the plant cell walls are damaged. This is why the foliage may smell of Almonds. The seeds have been responsible for a number of human deaths, while the foliage is a common cause of livestock poisoning. See Flax (*Linum*) for more on cyanide poisoning.

Nutrients: Cherries are not merely a decoration for cocktails, they are a nutritious food, and have helped keep people alive when lost in the wilderness. They contain about 15% carbohydrate, vitamins A and C, and are rich in copper, calcium and potassium. They were an important food for Native Americans on the plains, where they were commonly used to make the staple food *pemmican*.

Gathering: The best time to look for cherries is not in late summer when they are ripe, but in spring when the trees are in conspicuous bloom. You then know exactly where to go when the fruit ripens. The trees may be quite tall, with the fruit up out of reach.

The quality of wild Cherries varies enormously, with every degree of palatability from sweet and delectable, to bitter and inedible, so taste any you find. Make sure they are soft and fully ripe, as even the best won't be very good if unripe.

Uses: The best fruits can be eaten out of hand, or added to cakes, drinks, desserts or soups. They can also be dried for later use, and make a good dried snack. You can dry them whole and remove the pits while you eat, or remove their pits first. The easiest way to extract the seeds is with a Cherry pitter (cooking also helps). For use as a trail food, it might be an advantage to leave the pits in, so you can't eat them so fast.

Native Americans crushed the whole fruits, pits and all, and dried them into small cakes for use in soups and sauces. The fact that the seeds contain toxins wasn't important, as drying and cooking destroys the toxins. The pits are a nutritious food also, as they contain about 30% protein and 40% oil.

Less palatable fruit are improved by cooking. Simply boil, strain out the skins and pits, sweeten and use the puree in pies, preserves, soups and sauces. They are good with apple or other fruits. A few pits may improve the flavor of many Cherry dishes by adding an almond flavor.

Drinks: Sweet Cherries are often used to flavor liqueurs such as brandy or rum (this is why the Black Cherry is sometimes known as Rum Cherry). A good drink can be made by boiling the dried fruit in water. You can also extract the juice as for Grapes (see *Vitis*).

Medicine: The bark of Black Cherry is used in commercial cough syrups as an expectorant, and was once listed in the USP for this. A tea of the bark has been used to soothe sore throats, and apparently was once favored by professional singers to keep their throats in good shape. The inner bark of the Chokecherry was used for diarrhea.

An interesting use for the fruits is to treat the pain of rheumatism and arthritis. Some people claim to have had almost instant relief from these chronic pains, simply by eating the fruits on a daily basis. You do need to eat quite a lot though, at least a half-pound of cherries daily. This is no hardship, and at the very least they would be a tasty and nutritious addition to the diet.

Cherries are often used to mask the unpleasant flavor of other medicines.

Other uses: Native Americans used the inner bark for cordage. A face pack for the skin has been made from the fruits. The pits were used for beads.

Animal food: Cherries are an important food for birds (many gardeners will attest to this), raccoons and numerous rodents. Some eat the flesh, others the seed kernels, and some the whole thing.

Wood: The wood of the Black Cherry is highly prized by cabinetmakers for its beauty and fine grain, and it is presently one of the most valuable and important American hardwoods. Properly seasoned it is very stable, and has been used for scientific and measuring instruments, patternmaking and engraving. Less valuable Cherry species have been used for pulpwood and boxes. Native Americans used Chokecherry wood for bows, spears and digging sticks.

Fuel: Many *Prunus* species are good firewood, burning with a pleasant odor, and giving as much as 20 million Btu per cord.

Cultivation: Cherries can be grown from seed, stratified for three months at forty degrees, though the fruit doesn't come true to type. Selected cultivars are propagated by grafting or budding. The trees are not as productive as their cousins the Plums, and are usually self-infertile, so several varieties must be planted for good fruit set. They can be very pretty when in bloom.

Best species include:
***P. avium* - Sweet Cherry**
***P. cerasus* - Sour Cherry**
These European species are the main progenitors of the cultivated Cherries. They are often found growing wild in this country, either as abandoned orchard trees or as seedling escapes (they are frequently sown by birds). Some bear fruit that is as good as their parents and are very good wild foods.

***P. virginiana* - Chokecherry**
***P. virginiana* ssp *demissa* - Western Chokecherry**
***P. virginiana* ssp *melanocarpa* - Rocky Mountain Cherry**
This is one of the most widely distributed trees in North America, and was an important food source for Native Americans. The fruit aren't really as bad as the common name suggests, though they are improved by cooking. A number of improved cultivars are available. The seed kernels were sometimes eaten, after leaching to remove toxins (see Hollyleaf Cherry (*Laurocerasus*).

***P. serotina* - Black Cherry**
The bitter fruits of the Black Cherry vary considerably from tree to tree and some aren't bad. The wood and the medicinal bark are more important than the fruits.

***P. emarginata* – Bitter Cherry**
I don't believe this species produces useful fruit. I have included it because small quantities of the dried bark and leaves have apparently been smoked as a mild sedative. I am only mentioning this out of scientific interest. I am not suggesting anyone actually try it, as the plant is known to contain cyanide and could be dangerous.

P. besseyi - Sand Cherry
This species is occasionally cultivated for its sweet purple fruits, and improved cultivars are available. It is hardy and drought resistant, and is sometimes used as rootstock for grafting cultivated Cherry varieties.

Prunus species / Plums

Throughout   *Rosaceae*
Much that has been said about the Cherries also applies to their cousins the Plums. In many ways these are even more valuable as food, being sweeter, larger and more nutritious. In some areas the trees become so laden with fruit their branches bend under the weight, and they become a major attraction for wildlife.

Fruit: The sweeter species of Wild Plums are among the best of all wild fruits, and may be used like cultivated plums. They are excellent raw, or cooked in pies, puddings, sauces and preserves. They are easily dried in the sun, or in a 150-degree oven, especially if you remove the pits first. Dried plums can be used in snacks and for baking. They are a good trail food for hikers, eaten alone, or added to energy bars (see *Juglans*).

The sour plums can be sweetened and cooked in pies, preserves and sauces.

Medicine: Plums are not important medicinally, though the fruits are a gentle laxative (of course prunes are famous for this). In excessive amounts the fresh fruits can cause diarrhea. The seeds are poisonous as they contain cyanide.

Cultivation: Propagation and growth requirements are much the same as for Cherries. However the trees are smaller and more productive, so are more useful for small gardens.

Best species include:
P. domestica - Garden Plum
P. institia - Bullace
P. spinosa - Blackthorn, Sloe
These European species were introduced into North America as cultivated varieties of Plums, and can now be found wild in many areas. Unfortunately they have reverted to their wild form, and rarely bear fruit of the same quality as their parents. You may find superior cultivated varieties around abandoned homesteads or orchards.

P. allagheniensis - Allagheny Plum
Good fresh or dried.

P. americana - Wild Plum
This is one of the best native plums, and is used in breeding new plum cultivars. The Wild Plum was encouraged, or even cultivated by Native Americans, as the sweet fruits were an important food.

P. angustifolia - Chickasaw Plum
This southeastern species is often very good. Native Americans probably cultivated it, and it can still be found on the sites of their settlements. European settlers often held plum gathering parties, unconsciously imitating the Native Americans before them, who celebrated the annual plum harvest as an important social event.

P. hortulana – Hog Plum
P. nigra - Canada Plum
P. mexicana Mexican Plum
P. munsonia -Wild Goose Plum
These species often bear fine fruit.

P. subcordata - Sierra Plum
There are several subspecies of Sierra Plums and their quality varies considerably (the best is probably var *kelloggii*). Growing conditions often determine their palatability. In arid dry areas they can be dry and not very good, but in moist areas they can be sweet and succulent. Improved cultivars are available.

P. umbellata - Flatwood Plum
The acid fruits are sometimes sold in markets in the southeast, for use in preserves.

P. maritima - Beach Plum
This coastal species thrives on windswept exposed sites, and often produces an abundance of sour fruit. These are sometimes sweet enough to eat raw, but are most often

sweetened and made into pies and preserves. Beach Plum jelly can often be purchased in tourist shops in coastal New England.

P. armeniaca – Apricot Syn *Armeniaca vulgaris*
The cultivated Apricot is found growing wild in parts of California, and elsewhere. The fruits can be used like domesticated Apricots, though fruit from seedling trees are rarely as good as that from cultivated varieties.

P. persica **– Peach** Syn *Amygdalus persica*
The Peach has been cultivated in North America for centuries and wild trees can often be found, either in abandoned orchards, or as seedlings grown from discarded pits. Unlike many seedling fruits, their quality is often very good, so sample any you find bearing fruit.

P. andersonii **- Desert peach.**
P. fremontii **- Desert Apricot** Syn *P. eriogyna*
The fruits of these species were eaten by Native Americans, but aren't very good.

P. fasciculata **- Desert Almond**
The seed kernels have been cooked and eaten.

Psoreala esculenta / Indian Breadroot
Plains   *Fabaceae*
Indian Breadroot was the most important edible wild root for some plains tribes. These plants were once very abundant on the plains, but (like Native Americans themselves) they have disappeared from much of their range, to be replaced by cultivated crops of wheat and corn. Consequently they are no longer common in many places, and in such cases should not be used.

Nutrients: The nutritious tubers grow from one to three inches in diameter and contain 70% starch, 7% protein and 5% sugar (also vitamin C). The explorer John Coulter lived off Breadroot and Thistle roots for a month, after escaping from his Native American captors.

Gathering: The Turnip-like roots were dug as they went dormant in midsummer, after the flowers have died down, but before the brittle tops disappear. The root is edible all of the time it is dormant, but it is difficult to locate for most of the year. This is because the top breaks off and blows away in the wind (this is how it disperses its seed). It is possible to locate and mark the plants when in flower, and return later to harvest. The roots can be difficult to dig if the soil is hard, so look for those growing in loose soil. The best tool for gathering the roots is the primitive, but effective, digging stick.

Preparation: The tough skin is peeled off and the interior is eaten raw, boiled, baked or roasted. They have a mild Turnip-like flavor, which is why they are also called Indian Turnip.

Native Americans gathered the roots in huge quantities for winter use. They dried the peeled roots in the sun and braided them into strings like Garlic. For faster drying they were sliced into discs. The dried roots were ground to flour for baking bread and biscuits, hence the common name.

Cultivation: This fine wild food has been suggested as a possible commercial food crop for the plains. It has occasionally been cultivated experimentally, but hasn't really caught on because the root takes two to four years to reach useful size from seed, and they are hard to propagate vegetatively. It does have potential for use in home gardens, where everything doesn't have to yield quickly. Native Americans probably encouraged the plants, by scattering the ripe seed from plants they dug. To hasten germination, nick the seed with a file to allow water to penetrate.

Related species:
No species is poisonous, and many have edible roots, though they usually aren't as good as the above. The best include:

P. castoria **- Beavers Psoreala**
P. cuspidata **- Large Bracted Psoreala**
P. epipsila
P. hypogaea **- Small Indian Breadroot**
P. megalantha
P. mephitica

The Uses of Wild Plants

P. macrostachya - Leather Root
P. lanceolata - Lance Leaved Psoreala
Native Americans used the inner bark of these two species as a source of fiber. This was pounded to separate it from the outer bark, and used for cordage, bags and twine.

Psoreala physodes / California Tea
This western species doesn't produce an edible root. It gets its common name because the aromatic leaves were used to make a tea. This was a favorite with Native Americans and the first European settlers.

Pteridium aquilinum / Bracken fern
North   *Polypodiaceae*
The Bracken Fern is found in northern temperate areas all around the globe, and is the commonest Fern in North America. It naturally occurs in open woodland, but in Britain it has become a dominant species on moorland. Moorland is impoverished land that has been deforested and then grazed by domestic livestock, which prevents forest regeneration. Bracken Fern is able to effectively take over large areas of moorland because it is toxic to most grazing animals, spreads aggressively by means of creeping rhizomes, and secretes allelopathic substances that inhibit the growth of most other plants.

Caution: The newly emerged fronds (often called fiddleheads because of their resemblance to the top of a violin) have been cooked and eaten before they uncurl. However this species contains a number of toxins, and is more often included in books on poisonous plants, than in books on edible ones.

In Japan, where fiddleheads are a popular food, they have been linked to stomach and esophageal cancer, when eaten over long periods. The whole plant contains the enzyme thiaminase, which destroys the vitamin thiamine. This can be fatal to animals that eat lots of raw plant, but usually isn't a problem for humans, as cooking inactivates the enzyme. The mature plant may also cause photosensitivity.

Fiddleheads: The above-mentioned problems are reason enough for most people to avoid using Bracken fiddleheads. Not all people though, Euell Gibbons cooked them like Ostrich Fern (*Matteucia*), and considered them to be one of the best of all wild vegetables. I would advise you to avoid them. If you want to eat fiddleheads, I suggest you try those of the similar, but less toxic, Ostrich Fern.

Bedding: The dead fronds have been used to make bedding for humans and animals. They can also be used as emergency blankets, by making a large pile of fronds and burrowing into it. Ideally this should be kept from

moving around in some way, such as by covering with evergreen branches. Never use such a bed near a fire, as the dry dead fronds are highly inflammable (they are often used for starting fires).

Packaging: The dry fronds were once commonly used as packing material for fragile items such as pottery, fruit or tiles.

Chemicals: The fronds were once burned for their ash, which was used for making soap and glass.

Fuel: The roots have been investigated as a possible source of starch for producing fuel alcohol.

Cultivation: Bracken is unpopular with European hill farmers, because it poisons livestock and crowds out more useful forage plants. Actually it is merely colonizing disturbed land prior to the re-establishment of forest, but of course young trees can't get established because livestock eat any succulent growth that isn't thorny or poisonous.

The plant is easily grown by root division, in rich moist soil, and thrives in both sun and shade. Spores can be used for propagation (it is a fern and produces these instead of seed), though this is slow. It can be eradicated by repeated cultivation.

Horticultural uses: Bracken might be planted to provide organic matter and cover for wildlife, but it has several drawbacks. It can be invasive, it dies down to the ground in winter (and becomes quite inflammable), and it gets very large. In good soil it may grow to be ten feet tall.

Fertilizer: The plants are a rich source of potassium, and ash from the burned plants has been used as a potash rich fertilizer. A better idea is to use the green or dry fronds as mulch, green manure or compost. Then one also gets the benefit of their organic matter and nitrogen content, as well as the potassium.

The dried foliage makes a good mulch. Its bulk and insulating properties make it useful for covering tender plants to protect them from frost.

Pueraria lobata / **Kudzu**
Southeast   *Fabaceae*

The notorious Kudzu was one of the first exports from Japan to North America. It was first welcomed as a miracle plant, but became too successful, aggressively out-competing and smothering everything in its path, including native species. It eventually came to dominate over 11,000 square miles of land in the southeastern states. The case of Kudzu is a classic example of what can happen when a plant is introduced into an ideal new habitat, with none of its natural controls.

Kudzu was first planted on a large scale in the 1930s, for its ability to rejuvenate land abused and worn out by the relentless cultivation of corn and cotton (two very demanding crops). This heat and drought resistant vine produces an abundance of nitrogen rich foliage to enrich the soil, and a dense root network that prevents soil erosion by even the heaviest rains. The deeply penetrating roots loosen compacted soil, bring nutrients to the surface, and even fix nitrogen by means of bacteria in root nodules.

By 1945, after a half million acres had been planted to Kudzu, people began to discover just how vigorous, aggressive and fast growing the plant was (it may grow a foot per day). It was not content to stay where it was planted. It first became a problem for foresters as it migrated from untended land. A vine can climb a hundred-foot tree in a single season, and eventually kill it by depriving it of light. The plants spread out in all directions, covering everything in their path, abandoned cars and buildings, power lines, railroad tracks, telephone poles (even occasionally bringing weakened ones down by the sheer weight of foliage).

When Kudzu was originally introduced into North America no-one had any idea that it would behave in this way. In Japan it is not unusually abundant, and presents no problem with excessive growth. In its native land it is kept in check by predators, and by cold weather, which cause it to die back to the ground every winter. In the much milder southeastern states, Kudzu merely sheds its leaves in fall and puts out new ones in spring. It may even send down new roots along the old stems.

Root starch: Kudzu is best known in Japan as the source of the very best food starch. The extraction of this starch from the roots is an important cottage industry in some areas.

Gathering: The tuberous roots can get very large. Those of very old plants have been known to weigh several hundred pounds, though most roots are much smaller. They are dug while dormant in winter, and are located at this time by the dead tops. For obvious reasons it is very important to make sure the tops have died naturally, and haven't been sprayed with toxic herbicides.

Starch preparation: The woody parts of the roots are discarded, and the starchy parts are cleaned, crushed and mixed with water. They are then macerated, agitated and squeezed to free the starch from the fibers, (a blender can be used on a very small scale). The milky, starch filled liquid is then strained to remove the fibers and left to stand until the starch settles out as sediment. The clear water is poured off, and fresh water is added to the sediment, which is then stirred and again left to settle. This step is then repeated for a third time, and after the water is poured off for the last time the starch is allowed to dry (or it may be used immediately for pancakes or bread).

Starch
There is probably more Kudzu growing in the southeastern United States than anywhere else in the world, which presents a great opportunity for some enterprising starch extractors. The roots are free for the taking and there is a ready market for this fine starch. It is presently imported from Japan and sold at premium prices in health food stores.

Uses: In Japan the starch is used like cornstarch, to thicken soups, sauces or drinks, and as a coating for fried foods. It is also added to various herb teas.

Root: The roots have been steamed or boiled for food, but aren't very good, and were considered a famine food.

Greens: The young shoots and leaves can be eaten raw or cooked. The dried powdered leaves have been used as a food supplement like Alfalfa.

Flowers: The flowers have been fried in tempura batter.

Medicine: In Asia Kudzu has long had a reputation as a medicinal plant, and is said to have an alkaline reaction in the body. The leaves were valued as a wound herb, for coughs, flu and headaches. They are also said to contain a substance that lowers blood pressure.

Fiber: In Japan the long slender vines were once an important source of fiber. They were prepared in much the same way as Flax (*Linum*). The fibers were separated into long strands, and used to make cloth and all kinds of cordage from sewing thread to bridge cables. It takes about fifty pounds of plants to produce a pound of fiber. The coarser fibers have been used for basket weaving and "grass cloth" wallpaper.

Other uses: Thrifty Japanese peasants used the fibers left over after starch extraction for binding plaster, stuffing mattresses, and to make fine paper.

Fuel: It has been estimated that a cubic foot of vine could be fermented to produce five cubic feet of methane gas, and a residue that is excellent fertilizer. The root could be used to produce alcohol.

The vigorous deciduous vines can be used to reduce energy consumption in hot climates, by training them to grow over roofs and windows. The thick blanket of foliage can reduce interior temperatures considerably.

Animal food: The foliage is as nutritious as Alfalfa, but causes fewer digestive problems. When grown as a fodder crop it only produces about one fourth as much as corn, but it builds up the soil rather than exhausting it. The flowers are a valuable source of nectar for bees and other insects.

Horticultural uses: Kudzu has so many virtues that some people are starting to change their minds about it once again. If properly looked after it need not present a problem, it only gets out of hand when it left to its own devices. It can be kept under control by grazing, repeated mowing or by digging the roots for food use. It can be grown in tubs if you really don't trust it.

The plant was first introduced to North America over 100 years ago as an ornamental, as it can be trained to make an attractive deciduous screen. It has occasionally been cultivated for its edible roots.

Fertilizer: Kudzu has also been grown as a drought resistant cover crop, to improve the soil. It is said that in fields where Kudzu has grown for three years, improved yields may be obtained for the next ten.

The abundant organic matter is good for mulch, or as compost material.

Caution: Most people still advise against planting Kudzu because of its imperialistic tendencies. A few people actually recoil in horror at the very thought.

Cultivation: Considering the plants reputation for vigor, it is somewhat ironic that Kudzu isn't always easy to get established. It may be grown from seed (nick the hard seed coat and soak overnight in water) or division when dormant. If you are harvesting a root, cut off the stem end and re-plant it. Kudzu can grow almost anywhere, but does best on rich soil.

Pyrus communis / Wild Pear
Escape   *Rosaceae*

The Pear isn't native but is commonly found as an escape, or a relic of cultivation. I have a neglected pear tree at the edge of my property that must have been planted by someone. Unfortunately it is covered in Poison Oak and so must remain neglected.

Most of what I have written about the uses and cultivation of Apples applies equally to their cousin the Pear (the Apple is often included in the *Pyrus* genus). As with Apple, the fruit of seedling trees are usually inferior to their cultivated parents, though it is worth sampling any you find. They might well be abandoned cultivars. Pears vary a lot anyway, and most need ripening off the tree to be really good. Do this by wrapping in paper and keeping in the dark for two weeks.

Quercus species / Oaks
Throughout   *Fagaceae*

Today the Oaks are best known for their strong, attractive wood (or as the best firewood), but for most of human history they have been far more important as a source of food. Acorns (Oak seeds) have been called the ancestral food for much of humanity, and have been a primary source of food for humans almost everywhere they grow; in America, Asia, Africa and Europe.

Many Native American tribes used acorns for food, but they are probably most associated with those in California. An indication of their importance to these people was the fact that families commonly held ancestral gathering rights to certain groves of trees. The acorn harvest was a major annual event in their lives, and (when the harvest was good) a time for celebration, feasting and dancing (even the men helped gather them). In some places one can still find mortar holes in large rocks, used by generations of women to grind their acorns. These stone mortars were too heavy to move around, so there were permanent ones at each campsite.

Nutrients: Leached acorns contain from 5 - 20% fat, 2 - 5% protein, 50 - 70% carbohydrate and lots of minerals. The unleached nuts are inedible because they contain up to 6% percent tannin. This is quite toxic if ingested in quantity and can damage the liver.

Food: One might imagine that acorns were a subsistence food, eaten out of necessity, and not very palatable, but this would be quite wrong. Certainly they don't taste very good in their raw state, but properly prepared acorns are a wholesome, if somewhat bland, food.

Gathering: In a good year a single Oak tree may give several bushels of acorns and in early autumn it is often possible to gather hundreds of pounds of food in a single day. Watch out for acorns with holes in the shells, as these contain insect larvae and should be discarded. There is an easy test to see if acorns are wholesome, just put them in water. The good ones will sink, the bad ones will float.

Where sweet and bitter acorns grow together they should be gathered separately. Don't mix them up, as they need different degrees of leaching. You might think its only worth gathering the low tannin White Oaks, as they need less leaching, but Native Americans often preferred the flavor of the Red Oaks.

You shouldn't feel guilty about destroying all those potential Oak trees. The tree produces far more seeds than it needs to reproduce itself, and at best only one in a thousand has any chance of becoming a new tree. If you do feel bad, you could plant a few of the very best acorns in a suitable spot.

Storage: Prepared acorn meal can be dried and stored, but it tastes much better when fresh, so usually only small amounts were ground and leached at one time. The tannin in the whole acorns helps preserve them and deters insects such as weevils. For storage they were dried in the sun, which also kills them so they don't germinate. In California they were often stored in granaries on stilts (to deter rodents), often with wood ashes or insect repellant herbs such as Mugwort or Sagebrush.

Preparation: Like their cousins the Chestnuts, acorns have a tough leathery skin rather than a hard shell. This was be removed from the dried acorns by cracking them between two rocks. You can also soak them overnight, which causes them to swell, soften and split. The easiest way to split them is with a pair of pruning shears. Removing the kernels from the shells is a rather tedious job, so it was often given to children and old people. The kernels can be leached whole, but the process is speeded up by first grinding them to meal. The easiest way to do this is with a blender.

Leaching: Though some acorns are sweet without any preparation, most need leaching to remove their tannin. There are a number of ways to do this.

1) The simplest method of leaching is to bury them in the ground over winter. By spring they should be black, but quite palatable. Native Americans dried, or roasted, them first, to kill the seeds so they wouldn't sprout.

2) Another easy method is to put the whole kernels or acorn meal (faster) in a bag and leave it in running water (or under a dripping tap). Squeeze the bag occasionally to hasten leaching, and in a few days (the exact number depends on the type of acorns) they should be sweet and palatable.

3) A quicker leaching method is to build a leaching apparatus, consisting of a piece of cloth forming a depression on top of a framework of twigs (or a colander). A half-inch thick paste of ground acorns was spread on the cloth and hot water was repeatedly poured on the meal for 2 - 3 hours, until it was sweet. Cold water can also be used, though this takes longer.

4) An even faster method is to boil the acorn meal in water, changing the water every time it turns dark brown. When the water no longer turns brown they are ready. An alternative is to repeatedly dip a bag of acorn meal into clean hot water. A recent innovation is to put the kernels in the blender with hot water and blend. Then drain, squeeze and add more water, repeating as necessary until the water is clear.

Use: Acorn mush, made by boiling the leached meal, was the staple food of many tribes. It swells up considerably with cooking, so that a quart of meal may yield five quarts of mush. It is quite bland, so they often added berries, ground seeds and nuts for additional flavor.

The prepared meal was also used to thicken soup, make tortillas. and to bake bread. Bread was made by mixing the meal with water, and forming it into little cakes, which were dried in the sun. It could also be made by baking the dough overnight in a fire pit (see *Camassia*). Pit baked bread was said to be sweet and dark brown, with excellent flavor and keeping qualities. John Muir often carried acorn bread on his treks, and claimed it gave more strength than wheat bread.

The leached whole nuts can be used in breads, cookies, trail mixes, roasted and cereals. The leached meal can be mixed with an equal amount of wheat flour for baking muffins, bread and pancakes.

New Crop

Today the Oaks are almost totally ignored as a food resource, but they could become important once again. They are probably the most valuable wild food of the northern Temperate Zone. It has been said that the Oaks produce more nuts annually than all other wild and cultivated nut trees combined. It is somewhat strange that we go to exotic distant lands to find Amaranth, Tef, Quinoa and Spirulina, while ignoring such valuable native plants sitting in our back yards. I think acorn flour has the flavor and nutritional value to be a viable commercial food product. Here is a good opportunity for some enterprising individuals to produce acorn flour, breads, muffins, pancake mix and cereals.

Oil: Some tribes apparently extracted oil from the acorns (they contain about 20% fat), by boiling and skimming as for Hickory (See *Carya*).

Medicine: An astringent decoction of Oak bark has been used as a douche, enema, gargle and to wash smelly feet. It is emetic so is not taken internally.

Native Americans used the mold that grew on old acorn mush to treat wounds and open sores. This sounds a lot like an antibiotic to me.

Tannin: Oak bark has long been an important source of tannin for tanning leather. In Britain this was one of the main products of Oak coppice. The tannin from an acorn food processing plant might be sold for this purpose. It has been said that the acorns with a high tannin content might be preferred by such enterprises, because the leached tannin is a valuable commodity in its own right.

Animal food: Oak trees provide food and shelter for innumerable creatures; insects, wild turkeys, raccoons, woodpeckers, jays, many rodents, peccaries, deer and bears. The acorn crop is an important factor in determining the population levels of many of these animals. Acorns are also valuable feed for livestock, and Europeans have allowed cattle and pigs to forage in Oak woods for centuries.

Wood: The Oak genus supplies more hardwood lumber than any other, though the quality of wood varies enormously with the various species. Quite a few species tend to have short trunks and gnarled branches and are useless as lumber.

Hardwood

The White Oak (*Q. alba*) is one of the best North American hardwoods. It has an unsurpassed combination of toughness, durability, hardness and ease of working, and is widely used for cabinetmaking, flooring, veneer, paneling and millwork. In earlier times it was also the first choice for building construction. Unlike most other Oaks, White Oak wood is non-porous, and was prized for whiskey barrels, shipbuilding, roof shingles and siding.

Coppice: Oak sprouts readily from the stump, and in Europe the trees were once widely coppiced for poles, fenceposts, basket materials, tanbark, charcoal and firewood (for more on coppicing see Hazel - *Corylus*).

Baskets: White Oak splits were a favorite material for making baskets. Saplings up to six inches in diameter were cut in spring or summer, trimmed to length and then split into strips of the desired width. These strips were split along the growth rings to make thin supple splits, ideal for weaving baskets.

Fuel: The Oaks are the most important firewood trees in North America, as they are excellent fuel, giving from 22 - 27 million Btu per cord, and are widely available. I mentioned timber rustling under Walnut (*Juglans*), but most timber rustling is of Oak, cut for firewood. In California even the legal cutting of the slow growing native Oaks is a problem, and native Oak woodlands are shrinking rapidly in many areas. Part of the solution to this problem could be Oak fuel wood plantations, as the trees coppice well.

Ink: Oak galls (swellings caused by insect larvae) were used for making ink, notably that used for printing money.

Propagation: Oaks are easily grown from seed. Select ripe acorns from the most suitable parent trees and plant immediately under a mulch, with protection from rodents. Acorns die if they dry out, so keep them moist. You can plant them in containers, for planting out at a later date. The seeds naturally germinate almost as soon as they fall to the ground, their strategy being to use up their food reserves up as quickly as possible, and so reduce their attractiveness as a food source. Seedlings are often abundant under Oak trees, and these can be transplanted successfully when very young. There are species of Oak for all soil types and growing conditions.

Fertilizer: Chopped Oak leaves (run them over with a power lawnmower to shred them) are invaluable as a soil building mulch or soil amendment. Sifted leaf mold from the forest is often used in potting soils, or for mulch. Contrary to popular belief Oak leaves don't acidify the soil very much, though you might want to add lime if your soil is already acid.

New crops: Oaks improve the soil, encourage wildlife and provide timber, fuel, fodder, fertilizer and tannin, as well as an edible crop. Such useful trees could be an important component of a future farm, which relies on a mix of trees, shrubs, herbs and grasses, rather than a single species monoculture. Some of the best food species are adapted to hot arid climates, and could be potentially valuable as multi-purpose crops for third world countries. There are already a number of improved cultivars, that bear sweet acorns with a low tannin content (notably of *Q. alba* and *Q. macrocarpa*).

Species include:
These trees are divided into two groups, the White Oaks and the Red Oaks. Species in each group may hybridize, in which case it may not be so easy to tell which species you have. Fortunately this doesn't matter, as any acorns can be eaten if leached properly.

White Oaks:
These species are distinguished by the rounded lobes on their leaves. They take only one year to produce acorns, and generally produce the sweetest types. A few species produce acorns that can be eaten without any leaching at all. The best species include:

Q. alba - **White Oak**
Q. douglasii - **Blue Oak**
Q. dumosa - **California Scrub Oak**
Q. emoryi - **Emory Oak**
Q. gambelii - **Gambel's Oak**
Q. prinus - **Chestnut Oak**
Q. macrocarpa - **Bur Oak**
Q. michauxii - **Swamp Chestnut Oak**

Q. lobata - **California White Oak**
This big tree can be very productive (one very large tree was observed to yield a ton of acorns), and its large acorns are of high quality. Consequently it was one of the most important Oaks to Native Americans. At least one improved cultivar is available (Ashworth).

Red Oaks
These species can be identified by their pointed leaf lobes. They take two years to form their acorns, and these contain a lot of tannin. Some bitter ones contain so much tannin as to be quite toxic. One benefit of a high tannin content is that they stay wholesome for a longer period. The best species include:

Q. agrifolia - **Coast Live Oak**
Q. kellogii - **California Black Oak**
These are two of the best tasting and most nutritious Acorns, and were among the most important species for Native Americans

Q. chrysolepis - **Canyon Live Oak**
Q. rubra - **Northern red Oak**
Q. wislizenii - **Interior Live Oak**

Rhamnus purshiana / Cascara Sagrada
Northwest   *Rhamnaceae*
The bark of this northwestern shrub contains a powerful purgative, and is an ingredient in many commercial laxatives. Five million pounds of bark is gathered from the wild annually for sale to drug companies. This has resulted in over-harvesting in many areas, so the plants are no longer as common as they once were.

Fruit: The plant is of very limited use as food. The red berries are edible in small quantities and were eaten by Native Americans. However they may turn your skin red, an apparently harmless, if somewhat alarming, effect.

Cultivation: Cascara is now cultivated commercially on a small scale. It can be propagated from seed or semi-ripe cuttings, and prefers moist woodland soil.

Medicine
The common name means Sacred Bark in Spanish and was given for its powerful medicinal properties. The bark must be aged for at least a year before use as a laxative, otherwise it is also strongly emetic. It is usually prepared by steeping the bark overnight in cold water, or infusing in hot water. The laxative effect is due to the arthraquinone glycosides, which stimulate the intestines. This is not really a substitute for a diet rich in fiber. A weaker tea is said to stimulate the appetite and act as a general tonic.

Related species include:
R. caroliniana - **Carolina Buckthorn**
R. crocea - **Hollyleaf Buckthorn**
These two species produce edible (but mildly laxative) berries. No other species produce edible berries.

R. frangula - **Glossy Buckthorn**
R. cathartica - **European Buckthorn**
R. californica - **Coffee Berry**
The bark of these species is used as a purgative as above. The seeds of the latter species have been roasted and drunk as a coffee substitute.

Rhodymenia palmata / **Dulse**

Syn *Palmaria palmata*

Both coasts   *Rhodophyta*

This is one of the most commonly eaten seaweeds. It is almost always found underwater, so must be gathered with a hooked stick or by diving. The fronds are at their best in spring.

The fronds are rubbery and tough when fresh, so are usually dried before use. The dried fronds are crumbled and used as a salt substitute (good on popcorn). They are also used in sauces, soup, baked in bread, fried in tempura and toasted. It is a source of carragheenan (see *Chondrus*). The natives of Kamchatka used to ferment the fronds to make an alcoholic drink.

Chewing gum: Dulse isn't chewing gum, but it was chewed like it. In Europe it was popular long before chewing gum was invented. It gets sweeter the longer it is chewed, because the saliva turns its starch into sugar.

Medicine: Seafaring people believed chewing Dulse could help prevent or cure seasickness. Dulse tea with lemon and honey was used for colds.

Rhus typhina / **Staghorn Sumac**

Throughout   *Anacardiaceae*

Caution: This species is a relative of Poison Ivy (*Toxicodendron*), and a few unfortunate people develop a rash after touching it.

Sumac lemonade

The fruits of this familiar shrub contain sour tasting malic acid, and can be used to make a kind of "lemonade" (Sumac-ade). The clusters of berries are gathered in mid-to-late summer, as soon as they are ripe (the earlier the better, as rain washes out the acid, and the flavor). Strip the smaller clusters from the main branch (these tend to have the best flavor) and use immediately, or dry them for later use.

Bruise the berry clusters, and steep them in cold water for a few minutes, to allow the flavor to come out. Don't leave them too long, or heat the water to hasten the process, as this will release tannins and spoils the flavor. Strain the liquid to remove any of the tiny, irritating hairs and other debris, sweeten as required and drink hot or cold.

If you keep adding fresh clusters of berries to the water (remove the old ones) you can make it almost as sour as lemon juice, and use it instead of lemon juice in salad dressings.

Seed: The seeds are quite nutritious, containing about 20% carbohydrate and 5% protein, but are covered in irritating hairs that shouldn't be eaten. Native Americans singed the hairs off the berries, and ground them to meal. This was used for drinks, baking (often mixed with cornmeal), or it was roasted and used like coffee. The fruits of some other species can be used in the same ways (notably *R. trilobata* and *R. ovata*).

Medicine: A decoction of the fruits, bark or leaves is rich in tannin, and has been used as an astringent for diarrhea, sore throats, urinary problems and bleeding. It is sometimes used to treat the rash caused by Poison Ivy.

Basket weaving: Many *Rhus* species have been used for basket weaving. The stems were split and soaked in water before use, to make them supple.

Other uses: The dried leaves have been smoked.

Cultivation: This handsome shrub is often grown as an ornamental. It is a typical pioneer species, fairly short lived, drought tolerant, fast growing, hardy, and able to thrive on poor soil. Most *Rhus* species are grown from root cuttings or ripe seed. The latter should be sown immediately, or scarified to remove the hard seed coat.

Sumac can be hard to eliminate once it is established. The best way to remove them is by shading them out with taller plants. Old plants can be rejuvenated by cutting them down to the ground, or by controlled burning.

Horticultural uses: Sumac has a fast spreading root network, which makes it useful for preventing erosion on disturbed sites. It also beautifies such places, acts as a nurse tree for less hardy plants, and provides cover and food for wildlife.

Related species include:
R. canadensis - **Fragrant Sumac**
R. copallina - **Shining Sumac**
R. glabra - **Smooth Sumac**
These eastern species can be used as above. The Smooth Sumac has been studied as a possible commercial source of useful tannins and polyphenols.

R. integrifolia - **Lemonade Sumac**
This species gets its name because of its use as a drink.

R. microphylla - **Desert Sumac**
R. ovata - **Sugar Sumac**
R. trilobata - **Squaw Bush**
These western species can be used as above. Squaw Bush was valued by the Navajo for basket weaving.

Ribes species / Currants

Throughout   Saxifragaceae
There are many native Currants in North America, and a few locally naturalized aliens. With a few exceptions (see below), they are either edible or harmless, so experiment with any you find. The difference between the Currants and the Gooseberries is that the former plants are smooth, while the latter have spines or bristles.

Ribes species are the alternate host for the White Pine Blister Rust (*Cronartium ribicola*) and consequently they may be uncommon in commercial Pine growing areas. As many as one and a half billion plants may have been destroyed over the years, to prevent the spread of this introduced disease However such eradication programs are not 100% successful, as the fruits are a favorite food for birds. This makes them very mobile and any plants that are overlooked can soon re-seed an area.
Interestingly it has been found that in many areas where the plants are left alone (such as in National Parks) there still remain healthy populations of White Pines.

Nutrients: The nutritious fruits contain up to 13% sugar, lots of calcium, copper, iron, potassium, pectin and vitamins A and C. The European Blackcurrant (*R. nigrum*) is one of the richest sources of vitamin C of all common fruits. It is also very rich in anti-oxidants.

Fruit: The palatability of the fruit varies considerably, some species can be very good, others are seedy and tasteless. You can sometimes gather the fruits in quantity by laying sheets under the shrubs and shaking the branches. Often the stalks must be removed from the berries individually, which is a lot of work.

The best tasting fruits can be eaten out of hand, or used raw in fruit salads. They should probably be used raw in moderation, as a few species may be emetic if eaten in quantity. Most Currants taste better cooked anyway, and can be very good in preserves, breads, muffins and pies. They are sometimes dried for later use.

Shoots: in spring the newly emerged leaf shoots can be eaten raw or cooked.

Flowers: The aromatic flowers have been used in add color to salads. Some kinds are full of sweet nectar.

Drink: The fresh or dried leaves can be used for tea by infusing them in boiling water for five minutes. Blackcurrant juice is a popular children's drink in Europe, and the concentrate is widely available commercially.

Medicine: The fruits are very rich in vitamin C and have long been used to treat scurvy. Their demulcent properties make them useful in treating coughs and sore throats. The leaves have been used as a diuretic.

European Blackcurrant seeds contain gamma linolenic acid, a nutrient that gives Evening Primrose oil its special value. I don't know whether any native species contain it.

Cultivation: In the cooler parts of Europe the fruits are widely grown as soft fruits, but in this country Pines are often more important, and it may be illegal to grow or ship them in certain areas. Fortunately Rust resistant varieties are now available, and these are becoming more popular in this country.

These hardy species are easily propagated from hardwood cuttings taken in fall, but they can also be grown from seed, tip or mound layering. They thrive in rich, moist, shady, well-drained soil. Many improved cultivars exist, including some delicious hybrids of Blackcurrant and Gooseberry. These are perfectly suited to growing in a forest garden.

The best species include:
R. americanum - **American Blackcurrant**
R. aureum - **Golden Currant**
R. petiolaria - **Blackcurrant**
All of these species are good.

R. nigrum - **European Blackcurrant**
This is perhaps the best all around Currant species, but is rare in this country. The best jam I ever tasted was made from this species.

Ribes odoratum - **Missouri Currant**
This species is good enough to have been domesticated for its tasty fruit, and several improved cultivars are available. With its scented yellow flowers and attractive foliage it is sometimes grown purely as an ornamental. It also makes a good hedge plant.

Caution:
***R. cereum* - Wax Currant**
***R. viscossimum* - Sticky Currant**
These species are emetic if eaten in quantity.

Ribes species / Gooseberries

Throughout
These small shrubs are often formidably spiny, to the point where even the fruits have spines. The fruits are succulent and often quite delicious. You know they are good if you find yourself gathering such fruit with bare hands – it can be painful. Fortunately the spines disappear with cooking.

The berries can be used in much the same ways as the Currants and are often better flavored. They can be used to make one of the best fruit pies.

Cultivation: Cultivation is much the same as for their cousins the Currants, Gooseberries are much more popular in Europe than in America, and many improved varieties are available there. The thorny plants are a useful addition to hedgerows.

Best species include:
***R. cyanosbati* - Pasture Gooseberry**
***R. grossularia* - Garden Gooseberry**
***R. roezli* - Sierra Gooseberry**

Robinia pseudoacacia / Black Locust

East   *Fabaceae*
Flowers: Almost all parts of the Black Locust are poisonous, because they contain a toxic alkaloid called robin. The only exceptions are the fragrant flowers, which are good raw in ice cream, drinks and salads, or fried in tempura batter.

Seeds: The beans contain only a small amount of toxin, and were cooked and eaten by Native Americans, usually in winter when other foods were scarce. This doesn't mean this is a good idea though, there have been some cases of poisoning from eating them. The beans were soaked overnight in water, and then cooked like dry beans for several hours until tender. The immature beans were sometimes cooked for 30 minutes and eaten like green beans.

Paper: These fast growing trees have been used for pulpwood, and they might be grown specifically for this.

Animal food: The flowers are an important source of nectar for bees. The green branches have been used for animal feed, and are said to be similar to Alfalfa in nutritional value.

Wood
The stiff, strong wood is highly durable, as it contains flavinoids that prevent decay. It's durability once made it important for shipbuilding, and it was exported to England for this. Presently it is most often used for outdoor purposes where rot-resistance is important, especially fence-posts. Locust posts are said to outlast almost all others and supposedly 100-year-old fence-posts have been sold for re-use. Native Americans used the wood for making bows.

Fuel: The wood is excellent firewood, giving about 26 million Btu per cord.

Crop Use: Despite its fine qualities Black Locust isn't an important lumber species in its native range, because it is vulnerable to attack by the Locust Borer (*Megacyllene robiniae*). Some strains of the trees have considerable resistance to this pest and there is hope that these might be profitably cultivated.

The tree has tremendous potential for cultivation in other areas, out of the range of the Borer. It is already cultivated as a crop in parts of Europe. It is an exceptionally good candidate for use in plantations (See *Populus*) for energy, paper, fence-posts or poles. It is widely adaptable, fast growing, fixes nitrogen, tolerates poor soil, and is drought and cold tolerant. Its thin lacy foliage allows a lot of sunlight to penetrate, enabling other plants to grow underneath it. It can be coppiced, but rather than sprouting from the stump (or stool) it more often sends up suckers.

Propagation: Black Locust can be grown from root cuttings or suckers. Special varieties can be propagated by whip grafting. Seed can also be used, and may remain viable for 15 years. The tree will grow in most soil types, even saline ones. Young trees are very vigorous and may grow 4 - 6 feet a year.

Horticultural uses: Nodules on the roots of the Black Locust are host to nitrogen fixing bacteria, so the tree enriches the soil in which it grows. For this reason it is highly prized as a soil builder to reclaim damaged or eroded land. The trees are also widely used for controlling erosion on steep slopes, and for reforestation. It also makes a good hedge plant and can provide high nitrogen organic matter for compost piles. It is a popular ornamental in Europe under the name False Acacia.

Related species:
R. neomexicana - **New Mexico Locust**
This western species is used as above. The flowers and pods were commonly eaten by the Apache people.

Rosa species / Wild Roses

Throughout   *Rosaceae*
Roses are best known as garden flowers, but there are wild species growing all over the country. Wild and cultivated Roses have a very long history of human use, for food, drink, perfume and ornament.

Nutrients: The fruits, commonly known as Rose hips, are so rich in vitamin C they are sometimes used as a commercial source. A cup of Rose Hip tea may contain as much vitamin C as six oranges. They are also rich in vitamin A, calcium, iron and phosphorus. The seeds contain vitamin E.

Gathering: The ripe fruits remain on the bushes for a long time, so you might well see old fruit still on the shrubs, when the next years hips are ripening. Their size and quality varies a lot, so you should try any ripe ones you find. Some are as small as peas, others as big as plums.

Uses: Prepare the hips by splitting them open and scooping out the seeds and tiny irritating hairs (ideally these shouldn't be eaten). The raw hips have a pleasant Apple flavor and are quite good. They can be chopped into salads (both fruit or green).

The Hips are often cooked to make preserves, syrup and sauces. Rose Hip syrup was widely used in Britain during World War Two, as a vitamin C supplement for children. One problem with such prepared foods is that the vitamin C breaks down quite rapidly, in only six months 50% of it may have disappeared.

The dried fruits can be added to cakes, cereals and trail mix. They may be used whole or ground to paste.

Drink: The most popular use of the hips is to make a tasty tea. Steep the fresh, or dried, hips in boiling water until they reach the desired strength, or simmer them for a few minutes. Don't throw the hips away after making one cup of tea, re-use them until their strength weakens. They are also good for sun tea.

Greens: The young leaf shoots can be added to salads.

Flowers: Rose petals are an aromatic addition to salads, sandwiches and pancakes, and have even been used to make uncooked jam. Collect them as they fall from the flowers. If you take the petals too early, the flowers won't be fertilized and won't produce fruit. The unopened flower buds have been pickled.

Medicine: The medicinal value of Rose hips is chiefly due to their high content of vitamin C. They have been used to treat scurvy, purify the blood, eliminate toxins and increase resistance to disease. The petals are said to benefit the intestinal flora. Rosewater makes a soothing eyewash.

Perfume
One of the best-loved characteristics of Roses is their scent, and Rose oil has long been prized as one of the finest and most expensive perfumes. It is expensive because as many as 250 pounds of petals must be distilled to produce an ounce of oil (known as Attar of Roses). The pure oil is too overpoweringly fragrant to be used by itself, so is blended with other oils, fixatives and alcohol to make perfume. The Damask Rose (*R. damascena*) is the most important commercial source of Rose oil.

The Uses of Wild Plants

The easy way to get the scent of Roses is by enfleurage, a simple procedure that consists of steeping the petals in oil until it picks up their scent. Pack a jar with petals and fill it to the top with sweet odorless vegetable oil. Leave this for about a month, then squeeze the oil from the petals, refill the jar with fresh petals and put the oil back in. Leave for another month and then again squeeze out the oil. This oil can then be used as perfume, alone or mixed with other oils.

Another way to get perfume is to macerate the petals in a solvent such as alcohol, then strain out the petals and evaporate off the solvent (don't use an open flame, this would be very dangerous). This leaves a strongly perfumed oily substance.

Rose petals are a basic ingredient in potpourri.

Cosmetics: Rosewater is made by distilling the petals in water. One pound of petals in a quart of water will produce about one cup of Rosewater. This is used for perfume, skin lotion and eyewash. The petals can also be used as a face pack to improve the complexion.

Rosaries: Rose petals were used to make the beads known as rosaries (hence the name). To make them simply crush the petals to paste, roll them into balls, thread on a string and leave to dry.

Cultivation: Wild Roses are generally fairly easy to grow and species exist for almost all soils and climates. They can be grown from ripe seed, sown immediately, or stratified at forty degrees for three months. Layering, tip layering and hardwood cuttings (taken early summer) also work well. Generally they prefer full sun, and need little care once established.

Horticultural uses: Roses come in many forms and have numerous landscaping uses. The larger ones make fine hedge plants, their stout thorns making them almost as impenetrable as barbed wire. They also provide food and refuge for wildlife. The climbing types make good ornamentals, while sprawling ones prevent erosion. All seem to attract beneficial birds and insects to the garden, as well as a few pests.

Some species do so well that they can become a nuisance. For example the Japanese Rose (*R. multiflora*) is a serious pest in parts of the East, as it crowds out native species.

Useful species include:
R. rugosa - Wrinkled Rose
This cultivated Asian species is naturalized in many areas. This is fortunate for the wild food gatherer, as its hips are among the largest, tastiest and richest in vitamin C. It is very tolerant of saline soils and is often found on (or near) beaches. It is a good windbreak plant for such areas. This is an amazingly vigorous and tenacious plant and quite hard to kill. There are even improved cultivars available, bred specifically for their edible hips.

Rubus species / Blackberries

Throughout   Rosaceae

What can you say about Blackberries? Incredibly vigorous and productive, they are a symbol of natures potential abundance. They are the most widely used wild fruits, and are still commonly gathered, even in cities (they are the only wild food many people gather). They were even more important to Native Americans, and families often held gathering rights to certain areas. On a good day a woman might gather a hundred pounds of the fruit. This could sometimes be hazardous, because Grizzly Bears often held gathering rights to those same areas.

There are no poisonous *Rubus* species, so you can use any you find that are worth gathering. This is fortunate as this is a confusing genus, with many similar species and hybrids between them. The genus can be roughly divided into two groups, the Blackberries and Raspberries. The only relevant difference for us is that the central core stays with a Blackberry when picked, whereas the core of the Raspberry stays on the bush, leaving a hollow fruit.

Fruit gathering: The Blackberries are a group of plants that have actually benefited from destructive human activities. They are pioneer species, and can be found in almost any open disturbed areas; waste ground, roadsides, hedges, and burned or logged areas. In a good season the fruits can be astonishingly abundant, almost coloring the bushes purple. This is a great plant to introduce children to wild food gathering, as it's so easy to gather the tasty fruits (so easy my dog would gather them for herself) and you can gather a lot of delicious fruit in a short time.

It's a good idea to wear tough old clothes while gathering Blackberries, as it's easy to tear your clothes on the spiny canes. Serious gatherers often carry a hooked stick to reach the inaccessible branches that always seem to have the best fruit. They also carry a picking can, which is simply a container with a wire loop attached to the rim. This is hung around you neck to leave your hands free for gathering and avoiding prickles. When full it is unloaded into a larger receptacle. Some people lay a board into the middle of a thicket, to allow them to walk right in and pick the most inaccessible berries.

Fruit uses: I used to think of Blackberries as slightly inferior to their cousins the Raspberries, but more valuable because they are more widely available and abundant. I changed my mind when I gathered them in northern California, where the luscious fruits, warmed in the sun, were up to two inches long, and as sweet, aromatic and delicious as any wild fruit I have ever eaten.

Blackberry junket
This is as simple a dessert as it is possible to make. Put the sweetest, ripest Blackberries you can find though a juicer, then leave the juice to sit for a few hours until it thickens and sets. It can then be eaten with shortcake and ice cream or whipped cream.

Almost all Blackberries are tasty enough to be eaten raw, though some are better than others. The best should be eaten out of hand, and can't be improved upon. Other types may be improved by cooking in pies and preserves. They are often cooked with other fruits such as apples. Native Americans mashed the berries into cakes and dried them in the sun, or dried them whole. The dried fruits are a great trail food for hiking and definitely have commercial potential.

Shoots: The tender new leaf shoots and tender suckers, were a favorite food of some Native American tribes in early spring, when other green foods are scarce. Their quality varies with species, so sample any you find. They are gathered by snapping them from the plant as low down as they break easily. If too woody to snap, they are too old to use.

The shoots can be eaten raw in salads and sandwiches, cooked like Asparagus, or even added to soup.

Drinks: The leaves have been steeped for 5 - 10 minutes for tea (add dried fruit for flavor). The berries can be made into excellent wine.

Medicine
Blackberry root bark tea is a famous remedy for diarrhea and dysentery, and it is credited with saving many lives during epidemics. However all other parts are rich in tannin too and can be used similarly. The leaves can be used externally to treat wounds, insect bites and scratches (including the ones received while gathering the fruit).

Canes: The flexible canes were stripped of their prickles, peeled and used for basket weaving. For fine work they were split lengthwise into quarters. They have also been used as cordage and twine for binding things.

Animal food: These species are exceptionally important as food for wildlife and all parts are eaten. Over a hundred species of birds and animals eat the fruit alone. The spiny thickets provide cover and secure shelter for many small creatures.

Cultivation: These species are easy to propagate. Root cuttings can be made from a three-inch piece of root, planted from fall to early spring. Suckers can be detached from the plant and replanted separately. They can also be grown from tip layering, simply peg down the tip, cover with a little soil and it will root (many species do this naturally, without any help). Seed can also be used, although it is slow and germinates irregularly. Plant it immediately, or stratify for three months at 35 degrees. Generally the plants do best on rich moist soils, with full sun or light shade.

If you don't have enough wild Blackberries growing around about, there are many superior cultivars available. These are cheap, grow fast and produce such large fruit that it's probably not worth transplanting wild plants into the garden. Wild plants may also carry virus diseases.

Horticultural uses: Blackberries are the ultimate pioneer plants. They are able to colonize disturbed land rapidly by means of bird-sown seed, and once established they can spread by rooting at the tips of the long arching canes. They are generally beneficial, if rather prickly, plants. They prevent erosion and improve the soil by adding humus. They also form spiny thickets that protect the seedlings of more tender and palatable trees. As these seedlings grow into trees the Blackberries beneath them eventually die out, or are reduced in vigor.

The Uses of Wild Plants

Blackberries attract birds to the garden, which then hopefully stay around to eat harmful insects. They also attract beneficial predatory insects. For example a parasite of the Grape Leafhopper spends part of its life cycle living on Blackberry Leafhoppers, and the rest living on Grape leafhoppers. This parasite can help keep Leafhopper populations under control.

There is a negative side to Blackberries, which I am dealing with in my present garden. They are prickly, invasive and persistent plants, easier to introduce than remove. Exhaust yourself hacking them down to the ground, and they simply grow back even more vigorously. Cardboard mulch can be used to eliminate them, or at least keep them under control.

Rubus species / Raspberries

Throughout   Rosaceae
Raspberries resemble their cousins the Blackberries, but aren't usually as vigorous or aggressive.

Gathering: The hollow fruits are easily crushed when gathering, so should be gathered into a shallow container. If you don't have one, try threading them on to a long blade of grass like a pearl necklace.

Preparation: Raspberries are never better than when eaten raw, but can also be cooked in pies, sauces and preserves. They can be frozen or dried for later use.

Shoots: The tender spring shoots can be eaten like those of the Blackberry and taste even better.

Drink: Raspberry vinegar used to be a popular cooling summer drink. Crush the fruits in white vinegar, steep to the desired strength, sweeten and mix with water to taste. Raspberry syrup is made by boiling the fruits with honey and water. A spoonful of syrup is mixed into a glass of water. Use sparkling mineral water for a special treat.

Raspberry leaf tea is sometimes drunk for pleasure, though I don't consider it to be very good.

Medicine: Raspberry leaf tea is still drunk regularly by many women during pregnancy, as it appears to make delivery easier. It is also used to relieve menstrual cramps. Apparently the leaves contain a substance that stimulates smooth muscle.

The leaves are used externally in ointment for burns. They can be used alone, but are often mixed with Slippery Elm bark (*Ulmus*), or Comfrey (*Symphytum*). The fruits are said to be beneficial for the throat, and were once eaten with honey for this. They are also a tasty and pleasant laxative. All Raspberries are very rich in anti-oxidants, but the Black ones are especially so.

Canes: The canes can be used like those of Blackberry for basket weaving.

Tooth cleaner: The fruits have been used like Strawberries (*Fragaria*) to clean the teeth.

Cultivation: Raspberries are cultivated in much the same ways as Blackberries, and have the same garden uses. Many cultivars are available, with red, yellow or black fruit. One interesting variety is a prostrate groundcover Raspberry from the Arctic.

Related species:
There are some other useful *Rubus* species.

R. spectabilis - Salmonberry
Often abundant, and available for several months in summer, I haven't found these yellow fruits to be very good, as they have a bitter aftertaste. It is said that they are much better cooked than raw, so don't give up on them. The green spring shoots can be quite good.

R. chamaemorus - Cloudberry
This yellow-fruited species is very good. It is found in the cool north, and on mountainsides up in the clouds.

Rumex crispus / Curled Dock

Throughout   *Polygonaceae*
The Docks are familiar to almost everyone, as they are among the commonest and most widespread of weeds. Their success is due in large part to their amazing fecundity: a single Curled Dock plant may produce 30,000 seeds (some of which may remain viable for up to fifty years). Often seed isn't even necessary for perpetuating the species, as many are tenacious perennials and can get along quite well by vegetative means alone. Needless to say they are unpopular with many gardeners.

No member of the *Rumex* genus is poisonous, though they do contain toxic oxalic acid (see *Oxalis*) and many species are too tough, bitter or astringent to be edible.

Nutrients: This species is very rich in vitamins A (up to 7000 i.u. per ounce) and C. It also contains many minerals and is one of the best plant sources of iron Unfortunately it is also high in toxic oxalic acid (see *Oxalis*), so should be used in moderation.

Greens: In mild climates this hardy plant grows right through the winter, and at this time it can be a very good potherb. The tender young leaves are a nice addition to salads, or may be boiled as a potherb for 5 - 10 minutes. Older leaves are bitter, but can be made more palatable by cooking in a change of water for 10 - 15 minutes. If they are astringent you might add a little milk to the cooking water. The leaves don't shrink much in cooking, so you don't need to gather a huge amount.

Seed: In autumn the abundantly produced seed can be threshed, winnowed and ground to meal. This can be used in bread, pancakes and gruel. It tastes better if it is toasted before grinding.

Medicine: Dock greens stimulate the liver and are slightly laxative. They have long been eaten as a spring tonic, to cleanse and purify the blood after a winter without fresh green vegetables. They were also used to treat anemia and are effective because of their high iron content.

The leaves and roots have been used as a soothing poultice for wounds, Poison Ivy rash and Nettle stings.

Cultivation: I can't imagine anyone wanting to grow this weed, though the related Patience Dock (*R. patienta*) is occasionally cultivated as a potherb. It can be grown from seed or root division, in almost any type of soil. Be careful where you put it however, as it can be hard to eradicate once established. Removing Docks is a problem because if any fragment of the brittle root is left in the ground, it will grow into a new plant. They can be eradicated by repeated cultivation, which eventually exhausts the roots, or by smothering with a mulch of cardboard, organic material or plastic.

Like many weeds, the Docks are be beneficial to the soil. Their deep roots mine the subsoil for nutrients, while the large fleshy leaves add organic matter.

Related species:
Any *Rumex* species with palatable leaves, or abundant seeds, can be eaten. The best include:

***R. aquaticus* - Red Dock**
R. arcticus
***R. hymenosepalus* - Canaigre**
The large astringent root of Canaigre contains up to 35% tannin, and has been used to treat wounds and diarrhea. It has been cultivated as a source of tannin for tanning leather.

Rumex acetosa / **Common Sorrel**
Throughout
Caution: The characteristic sour flavor of Sorrel is produced by oxalic acid, which makes the plant mildly toxic if eaten raw in large quantity (cooking reduces this considerably). Oxalic acid can damage the kidneys, and inhibits the absorption of calcium.

Greens: This hardy plant often stays green all winter, and doesn't get bitter in summer, so can provide food

year round. The arrowhead shaped leaves are a good minor addition to salads, and can even be used in salad dressings instead of lemon or vinegar.

Sorrel is also a fine potherb if you change the cooking water once or twice, to reduce the sour flavor. This also reduces the oxalic acid content. It is recommended that you don't use aluminum or copper cooking pots when cooking Sorrel, as the acid may react with them (I wouldn't use them to cook anything else in for that matter). Sorrel soup is a delicacy in France.

Medicine: Sorrel leaves were used as an antiseptic poultice, or wash, for wounds and sores.

Cleaner: Sorrel leaves have been used to remove stains from the hands, and are probably effective because of the oxalic acid. This acid is used as an industrial metal cleaner.

Cultivation: Common Sorrel has been cultivated as a potherb, though not as often as its cousin French Sorrel (R. scutatus). It is easily grown from seed, or division, in most soil types, though it prefers slightly acid ones. It will grow in full sun or part shade. If you are growing it as a potherb, cut off the flower stalk as it appears, otherwise energy will be channeled away from leaf production.

Related species:
***R. scutatus* - French Sorrel**
This species is highly esteemed in France, and a few cultivated varieties exist. It is sometimes found as an escape.

R. acetosella - Sheep's Sorrel

This species is smaller than the Common Sorrel, but can be used in the same ways. It can become a weed in gardens if you let it get out of hand. It is an indicator of acid soil, and might be eliminated by making the soil more alkaline. Do this by adding a liming agent such as wood ashes or ground limestone.

Sabal palmetto / Cabbage Palm

Southeast   *Arecaceae*

Almost all members of the Palm family are found in the tropics; only a few venture as far north as the United States. This is the most northerly growing of them all.

The Palms have the same growth pattern as the Agaves and Yuccas (no coincidence, they are all Monocots). The plant grows from a single bud that slowly enlarges in size for a number of years and then starts to grow upward. Once it begins to elongate the trunk never gets any wider, but stays the same width the whole way up. If this growing bud (heart) is removed, the plant dies.

Hearts: The tasty and nutritious heart is the reason the tree is called the Cabbage Palm, though it doesn't taste anything like a Cabbage. Though the hearts are very good, their practical value is limited because eating the heart kills the tree. Obviously this is inexcusable (not to mention probably illegal) unless the tree is going to be destroyed anyway. The heart may be a foot in diameter, and is good raw in salads, cooked as a vegetable and in soups.

Fruit: Native Americans ate the blackish berries, though they aren't particularly good.

Fronds: The leaves can be used like other Palms, for roofing, and for weaving mats, hats, sandals, baskets and chair seats. The tough fibers can be freed from the leaves by steaming and pounding, and used for cordage and rope. In the past they have been of minor commercial importance for these uses.

Cultivation This Palm is often grown as an ornamental, or street tree, in areas with very mild winters. It doesn't have a very large root network and transplants easily, even when quite large. It is often used as an "instant tree" for shopping centers and resort complexes. These trees are frequently obtained from areas about to be "developed", which means even less chance for foragers to get edible hearts.

It has been suggested that this species might be cultivated commercially as a source of palm hearts.

Related species:
S. etonia - Scrub Palmetto

S. minor - Bush Palmetto
S. texana - Texas Palmetto
These species can be used as above.

Sagittaria species / Arrowheads

Throughout   Alismataceae

Known as Wapatoo by Native Americans, the Arrowheads provide one of the best wild edible tubers. These were a staple winter food of some tribes and were gathered in large quantities for winter use. In Asia the related *S. sagittifolia* is cultivated as a food crop. The plants are common in the shallow water of lakes and slow moving rivers, and various species can be found right across the country.

The tubers of any species can be eaten, though they vary considerably in size, according to species and growing conditions. Some are as small as a pea, others as big as a hens egg.

Gathering: The tubers are at their best while dormant, in late fall and winter, when they swell with stored food. They grow in mud or shallow water, with the tubers often several feet from the visible plant. You can't pull on a plant to uproot the tubers, as the roots will simply break off. Instead you must carefully work your way along the roots. Native American women used to wade in the mud and loosen the tubers with their feet, whereupon they rise to the surface, but this can be a cold job at that time of year. Modern foragers usually wear rubber boots and use a potato hook (or at least a hooked stick).

Gathering the tubers may seem destructive, but many tubers will remain in the mud to grow into new plants, so it usually doesn't do any harm.

Preparation: The tubers are acrid and unpleasant when raw, but develops a sweet flavor when cooked. They are quite a substantial food, and can be used in the same ways as potatoes: boiled (15 minutes), baked (30 minutes at 350 degrees) or fried. You don't need to peel them, but if you really want to it's easier after cooking. Native Americans mashed and dried them in large quantities for winter use.

Horticultural uses: These attractive, aquatic perennials are often planted as ornamentals in shallow, slow moving water. In China their native species is commonly cultivated for food in irrigated fields and improved cultivars are available. It has been grown around San Francisco for the large Chinese population there. These tubers have the potential to be a popular food for the rest of the population.

Cultivation: Probably the easiest way to grow Arrowheads is from wild tubers, planted three inches deep in shallow water. Seed can also be used. Start it two inches deep in a nursery bed, and transplant to its permanent position when the plants are a year old.

Species include:
S. latifolia – Wapatoo
This is probably the best food producing species.

Caution:
S. fasciculata - Bunched Arrowhead
This is a threatened species and should never be used.

Salicornia species / Glassworts

Coasts   *Chenopodiaceae*

These odd looking plants are adapted to grow in the hostile conditions found on the seashore, salt marshes and saline soils inland. Their leaves have been reduced to small scales to reduce water loss, and the thick succulent stems help them to tolerate high salt levels.

Greens: These distinctive and easily identified plants are a very good wild food. The stems of young plants are a pleasant (if slightly salty) addition to salads and sandwiches. You can reduce their salinity by washing thoroughly, or by soaking in fresh water.

The young plants, or the tender growing tips of older plants, can be steamed for a few minutes as a potherb. Don't cook too long or they will turn to mush. They can be added to other greens or soups, at the end of cooking, as a combined vegetable and seasoning (they contain all the salt you would need). They have also been pickled.

Older parts still have good flavor, but develop a wiry core that isn't very pleasant. To solve this problem some

foragers make a puree of cooked shoots and discard the fibrous parts.

Seed: The edible seed has been used like that of its cousin, Lambs Quarters (*Chenopodium*).

Chemicals: In the past the plants were dried and burned in large quantities, and the resulting ash (mostly sodium carbonate) was used for making glass and soap. This is how they got their common name. This could be leached with limewater to make sodium hydroxide, which could then be used as an ingredient in wild biodiesel.

Animal food: These plants have been used as forage for livestock, notably sheep.

New crop

In addition to being halophytic (adapted to saline soils), Glassworts are also xerophytic (adopted to dry conditions). This means they can grow in areas of low rainfall, and on land where irrigation has caused salt to accumulate to toxic levels. They have been investigated as a potential crop plant for such areas. They may also be worth investigating as a garden crop, as they actually grow better, and taste better, if irrigated with fresh water.

Cultivation: Propagate from seed. Some species will actually germinate in seawater, although they prefer fresh water.

Salix species / Willows

Throughout   *Salicaceae*

The Willows aren't of much use as food, but have several unique and important uses. They prefer wet soils near water, and are some of the most reliable indicators of wet ground. They are mostly pioneer species, fast growing, short lived, needing full sun to thrive (they are intolerant of shade) and reproducing readily by seed and vegetative means. They are among the first trees to get established on marshlands, and help to dry them out for other plants.

Famine food: Most Willows aren't really edible, though they have been used as survival food, (for some notable exceptions see below). The young catkins, leaf shoots and inner bark, have all been eaten raw, or cooked for 10 minutes, but they aren't very good.

Medicine: The plant has been used externally as an antiseptic wash or poultice for wounds.

Native American Uses: The finest Willow shoots were a trade item among some tribes. Small shoots were used for baskets, while longer ones were used for wigwams, sweat lodges, wickiups and small boats. Very small shoots were used for emergency cord.

Willow and aspirin

Willow bark tea was once an important medicine. It is a diaphoretic, and reduces fevers by increasing the flow of blood to the skin and causing sweating. It also kills pain, and reduces muscle and joint inflammation, such as is experienced in arthritis. It is now known that the bark contains salicylic acid, which is a close chemical relative of aspirin. Aspirin was actually developed as a gentler substitute for Willow bark.

Willow bark tea is usually made from the bark of 2 - 5 year old twigs. Steep two teaspoons of bark, or a quarter cup of chopped twigs, in a cup of water for ten minutes. A cup of tea is equal to two or three aspirins. It tastes pretty awful, though honey and milk may be added to reduce its astringency, and make it more palatable. It may also upset your stomach, so you probably won't use it unless you really need it.

Fuel: Willow wood contains a lot of water, which makes it poor firewood. It gives about 13 million Btu per cord on average (about half the fuel value of Oak). However the wood has long been prized for making charcoal for drawing, gunpowder and medicinal purposes.

Some strains of Willow grow twice as fast as others of the same species, and have been used experimentally in energy plantations. They are coppiced on a short rotation of 2 - 4 years, and converted to chips for use as fuel. An acre of these plants might yield the energy equivalent of about 25 barrels of oil annually. If fertilized with sewage sludge (which is generally unsuitable for food crops), these could be a useful source of energy.

Chemicals: Though the Willows are poor firewood, they have potential as a source of fuel and chemicals, extracted by wood pyrolysis (distillation). This yields methanol, methane, wood oil, tar, pitch, creosote, charcoal, acetic acid and other valuable chemicals.

Wood: Willow wood is light and weak, but very shock resistant, and has been used for sports equipment (English cricket bats are made of Willow), artificial limbs and polo balls. It is durable if kept wet, so is sometimes used for pilings and revetments. In the middle ages the long, supple shoots were widely used to build scaffolding for the construction of large buildings such as cathedrals. It was lashed or woven together, much as bamboo is still used in Asia.

Tanning: Willow bark was used to tan some of the very finest leathers.

Down: The downy seed has been used like that of Cattail (*Typha*), for stuffing clothing and pillows.

Basket Weaving

Basket weavers prize the slender, supple shoots as perhaps the best of all materials for their craft. The shoots are usually cut in winter, or early spring before the leaves appear, but for rough work they were sometimes harvested in summer. The cut stems were stored upright, with their butt ends in water. For fine basketwork the bark must be peeled off, which is most easily done in spring, when the sap is rising. If gathered at other times it is necessary to boil the shoots to loosen the skin. They are peeled by pulling through a V shaped notch in a board and are then dried for storage. They are soaked in water overnight prior to use, to make them supple.

Larger poles and shoots were used for weaving wattle fencing and walls, gates, cart sides, boats, fish and eel traps and chairs.

Animal food: These species are an important source of food for wildlife, including deer, beaver, moose, hares, ptarmigan and many insects. Goats and cattle will eat the foliage quite enthusiastically, and it can be dried for winter use. The pollen is a source of food for bees early in the year.

Propagation: Willows are easily propagated vegetatively. Even in the wild cuttings are an important method of reproduction, as the brittle twigs break off in storms and float off downstream to take root anywhere suitable conditions exist. Willows logs used for fenceposts and revetments have been known to sprout and grow into trees.

Propagate the trees while dormant, by simply hammering a 2 - 3 foot long shoot half way into the ground. Take care to plant it the right way up and not to split the top. Smaller shoots can be pushed directly into the soil. If given rich, moist soil and full sun, they grow rapidly.

They can be grown from seed, but this must be planted immediately, as it doesn't remain viable for very long.

Horticultural uses: Willows are often unpopular with homeowners because they continuously drop branches, twigs and other debris. Another drawback is their tendency to clog drains and ditches, as their roots go searching for water.

Their affinity for water makes them useful for preventing erosion of stream banks and levees, and they are often planted for this purpose. They may increase fish populations by providing shade, and attracting edible insects. The low shrubby types are best for this, as large trees may dry up small streams in dry summers.

An interesting idea is to grow a coppiced Willow hedge, by planting two rows of cuttings. Plant them 12" apart in the rows, with 36" between the rows. These can be cut every year for basket making materials, or every 3 years for biomass. This gives you a productive summer hedge, which also makes an attractive screen.

Rooting substance
Willows are able to root so easily because they contain a growth promoting substance. Professor Makota Kawase at the Ohio Agricultural station discovered that an effective rooting substance can be prepared by steeping the chopped shoots in water for 24 hours. This was also found to increase the effectiveness of commercial rooting hormones. It is also useful for pre-soaking seeds and for watering seedlings.

Coppice: Willows sprout readily from the stump and were some of the most important species for coppicing. Growing Willow for basket making was once a major industry in Europe. In some parts Willow gardens were almost as common as vegetable gardens. They supplied material for baskets for household use and for sale to provide income. Such a garden can still be profitable today. You could sell the shoots, or make baskets from them and sell those.

If you plant the cuttings 12 inches apart, you can get as many as 20,000 on an acre of land. Once established these may grow 10-12 feet in one season and can be cut annually. This is so easy that anyone into basket weaving should grow their own (even if it means planting the cuttings on land you don't own). See Hazel (*Corylus*) for more on coppicing.

Pollarding: In parts of Europe with a lot of livestock Willows in hedgerows were commonly pollarded instead of being coppiced. This consists of cutting the top off the tree, leaving only the trunk, about 6 – 10 feet tall. This causes the tree to send up a cluster of shoots, well up out of the reach of livestock or deer. These shoots were cut annually just like those from coppiced plants.

Useful species include:
S. alaxensis - **Feltleaf Willow**
S. pulchra

These northern shrubs are the only Willow species that are worth using for human food under most circumstances. Their shoots are actually quite pleasant, and were an important survival food in the far north. They are very rich in vitamin C, containing over 500 mg in 100 grams. Native Americans also ate the sweetish inner bark.

S. gooddingii - **Goodding Willow**
The sweet catkins can be eaten raw or cooked.

S. lasiolepis - **Arroyo Willow**
Native Americans used the inner bark fibers for making rope and cord.

S. nigra - **Black Willow**
This is probably the best lumber species of all the Willows. It is a very fast growing tree, sometimes reaching a height of fifty feet in only ten years.

S. viminalis - **Osier**
Also known as Basket Willow, this European species is naturalized in the northeast (and perhaps elsewhere). It is one of the best Willow species for basket weaving and was once widely cultivated for this.

Salsola kali / **Russian Thistle**   Syn *S. iberica*
Throughout   *Chenopodiaceae*
This pioneer species was introduced into North America about a century ago in Flaxseed imported from the Middle East. It is often called Tumbleweed, for its habit of snapping off at the base when dead and rolling away in the wind, slowly spreading seed as it goes (as many as 100,000 from a single plant). Tumbleweeds may occasionally accumulate in sheltered low-lying areas and gather wind blown about them. These piles have been known to block streams, ditches and even railroads.

Russian Thistle is now considered a serious pest of overgrazed rangeland, as livestock will only eat it when it is very young. Attempts have been made to eliminate Russian Thistle by introducing an Asian moth (*Coleophora parthenica*), which tunnels into members of the *Chenopodiaceae*, weakening or killing them.

Caution: All parts of the plant contain oxalic acid, so should be eaten in moderation. In some soils they may also become toxic by concentrating nitrates.

Greens: This plant is only edible for a short period in spring, when it first appears. At this time it produces what is considered to be one of the very best wild potherbs. The grass-like 2 - 5 inch shoots can be cooked like Asparagus; boiled, steamed, sautéed or added to soups. They have also been eaten in salads, but must be chopped very finely, as they can be irritating. The tender growing tips of older plants have been eaten later in the year, but aren't as good.

Seed: The abundant seed can be used like that of the related Lambs Quarters (*Chenopodium album*).

Glass: These species have been used like the related Glassworts (*Salicornia*), as a source of ash for making glass and soap.

Fuel
The abundant Tumbleweeds have been pressed into logs for use as firewood. It has been estimated that this could produce an income of 300 dollars per acre, on otherwise "useless" desert land. They might also be pressed into wallboard, or made into paper.

Animal food: Ironically this despised range weed is almost as good as Alfalfa as a livestock food. Young plants can be eaten directly, while older ones have been used to make protein rich silage. Since the plant grows better than almost anything else in some arid areas, it might profitably be cultivated as a forage crop.

Cultivation: This hardy and drought resistant plant is often the last green growing thing in a parched brown landscape. It can be grown from seed in most soils, even very alkaline ones, and self-sows easily enough to become a nuisance. The plant is an alternate host for the Grape Leaf Hopper so is discouraged near vineyards.

Related species:
S. collina - Used as above.

Salvia columbariae / Chia
West   *Lamiaceae*
Chia is native to desert areas of the southwest, but has now spread throughout much of the west. It is a close relative of the garden Sage, but is not used like that herb. Instead it is prized as a source of edible seed.

Gathering: Chia blooms in late winter, and the seed ripens in early spring. By this time the plants are practically dead, and are only identifiable by their spiny seed heads. Gather the seed by bending the ripe heads over a basket, and beating them to free the seed. Alternatively you can lay the whole heads out to dry on a sheet in the sun, or put in a paper bag in a warm place. When the heads are dry and brittle, crush them to release the seed. Then winnow and dry the cleaned seed. It is possible to gather several quarts of seed on a good day.

Uses: Native Americans used to say that a person could live on a spoonful of Chia seeds per day. This may be an exaggeration, but the seed is very nutritious, containing about 25% protein and 35% fat.

When traveling, Native Americans sometimes carried Chia seeds as emergency food rations. When mixed with water the mucilaginous seed coat absorbs a considerable amount of water and forms a thick slimy jelly. This was eaten as a combination food and drink.

Flour: Native Americans roasted the seeds (you can toast them in a skillet) to reduce their slimy quality and then ground them to flour. This can be mixed with an equal amount of corn or wheat flour, for gruel, bread, pancakes and piecrust.

Sprouts: The seed can also be sprouted for salad greens, though one can't simply soak them in water like you would most seed; they will form a solid mucilaginous glob and rot. You must gently sprinkle drops of water onto the seeds at regular intervals. The sprouts are best when about an inch long. Should I should mention Chia pets?, no probably not.

Tea: Chia seed tea is made by steeping the crushed seeds in hot water for twenty minutes. It is slimy and tasteless, so usually mixed with lemon, honey and tastier herbs.

Medicine: Native Americans used the seeds as a poultice for wounds. They also used them to remove foreign bodies from the eyes. Apparently if you put a seed in the eye, any particles will adhere to its sticky coat and it can then be removed.

Cultivation: Chia is easily grown from seed, in well-drained soil and full sun. Some Native Americans actively cultivated the plants, while others encouraged its growth. It could be a useful crop plant for arid areas, as the seed is quite valuable. The Chia seed sold in stores is usually from the much larger *S. Hispanica,* rather than this species.

Related species include:
S. arizonica
S. carnosa - **Grey Ball Sage**
S. carduaceae - **Thistle Sage**
Used as above.

Salvia apiana / White Sage
Syn **Audibertia polystachya**
Southwest
Flavoring: This highly aromatic species can be used as flavoring like its cousin the Garden Sage (*S. officinalis*). The leaves are best before flowering and can be used fresh or dried.

Seed: Native Americans ground the seed to meal for gruel and bread. It is not mucilaginous like Chia seed.

Medicine: White Sage tea was drunk to aid the digestion. It was also used externally as a poultice for wounds and insect bites.

Incense: Native Americans burned White Sage to purify places, things and people. They occasionally smoked the leaves also.

Cosmetics: A strong tea of the leaves can be used to make a beautifying hair rinse.

Propagation: Cultivate in the same way as Chia (above).

Related species:
S. leucophylla - **Purple Sage**
S. mellifera - **Black Sage**
Used as above. These species are important sources of nectar for bees.

Sambucus species / Elders
Throughout   *Caprifoliaceae*
Caution: The blue fruited species of Elder are edible, but those with Red berries may be purgative and should be avoided. Native Americans also ate the young spring shoots of Elders, but all green parts contain toxins and are generally considered to be unsafe to eat.

Fruit: These bushes often produce an abundance of fruit, but this varies greatly in quality, according to species. Some have a weedy taste and are quite unpleasant, but others are pretty good and well worth gathering.

Gather the fruits by picking the whole cymes of berries. Take these home and strip the berries off individually with a fork (this can be rather tedious).

Flowers: The flowers of some Elder species are bitter, but others are quite palatable, and have been used as flavoring for cakes, fruit preserves, ice cream and fruit pies. In Germany the whole flower heads are dipped in batter and deep-fried as a dessert.

The fruits of the best species are reasonably palatable raw, though some people have trouble digesting them. Most kinds are better cooked like Blueberries (sometimes mixed with them), in preserves, pies and sauces. Drying also improves their flavor and of course helps preserve them. The berries have also been used as purple food coloring.

Drink: In Europe Elderberry syrup is mixed with water and lemon juice to make a cooling summer drink. The berries and flowers have both been used to make exceptionally good wines. The dried flowers make pleasant tea, alone or with other herbs (they are often mixed with black Tea). A carbonated drink called Elderflower presse is sometimes available commercially. It reminds me of childhood walks on summer evenings.

Medicine: Elder was once used for respiratory, liver and kidney problems, menstrual cramps and as a blood cleanser, diuretic and a mouthwash. The berries are a mild laxative. Elderberry extract has been found to decrease the duration and severity of influenza, by inhibiting virus replication, and boosting the immune system

A tea of the flowers has been used as an antiseptic wash for burns, skin infections and wounds. A tea of the leaves has been used to treat Poison Ivy rash.

The fruits contain a sugar (3-rhamnoglucoside) that is very beneficial to the eyes. It may even help slow eye degeneration caused by ageing. They also contains substances that may be beneficial to the brain, and other substances that help to detoxify the body.

Wood: In Europe it was considered unlucky to use Elder wood, as it was a magical plant, protected by fairies and witches. This is no real loss, as it is poor fuel and usually too small for anything else.

Animal food: Elders are important food plants for many birds. The flowers provide food for many small insects.

Cosmetics: The berries were used as hair coloring by the Romans. They will also color your skin, so be careful. A wash of the flowers has been used to lighten the hair and skin.

Twigs: The twigs are easily hollowed out to make a tube, simply remove the core of light pith. These tubes have been used as spiles for tapping Maple sap, and also for whistles, flutes and blowpipes. They were also used for bellows for stoking a fire, and this may be the origin of the common name, which is derived from *aeld*, an Anglo-Saxon word meaning fire. An alternative explanation of the name is that the wood was once used for making fire by friction. The pith is one of the lightest solids known and is useful as tinder.

Cultivation: Though Elders can grow almost anywhere, they prefer rich moist soil, with full sun or part shade. They are most easily propagated from hardwood or semi-ripe cuttings, preferably 12 - 18 inches long with several buds. You can plant the ripe berries, but they may not germinate for two years. They can also be grown by layering, or by detaching suckers from the main plant.

Old bushes can be rejuvenated by cutting them down to the ground. This stimulates the emergence of vigorous new shoots.

Horticultural uses: Elder commonly occurs in the hedgerows of Europe, but it isn't a good barrier plant, and is often removed when laying them. It is useful in other ways though, as a source of the many materials mentioned above. In pagan times it was thought to protect the garden and fields from evil. Some species are grown as garden ornamentals, or to attract wildlife with their flowers and fruit.

Their spreading habit has been put to good use by planting them on eroded, burned, strip-mined or otherwise damaged land. They are a good source of organic matter.

A number of improved cultivars are available that bear superior quality fruits, and these are quite popular in cool climates. They are productive, attractive, hardy and little bothered by pests. They fruit on second year wood.

Useful species include:
S. cerulea - **Blue Elder** Syn *S. glauca*
S. canadensis - **American Elder**
S. melanocarpa - **Black Elder**
S. mexicana - **Mexican Elder**
These species can all produce good fruit.

Sanguisorba officinalis / Great Burnet
Throughout   *Rosaceae*
The young tender leaves, gathered before the flowers appear, will add a cucumber flavor to salads. They can also be cooked as a potherb, or added to soup and wine.

Medicine: The genus name is derived from the Latin word sanguis (blood) and sorbere (drink), which indicates the plants most important medicinal use. The astringent root has long been used as a poultice for wounds, bites, stings and burns. Always sterilize such poultices to ensure they are perfectly clean, otherwise you could introduce tetanus or other infections into a wound. Other parts of the plant have been used in the same ways, but aren't as good.

Cultivation: Great Burnet is attractive enough to be used as an ornamental. It is easily grown from seed, or root division, and prefers poor dry soils, with part shade.

Related species:
S. canadensis - **American Burnet**
S. occidentalis
S. menziesii
S. stipulata
S. minor - **Lesser Burnet**
S. officinalis - **Great Burnet**
These species may be used as above. Lesser Burnet is probably the best.

Saponaria officinalis / Soapwort
Northeast   *Caryophyllaceae*
Soapwort has been cultivated for its beauty and utility. It is naturalized in the northeast and locally elsewhere.

Caution. Soapwort is actually quite poisonous, as it contains up to 30% dry weight of toxic saponins.

Medicine: The entire plant is useful for skin problems, cleaning wounds, and as a poultice for Poison Ivy rash.

Soap: The saponins in the plant make it a useful soap substitute, which explains the common and generic names. If you take a handful of stems, leaves or roots and rub them on your hands with water, you will get a cleansing lather. The whole plant (fresh or dried) can be used as soap, shampoo or a general cleanser.

A good way to use Soapwort is to boil the clean chopped roots in water, then strain and use the liquid like detergent. This liquid makes an excellent shampoo, and can be mixed with other "hair herbs", like Nettle, Comfrey or Yarrow, to make your own shampoo.

The plant was once known as Fullers Herb in Britain (a fuller is someone who dyes cloth), because of its importance to the textile industry there. Prior to the introduction of modern detergents it was used in large quantities to soften water, and clean fabrics prior to dyeing. It was also used domestically to clean clothes. It has a very gentle cleansing action, and has been used in museums to wash fragile old fabrics. It may even help to preserve them, as it contains a fungicide. The plant was also known as Bouncing Bet, but I don't know why.

Other uses: Extracts of the plant have been used to give beer a foamy head. The sweetly scented flowers have been added to potpourri.

Cultivation: With its sweet scent, and long blooming season, Soapwort is an attractive ornamental, but it is too invasive for small gardens. It was commonly grown in the cottage gardens of England, probably tolerated because of its special properties. It can be grown from seed, or creeping rhizomes, and thrives in almost any soil. Take care to confine it, or it will spread energetically.

Sassafras albidum / Sassafras
East *Lauraceae*

This distinctive tree is easily identified by its uniquely shaped leaves, which take three distinct forms, elliptical, single lobed (mitten shaped) and double lobed. Another unique feature is the "root beer" scent of the bark, which is due to an aromatic oil composed mostly of *safrole* (this is most concentrated in the root bark). The tree has long been prized as medicine, even a panacea, and was one of the first exports from the New World colonies. It even provided an incentive for early exploration of the new world, until people realized how common it was.

Caution: *Safrole* is toxic when taken in quantity and can cause central nervous system depression, nausea and vomiting. It also inhibits liver enzymes, and in large amounts has been found to cause liver cancer. Sassafras oil is banned from use as a food additive in the U.S.A. In a few individuals the plant may also cause dermatitis. I will tell you how Sassafras can be used, but this is not a recommendation that you use it.

Gathering: The bark is at its best in winter and is usually gathered at this time. Dig around in the soil to find the shallow running roots and pull them up. They sometimes travel just beneath the surface for quite a distance. Wash the root carefully, then peel off the bark and dry it. Thin roots can be dried whole.

Tea: Sassafras produces one of the best wild teas. The best tea is made from the root bark, though the actual root wood can also be used. It is steeped in boiling water for about ten minutes, until it reaches the desired strength. Don't discard the bark after one use; it can be re-used several times before it loses strength. Sassafras sun tea with lemon is a nice cooling summer drink. The root was once widely used in root beer.

Culinary herb: The dried powdered leaves are an important seasoning in the southeast, where they are known as *gumbo file*, and are used to thicken and flavor soups and sauces. The tender new spring leaves have occasionally been eaten in salads. The powdered root bark is sometimes used as a culinary spice like Cinnamon (as are the ripe berries, though these aren't really edible).

Medicine: Sassafras was once an important medicinal plant. The tea was used as a diaphoretic, a carminative, and as a spring tonic to cleanse the blood (this is the origin of root beer - see *Betula*). It was used externally as an antiseptic wash for wound and burns.

Chewing sticks: The chewed ends of twigs have been used to clean the teeth. This is a good way to clean the teeth and remove plaque, as the plant is antiseptic. Sassafras has even found its way into modern root canal disinfectants. The tea was used as a mouthwash.

Smoke: Native Americans smoked the bark, usually with other herbs.

Perfume: Oil distilled from the bark has been used in perfumes, soaps, cosmetics and insect repellant. The bark has been added to potpourri,

Animal food: The foliage is eaten by deer, rabbits and bears. Birds eat the fruits and distribute the seed.

Wood: Sassafras wood is soft and brittle, but quite resistant to insect attack. It is most often used for fence-posts and other outdoor uses. It resembles Ash in appearance, and small amounts are occasionally used for cabinetmaking. The wood is poor fuel and sends out lots of sparks. Burning it is sometimes considered unlucky, a belief that probably originated with Native Americans, who considered it a sacred tree.

Cultivation: With its unusual foliage, and bright fall colors, Sassafras is a handsome shade tree. Plant the short-lived seed when ripe, or stratify for three months at 35 degrees. It can also be propagated from root cuttings (6 inch pieces of root) or suckers (detach from the parent plant in spring and move the following fall). This fast growing tree thrives on rich moist soils, though it will grow in most types. The numerous suckers can be a drawback in the garden as they are quite invasive, often emerging where you don't want them.

Satureja douglasii / Yerba Buena
West   *Lamiaceae*

This is one of several unrelated plants known as Yerba Buena, which means "good herb" in Spanish. The city of San Francisco was once known as Yerba Buena, and there is still an island in the bay by that name.

Flavoring: This delicate little plant is a close relative of the garden herb Summer Savory, but has its own uniquely delicious scent.

Drink: Yerba Buena is an excellent tea plant, and is sometimes known as Oregon tea for this reason. Use it like the related Mints (*Mentha*).

Cultivation: Yerba Buena can be grown from seed, cuttings or division, in well-drained soil, with full sun or part shade. It makes a beautifully scented low growing groundcover.

Related species include:
S. acinos
S. arkansana - **Calamint**
S. hortensis - **Summer savory**
S. rigidus
S. vulgaris - **Wild Basil**
The aromatic leaves of these plants can be used as culinary flavoring and tea.

Schoenoplectus species / Bulrush, Tule
Syn *Scirpus* spp
Throughout   *Cyperaceae*

These aquatic species are found all around the Northern Hemisphere. They are among the most useful of all wild plants, and supplied primitive peoples with many of the necessities of life.

Caution: If there is any possibility of biological contamination from polluted water, don't eat any part of these plants raw. If chemical pollutants are suspected, don't eat them at all.

Roots: All of these species have starchy edible rhizomes, though their usefulness for food varies. The best part is the newest growth at the end of the rhizome. This contains a lot of sugar, and can be peeled and eaten raw.

Native Americans roasted the roots for several hours in a fire pit (see *Camassia*), then peeled off the skin and ate the interior. They also boiled the peeled and chopped roots for 30 minutes. These were eaten as a vegetable, added to soup, or boiled down to a kind of gruel.

At the base of the old stem, there is a tender starchy core that can be eaten raw or cooked.

Flour: Native Americans gathered the dormant roots from fall to early spring, and extracted a sweet flour from them in the same way as for Kudzu (*Pueraria*). Flour can also be obtained by grinding the dried roots, and then sifting them to remove the fibrous parts.

The flour can be used like cornstarch, or mixed with wheat flour for bread and pancakes.

Buds: New buds develop on the roots in autumn. These can be eaten, raw or cooked, right through the winter, up until they start to elongate the following spring.

Seed: Bulrushes also provide edible seeds, though the harvest is very irregular. In some years none is produced at all, while others bring an abundance. It is prepared and used like Wild Rice (*Zizania*).

Pollen: The pollen has been gathered and used like that of Cattail, for bread, pancakes and gruel.

Stems and leaves: These have been used in much the same ways as the Cattail (*Typha*) and Reed (*Phragmites*), for thatch, boats, mats, baskets and cordage.

The stems and leaves are at their best for weaving in early summer when most flexible. They are gathered at that time and dried until needed. They are soaked in water overnight, prior to use, to make them flexible.

Animal food: Bulrushes are important to wildlife for food and as cover from predators. Young green plants have been used as livestock forage.

Pollution cleanup: Some of these species (notably. *S. lacustris*) are very efficient at removing suspended solids (phosphates, nitrates and other organic and inorganic compounds) from water, and potentially have great value for cleaning up polluted water. In Europe they have been used successfully in sewage treatment plants, to decompose sewage and eliminate harmful bacteria. They have also been used in domestic greywater treatment systems. See *Phragmites* for more on this. The plants grow quickly on a rich diet of phosphates and nitrates (up to twenty times faster than normal) and produce large amounts of organic matter. This has many potential uses.

Fuel: The abundant organic matter produced by sewage treatment plants could be fermented to produce methane and organic fertilizer. The starchy roots could be used to produce alcohol.

Fertilizer: The abundant foliage is good mulch or compost material.

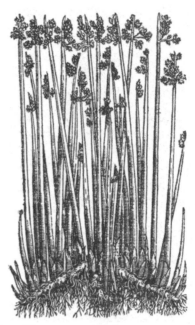

Cultivation: These perennial plants are most easily propagated from pieces of rhizome. They prefer very wet soils, or shallow water. Unlike Cattails they can grow in slow moving water.

Useful species include:
No *Schoenoplectus* species is toxic and probably all are edible. Definitely so are:

S. californicus - **California Bulrush**
S, lacustris - **Common Bulrush** Syn *S. acutus*
S. paludosus - **Alkali Bulrush**
S. validus - **Soft Stem Bulrush**

Sedum purpureum / Live-Forever
Escape   *Crassulaceae*
Live-Forever was originally introduced into North America as an ornamental, but is now naturalized in many areas. It gets its common name because an uprooted plant can live for a long time on the nutrients, and moisture, stored in the fleshy leaves.

Caution: Use in moderation, as they may be emetic if eaten in quantity.

Greens: The succulent young leaves are best when eaten in spring, before the flowers appear. They have been used raw, cooked or pickled.

Roots: The tuberous roots are dug while dormant and eaten raw, cooked or pickled.

Medicine: The leaves have been used as a poultice for burns wounds, skin irritation and even cancer. They have been taken internally for diarrhea.

The Uses of Wild Plants

Cultivation: Live-Forever is a favorite ornamental perennial for rock gardens. Some species have been grown as salad plants. Propagate by division, seed or cuttings (taken in late summer) in well-drained soil.

Related species include:
Only a few species are good enough to be worth eating. They tend to be more highly esteemed in northern areas, where wild greens are less abundant. The best include:

S. roseum - **Roseroot**
This species has edible roots that smell something like Roses. The leaves are also good. Use as above.

S. divergens - **Spreading Stonecrop**
Used as above.

Serenoa repens / Saw Palmetto

Southeast   *Arecaceae*
This, the sole member of the *Serenoa* genus, is our commonest native Palm tree. It is more of a shrub than a tree, and is often considered a weed for its habit of colonizing waste ground.

Despite its diminutive size, this is perhaps the most useful food bearing native Palm, for the simple reason you can gather the hearts without killing it. This is because it grows as a shrub, sending up multiple stems rather than just one. You can take the hearts from some stems and the plant will continue to grow (leave some hearts to put out new stems). Thinning may even be beneficial.

Medicine
Saw Palmetto berries have significant medicinal uses. They are still commonly used as a diuretic and are said to be a tonic for the reproductive organs. They may stimulate the production of male sex hormones, which could be why they have long been considered to be an aphrodisiac. They have also been found to have the ability to reduce enlarged prostate glands, and many men take them regularly to maintain prostate health. A tea of the berries has been used as an expectorant for pulmonary ailments.

Gathering: The small individual hearts are found at the center of the growing point, and must be carefully dug out with a knife.

Preparation: Palm hearts are a delicacy fully equal to Artichokes and are used in many of the same ways. They can be eaten raw, but are better cooked as a vegetable (add cold to salads) or added to soups.

Fiber: The large leaves have been used for thatch, mats, baskets and cordage.

Fruit: Native Americans ate the berries occasionally, but they aren't very good. The seeds are also edible.

Cultivation: This species is easily grown from seed, and does well in most soil types. Though hardier than most Palms, Saw Palmetto is still pretty frost tender and can't stand prolonged cold. In the north it is sometimes grown as an indoor plant.

New crop: The medicinal use of the berries has made gathering them a minor cottage industry in parts of Florida. Thousands of tons of berries are gathered annually, and this must eventually have an effect on these wild plants. It may soon become a profitable new crop for marginal areas.

Shepherdia argentea / Silver Buffaloberry

West   *Eleagneaceae*
Fruit: These plants often produce so much fruit that their branches bend with the weight. Unfortunately the berries are usually too bitter to be eaten raw, and may even be mildly toxic (they contain a lot of saponins). They are much improved by cooking them with sugar, and are then used like Cranberries in sauces, pies and soup. They are sometimes sold in markets in parts of the northwest.

Native Americans mixed the berries with Buffalo meat and fat to make pemmican. This is probably how they received their common name.

Animal food: The berries are important for wildlife.

Cultivation: With its characteristic silvery leaves (which give the plant its name), this species is attractive enough to be grown as a combination ornamental and fruit producer. It has been planted in hedges and shelterbelts, and used to control erosion. A number of improved cultivars are available.

This species is easily grown from seed, fruits abundantly, thrives in poor soils, is very hardy and may even contain nitrogen-fixing bacteria in its roots (its cousin *S. canadensis* certainly does).

Related species:
S. canadensis - **Russet Buffaloberry**
This species also produced an abundance of fruit. Unfortunately the berries are even more bitter and unpleasant than those of the above. They contain so much saponin they can be used as soap. Cooking helps destroy the saponins, and you can add sweetener, but they still aren't very good. Native Americans didn't mind their bitterness and ate them a lot. They even took

advantage of the saponins by whipping the berries with water and sweet berries to make a foamy dessert.

S. rotundifolia - Roundleaf Buffaloberry
Used as above.

Silybum marianum / Milk Thistle
Escape   *Asteraceae*
This biennial species is used in the same way as the *Cirsium* and *Carduus* species, and is occasionally included in the latter genus.

Food: All parts of this wholesome and nutritious plant have been eaten, raw or cooked, like the other Thistles (see *Cirsium*). Beware of plants growing in chemically fertilized fields, as they can concentrate nitrates from the soil and become somewhat toxic.

Medicine: This was the most important Thistle for medicinal purposes. Traditionally it was thought to be beneficial for the liver, and was used as a spring tonic to cleanse the blood and improve the appetite. It is also useful as a mild laxative and febrifuge (fever reducer).

The bruised leaves are a good poultice for wounds and skin sores.

Milk Thistle seed
It has recently been discovered that Milk Thistle really is beneficial to the liver. The seeds contain substances that protect the liver from toxins, and help it to recover from damage. An extract of the seeds has been used experimentally to treat poisoning by the deadly Death Cap fungus (*Amanita phalloides*) and also for hepatitis and cirrhosis of the liver. The seed tea has been used to treat nausea, motion sickness and allergies.

Stuffing: The downy seed can be used like that of Cattail (*Typha)* for stuffing pillows and clothing.

Cultivation: This attractive plant has been cultivated as an ornamental, as a vegetable and for its medicinal properties. It attracts many beneficial insects and birds to the garden. Milk Thistle is easily grown from seed in most soil types and self-seeds readily.

Simmondsia chinensis / Jojoba
Southwest   *Buxaceae*
The specific name *chinensis* indicates that Jojoba (pronounced ho-ho-ba is native to China, but it is actually a native American plant. The misleading name is the result of an error by the botanist who first named it. His specimen somehow got mixed up with some plants from China, so he naturally assumed it came from there. It has also (more appropriately) been called *S. californica*, but by the rules of botanical nomenclature the first specific name given to a plant has precedence.

Seed: The seeds are bitter and rather indigestible, but were eaten (in moderation) by Native Americans. They contain about 50% oil and 35% protein, so are quite nutritious. Gather the ripe seed when the husk is loose. It can be eaten raw, but is more palatable when roasted in a campfire (or in an oven at 250 degree for an hour). This removes some of the oil and tannin. Native Americans ate the roasted seeds like peanuts, or ground them to meal for baking. They were also used as a coffee substitute.

Cooking oil: Jojoba oil is not very digestible and only about 20% of the oil is assimilated by the body. It has been suggested that it could be used as a low calorie cooking oil. It is rather laxative if eaten in quantity however. It is a very stable oil, and doesn't go rancid for a long time.

Jojoba oil
Jojoba) was important to Native Americans in the southwest, for food, cosmetics and medicine. It has now become important worldwide, because the oil in its seeds is almost identical to that produced by the now protected Sperm Whale. Whales are no longer a source of oil, and it can't be synthesized economically, so demand for Jojoba oil is high.

Medicine: Native Americans used a paste of the toasted seeds as an ointment for scratches, wounds and sore eyes. The oil has been used to treat some kinds of acne.

The indigestible oil has been used as a coating for time-release drugs. As this coat is slowly digested, the drug is released into the bloodstream.

Oil extraction: The highest quality oil is extracted by mechanically pressing the seed. The remaining inferior oil is obtained by using solvents. The leftover solids are used as a high protein animal feed.

Industrial uses: Jojoba oil isn't actually an oil, but a liquid wax, consisting of straight chain mono-unsaturated alcohols and acids, and has special characteristics that make it very useful to industry. It is so important that it is stockpiled by the United States as a strategic material. It has a high flashpoint, viscosity and dielectric constant, and is used as a lubricant for gearboxes, high-pressure machinery, scientific instruments and even artificial hearts. It has been used as a coolant for transformers, in oil for sharpening tools, for treating leather and in soaps, inks, rubber, lamp oil and adhesives. It also has industrial applications as an emulsifier, corrosion inhibitor and detergent. The hydrogenated oil can be used as a substitute for Carnauba wax, in wood polish, food containers and candles.

Cosmetics: Native Americans used the oil as a hair treatment, and for dandruff (it dissolves sebum from the scalp). There has been quite a rush by the cosmetics industry to include the oil in their products, but these often contain so little of the oil as to be of doubtful benefit. Their only purpose being to enable the producer to legally put the word Jojoba on the bottle in big letters.

The oil is beneficial for the skin, and is of potential value for treating weather-damaged skin. It has been used in lipsticks, face creams, soaps and suntan preparations.

New crop

The plant has considerable promise as a crop for arid lands. It is a high value crop, can be easily stored and transported, and thrives in conditions where few other crops do well. Jojoba plantations have sprung up across the Southwest (at least 30,000 acres have been planted), and it has also been planted in Australia, Mexico, Africa and the Middle East (much valuable Jojoba research has been done in Israel). It has been estimated that at least 250,000 acres of Jojoba will be needed to meet worldwide demand.

Wildlife: Jojoba is an important food source for wildlife.

Cultivation: Jojoba is easily grown from seed, planted an inch deep in well-drained soil. It should germinate within a week or so. Seedlings don't transplant well because of their long root system, a three year old plant may have a root thirty feet long. For commercial purposes they are usually grown in cardboard tubes, and planted out as soon as possible.

The plants are dioecious, which is a problem when growing the plants from seed, as only the females produce seed (approximately one male is needed for every six females to ensure pollination). For this reason commercial growers usually propagate Jojoba vegetatively from cuttings, though it can be difficult to root. Another advantage of vegetative propagation is that varieties with a high oil content can be used. A disadvantage is that the plants are genetically identical and so vulnerable to the same pests.

Jojoba can survive on as little as five inches of rain per year and may survive for several years with no water at all (it simply goes dormant). It naturally puts on a spurt of growth in spring and goes dormant in summer when water becomes scarce. When cultivated it is usually given about 20 inches of water annually, for optimum growth and maximum seed production. It dislikes cold temperatures, and the flowers will be killed if temperatures go much below 40 degrees Fahrenheit. The wild plants are rarely bothered by pests, though some problems have appeared when it is grown in large monocultures. It is a slow growing plant, but may live up to 200 years. In hot dry areas it is occasionally planted as an ornamental shrub.

Jojoba bears its first seed when only five or six years old and can eventually produce about 10 pounds of seed annually. An acre of mature plants might produce up to 6,000 pounds of seed (or 2,000 pounds of oil) annually.

Sium sauve / Water Parsnip
Throughout   *Apiaceae*
Caution: The roots of this species are edible, but the plant is quite similar to the deadly Water Hemlocks (*Cicuta douglasii* or *C. maculata*). These are perhaps the most poisonous plants in North America (a tablespoonful could kill you), so it's really not worth taking the chance on eating them. Quite a few people have died after mixing these plants up.

Root: If you can safely and positively identify this plant, the roots can be gathered in late autumn and cooked like Parsnips. They are very good, but not good enough to take any kind of risk.

Greens: The young leaves have occasionally been eaten.

Cultivation: The Eurasian Skirret (*S. sisarum*) was once widely cultivated as a root vegetable and this species could be too. This would certainly be safer than gathering wild plants. It is easily grown from seed or division, in rich moist soil.

Smilax species / Greenbriars
Throughout   *Smilacaceae*
There are *Smilax* species growing in most areas of the country, but they are most useful for food in the Southeast. They are distinctive as the only vines that bear both thorns and tendrils.

Shoots: The tender young leaves, and growing tips, can be eaten raw in salads and sandwiches, or they can be cooked like Asparagus. The shoots are best in spring, but useful new growth can be found for most of the summer.

They are gathered by snapping them off as far back on the plant as they will break easily.

Flour: The roots of several species contain a starchy gelatinous flour that can be extracted in the same way as Kudzu starch (*Pueraria*). The roots are at their best while dormant, so are gathered in late fall or winter. The flour can be used to thicken soup, make a kind of jelly (mix a half cup of flour with one pint of water), or it can be mixed with wheat or corn flour for pancakes or bread. Native Americans dissolved the flour in water to make a drink.

Drink: Though only a few species are good enough to make flour, most can be used to make tea or root beer (even very woody ones). Their flavor resembles that of the closely related Sarsaparilla (*S. officinalis*). Prepare a tea from the chopped root (or shave pieces from a root), infused in boiling water.

Fruit: The berries are not very good, but are rich in pectin and have been added to fruit preserves to make them set.

Medicine: A tea of the roots was once a popular spring tonic and blood purifier (the original purpose of root beer). The roots were used externally for skin diseases.

Fiber: Native Americans prepared cordage from the fibrous stems.

Chewing sticks: The thicker stems were used as chewing sticks to clean the teeth.

Animal food: Dense thickets of Greenbriars are important to wildlife for both food and shelter.

Cultivation: These pioneer species grow best in sunny open sites, though some will take part shade. Propagate from stem cuttings (in spring), root division, or ripe seed (this should be sown immediately). Old clumps can be rejuvenated by cutting down to the ground or burning. These vines sometimes kill trees by strangulation, or by depriving them of light, so be careful where you put them.

Well-armed species such as the Greenbriar (*S. rotundifolia*) could be planted in hedgerows to make them more impenetrable and more productive.

Edible species include:
S. bona - nox - **Bull Briar**
S. californica - **California Greenbriar**
S. laurifolia - **Laurel Greenbriar**
S. tamnoides - **China Root**
The fleshy roots of these species can be used as a source of flour. Bull Briar is probably the best.

S. herbacea - **Carrion Flower**
S. smalli
S. walterii - **Walters Greenbriar**
These species produce edible shoots.

Solanum nigrum / Black Nightshade
Throughout   *Solanaceae*
Caution: This species is somewhat confusing for the wild food forager. The berries have been eaten in pies, and preserves, and sometimes even raw; but some people say they are poisonous and warn of the dire consequences of eating them. Even the leaves have been eaten in some places, though all green parts, including the unripe berries, are generally considered to be toxic, due to their content of solanine.

The answer to this confusing state of affairs is probably quite simple, the plant is sometimes edible and sometimes poisonous (well okay it's not simple). There are number of possible reasons for this. It could be due to genetic variation in the plants of different areas, or the effects of different climates. The age or ripeness of the plants parts could also be a factor; young leaves contain much less toxin than older ones. Certain people, such as children with their smaller body weight, or people habitually eating certain plants, could be more or less sensitive to the toxins. It is also relevant that solanine is water-soluble, so the cooked berries are less toxic than raw ones.

Fruits: It is probable you could eat small quantities of the cooked berries with no ill effect, though I can't recommend them (they aren't even particularly good). They are best when cooked in a change of water (to remove any bitterness) and sweetened with honey or sugar. They have been used like Blueberries in pies and preserves.

The Uses of Wild Plants

Cultivation: Black Nightshade is a common weed of gardens and disturbed places, but it isn't usually a serious pest. It has been grown in gardens to attract Colorado Potato Beetles away from potatoes.

The plant breeder Luther Burbank apparently produced a fruit he called Wonderberry from this species and some related ones. This later became known as the Garden Huckleberry but never achieved much popularity, despite the fact that it fruits abundantly and is easy to grow. This is probably because it doesn't taste very good.

Related species:
S. douglasii - **Black Nightshade**
S. eleagnifolium - **Silverleaf Nightshade**
Used as above.

Solanum fendlerii, S. jamesii / Wild Potatoes

Southwest   *Solanaceae*
These species are close relatives of the Potato (*S. tuberosum*) and their small tubers were an important food for the Navajo and surrounding tribes. They can be used in the same way as potatoes and like them are not good raw. Green tubers contain solanine and should not be eaten. If the outer skin is bitter peel it away.

Cultivation: *S. jamesii* has been cultivated experimentally as a root vegetable. It may one day be hybridized with the Potato to produce new crop varieties.

Solidago odora / Sweet Goldenrod

East   *Asteraceae*
Though the many species of Goldenrod can be hard to differentiate, this one is distinctive because its crushed leaves give off a sweet Anise scent (hence the name).

Food: The new spring leaves have been eaten raw, or cooked as a potherb. The flowers have been used for flavoring soups and added to salads.

Tea

The flowering tops of Sweet Goldenrod can be used to make one of the best of all wild teas. This was especially popular when oriental tea was boycotted during pre-independence days, and gathering the wild plants was once a minor industry. The tops are at their best when the flowers first open in late summer. They can be used immediately, or dried for later use. The dried leaves aren't as good though.

Medicine: The tea is carminative and diaphoretic, and was once commonly used to allay nausea. A poultice, or wash, of the leaves has been used for wounds and insect bites. Goldenrods are often erroneously accused of causing hay fever, because they produce their showy flowers at the same time as the real culprits, the inconspicuous Ragweeds (*Ambrosia*).

Rubber: These species are related to the Guayule (*Parthenium*) and have been studied as possible commercial source of rubber. A few have even been cultivated experimentally and yielded a few hundred pounds of rubber per acre. Thomas Edison was very interested in the uses of these (and other) wild plants and actually produced tires from them. He apparently found a variety of *S. leavenworthii* growing in Florida that grew twelve feet high and contained 12% latex. These interesting experiments never resulted in commercially viable crops, because of lower production costs for other types of rubber.

Wildlife: Many insects get food from the Goldenrods, including butterflies, aphids, bees, wasps and spiders. The Goldenrod Ball Gall makes large bulbous swellings in the stem, each containing a grub. These are sometimes used as bait for fishing.

Cultivation: This species can be grown from seed or division, and thrives in light, well-drained sunny soil. It is rather invasive, but can be controlled by using it for tea.

Related species include:
The flowering tops of any of the Goldenrods can be used for tea, though none are as nice as the Sweet Goldenrod.

S. altissima - **Tall Goldenrod**
S. fistulosa - **Pine Barren Goldenrod**
S. leavenworthii
These species are the most promising rubber producers, containing 5 - 7% latex.

Sonchus species / Sow Thistle

Throughout   *Asteraceae*
These useful food plants are more closely related to the Lettuces (*Lactuca*) than to other Thistles. They are nutritious (rich in vitamins A and C), and no species is poisonous, so any with tender foliage can be eaten. Be aware that when growing in chemically fertilized soils, they may accumulate toxic amounts of nitrates.

Leaves: The mildly flavored young leaves are a good potherb, and can even be used for salads, if their spines are trimmed off. Native Americans rolled the leaves into small balls to crush the spines and then ate them. Older leaves are bitter, but have been eaten after cooking in several changes of water (I am not sure they have any nutrients left after this much cooking though). They can also be blanched to reduce their bitterness, by covering with a bucket for a few days to exclude light.

Flower stalk: The succulent flower stalks can be eaten until the flowers appear. Peel and eat raw or cooked.

Coffee substitute: The roots of some species can be used as a coffee substitute. Prepare like Chicory *Cicorium*).

Animal food: The seeds are important food for birds.

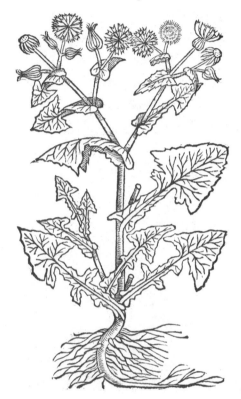

Weeds: All of these species have the potential to become weeds, but the worst is the Creeping Sow Thistle (*S. arvensis*). This species is a serious weed of gardens, fields and grazing land, as it spreads by means of creeping roots, as well as airborne seed.

Best species include:
S. oleraceus - **Common Sow Thistle**
S. asper - **Spiny Leaved Sow Thistle**

Sphagnum species / Sphagnum Moss
Throughout   *Lichenes*
The *Sphagnum* species are the most useful and commercially important of the mosses. They are significant because they are highly absorbent, holding up to twenty times their own weight in water (the moss would not make a good stuffing for life preservers).

Caution: Before use as a wound dressing the moss must be sterilized by boiling, as the spores of a disease causing fungus (*Sporotrichum schenkii*) are often found in the plant.

Peat moss: Sphagnum Moss is now most important in the form of Peat moss. This is formed in peat bogs, where the unique combination of high acidity, and a lack of oxygen (they are waterlogged all the time), inhibits decay causing organisms. When the mosses die in a peat bog they don't rot, but instead accumulate to form thick deposits of organic matter. Even animal matter doesn't rot in these bogs, and peat cutters have found a number of well-preserved human corpses, at first thought to be murder victims, but subsequently found to be up to 2000 years old. These bodies have given archaeologists fascinating insights into how humans lived in the past.

Wound Dressing
Pads of sterilized Sphagnum moss were once commonly used as an absorbent wound dressing. It's said that an ounce of moss will absorb an ounce of blood. During World War One a minor industry grew up in several European countries, whereby volunteers gathered and processed the moss for military use. It was sterilized by boiling and then dried, shredded and sewn into pads (often it was soaked in antiseptic before use). Britain alone was processing a million pounds of moss a month by the time the war ended. Happily, the end of the war saw a drastic decline in the demand for blood absorbing materials. The moss worked better than anything else that was available, but without volunteer labor for gathering it wasn't economical for use in peacetime.

Fuel: Dried peat moss was once widely used as fuel in northern areas, where trees are scarce. It is actually better than many types of wood, containing about 5000 Btu per pound. It was cut in winter when there was little farm work to be done and so free time was available. It was left in stacks to dry out for a year and then burned the following winter.

Peat moss is still used as a source of energy. Russia has about 75 centralized peat fired electric power stations. They are said to be cleaner than coal fired power stations. Some people advocate the United States should construct similar plants, pointing out that there are over 250 million acres of peat in the country, equal in energy terms to about 240 billion barrels of oil.

Another way to get energy from the plants is to ferment them to produce alcohol or methane gas. This has been done experimentally, but never on a large scale.

The Uses of Wild Plants

Of course you could argue that peat is too valuable as a unique habitat for it to be consumed on such a massive industrial scale as this.

Building construction: Another unlikely use for these plants is in building houses. The idea of a tiny moss being made into houses sounds ridiculous, but the same blocks of peat used for fuel also make fine building blocks. The resulting houses are quite similar to the sod houses built by the first European settlers on the plains. The moss was once a favorite material for chinking log cabins.

Peat / cement
A new use of peat is for making concrete blocks for building construction. The absorbent fibers readily absorb cement to produce stiff, light, easily cut blocks with a high insulating value.

Gardeners use a mixture of cement, sand and peat moss (known as hypertufa) to make artificial stone planting containers.

Absorbent: The fibers have been used in industry to absorb spilled oil, chemicals and other materials.

Diapers: The moss has been used to fill disposable diapers and menstrual pads. These can be completely biodegradable and may be disposed of into the soil after use, with their fertility no doubt enhanced.

Other uses: The whole plants were once commonly used as packing material for fragile objects and for stuffing mattresses. The fibers have been used for making paper and cloth.

Horticultural uses: Peat moss is best known in North America as a soil amendment. It is added to clay soils to improve porosity and drainage. In sandy soil the absorbent fibers increase water retention. It is quite acid, and when used in quantity a liming agent should be added to balance the pH.

Peat moss is widely used in potting and seed starting mixes (with sand, compost, vermiculite, leaf mold, etc). It is valued for seed starting because it holds a lot of water, is free of weed seeds, sterile and slightly antiseptic (which is said to deter damping off disease). Newly sown seeds are sometimes covered with a thin layer of moss for this reason. Horticulturists have used the fresh moss for similar purposes, but it is more expensive than peat moss.

Peat moss is widely used to pack plants for shipment. It is ideally suited for this, because it not only protects the plants from impact, but also holds water which keeps them from drying out.

Cultivation: In the West we generally use only the dead plants in our gardens, but in Japan the mosses are widely cultivated for their beauty. They can add a whole new dimension to gardening on moist shady sites. The plants can be propagated by transplanting small clumps of moss in a chessboard fashion. If they are kept moist, and like the growing conditions, they soon fill in the bare spots.

Stachys palustris / Woundwort
Throughout   *Lamiaceae*

Roots: Woundwort is a member of the Mint family, but is important for its edible tuberous roots, rather than as flavoring. These tubers are gathered after the plants go dormant in late fall or winter, which presents the problem of finding and identifying the dead plants. They are a valuable winter food, and can be eaten raw, boiled, fried in tempura or pickled.

Greens: The new leaf shoots can be eaten raw, or cooked, in spring.

Medicine: A wash, or poultice, of the leaves has long been used as a wound herb to stop bleeding. This explains the common name.

Smoke: The leaves of some species have been added to herbal smoking mixtures.

Cultivation: In China and France the related *S. sieboldii* is cultivated as a root vegetable, and other species could be. They are grown from seed or tubers in light, moist soil. Be careful where you put them, as they can become weeds. Keep them confined, and try not to spread the tubers around when you harvest.

Other species include:
S. hyssopifolia - **Hyssop Hedge Nettle**
This is one of the best tuber-bearing species.

S. sieboldii - **Chinese Artichoke**
This Asian species is occasionally cultivated in this country, and may be found as an escape.

Stellaria media / Chickweed
Throughout   *Caryophyllaceae*
It has been suggested that Chickweed may be the commonest plant on earth. It has spread far from its native Eurasia and is now found around the world. The plants delicate appearance is deceiving, as this is one of the hardiest of all annuals. It can survive temperatures as low as 10 degrees Fahrenheit and in chilly 40-degree weather will produce a luxuriant green carpet. The plant

is actually happiest in such cool temperatures, as the cold suppresses larger plants that would otherwise out-compete them. It usually disappears altogether in hot weather. Another factor in the plants success is its fast growth; it can grow from seed, and produce seed of its own, in as little as thirty days.

Greens: Chickweed is highly regarded as a source of wild greens. It is common, easily identified, mildly flavored, rich in vitamin C and in mild climates will provide food right through the winter. The tender growing tips can be used as a base for a fine salad, simply add pungent, sour and aromatic leaves to give more flavor. They are also an attractive garnish.

The young tops can also be used as a potherb, though you will need to gather a lot, as it shrinks when cooked. The tops of older plants can also be used as a potherb, though you may need to discard the tougher stems.

The dried, powdered plants have been added to baked goods, to increase their nutritional value.

Seed: Chickweed seed can be sprouted like Alfalfa, or ground to meal for baking. You might be able to gather the seed by uprooting the plants and leaving them to dry out as for Purslane (see *Portulaca*).

Medicine: The leaves were once commonly used as a poultice, or ointment, for burns and to stop bleeding. The potherb is a mild laxative, and has been eaten as a spring tonic to purify the blood.

Animal food: As the common name suggests the plant is an important food for birds and was once fed to domestic chickens.

Cultivation: Wherever you live in North America, you probably have the plant growing near you at some time in the year. Look for it in cool weather, when it will be one of the last green growing plants. Chickweed could easily be grown from seed, but there seems little point.

Related species include:
S. pubera - **Star Chickweed**
S. jamesiana - **Sticky Starwort**
Used as above. The latter species also produces edible tubers, that can be eaten raw or cooked.

Stokesia laevis / **Stokes Aster**
South   *Asteraceae*
This perennial is noteworthy because the oil in its seeds is rich in epoxy fatty acids. These have important industrial uses, and the plant may become an important oilseed crop in the future.

Suaeda species / **Sea Blite, Seepweed**
Coastal & saline soils   *Chenopodiaceae*
Leaves: The Sea Blites are halophytes, which means they can tolerate soils containing lots of salt. Like many halophytes they produce fleshy leaves that can be used sparingly in salads. They can also be used as a potherb, but must be cooked in at least one change of water to reduce their salinity. They can also be added to soups, blander greens, or other foods, as a combination vegetable and seasoning.

Seed: The Paiutes gathered the seed of Seepweed (*S. torreyana*) and used it like that of Lambs Quarters (*Chenopodium*).

Salt: Native Americans living away from the coasts prized the plants as a source of salt.

Ash: The plants have been burned, and the ash used like that of Glasswort (*Salicornia*) for making glass and soap.

Species include:
S. torreyana
This species is cultivated for greens in Mexico.

Symphytum officinale / **Comfrey**
Escape   *Boraginaceae*
This persistent European is planted in gardens across the North America, and often occurs as an escape from cultivation. This is fortunate because Comfrey is something of a wonder plant.

The Uses of Wild Plants

Caution: Though Comfrey has been eaten as a potherb in the past, there is some controversy as to whether it is really safe to eat. It has been found that the leaves and roots contain toxic pyrrolidizine alkaloids. Some plants containing these substances are dangerously toxic, and are often responsible for poisoning domestic livestock.

There are no records of Comfrey causing poisoning in humans or animals. On the contrary it is generally considered to be a very beneficial forage plant, and has even been fed to racehorses and show animals, to bring them into peak condition. Proponents of the plant claim that the evidence of toxicity is almost purely from a laboratory, when extracts were injected, and that it is perfectly safe to eat in moderation.

I will remain on the fence on the question of toxicity. Even though I talk about eating Comfrey, this is not a recommendation for you to do so.

Nutrients: Comfrey is one of the world's most efficient producers of plant protein, yielding up to six times as much per acre as Soybean. It is one of the few vegetable sources of vitamin B12, and is also rich in vitamins A and C, and calcium, phosphorus and potassium.

Green drink

I most often use Comfrey leaves in a green drink, which is a form of smoothie. I don't have a specific recipe, because it all depends upon what's available. Here is my basic method:

Fruit juice (I like Orange, but some people use raw Pineapple juice, as its enzymes may help to digest the proteins in the drink. You could also use soymilk).

Green leaves (Comfrey, Dandelion, Violet, Gotu Kola, Strawberry or whatever you have).

Banana (to sweeten. You might try *Stevia*).

Seeds (Sunflower, Pumpkin, Sesame, Evening Primrose, Flax, Chia).

Antioxidant berries (Blueberry, Wolfberry).

Other ingredients (Flaxseed oil, Elderberries, Kelp, Brewers yeast, Bee pollen, lecithin).

Put the Sunflower seeds in the blender with a small amount of fruit juice, and puree them to a cream. Add more fruit juice, the leaves and everything else, and blend until smooth. The whole thing tastes surprisingly good, and is a great way to take in a lot of extra nutrients.

Greens: The leaves are too rough to be good raw, but make a fair potherb, and were once popular fried in tempura batter. Young leaves are best, but older ones can be used. The dried leaves have been ground to powder, for use as a food supplement.

Drinks: The dried leaves have been used for tea, but are better mixed with other herbs, rather than used alone.

Medicine: The herbalists of old considered Comfrey a panacea, of help for almost everything, and it is still considered a very special medicinal plant. The growing parts contain a substance called allantoin that stimulates cell growth. This makes Comfrey one of the best plants to hasten the healing of burns, wounds, ulcers, sprains, bruises and infected sores. It is also used to stop bleeding. The leaves or roots can be used as a poultice, or mixed with oil and beeswax to make a wonderful salve. Be sure the plant parts are perfectly clean, as dirty material on a wound could lead to infections such as tetanus.

I have read that the mashed root was once used as a poultice for broken bones, and that it will set hard like a cast. I don't know how it was used. The dried powdered root was eaten to hasten the healing of broken bones.

Healing Salve

2 ounces of Comfrey leaves
1 pint of olive oil
1½ ounces of beeswax
½ teaspoon benzoin (a preservative)

Gently simmer the Comfrey leaves in the oil in a covered pot for about an hour. Make sure the oil doesn't overheat, otherwise it may catch fire (for this reason I advise you to do this outside). Overheating the oil may also impair the healing qualities of the salve. The next step is to add the beeswax and benzoin and stir thoroughly. Take out a spoonful of the mix and allow to cool, so you can check its consistency. If it is too thick add more oil, if too thin add more wax. Finally pour it into wide mouth jars and allow to cool fully. If stored in a cool place it may stay good for several years.

This same basic recipe can be used with many other healing plants, such as Plantain (*Plantago*), Yarrow (*Achillea*), Chickweed (*Stellaria*) and St Johns Wort (*Hypericum*). Those plants can also be added to this recipe.

Animal food: Comfrey has been cultivated for use as animal feed, and then returned to the land in the form of manure.

Cosmetics: The juice of the plant is said to be beneficial for the hair and skin.

Fuel: Comfrey may produce up to 50 tons of green matter per acre in a season, so it has been suggested as a possible source of vegetation for methane production. This would also give nitrogen rich fertilizer as a by-product.

Cultivation: Comfrey is very easy to propagate vegetatively by means of root cuttings. They grow whatever you do. You could start with a single root cutting and within two or three years you would have more Comfrey than you could possibly use. Seed is not used for propagation because the plants don't normally produce viable seed. The plants are said to prefer rich moist soil, though I have seen them growing on dry mine spoil heaps that couldn't really be called soil at all. They will grow in part shade, but do much better in full sun. Established plants are rarely bothered by pests or disease (except for Comfrey Rust in some areas).

Horticultural uses: The plants are quite attractive, and several species have been used as ornamentals. A number of superior cultivars exist, but they are hard to obtain. Fortunately even wild forms are very productive.

Eradication: One problem with Comfrey is that it is very persistent, and can be hard to eradicate once established. It doesn't spread aggressively, but is easily chopped up and spread around while digging. If it becomes a pest, it can be eliminated by solarization, or a mulch of cardboard, black plastic or carpet. You might also try repeated cutting to exhaust the roots, but you will probably get exhausted before the plant does.

Fertilizer

Of all its many uses, Comfrey is perhaps most valuable as a fertilizer and soil builder (this is certainly its safest use). Its vigorous root system breaks up compacted soil and mines the subsoil for nutrients. Poor soils can be improved by planting Comfrey on them (perhaps with Clover or other nitrogen fixing herbs).

The high nitrogen content of the leaves makes them an excellent green manure and compost material. They can also be used as the nitrogen component of compost piles. For maximum productivity the leaves should be cut regularly.

A great way to use Comfrey as fertilizer is to make a liquid foliar feed. Just fill a bucket with as many leaves as it will hold, top it up with water, cover and leave to ferment for 2 - 3 days. Then strain out the remaining fibers, dilute with an equal amount of water and apply with a watering can. Like any anaerobic fermentation it smells horrible, but for a serious gardener that's a small price to pay.

Related species:
S. tuberosum
S. uglinosum
S. uplandicum
These species may also be found as escapes and are used in the same ways. The last species is the most common. and I have read that it contains less of the toxic alkaloids, but I can't vouch for this.

Tagetes minuta / African Marigold
Southeast   *Asteraceae*
This species is naturalized in the southeast and locally elsewhere. The specific name minuta refers to the flowers not the plants, as this plant may grow to 12 feet in height. I don't find the smell of this very aromatic plant very appealing, but apparently it has been used as a culinary herb.

Nematocide: This species is probably best known for its nematocidal properties. Exudations of thiophenes from the roots can kill nematodes in the soil up to three feet away. For maximum effectiveness the plants must be sown in a solid block like a cover crop, covering the entire affected area. It may also kill fungal spores and inhibit some seeds. The plant is also a good compost or smother crop, as it produces a lot of biomass, in which case you can kill several birds with one stone.

Cultivation: This species is easily grown from seed, in almost any soil. It self-seeds readily and can become a weed (in fact it is a naturalized weed in the southeast).

Taraxacum officinale / Dandelion

Throughout   *Asteraceae*

Dandelion is a familiar plant to many urban and suburban dwellers. The acquaintance is usually pretty superficial though, often just how to recognize and kill it. Most people wouldn't dream that the Dandelion is one of the most nutritious of green plant foods. It also has numerous other uses, is an important wildlife food and is beautiful as well.

This highly efficient plant has spread to all temperate areas of the world. The wind borne seed can travel huge distances to colonize disturbed ground, such as gardens, roadsides, cultivated fields and waste ground. The seed has no dormancy period so can germinate immediately, and a plant can produce seed of its own within three months of germination. This might not sound very impressive compared to some annuals, but Dandelion is a persistent perennial, and doesn't really need to produce seed at all. Its deep taproot enables it to survive on poor soil and through drought. As any gardener knows it also makes the plant hard to remove, as any piece of root left in the ground can quickly become a new plant. Careless weeding can be a form of propagation, rather than eradication.

Nutrients

Dandelion leaves are much more nutritious than most common vegetables. They contain up to 14,000 i.u. of vitamin A per hundred grams, along with lots of Vitamin C, B vitamins and many minerals, including calcium, chlorine, copper, iron, phosphorus, magnesium, silicon and sulfur. They are one of the richest plant sources of potassium.

Greens: Considering its great food value, it's a shame that for most of the year the Dandelion is too bitter for most palates, and is only really good in cold weather. It is usually eaten in spring, from the time it first appears above ground, until the flowers stalks appear. It may also be good for a while in late autumn. In milder areas it may remain green and palatable all winter.

The young leaves can be used in salads, or cooked for 5 - 10 minutes as a potherb. If they are too bitter, change the cooking water at least once. Some people blanch the

leaves by covering them with a box for a few days, as this makes them less bitter and more tender (it also reduces their vitamin content).

Crown: The crown of the plant is also edible in early spring. Cut the green top off of the root, just far enough down so it holds together, and then cut off the leaves. These are naturally partly blanched, and are often still palatable after the green leaves have become too bitter to eat. They can be eaten raw, boiled, or fried in tempura batter. If they are too bitter try cooking them in a change of water.

Winter Greens: The roots have been forced indoors like Chicory, as a source of winter greens. See (*Cicorium*), for more on this.

Flower buds: You can find these huddled down inside the leaf rosette, soon after the leaves appear, waiting for warmer weather to make their appearance. These make good salad material, or can be boiled or steamed.

Roots: The dormant roots have been eaten like Salsify (*Tragopogon*).

Green drink: I often add a few Dandelion leaves to a green blender drink. They can be used for this at any time of year. Their bitterness usually isn't noticeable, and they add a lot of nutrients. See (*Symphytum*) for more on these

Coffee: The roasted roots have been used like Chicory as a coffee extender or substitute. Done properly this is aromatic and quite good.

Medicine: Dandelion is mainly of value as a nutritive tonic. The chlorophyll, enzymes and high vitamin and mineral content of the leaves make them one of the best spring tonics. These were thought to purify the blood, and aid in the neutralization and elimination of toxins accumulated over the winter. They are also a powerful diuretic, as suggested by the old common names Piss-A-Bed and Wet Weed.

The very high vitamin A content of the leaves makes them a potent cancer preventive if eaten regularly. The leaves, or their extracted juice, have been used to treat anemia and rebuild the teeth and bones. They have also been used as a poultice for wounds and skin ailments.

The roots have been used to treat jaundice, hepatitis, gallstones, diabetes and hypoglycemia.

Rubber: All *Taraxacum* species contain large amounts of rubber latex, and one species (*T. kok-sayghiz*) was cultivated in the Soviet Union during World War Two as a source of rubber. It provided that country with 80% of the rubber used during that time.

Animal food: Though an introduced species, the Dandelion is an important source of nectar and pollen for many native insects. Many birds eat the seed. Both domestic and wild animals eat the foliage.

Cultivation: If Dandelions don't grow in your garden they are worth cultivating, as they provide a reliable source of greens every spring. Improved varieties are available, with larger more succulent leaves, but which still retain much of the vigor and independence of wild plants. They are easily grown from seed or root division, in most soil types. Be warned they will self- seed freely, maybe more freely than you might like.

Garden uses: Dandelion is often a hated weed, and huge quantities of toxic chemicals are used annually to eliminate it from lawns. At the same time it is cultivated in some areas, and sold in markets as a salad herb. It is equal to Chicory or Endive in flavor, yet easier to grow.

The plant is generally beneficial in the garden. It attracts bees and predatory insects, its deep roots break up compacted soil and bring nutrients to the surface. The whole plants are fine compost material.

I think it is time for plant breeders to create some ornamental Dandelions. They are certainly pretty enough.

Taxus canadensis, T. brevofolia / Yews
Throughout   *Taxaceae*
The Yew is probably more familiar as a landscape plant

than in the wild, as it is widely planted around public buildings and in gardens.

Caution: Almost all parts of the Yew are toxic. They contain the dangerously heart depressing alkaloid taxine, and have caused deaths in both livestock and humans. Interestingly deer can eat it with impunity and actually seek it out.

Food: The only exception to the plants toxicity is the sweet red flesh that surrounds the seed, (the seed itself is poisonous). This is usually eaten out of hand as a snack, but has occasionally been used to make preserves.

Medicine

Taxol from the bark of *T. brevifolia*, has been found to be effective in treating breast and ovarian cancers (and perhaps others) and is now widely prescribed for this. This has resulted in considerable demand for the foliage by pharmaceutical companies, resulting in increased gathering from the wild. Fortunately this substance has now been found in the leaves of other *Taxus* species, along with substances that can be converted into taxol. It is now being cultivated to meet the demand.

Wood: Yews are conifers, and so botanically classified as softwoods, though the wood of these slow growing plants is certainly not soft. It is hard, heavy and very elastic, and was once prized for making bows. It was the favored wood for the longbows of the English archers who dominated medieval European warfare until the perfection of firearms. Native Americans used it for paddles, harpoons and spears, as well as bows.

Fuel: Yew is excellent firewood, but slow growing and uncommon, so it is rarely used.

Insecticide: The leaves are toxic to insects, and a decoction has been used as a dip to kill external parasites on livestock.

Cultivation: Yews can be grown from seed, planted as soon as it is ripe, or from hardwood cuttings. They prefer cool moist conditions, with some shade.

These evergreen trees are widely planted as ornamentals, and cultivars have been developed for every purpose, from large upright trees to prostrate groundcovers. They are also good as hedge and windbreak plants.

Yews are now cultivated as a source of medical drugs. They can be coppiced, which allows them to be cut at regular intervals. See Hazel (*Corylus*) for more on coppicing.

Tephrosia virginiana / **Devils Shoestring**
East   *Fabaceae*
Cordage: The flexible roots are tough enough to use for cord or string. They are probably responsible for the plants common name.

Insecticide
This toxic species is of interest because it contains up to 5% rotenone in its roots (probably the only native species to do so). Also known as derris, this is a powerful insecticide, acting as a stomach poison to many insects, but being relatively harmless to warm blooded animals. It is popular with many organic gardeners as a "natural" pesticide, that breaks down quickly in the environment to become harmless. Nevertheless it is still a powerful poison and upsets natural balances, often killing beneficial insects as well as "pest" species.

Fish poison: Rotenone is also poisonous to fish and the root has been used to catch fish. The African species (*T. vogelii*) is known as Fish Poison plant.

Cultivation: Some related African species are used as green manure crops, and to smother weeds. As legumes they probably contain nitrogen-fixing bacteria. They are easily grown from seed.

Tetragonia tetragonoides / **New Zealand Spinach**   Syn *T. expansa*
West coast   *Aizoaceae*
This creeping succulent plant is cultivated as a warm weather spinach substitute, as it doesn't bolt to seed in hot weather. It has naturalized in the mild climate of the West Coast, and is now quite common in coastal areas. It is occasionally found as an escape elsewhere.

Greens: The tender growing tips can be gathered all summer, and used as a potherb or in soups. They have been eaten raw in salads, but aren't very good. Older parts are acrid and unpleasant.

Cultivation: This species is easily grown from seed, in deep rich soil, and is tolerant of saline soils. It is very frost tender, and in cold climates it must be started indoors in early spring. It is slow to get started, but once established it produces freely with little attention. It also self-sows readily.

This species has been grown as an ornamental groundcover, or to add foliage to hanging baskets.

Thelesperma species / **Navajo Tea**
West   *Asteraceae*
Greens: The young spring leaves can be used as a salad or potherb. Like many members of the *Asteraceae*, they are often bitter unless cooked in a change of water.

Tea: Native Americans prized the leaves for tea (hence the name) and often traveled long distances to gather, or trade, for it. They would boil a single stalk of fresh or dried plant in a cup of water for 5 minutes or so.

Useful species include:

T. filifolium - **Greenthread**
T. gracile - **Navajo Tea** Syn *T. magapotamicum*
T. longipes
These species are all good. Greenthread has been called one of the best wild tea plants.

Thuja occidentalis / **Arborvitae**
Northeast   Cupressaceae
This was one of the first North American trees to be planted in Europe, and a tree was recorded as growing near Paris in 1536. It can live up to 400 years, which may account for the common name; which means Tree of Life.

The young tips have been added to soups, for a few minutes before serving (and then removed), but why is anybodies guess, as it isn't very pleasant. It should be used very sparingly (if at all), as it contains the same toxic oil (thujone) that is found in Wormwood (*Artemisia*).

Tea: The growing tips were used to make tea by Native Americans, and some white men (notably lumberjacks), however it is not very palatable. I suspect lumberjacks drank it to prove what a macho and elite group they were. The unpleasant flavor is not such a bad thing, as the plant is rather toxic and should be used in moderation, if at all.

Medicine: About the only good thing you can say about the tea, is that it is rich in vitamin C. Native Americans frequently used it as a cure for scurvy, and it has saved many lives (including the crew of Jacques Cartier's ship on one of his Canadian voyages).

The green boughs have antiseptic and antibiotic properties, and can be used as disinfectant. They were also used to treat pulmonary complaints, rheumatism and muscle pains. They are quite aromatic so were used for incense, and to scent sweat lodges.

Wood: The aromatic wood is rot resistant, tough, light and splits easily. It is often used for fenceposts, siding and other outdoor uses. Native Americans favored it for building the frames of their Birch bark canoes.

Other uses: The shredded inner bark was commonly used as tinder and cordage. Oil from the wood has been used in perfumes.

Cultivation: A number of *Thuja* species are used as ornamentals. They like moist, acid soil with some shade, and are propagated from seed or semi-ripe cuttings.

Thuja plicata / Western Red Cedar
This is the giant of the *Thuja* genus and one of the most massive of all trees. In its native northwest it used to reach 200 feet in height, and have a diameter of 20 feet. The leaves have been used for tea as above.

Medicine: Used as above.

Wood: The wood of Western Red Cedar is extremely durable, as it contains an antibiotic that kills wood decomposing organisms. It has been used for all purposes where rot resistance is important, including fenceposts, boatbuilding, greenhouses and telephone poles. I wonder if this antibiotic could somehow be used as a natural wood preservative? This might be less polluting to manufacture, and less injurious to health, than the preservatives we presently use. Though like synthetic preservatives it is still quite toxic to humans, and the wood dust often causes allergies such as dermatitis and respiratory problems.

The durable wood works and splits easily, and these qualities make it the most important wood for making shingles and siding. Shingle splitting was once an important industry in many areas, but is now declining rapidly in most places, as almost all of the straight grained old growth trees outside of parks and preserves have been cut down. Cedars are rarely planted to replace those felled, as they take too long to mature, so Douglas Fir usually replaces it. Ironically, loggers in the past had little use for these trees, but often had to cut them so they could remove the Douglas Firs they wanted. They just left the Cedars where they fell. Some of these huge old trees are still sound, despite the years they have spent on the damp forest floor. They are now very valuable, and many are being salvaged by independent loggers, often from places so inaccessible they are split into shingles on the spot, and transported from the site by helicopter.

This species was very important to Native Americans because the wood splits easily, and even with primitive tools they could obtain boards up to two feet wide and forty feet long (they often cut planks from standing trees without cutting down or killing them). They used these planks to construct some of the most sophisticated buildings of all the northern tribes. They also hollowed out the trunks to make large sea-going war canoes.

Inner bark: This was an important material for Native Americans, and had many uses. It was used for cordage, rope, baskets, lamp wicks, disposable diapers, menstrual pads and even clothes.

Cultivation: This attractive species has been planted as an ornamental. It is propagated as for the Arborvitae.

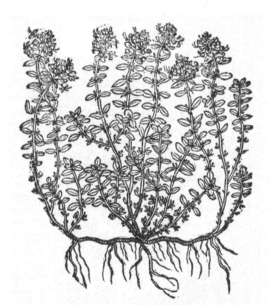

Thymus serpyllum / Wild Thyme
Throughout *Lamiaceae*
This species is widely grown in gardens under the name Creeping Thyme, and is often locally common as an escape. It can be used like Garden Thyme (*T. vulgaris*) as a culinary herb or tea, though it isn't as good.

The Uses of Wild Plants

Medicine: The plant contains the antiseptic thymol and has been used as a wound herb. It is also fungicidal and was used for skin diseases such as athletes foot. Thyme tea is a carminative, digestive, expectorant and tonic. It was once recommended for hangover headaches (remember: wild time - Wild Thyme).

Animal food: Fairies and bees are fond of Thyme.

Cultivation: The plant can be grown from seed, division or cuttings, in well-drained sunny soil. It makes a good ground cover.

Tilia americana / **Basswood**
East   *Tiliaceae*

Greens: The leaf buds and new leaves are a minor addition to spring salads, and have occasionally been used as a potherb.

Flowers: The flower buds and flowers can be eaten in salads, or fried in tempura batter. More importantly they were used to make tea. This was once one of the most popular herbal teas, but seems to have declined in popularity of late

Medicine: Basswood tea is considered to be a mild sedative and tranquilizer, and makes a good bedtime drink. It was once prescribed for coughs and sore throats, and to settle the digestive system.

The mucilaginous inner bark has been used as a poultice for skin ailments and burns. Native Americans used it to bandage wounds.

Honey: Basswood is an important nectar producing plant. The trees attract so many bees while blooming that it is said you can find them by the buzzing. Connoisseurs consider Basswood honey to be some of the best. Bees attracted to trees in your yard will stay and pollinate other plants.

Cosmetics: The flowers have been added to bathwater as a skin treatment, and an aid to relaxation. The easiest way to do this is to make a tea and pour it into the bath. This was also used to wash hair, babies and babies hair.

Wood: Basswood wood is light, soft, evenly grained and doesn't split easily. These qualities make it a favorite of woodcarvers, turners and cabinetmakers. It is also prized by luthiers (guitar makers) as it is acoustically dead. The wood has also been used for pulpwood. It is poor firewood, giving only about 14 million Btu per cord.

Fiber: Basswood was a valuable source of fiber for Native Americans. They separated the useful inner bark from the outer part, and boiled it in wood ashes to separate the fibers. The resulting fiber is very strong and can be used for cord, rope and sandals. In Russia it has been used to make paper and cloth. A narrow strip of inner bark can be used as emergency cord if nothing else is available. Strips of whole bark have been used as roof shingles, and wide sheets were used for covering wigwams.

Tanning: The tannin rich bark has been used for tanning leather.

Cultivation: Basswood likes rich moist soil, and can be propagated from cuttings or layering. Seed can also be used, but it is slow to germinate unless the hard seed coat is removed.

Horticultural uses: Basswood is an attractive shade tree, but it has one drawback; aphids feeding on the leaves drop copious amounts of honeydew. This can make a mess underneath the trees, coating cars, furniture, windows and other surfaces. It has even been known to make road surfaces slippery. One would imagine that so many sap-sucking insects must be detrimental to the trees, but they are actually beneficial in an unlikely way. The honeydew apparently stimulates nitrogen fixing bacteria in the soil, and much of the nitrogen they fix eventually finds its way into the plants. This illustrates very well how our immediate assumptions and prejudices about insects can be quite wrong.

These species sprout readily from the stump after being cut down, and in Europe related species have been coppiced for poles, tan bark and firewood. It is cut on a 10 - 25 year rotation. See Hazel (*Corylus*) for more on coppicing.

Related species:
All other *Tilia* species can be used in the same ways.

Torreya californica / **California Nutmeg**
California   *Taxaceae*

This rather uncommon tree is scattered sparsely over much of California. Its scarcity is rather unfortunate, as this is an attractive and useful tree.

Food: The oily nuts were eaten raw or roasted by Native Americans, but have a bitter astringent covering that is hard to remove. They contain about 50% oil, which can be extracted by pressing, or by boiling as for Hickory (*Carya*). An Asian species (*T. nucifera*) has been cultivated as a source of oil.

Wood: The strong, durable wood is used locally for fenceposts, but it is not common enough to be commercially significant. Native Americans used it for bows. The roots have been used for basket weaving.

Cultivation: The handsome foliage of this species somewhat resembles that of a Coast Redwood or Yew, but has a very strong and distinctive odor. Propagate from seed or semi ripe cuttings. This species and its hardier Asian cousin *T. nucifera*, have been planted as ornamentals, and occasionally for their edible nuts.

Toxicodendron species / Poison Ivy, Oak, Sumac Syn *Rhus* spp

Throughout   *Anacardiaceae*
Caution: These species are poisonous, and don't have any properties we can easily make use of. I have included them here because so many misconceptions exist about them, and you will no doubt encounter them when looking for other plants mentioned in this book.

Rash: You probably already know that touching any of these species can cause an unpleasant rash (known as Rhus dermatitis), with redness, itching, blistering and worse. This is caused by a toxic resin called *urushiol*, which is found in all parts of the plant. As little as a billionth of a gram can cause a reaction (it takes less than that in my case). As with other allergies the first exposure to the toxin doesn't produce any rash, but can sensitize the person so that a subsequent exposure will produce the symptomatic reaction and associated rash. This is caused by the body's immune system attacking the infected skin as if it were not part of the body. It may occur within a few hours of contact, or it may take several days. Sensitization may not occur with the first exposure, but the tenth or the fiftieth exposure may do it. Perhaps 70% of people are affected by these species to some degree. People often think they are immune, but it's simply that they don't come into contact with it. It isn't too hard to avoid the plants when they are in leaf, but in winter and early spring the inconspicuous leafless (but equally toxic) plants are more of a problem.

Treatment: The toxic resin quickly binds to the skin, so wash affected areas with soap and water as soon as possible. This washes off any excess resin and may reduce the seriousness of the rash. It is particularly important to wash your hands thoroughly, so you don't spread it to every part of your body you touch.

A common misconception is that the clear yellow pus from the blisters can spread the rash to other parts of the body; it can't. What very often happens, and probably causes the confusion, is that clothes become contaminated with the resin, and this can be spread to anything it touches. This can happen days, or even weeks, after initial contact and is the reason you should wash all clothes thoroughly after exposure.

The conventional remedy for the Rash is cortisone, which works by suppressing the immune system.

Unfortunately this is a powerful drug with many possible side effects, and the cure can be worse than the problem. I have only succumbed to using cortisone once, and only after I couldn't bend my arm because of the swelling.

There are many herbal remedies for alleviating the misery of the rash. The best known of these is Jewelweed (see *Impatiens*); others include Aloe Vera, Comfrey and Goldenseal. A Native American remedy was to rub soil from near the plant onto the rash. This sounds crazy, but such soil may actually contain substances that neutralize the resin. You must do this soon after exposure though, as one can hardly rub soil into weeping blisters.

Another possible treatment for the rash involves the use of homeopathic preparations, several of which have been used. I once tried a preparation made from Poison Ivy known as Rhus Tox, and it seemed to have a beneficial effect, stopping my weeping blisters and itching within 24 hours (whether it would have stopped anyway is of course an open question). The homeopathic literature says that if taken properly it can actually make you immune to the plant. I can't argue with success, especially when it's non-toxic, and I think it's worth trying if you are particularly sensitive to the plants.

Some people claim to make themselves immune by swallowing a tiny leaflet from the plant every day for a month in spring. Conceivably this may work by stimulating the body's immune system, but ingesting any part of the plant can hardly be recommended.

Medicine: Native Americans used the toxic resin to remove warts, by cutting the top from the wart and spreading the juice on it. They were often immune to the plants allergenic effect however.

Other uses: Native Americans commonly used the vines for basket weaving. The toxic resin from the closely related Japanese Lacquer Tree is used as varnish for woodenware, and it has been suggested that native species could be used in the same ways.

Animal food: I have a certain admiration for these plants, because of their ability to aggressively stand up to human intrusion. They are quite important as food and shelter for wildlife. Deer and goats eat the leaves and the berries provide food for many birds (they distribute the seeds). The flowers produce nectar for bees.

Cultivation: It's stretching the imagination to imagine cultivating Poison Ivy or Oak, though I can see at least one potential use: growing it along walls or fences to keep out human intruders. If you want to propagate these species, seed or cuttings are effective.

Eradication: Of more interest to most people is eradicating the plants, and while poisoning Poison Ivy does have a certain poetic justice, I hesitate to use herbicides. The plant can be eliminated by repeated cultivation, smothering with a thick mulch, grazing by goats, or simply uprooting. Of course all of these can be problematic if you are susceptible to its effects.

It is said that burning the plants will cause the resin to be vaporized in the smoke. Apparently this can cause potentially serious irritation to the eyes, throat and lungs. Nearly everything I have read on this topic claims this to be true, except for one, seemingly authoritative, opinion which stated flatly that this is wrong. Either way it would seem prudent to avoid getting into the smoke.

Species are:
T. radicans - **Poison Ivy**
T. vernix - **Poison Sumac** (the most virulent species)
T. quercifolia - **Poison Oak** (the commonest shrub in California)
T. diversilobum - **Oakleaf Poison Ivy**

Tradescantia virginiana / Spiderwort
Syn. *T. ohioensis*
East   *Commelinaceae*
Greens: The tender young leaves and stems can be used in salads, or as a potherb. Older leaves can also be used as a potherb. They are quite slimy, hence the rather uncomplimentary common name "Snotweed" (try taking Snotweed quiche to your next potluck).

Flowers: These may be added to salads or candied.

Medicine: The plant is a useful wound herb to stop bleeding. It has also been used for urinary problems.

Other uses: The hairs on the stamens are useful to botanists. They consist of a chain of 22 large cells, and are frequently used in botany classes to study cell nuclei.

Pollution indicator
One unusual use of the plant is in studying pollution. The blue hairs on the flower stamens are very sensitive to some pollutants (including vinyl chloride, ethylene dibromide, sulfur dioxide, auto emissions and low level radiation). If exposed to these pollutants they can turn pink in as little as 2 - 3 weeks. People living close to major sources of pollution might want to have Spiderwort in their gardens (or they might consider moving elsewhere).

Cultivation: This popular perennial ornamental can be grown from cuttings, seed or division, and thrives in part shade or full sun. It grows in most soil types, multiplies quickly, needs no maintenance, and grows so vigorously it can become a pest.

Related species include:
T. occidentalis - **Western Spiderwort**
T. pinetorum
Used as above.

Tragopogon species / Goatsbeard
Throughout   *Asteraceae*
Roots: The roots of these biennials can be eaten while dormant, from the end of their first year of growth, until they start growing in the spring of their second year. The rosettes of grass-like leaves are quite inconspicuous at this time, so you must look for the old second year plants. Close by you will find the new rosettes.

The roots are scraped, or peeled, and eaten raw or cooked like Carrot. If they are bitter try cooking them in at least one change of water.

Greens: In the spring of their second year, the new leaves and crowns can be used like those of Dandelion (*Taraxacum*), raw or cooked. The flower buds have been steamed or fried in tempura batter.

Drink: The roasted root is used like Chicory (*Cicorium*) as a coffee substitute.

Medicine: The leaves have been used to treat wounds.

Ornament: The attractive, downy seed heads resemble those of the related Dandelion. They have been sprayed with hair spray to hold them together, and used in dried flower arrangements.

Cultivation: These species are easily grown from seed in any good garden soil, and often self-seed.

Species include:
T. dubius - Yellow Goatsbeard
T. pratensis - Meadow Salsify (best)
T. Porrifolius - Salsify
Cultivated for its roots, Salsify is often found as an escape. The wild roots are smaller and less succulent than cultivated ones, but are used in the same ways.

Trapa natans / Water Chestnut
Escape   Hydrocaryaceae
Seed: This is not the tropical Water Chestnut (*Eleocharis dulcis*) which is only found in Chinese restaurants in North America. This species bears edible seeds in large two horned fruits. These are a substantial food, with about 15% starch, 3% protein and lots of manganese, calcium, phosphorus and iron. They can be dried and ground to flour, cooked as a vegetable or candied.

Cultivation: Related *Trapa* species have been dietary staples in parts of their Asian homeland, and are commonly cultivated. Apparently they have yielded as much as 10,000 pounds of seed per acre. This species is hardy enough to have naturalized as far north as New England. It is fairly easy to grow from seed (which should be kept moist at all times) in warm, shallow, slow moving water. It spreads easily and rapidly by means of floating seed, and can become a pest, crowding out native species. If you plant it you have a responsibility to ensure it doesn't escape and become a problem.

Trifolium pratense / Red Clover
Throughout   *Fabaceae*
Red Clover was originally introduced from Europe as a fodder crop, and is now one of the commonest *Trifolium* species in the country. Like many members of the *Fabaceae* it contains nitrogen fixing bacteria in nodules on its roots, and enriches the soil it grows in. The name

Clover is derived from the Latin clava meaning club, which explains why the playing card club symbol is a clover.

Greens: Clover is common and nutritious, but not very good, so I would classify it as a "survival food". Native Americans in California (and elsewhere) thought differently, and ate the young spring leaves in large quantities. The first white explorers were astonished to see them grazing in the fields like deer.

The young spring leaves can be eaten raw, but are more easily digested if cooked for 5 - 10 minutes. They are better when mixed with other greens. I sometimes add a few leaves to green blender drinks (see *Symphytum*).

Bloat is a common problem for livestock (and humans) when eating a lot of Clover. It is caused when digestive gases combine with substances in the plant to form a foam. Native Americans sometimes dipped the leaves in salt water to prevent this, or they ate them with California Bay Laurel nuts (*Umbellularia*).

Flowers: The newly opened individual flowers have been added to salads.

Seeds: The cleaned seed can be sprouted for salad greens like Alfalfa. It has also been ground to flour, and mixed with wheat flour for baking bread.

Drink: The nectar rich blossoms have a faintly sweet flavor, and are used (fresh or dried) for make tea.

Medicine: Clover blossom tea is thought to stimulate the liver and bladder, and is sometimes used as a diuretic. It is also a carminative and possibly a mild sedative. The plant was used externally for skin diseases, and to treat some forms of cancer (it may have some tumor-inhibiting properties).

Animal food: Red Clover was once the most important commercial forage crop in North America, and is still very important. However the protein rich leaves can cause digestive problems, so must be used in moderation. They also contain minute amounts of estrogen and have caused animals to abort. Clovers are an important source of nectar for bees.

Nitrogen Fertilizer

In the 16th and 17th centuries the use of nitrogen fixing Clovers in crop rotation caused a revolution in European agriculture and increased production enormously. They were used to return nitrogen to the soil, to replace that taken by growing crops. An acre planted in Clover may receive 100 - 500 pounds of nitrogen annually, which is the equivalent of up to ten tons of manure.

A Japanese farmer named Masanobu Fukuoka claims to have farmed the same piece of land for over forty years, obtaining two crops of grain annually, with only the nitrogen obtained from interplanted crops of Clover.

Clovers are excellent for improving the soil, either as a green manure, or cover crop, and a large number of species and varieties are available. They also suppress weeds, encourage worms and give nectar for bees.

Lawns: If you can live without a 100% pure grass lawn, Red Clover is an excellent lawn plant. It fixes its own nitrogen, so feeds itself and its neighbors, and stays green long after grass has turned brown. The clippings can be used for green manure, mulch or compost.

Clover can be combined with herbs such as Chamomile, Thyme and Yarrow, to make an herbal lawn.

Cultivation: This species is easily grown from seed, and does well in average garden soils. It can become a weed.

Related species:
Almost all *Trifolium* species can be used for food as above, but most aren't very good. The best include:

T. obtusiflorum - **Clammy Clover**
T. virescens - **Bear Clover**
These annual species are among the best flavored.

T. bifidum - **Pinole Clover**
T. dichotomum - **Indian Clover**
These species are good seed bearers. No doubt they received their common names because of their importance to Native Americans.

T. repens - **White Clover**
T. wormskioldii - **Cow Clover**
The thin rhizomes were gathered while dormant from fall to early spring. They were usually boiled or steamed, and are said to taste quite good (I'm not convinced though).

Caution: *T. arvense* - **Rabbits Foot Clover**
This species is not edible.

Tropaeolum majus / Nasturtium
West coast   *Tropaeolaceae*
This popular garden ornamental has escaped and naturalized along the west coast, and locally elsewhere. It shares the name Nasturtium with the unrelated Watercress (*Nasturtium officinale*), because they both have the same pungent mustard flavor.

Greens: The leaves can often be found growing year round in mild climates. They can be used in the same ways as Watercress. They are good raw in salads and sandwiches, cooked as a potherb, and in soups and stir fries.

Flowers: The large, brightly colored flowers are sweet, pungent and slightly aromatic. With good reason they are probably the most commonly eaten edible flower. They can transform a dull green salad into a work of art. You can suck the nectar out of the spur on the flower.

Seeds: The unripe seeds can be eaten in salads and soups. They have also been pickled like Capers.

Cultivation: The Nasturtium is a very useful edible ornamental. It is beautiful, easily grown from seed, grows vigorously in poor soil, and often self-seeds.

Tsuga species / Hemlocks
Throughout   *Pinaceae*
Caution: These Hemlocks are large, long-lived coniferous trees, and have nothing in common with the dangerous Poison Hemlock (*Conium maculatum*).

Cambium: Like many conifers, the inner bark is edible, if not particularly palatable, and is generally considered a survival food. However Native Alaskans actually acquired a taste for it, and gathered and ate it regularly each spring. They stripped the bark from the Western Hemlock, separated the soft inner bark from the woody outer layer, and cooked it in a fire pit (see *Camassia*).

The cooked inner bark was then eaten alone, or mixed with berries and made into cakes. These were often dried for later use.

Tea: The tender, young, light green needles can be used to make an antiscorbutic tea, or brewed into a drink somewhat like Spruce beer.

Medicine: Oil from the leaves has been used as a liniment for muscle pain. A tea of the bark has been used to wash wounds. The vitamin C rich leaf tea has been used to treat scurvy. It is quite astringent, so has also been used as a gargle for sore throats, and as an enema.

Beds: The green boughs were once used to make camp beds, but this destructive practice is not really acceptable anymore. See *Pinus* for a more acceptable modern substitute.

Wood: All species can be used as lumber. They were not considered particularly valuable in the past, but as large trees of more desirable species become scarce, they have become more important. The Western Hemlock (*T. heterophylla*) is the largest and most important species, and is now one of the most valuable lumber trees in the northwest. The wood is similar to pine, and is mostly used in building construction and millwork.

Hemlocks are often used for pulpwood, and for making synthetic fibers such as rayon. They are not particularly good firewood, giving about 15 million Btu per cord.

Other uses: The bark has been used as a commercial source of tannin, for brown dye and for garden mulch.

Cultivation: Propagate these species from seed, in moist woodland soil. They transplant well, grow quickly and tolerate deep shade. They are quite hardy, but dislike extreme heat and drought. The seedlings grow well in the shade of other trees, and eventually come to dominate them in the climax forest. They are long-lived trees, some lasting up to 1000 years. The graceful Hemlocks are popular specimen trees, and are also commonly clipped to make dense evergreen hedges.

Turnera aphrodisiaca, T. diffusa / Damiana
Texas *Turneraceae*

These species only occur in the United States in Texas. They aren't really edible, but I have included them because they have received attention for their reputed aphrodisiac, and intoxicating effects, and they are becoming less common in the wild because of this.

Tea: The leaves have been used as a substitute for oriental tea.

Medicine: A tea of the bitter leaves is used as a tonic for the genito-urinary tract. They are often mixed with an equal amount of Saw Palmetto berries (*Serenoa*) for this. The leaves are a mild sedative, but smoking them is more likely to arouse your lungs than anything else.

Cultivation: Damiana can be grown from seed or semi-ripe cuttings. It likes a well-drained sunny location.

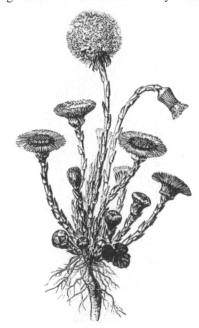

Tussilago farfara / Coltsfoot
Northeast *Asteraceae*

The Dandelion-like flowers are among the first flowers of spring, appearing even before their own leaves.

Greens: The young leaves and flower stalks are edible when cooked as a potherb, but are not very good, and contain potentially toxic pyrrolizidine alkaloids.

Roots: The roots have been boiled as a vegetable. They have also been candied by boiling them in sugar.

Smoking mixture

In Europe the dried leaves were once widely smoked as a tobacco substitute. They formed the basis of many herbal smoking mixtures, to which were added such herbs as Thyme, Mullein, Buckbean, Rosemary and Bearberry. The smoke of these mixtures is wonderfully fragrant, but I imagine it is still pretty harmful to the lungs.

Salt substitute: Native Americans rolled the dried leaves into balls, dried them in the sun, and then toasted them on rocks around the fire (try using a skillet). The resulting ash was crushed to powder for use as a salt substitute. An even better product was made by dissolving the ash in water, and then straining and evaporating it.

Medicine: The generic name means cough dispeller and was given because the plant was once used as an expectorant and to soothe mucus membranes in all kinds of respiratory ailments. The root may be used as tea, candied, or made into syrup. The dried leaves were once commonly smoked to relieve asthma.

Cultivation: Coltsfoot was originally introduced as a medicinal herb, but soon escaped from cultivation. It is now a common weed in many areas. It can be grown from seed or division, in almost any soil. It can be eradicated by improving the soil, which gives more vigorous competitors an edge.

Typha species / Cattail Flag

Throughout   *Typhaceae*
Cattails are one of my favorite useful wild plants. They have all the necessary attributes for a good wild food, they are common, easily identified, widely available, nutritious, tasty, available year round, aren't harmed by harvesting (indeed thinning may be beneficial) and can't be confused with any poisonous plants.

Caution: Don't eat raw Cattails if there is any danger of contamination from polluted water. For example the plants often stretch for miles in poorly drained roadside ditches, but may be contaminated by car exhaust emissions.

Shoots: In winter the dormant roots develop claw-like shoots that will develop into new stems in the coming year. Snap these from the rhizome, peel and eat raw in salads, boil for ten minutes as a vegetable, or add to soups and stews.

In late winter and early spring these shoots start to elongate, and can be eaten until they are about two feet long. Longer shoots may be too acrid to be palatable, as may the new shoots that emerge later in the year. These shoots break from the root quite easily. Peel off the tough outer leaves, to leave the white tender core, which can be eaten raw in salads, boiled for 5 - 10 minutes, steamed, stir fried (with Wild Onions, Watercress, Arrowhead), or added to soups (good with miso and seaweed).

Flowers: My favorite Cattail food is the immature flower spike, which appears over a few weeks in early summer (May - June). It's gathered while still tightly wrapped in the sheath, boiled for 5 - 10 minutes, and eaten like Sweet Corn, which it somewhat resembles. The edible part can also be scraped from the wiry core and cooked as a vegetable, or added to soup.

Pollen: When the flowers mature in June and July they produce an abundance of edible pollen. Gather it by bending the flower spike over a bag, and gently rubbing off the pollen. Sift carefully to remove insects, and any debris, and its ready to use. Pollen might seem like a pretty insubstantial food, but Native Americans gathered it by the basketful. If dried thoroughly the pollen may stay wholesome for 12 months.

This fine powder can be mixed with an equal amount of wheat or corn flour, to add flavor and nutrients to bread, cakes, pancakes and muffins. Native Americans made cakes of pollen and water, wrapped them in Cattail leaves and baked them in the coals of a fire. It can also be used for thickening soup, or made into gruel (boil two parts of pollen with one of wheat flour). It colors everything bright yellow.

Seed: Native Americans ate the tiny seeds, after burning them to remove the down. They sprinkled water on the piles of fluffy seeds, so the resulting fire wouldn't be so fierce as to destroy the seed. The cleaned seed was used to make a nutritious gruel.

Roots: The fleshy rope-like rhizomes provide the most substantial food. They can be an important survival food, as they are nutritious, often abundant and are available year round. They are actually more nutritious in winter, when other foods are scarce, as they are full of stored starch at this time. The rhizomes can be eaten raw, boiled, or roasted in a fire (eat the starchy interior and discard the tough fibers).

Flour: The roots contain 20 - 40% starch which can be extracted from the roots by the process described for Kudzu (see *Pueraria*). The wet meal can be used immediately for pancakes, bread and gruel, or to thicken soups and sauces. It can be dried for storage. The flour contains about 80% starch and 7% protein, and has potential as a new commercial food product. It has been estimated that an acre of plants might yield three tons of starch annually.

Medicine: The downy seeds were soaked in the juice of healing herbs and used to dress wounds. The root starch has been used as a poultice for burns. The pollen has been used to stop bleeding.

Stems and leaves: The fibrous stems and leaves can be used for thatch, baskets, mats, sandals, rafts, hats, belts, screens and many other things. The leaves have been used as caulking between barrel staves, boat planks and the logs of cabins.

Cattail leaves are the best material for woven rush seating, and they were once widely used for this. They are gathered as soon as they reach full size, and dried for later use. They are soaked overnight prior to use, to make them supple.

Down: The fluffy seeds can be used to stuff pillows (especially for dream pillows - see *Humulus*), lifejackets, sleeping bags, life preservers, walls of huts, mattresses, insulated clothing and quilts. Some people buy do-it-yourself down clothing kits, and substitute Cattail down for goose down. Native Americans used the absorbent down for diapers.

To keep warm in an emergency, stuff handfuls of the down into your boots and clothing (but don't get wet gathering it).

Gather the ripe seed heads as they begin to disintegrate in late summer, break them up and dry thoroughly before use. A potential problem in some cases may be infestation with insects. A possible solution to this might be to add a powdered insect repelling plant such as Tansy (*Tanacetum*) or Wormwood (*Artemisia*).

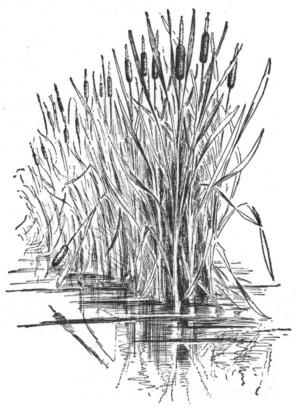

Tinder: The down and pollen were used to catch sparks for starting fires without matches.

Pollen: Native Americans often used the powdery pollen to decorate their bodies, and as baby powder.

Pollution cleanup: These fast-growing plants take most of the available plant nutrients (especially nitrogen and phosphorus) from the water in which they grow, and

convert them into vegetation. Consequently they can be used to clean up water polluted by chemical fertilizers and sewage sludge. They aren't as efficient as Water Hyacinth (*Eichornia*), but they are much hardier and can grow farther north. They have been used in wastewater treatment marshes, to purify wastewater from sewage treatment plants. On a smaller scale they have been used in domestic greywater treatment beds. In Egypt they have been used to desalinate soil for agriculture.

Light: The whole head can be wired on to a stick, dipped in oil or wax, and used as a torch. They may last up to 30 minutes.

Fuel

Growing Cattails in sewage treatment plants would result in the production of enormous quantities of organic matter. This biomass could be fermented to produce methane. An acre of the plants could yield as much as 250,000 cubic feet of gas annually. The starchy roots could be fermented to produce alcohol for fuel. The residue left after both of these forms of fermentation is excellent fertilizer, and could return a lot of leached nutrients back to dry land.

Ornament: Urban dwellers are probably most familiar with Cattails as dried floral decorations. Some people recommend spraying them with hair spray to hold the head together, but this only works if you gather them early enough.

Animal food: The plants are very important to wildlife for food and shelter.

Culture medium: Starch from the roots has been used as a bacterial culture medium.

Cultivation: Cattails are easily propagated from sections of rhizome, moved when dormant. They grow in the still shallow water of ditches and lake margins, or any very wet soil. In suitable conditions they spread rapidly, a single plant has been known to produce 35 offsets in a single summer.

Fertilizer: The abundant organic matter produced by the plants can be used as mulch, compost material or green manure. Green parts contain 2% nitrogen, 1% phosphorus and 3% potassium.

Potential crop use: These plants not only produce a wide variety of useful products, but also produce them in large quantities. They could be a useful crop for land that is unsuited to most conventional crops. They are rarely bothered by pests or disease, are perennial (so don't need re-planting every year) and don't mind growing in monocultures.

Useful species include:
All *Typha* species can be used in the same ways. The commonest are:

T. angustifolia - **Narrow Leaved Cattail**
T. latifolia - **Common Cattail**

Ulmus rubra / Slippery Elm Syn *U. fulva*

East   *Ulmaceae*

The Slippery Elm was once a common tree through much of the east, but sadly this is no longer the case. It has been badly hit by Dutch Elm disease, a disease spread by a lethal combination of the tunneling Elm Bark Beetle (*Scolytus*) and a fungus (*Ceratocystis ulmi*). This may have killed as many as 15 billion Elms (15,000,000,000) of various species, since it was introduced into North America on veneer logs in the 1930's. One hopeful note is the isolation of a bacterium that inhibits the lethal fungus, and may eventually be of help in halting the disease.

Though Slippery Elm is much less abundant than it once was, it is by no means rare, and in some places is still quite common. The nutritious and rather mucilaginous, inner bark (cambium layer) was frequently used by Native Americans for food and medicine.

Gathering: Never strip the bark from the trunk of a tree, as this would kill or seriously injure it. The only exception to this would be if a tree were being cut down anyway. The least destructive way to get the bark is to trim off some branches and strip it from them. The bark is usually gathered in spring, when it is easiest to peel and contains the most sugars. The edible inner part is separated from the woody outer bark, and eaten fresh, or dried for later use.

Preparation: The sweetish inner bark may be eaten raw or cooked, but is not a very attractive food. Native Americans dried and ground it to flour, for use in thickening soup and making gruel. This was considered good for invalids who couldn't eat solid food.

Drink: The fresh or dried bark can be used to make a tea. This is often mixed with more flavorful herbs.

Medicine: A poultice of the mucilaginous inner bark was once widely used to treat skin problems, sores, acne, burns, wounds, cancer and gangrene. It can be used alone, or mixed with healing herbs such as Comfrey (*Symphytum*) or Chickweed (*Stellaria*). Some herbalists moisten the dried bark with a tea of Wormwood (*Artemisia*) or other herbs.

The inner bark has been used internally for lung, throat, digestive and urinary problems, and for diarrhea.

Native American women used the inner bark to aid in childbirth, and to induce abortion. Interestingly it has now been found to contain a glucocorticosteroid similar to those found in Wild Yams (*see Dioscorea*), and which are used to create birth control pills.

Animal food: Cattle have been fed the dried inner bark when little else was available.

Cultivation: Elms prefer rich, moist, neutral soil and can be grown from ripe seed, planted immediately, or stratified at 40 degrees for three months. Suckers and layering can also be used. They transplant quite well.

U. americana / American Elm

Wood: This species has few of the medicinal benefits of the Slippery Elm, but its wood is much more important. It is tough, resists splitting, holds nails well, bends well, is durable if kept wet, and has an attractive grain. It has been used for making boats, wheels, carts, paneling, fenceposts and veneer. Elm was not very highly regarded for cabinetmaking in the past, when there was such an abundance of fine timber, but in recent years it has become more popular. Dutch Elm disease has also increased its availability.

Fuel: Elm is not considered to be very good firewood (it gives about 20 million Btu per cord), but it has been widely available in some areas, due to the Dutch Elm disease.

Fiber: The inner bark of the American Elm was an important source of fiber for Native Americans, and was used for cloth, mats, baskets, ropes and cordage. The outer bark was used for making canoes, though these were inferior to those of Birch bark. White pioneer craftsmen wove the bark into chair seats, in the same way as the Hickory (*Carya*).

Horticultural uses: There are vigorous, disease resistant hybrids of American and Chinese Elms, which are said to grow 8 - 14 feet a year, and coppice well. They have potential for use in energy plantations, to produce firewood, alcohol or methane. Elms tend to be very wind resistant, and make good windbreak or shelterbelt trees.

Ulva lactuca / Sea Lettuce

Atlantic   *Chlorophyta*

This common green seaweed is one of the most photosynthetically active of all seaweeds, and in confined pools it may become the dominant plant. It is easy to gather in quantity, but be careful where you gather it, as it thrives in polluted water near sewage pipes, or where nutrient rich fertilizer runoff enters the sea.

Food: This species is best in spring. It is sometimes known as Green Laver, because it is used in the same ways as Laver (*Porphyra*). It is not as useful however, as it is tougher and less palatable. It is often dried and ground to powder, as a nutritional supplement and salt substitute.

Related species: Several West Coast species can be used in the same ways, including:

U. fenestrata
U. rigida

Umbellularia californica / California Bay Laurel

West coast   *Lauraceae*
This species is widely distributed along the West Coast, and quite variable in its form. In the hot arid interior of California it grows as a shrub, but on the cool moist Oregon coast it becomes a handsome 100-foot tall tree.

Caution: Like many members of the *Lauraceae*, the Bay Laurel has aromatic evergreen leaves. These contain safrole, which is toxic in large amounts, so they should be used in moderation (see *Sassafras*).

Nuts: The Bay Laurel also produces quantities of oily, thin-shelled edible nuts (sometimes called Kettlewood nuts). These are bitter when raw, but supposedly become quite palatable when roasted like Peanuts. I have found them to have a good flavor, but a bitter aftertaste (maybe leaching would help?) I used to gather them from a bike path where they had been gently run over, already cleaned of the fleshy part and sun dried. Native Americans gathered them in large quantities for winter use. They roasted them as a snack, or parched and ground them to meal for baking and gruel.

Drink: Native Americans used the leaves for tea.

Bay Leaves

The aromatic leaves are similar to those of Sweet Bay (*Laurus nobilis*) in appearance and flavor, though they are more strongly flavored. They can be gathered year round and used fresh or dried. The dried leaves are commonly sold as a substitute for Bay on the West Coast.

The leaves can be used in exactly the same way as Sweet Bay. They are added to the pot for the duration of cooking and removed just before serving (they are too leathery to actually eat). Native Americans ground the dried leaves to powder for use as flavoring.

Medicine: The aromatic oil is antiseptic, but rather irritating to skin and mucus membranes. Merely inhaling the odor of a crushed leaf can cause sneezing. The pungent odor of the crushed leaf was once thought to cure headaches. A tea of the leaves has been used as a wash for wounds and skin parasites.

Other uses: The leaves have insecticidal properties. They have been stored with food to repel insects. They have also been burned to eliminate fleas from people, animals and places. Oil has been extracted from them, for use as an insecticide. The leaves have been used to scent the water in sweat lodges and saunas.

Wood: The wood is often known as Oregon Myrtle. It is hard, heavy and polishes to a rich brown color, but is rather difficult to season. It is often used in cabinetmaking, and burlwood with its unusual curly grain patterns is particularly prized. It has also been used for boatbuilding, paneling, veneer and turning. Making tourist souvenirs, such as candlesticks and bowls, is a cottage industry in parts of Oregon. This is not an important commercial tree to the large lumber companies, though they do cut and sell it. Often because it is in the way of the Douglas Fir they want. The supply of lumber sized trees is now rapidly nearing exhaustion.

Cultivation: Bay Laurel is attractive in both its tree and shrub forms, and makes a fine garden ornamental. It may be propagated from seed (file it to allow water to penetrate the hard seed coat), semi ripe cutting or layering. It is slow growing, but lives up to 300 years.

Umblicaria species / Rock Tripe

North and mountains   *Lichenes*
Survival food: The Rock Tripes have often been eaten in the far north in times of necessity, but are usually

described as revolting, and only slightly preferable to death by starvation. The fresh plants contain acids that cause severe gastrointestinal irritation, and must be leached to make them edible. See Iceland Moss (*Cetraria*) for details on the preparation, other uses, and cultivation of Lichens.

In Japan the native species (*U. esculenta*) is considered a delicacy, and is sold in markets under the name *Iwatake*. It is soaked in water to leach out the irritating acids, boiled until tender, seasoned and served in salads and tempura.

Species include:
U. muhlenbergii
Native Americans used this species for soup.

Urtica dioica / **Stinging Nettle**

Throughout   *Urticaceae*
The Stinging Nettle has all of the attributes of a valuable wild food plant. It is highly nutritious, easy to identify, doesn't resemble any poisonous plants, is widely distributed, very vigorous and often available in abundance. It also tastes good enough to have been cultivated as a food crop.

The specific name is derived from the Latin word *Ure* meaning burn, while the common name Nettle is from the Anglo Saxon word for needle. These names are a good clue to the plants most obvious asset (as is the word "stinging" of course. The Nettle is covered hollow hairs which act like tiny hypodermic needles. When these are touched they inject a stinging substance containing formic acid. The plant is avoided by most mammalian herbivores, though not insects, it is a very important food plant for many of them.

The sting of the Nettle is unpleasant, but usually wears off fairly quickly, and it is a lot less irritating than Poison Ivy. Apparently some tropical Nettles can immobilize one for days, and perhaps even kill.

Nutrients: The Nettle has a good reason for protecting itself as it does: this tasty herb is one of the most nutritious of all green plants. It contains more protein than almost any other green leaf, large amounts of chlorophyll, vitamin A, several B's, lots of C and D and an abundance of minerals including calcium, iron (one of the richest plant sources), manganese, phosphorus, potassium, silicon and sulfur.

Gathering greens: The drawback to the use of Nettles as food is that they are only edible when young, for a short time in early to late spring. Not only does the plant get tougher as summer progresses, but inedible crystal deposits form in the leaves.

You need to protect your hand when gathering Nettles, so wear gloves (or anything that comes to hand).

Preparing greens: Obviously this ferocious plant can't be eaten raw, but it actually takes only a few seconds of cooking to render the sting impotent. A few minutes of boiling, steaming or stir-frying produce an excellent potherb. The greens can be used as a substitute for Spinach in any recipe.

The dried, powdered leaves have been added to bread, soups and sauces to increase their nutritional value.

Winter greens: The roots have been taken indoors in autumn and forced like Chicory to produce winter greens (see *Cicorium* for more on forcing).

Drink: The dried leaves can be used to make a nutritious tea. This is usually mixed with tastier herbs to improve its flavor. In Europe the young leaves are used to make a palatable non-alcoholic soft drink called Nettle Beer.

Rennet: Fresh Nettle juice has been used like rennet for making cheese.

Medicine: The plant has traditionally been used as a detoxifying spring tonic, so it's interesting that it contains secretin, a substance that helps the bowels to eliminate mucus. It has also been used to treat arthritis and gout. It was thought to stimulate the kidneys, gall bladder, prostate gland, liver and digestive tract. The greens are a mild laxative, and their high nutritive value makes them a useful food for those suffering from anemia.

The fresh juice, and powdered leaves, have been used externally as a styptic wound herb. The sting was thought to be beneficial for treating rheumatism, stiff muscles and frostbite. Freeze dried nettles has been found to reduce the symptoms of hay fever.

Nettle rash: The plant is frequently the cause of injury in the form of Nettle rash. The traditional treatment for this is to rub the affected area with the crushed leaves of soothing plants, such as Dock (*Rumex*), Jewelweed (*Impatiens*), or Mugwort (*Artemisia*).

Fiber: Nettle is closely related to Indian Hemp (*Apocynum*), and like that plant it is an excellent source of fiber for cordage, rope, netting, paper, sail cloth, sack cloth and fine fabrics (it was said to be better than Flax). The fibers can be extracted and prepared in the same way as Flax (*Linum*). Nettles were among the most important fiber plants for Native Americans.

Animal food: For obvious reasons animals avoid fresh Nettles, but the dried plants lose their sting, and are a valuable animal feed. Nettle hay is actually too rich in protein (about 25% dry weight) to be used alone, so is added to other feed as a nutritional supplement. It is said to increase the disease resistance, weight and general health of cows, poultry and most other animals. Gypsies once fed Nettles to horses to improve their appearance prior to sale.

Shampoo: Nettle tea makes a good hair rinse (sometimes mixed with vinegar), to add shine and body and remove dandruff.

Other uses: The dark green leaves have been used as a green dye, and as a commercial source of chlorophyll.

Companion Plant: Stinging Nettle is considered to be one of the best companion plants for the garden. When grown with aromatic herbs such as Valerian and Mint, it is said to increase their production of aromatic oils. It is also believed to make neighboring plants more resistant to disease, and attacks by insect pests.

Cultivation: With so many valuable uses for the plants, they are well worth having around the garden. It has occasionally been cultivated as a perennial potherb. If you are lucky you will have it (or a related species) growing nearby. In which case you can divide and transplant some (or take root cuttings), otherwise you will have to grow your own from seed. The plants like rich moist soil, and will grow in full sun or deep shade.

Their high chlorophyll content enables them to grow with as little as ten percent of daylight.

Nettles can be invasive, so it is best to put them somewhere they can be allowed to run wild without stinging too many people. It has been suggested as a possible cover crop for orchards. An ingenious gardener might use the plant to deter intruders, especially children, or to keep people from getting too near especially cherished plantings.

Fertilizer

Stinging Nettles love nitrogen rich soils, and often their presence indicates the site of old human habitations, such as animal pens, dung heaps or abandoned privies. The plant enriches the soil it grows in, as its leaf litter decays into especially rich humus (with an abundance of nitrogen, potassium and other minerals). It was once said that you should plant fruit trees where Nettles grow abundantly.

Biodynamic gardeners have an especially high regard for the plant, and use it in many of their formulations. You can make an excellent liquid fertilizer from Nettles (See Comfrey *Symphytum* for details on how to do this). The same liquid (or the whole plant) is said to stimulate fermentation in the compost pile.

Related species:
All native *Urtica* species can be used in the same ways, though they may not be as good.

U. lyalli - Tall Nettle
The roots of this species are edible.

Vaccinium species / Blueberries

Throughout   *Ericaceae*

Blueberries are most common in cool northern regions and have long been one of the most important wild foods to be found there. They are mostly pioneer plants and can often be found in abundance after fires or logging have disturbed the forest ecosystem. Remember this when looking for them. The quantity and quality of the fruits varies according to species, but most are pretty good.

The fruits were very important to some Native American tribes, and families held gathering rights to particular locations. The annual harvest was often an important social event, as scattered bands came together at the best gathering grounds. It was a time for talking with old friends and relatives, feasting, trading, gambling, dancing and courting. Large quantities of fruit were eaten fresh, but most were sun dried for winter use.

The Uses of Wild Plants

Fruit gathering: The berries ripen in mid-to-late summer, and must be gathered as soon as they are ripe, otherwise birds and other forest creatures will take them. Native Americans often used berry combs to gather these (and other small) berries. These are much more efficient than hand picking, and greatly speed up the process of gathering small, widely dispersed berries. One can sometimes gather the ripe berries quickly by putting a poncho or tarp on the ground under the bushes and shaking them. Be gentle with the ripe fruits however, as they crush easily.

If you gather more berries than you can use at one time, dry them in a warm dark place, or freeze them whole.

Fruit preparation: The berries are smaller than their cultivated counterparts, but also sweeter. They are great eaten raw straight from the bush, or in fruit salads, ice cream, etc. They can also be cooked, in pies, preserves, muffins, sauces, pancakes and fritters.

Drinks: The fruits can be used to make wine, and to flavor liqueurs.

Antioxidants
Blueberries are one of the richest sources of antioxidants yet discovered. These important nutrients help eliminate toxins, prevent cell damage, and may even help to prevent cancer. Everyone should eat more antioxidants.

Medicine: A tea of the leaves was once widely used as a remedy for diabetes, and can actually reduce blood sugar levels. This is not a home remedy however, as this effect makes the tea somewhat toxic when drunk in quantity.

The tannin rich berries have been used to treat diarrhea. Paradoxically they have also been used as a mild laxative. They are also said to prevent flatulence, and to have a blood-cleansing effect.

Smoke: The leaves of *V. uliginosum* (and perhaps others) have been smoked like those of the related Bearberry (*Arctostaphylos*).

Dye: The juice of the berries has been used to dye food, wine, cloth, leather and people.

Animal food: The plants provide food for many wild creatures. The berries (bears, birds, rodents) and foliage (deer) are both important.

Cultivation: Blueberries can be grown from seed, but it is slow, so cuttings, suckers and layering are more commonly used. They like well-drained, moist, humus rich, acid woodland soil. If the soil isn't acid enough you can add sawdust or pine needles to lower the pH. These plants often form an association with nitrogen fixing fungi, which helps them to survive in poor acid soils. As pioneer plants they prefer fairly open conditions, with lots of sun.

Many improved Blueberry cultivars are available for different parts of the country. They are not self-fertile, so several types should be planted for maximum fruit set.

Horticultural uses: Blueberries were only domesticated in the early twentieth century, and are one of the few North American plants grown as a commercial crop. Some Blueberry species have also been grown as ornamentals, groundcover, windbreaks and hedges. They are not much bothered by insect pests or disease, but birds love them, and will eat every fruit on the bush if given the opportunity.

Species include:
V. corymbosum - Highbush Blueberry
A single large shrub (up to 15 feet tall) may produce as much as ten pints of berries. It has been the subject of intensive plant breeding and many fine cultivars exist.

V. angustifolium - Sugar Blueberry
This species is small, but very sweet. Several improved cultivars are available as Lowbush Blueberries.

V. ashei – Rabbiteye Blueberry
This southern species is much more heat tolerant than the other Blueberries, and has been used to breed cultivars that thrive in warmer climates.

V. stamineum - Squaw Huckleberry
This isn't called a Blueberry because the fruits are greenish purple when ripe. These are rather acid and taste best when cooked with sweetener.

V. deliciosum - **Rainier Bilberry**
V. ovalifolium – **Mountain Huckleberry**
V. ovatum – **Evergreen Huckleberry**
V. pennsylvanica - **Lowbush Blueberry**
V. uliginosum - **Bog Bilberry**
These species all bear excellent fruits.

V. parvifolium - **Red Huckleberry**
The sour fruits aren't bad raw, but are better cooked.

Vaccinium macrocarpon, V. oxycoccus / **Cranberry** Syn **Oxycoccus** spp

North   *Ericaceae*

You might think of Cranberries as an archetypal American food, yet *V. oxycoccus* is actually circumboreal, which means it grows all around the northern part of the globe. These species certainly thrive in North America however, and were one of the first exports from the New World colonies to Britain. Unfortunately these evergreen plants are becoming less common in the wild, as their boggy habitat is drained for agriculture and building.

Gathering: The berries ripen in late fall, and may remain in good condition right through until spring if not eaten. Winter is the best time to gather them, as the boggy ground is then frozen solid, and the red berries are easier to see. They may even be improved by exposure to frost.

Uses: The red berries are too sour to be pleasant raw, though their juice can be extracted and mixed with other fruit juices in cocktails. Most often they are cooked with sugar to make Cranberry sauce or jelly (the fruits contain a lot of pectin). The whole fruits freeze well.

Native Americans boiled the berries with Maple sauce to produce a kind of jelly, which was used as a traveling food. They also dried the fruits in the sun, and ground them to meal for baking. The dried fruits are now widely available commercially, and can be used like raisins in muffins and other baked goods.

Medicine: The fruits are rich in vitamin C and available in winter, so have long been used to treat scurvy. European sailors sometimes carried barrels of Cranberries in water aboard their sailing ships to prevent that dreaded affliction. It is sometimes claimed that the fruits can aid in relieving asthma and arthritis. They may also inactivate some antibiotics.

Urinary problems

Cranberries have long been used to treat urinary tract problems such as cystitis. The active ingredient is probably arbutin, which is a potent antiseptic (see *Arctostaphylos*)

Metal polish: Cranberries can be used as metal polish to remove the tarnish from silver.

Horticultural uses: The berries were gathered commercially from the wild for years before a man named Henry Hall first thought of cultivating them in the early nineteenth century. They have proved to be a useful crop for land on which few commercial crops can be grown without extensive drainage. Many improved cultivars have been produced over the years (mostly from *V. macrocarpon*), especially in Eastern Europe.

Propagation: The plants can be propagated from cuttings (easy), or seed (slow and less dependable). They like wet, acid soil, with a high humus content and part shade. They are hardy, but in the far north they may need the protection of snow, or water, to prevent frost damage. They are mostly self-fertile, but planting several varieties increases yields. In ideal conditions they are highly productive, giving as many as 400 bushels per acre.

Related species include:
Vaccinium vitis idaea - **Mountain Cranberry**
The leaves have been used for tea. Also known as the Lingonberry, this species is an important source of fruit in the far north, where few other fruits grow well. It is very popular in Scandinavia, where it is used in pickles, candy, wine, liqueurs, preserves, ice creams and sauces. It is widely cultivated there, and a number of cultivars are available. It is actually a better fruit than the Cranberry, and has potential as a new crop for the colder areas of North America.

This low growing plant can be used as a productive groundcover.

Valeriana edulis / **Tobacco Root**

West   *Valerianaceae*

This species resembles its cultivated cousin the European Valerian (*V. officinalis*) in appearance and properties, and its root has the same characteristic overpowering smell. Many people can't stand the smell of the root, but you can get used to it, I used to think it was nauseating, but now I quite like it.

The name Valerian is derived from the Latin valere, meaning to be strong, though whether this refers to its medicinal properties, or its overpowering odor is unclear. Apparently it gets its common name because the root was though to smell something like tobacco. It wasn't smoked that I know of.

Caution: The roots may be slightly toxic raw. This might just be their sedative effect, but the plant should probably be eaten in moderation.

Root: The roots can grow to 18 inches in length and two inches in diameter. They were a staple food for Native Americans in parts of the northwest. The roots were dug while dormant from fall to spring, and baked in a fire-pit in the same way as Camas (see *Camassia*s). If the flavor is too strong they can be boiled in a change of water. The cooked roots can be eaten immediately, added to soups, or dried and ground to flour for baking.

Greens: The young leaves have occasionally been cooked as a potherb.

Tea: The root makes an excellent tea, though it is rather a cultivated taste. It should probably be used in moderation because of its medicinal properties.

Medicine: A tea of the roots is a mild sedative and makes an ideal bedtime tea. It has also been added to dream pillows, and baths, for this effect.

Cultivation: This species has occasionally been cultivated for its medicinal root. Propagate from seed, soft cuttings or division, in a good garden soil.

Related species include:
V. ciliata
V. dioica - **Woods Valerian**
V. obovata
V. occidentalis
V. sitchensis - **Sitka Valerian**
Used as above.

Veronica **species** / **Brooklimes**

Throughout   *Scrophulariaceae*

Caution: The same caution I gave for Watercress, about gathering from clean water, also applies to Brooklime. If the water is polluted or contaminated, the plant will be also, and washing won't clean it. Of course cooking will kill any harmful organisms, though it won't eliminate chemical pollutants. I don't know whether parasite eggs can live in this plant, as they do in Watercress.

Greens: These plants like the same conditions as the Watercress (*Nasturtium*), and the two plants are often found growing together. Appropriately enough, they can be used together to make a tasty salad. Brooklime is rather bitter in flavor, but I don't find it unpleasantly so. The tender young leaves can be gathered from early spring until the flowers appear, and used in salads. Older leaves can be gathered anytime for use as a potherb, though you will probably have to change the cooking water at least once to reduce their bitterness.

Medicine: Brooklime was once greatly valued as a medicinal herb for treating scurvy, and respiratory problems. It is also a good wound poultice.

Cultivation: These plants are cultivated like Watercress.

Useful species include:
V. americana - **American Brooklime**
V. anagallis-aquatica - **Water Speedwell**
V. beccabunga - **European Brooklime**
V. comosa
All of these species are good.

Viburnum trilobum / **Highbush Cranberry**

Syn *V. opulus var trilobum*

North   *Caprifoliaceae*

Many or the twenty or so *Viburnum* species in North America bear edible fruits, though their palatability varies greatly. Sample any you come across to find the best flavored ones. This species is sometimes considered a subspecies of the European Guelder Rose. It is almost identical to that plant, except for one important point; the fruit is sour but palatable, while that of the Guelder Rose is so bitter as to be pretty much inedible. The fruits were quite important to Native Americans and gathering rights were sometimes divided among families of a tribe.

Fruit: The berries often remain on the bush well into winter, and may be improved by repeated frosts. As the common name suggests, the sour berries taste rather like Cranberries and can be used like them in preserves, jelly (they are rich in pectin), sauces and juice cocktails. They are usually too sour to eat raw, except as a nibble. Some people prefer the slightly under- ripe fruits.

Drink: A nice drink can be prepared by simmering the fruits in water with citrus peel and honey to taste (or aromatic herbs). They can also be fermented to make wine.

Medicine: The bark has been used medicinally like that of the Black Haw (below), but isn't considered to be as good. The fruits are rich in vitamin C and have been used to treat scurvy.

Animal food: Birds and rodents eat the berries. The foliage is eaten by deer and other herbivores.

Cultivation: The European and American species are both cultivated as ornamentals, for their pretty flowers, bright red berries and fall foliage. They are very hardy, self-fertile, and may be grown from seed, cuttings or layering. They like moist soil and sun or part shade. They need little attention once established and make a fine hedge or screen.

Plant breeders have worked to improve the fruit, and a number of superior cultivars are available.

Related species include:
V. opulus - **Guelder Rose**
This species may be found as an escape. The bitter fruits have been eaten in Europe, but usually only when better fruit was unavailable.

V. edule - **Squashberry**
V. pauciflorum - **Mooseberry**
The berries of these species are quite palatable raw and were important to some northern tribes. Use as above.

Viburnum prunifolium / **Black Haw**
East   *Caprifoliaceae*
Fruit: The dark blue fruits of the Black Haw are quite unlike those of the closely related Highbush Cranberry (see above). They consist of a large seed and a thin pulp

that tastes rather like raisins or dates. The quality varies with individual plants; some are much better than others, so one has to experiment to find those worth eating. They are all improved by frost.

The fruits are often good enough to eat raw as a snack, but their large seeds are a problem. The best way to cook them is to bring to a boil, simmer for 20 - 30 minutes, then put through a strainer to remove the seeds. Use the pulp in preserves, sauces and pies.

> ### Cramp Bark
> Black Haw was once commonly known as Cramp bark, because a tea of the bark was used to relieve menstrual cramps. Women also drank it in the last few weeks of pregnancy, in the belief it could help prevent miscarriage. It was once in the USP as a uterine relaxant, antispasmodic, diuretic, nervine and tonic.

Cultivation: Cultivate in the same way as the Highbush Cranberry.

Related species include:
V. alnifolium - **Hobblebush**
V. cassinoides - **Witherod**
V. lentago - **Wild Raisin**
V. nudum - **Large Witherod**
V. rufidulum - **Rusty Black Haw**
All of these species can be used as above, though their fruit is not usually as good.

Viola species / Violets
Throughout   *Violaceae*
There are over 400 species (and many hybrids) in the *Viola* genus. The ones with blue or white flowers are generally considered to be edible, while those with yellow flowers are said to be inedible or cathartic.

Greens: The tender spring leaves are very rich in vitamins A and C, and can be used in salads, or as a potherb. Older leaves are rather astringent, but have been used as a potherb (usually mixed with other greens).

Flowers: All of the blue flowered species can be eaten, though none are as good as the scented flowers of the European Sweet Violet (*V. odorata*). This species is commonly cultivated for its flowers. Don't worry that gathering the flowers will prevent the plants from perpetuating themselves, as these showy flowers rarely produce seeds. In summer these plants produce a flush of inconspicuous cleistogamous flowers, and these produce an abundance of seed.

The flowers can be added to salads to make them more attractive. They can also be cooked with the leaves as a potherb.

Tea: The leaves and flowers can be used to make a passable tea.

Medicine: The Sweet Violet is the most important species for herbalists. Its leaves have been used internally as an expectorant, demulcent and laxative. They have been used externally as a poultice for skin diseases (they contain beta-ionone - a natural fungicide), wounds and even cancer. It is probable that native species share similar uses.

Cultivation: Violets are popular ornamentals and many attractive cultivars are available. They are mostly woodland plants, and like rich, moist soil, with some shade. Propagate by means of seed, cuttings or division.

Some species are quite invasive, as they can spread vegetatively and by self-sown seed. I wouldn't consider them to be serious weeds though.

Vitis species / Wild Grapes

Throughout   *Vitaceae*

There are a large number of native grape species and hybrids, but no species is poisonous, so you can use any you find palatable.

Nutrients: Grapes are rich in sugars (particularly dextrose, which is sometimes called grape sugar) and the minerals iron, phosphorus, potassium and magnesium.

Gathering: It is sometimes possible to smell wild Grapes before you can see them. The yield of fruits varies considerably according to species, variety, soil, location, climate or age of plants (generally the younger plants seem to produce fruit more freely). Exposure to frost may make them sweeter.

Uses: Some wild grapes can be eaten straight from the vine and are often eaten seeds and all. Others are too tough skinned, sour, seedy or strongly flavored to be eaten in this way. These can be cooked, strained and sweetened, and used in preserves and pies.

You can dry the best-flavored grapes to make your own raisins. Dry in a warm, well-ventilated place or in the sun. Puncturing the skins will hasten drying, by letting the moisture escape faster. They will still have seeds of course.

Seed: Native Americans ground the dried seed to flour for baking and gruel.

Oil: Though Grape seeds are not very palatable, they provide one of the best edible vegetable oils. This is commonly used in the wine growing areas of Europe, where huge quantities of seeds are left over after juice extraction.

Grape Juice

Many types of wild grapes have tough skins and lots of seeds, and the best way to use them is as juice. Use the fresh juice as soon as possible, otherwise it will ferment and become wine or vinegar (unless that is what you want of course).

The easiest way to extract juice from grapes is with a fruit or vegetable juicer. It is also possible to obtain tasty juice with only a piece of cloth. Mash the fruits, then wrap them in a piece of muslin or porous cloth. Squeeze and knead this until the juice comes through the cloth, and is caught in a bowl. Another way to obtain juice is to simmer the berries in a little water, then strain and use the juice.

Wine: The most important use for Grapes is to make wine. Though most wine is made from the fruit of the European Grape (*V. vinifera*), all of the wild American species can be used in the same way. The bloom that covers the fruit is wild yeast, so no additional yeast is necessary.

Greens: While most people are familiar with the fruits, many don't know that the leaves are also edible. These are at their best in late spring and early summer while still young and tender. They can be gathered at this time and preserved in dry salt for later use.

The fresh greens can be cooked for 10 - 15 minutes as a potherb. In Mediterranean countries they are cooked for a few minutes, and then wrapped around food to impart their own tart flavor to it. They can also be fried in tempura batter.

The young growing vine tips can be added to salads any time they are available. They are also a nice snack while hiking.

Medicine: Grapes have a cleansing and purifying action on the body, and are sometimes used as the basis for a fruit fast, whereby one consumes only the fruit (in the form of juice or whole grapes) for a limited period. They are well suited for this purpose because of their laxative, diuretic, demulcent and nutritive properties.

The leaves have been used as a wound poultice.

Vines: The woody vines can be peeled, split and used for basket weaving. They are frequently used as the framework for floral wreaths and other decorations. The strong and supple vines have been used for cordage, and have even been twisted into ropes.

Industrial oil: Non-drying Grapeseed oil has been used for making paint. It has also been burned in oil lamps.

Animal food: The fruits and leaves are important food for wildlife, and in return many creatures help distribute the seeds.

Cultivation: There are native Grape species growing in almost all parts of the country. These are well adapted to local growing conditions and easy to grow.

European Grapes were introduced into the North American colonies very early, but often didn't thrive as they had little resistance to native insects and disease. It was then discovered that if European scions were grafted onto native roots, they would receive natural resistance to many pests. When a pest of American Grapes (*Phylloxera vastatrix*) was accidentally introduced into Europe, it devastated many vineyards and killed over two million plants. The vineyards were saved from ruin by grafting the choice European scions onto resistant American rootstocks.

Propagation: Generally the Grapes prefer deep, rich soil, with lots of sun. Some species are very drought resistant. They are so easily propagated from cuttings

while dormant that other methods are rarely used. Though they can also be grown from seed (cultivars don't breed true), or layering (in early spring). The plants take 3 - 5 years to start bearing fruit.

Grapes are useful for the small garden because they are vines and can be trained to grow vertically, thus using space that might otherwise be wasted.

Best species include: All are edible, but some are much better than others. The best include:
V. argentifolia
V. arizonica- Arizona Grape
V. californica - California Grape
V. labrusca - Northern Fox Grape
V. riparia - Riverside Grape
V. rotundifolia - Muscadine Grape
V. vulpina - Frost Grape

Washingtonia filifera / California Fan Palm
Southwest   *Arecaceae*
This is the only native western Palm, and the largest indigenous species, sometimes reaching 80 feet in height. Though originally of tropical origin, it is found naturally in moist places in the canyons of southern California, Arizona and south into Mexico. It gave its name to many places in that area, including Palm Springs and Twentynine Palms.

The Fan Palm is a thirsty plant that needs constant water, so it is a useful indicator of nearby water (though this will often be underground). It grows naturally in small oases, scattered around desert springs and watercourses. Wild Palms were quite common before Europeans arrived, but began to decline with the appearance of the first European settlers, who ate the hearts, and used the trunks for lumber. It is now quite scarce in the wild, because its natural habitat is also the natural habitat of retirees, golfers and aging movie stars. A major factor in its disappearance is the increased pumping of groundwater in these areas. This is lowering the water table to the point where these thirsty plants can no longer reach it, and without enough water they die.

Though natural Palm oases are becoming rare, the plant is in no danger of extinction, as it is a commonly planted as an ornamental in warm places around the world. Its new habitat is golf courses and condominium complexes.

The trees were very important to the Cahuilla and other desert peoples, as they provided food, fiber, thatching material and shade (an important commodity in the desert). Palm groves, with their steady source of fresh water, were a favorite site for their villages. This is certainly understandable, as they are wonderful places to be. Native Americans may have transplanted the Palms to suitable growing sites and helped extend its range.

Berries: The blackish fruits ripen mid-to-later summer and are often produced prolifically (some clusters may weight 10 pounds or more). Native Americans used long poles to get them from the trees.

The fruits have a large edible seed, and a thin sweet pulp which is somewhat reminiscent of Dates, but they aren't really very good. Native Americans often ground the whole fruit to meal, and then boiled it for 30 minutes to make gruel. The pulp was sometimes boiled to make a kind of syrup, or soaked in water for a beverage. The seeds were ground separately for baking bread

Heart: The growing heart can be eaten like that of the Cabbage Palm (*Sabal*), but taking it kills the tree, which would be unforgivable. Native Americans rarely ate the hearts for this reason.

Fiber: The large fan-like leaves can be used like those of the Cabbage Palm (*Sabal*) for cordage, thatch and weaving baskets, hats, mats and sandals.

Wood: The trunks have been used locally for shelters, huts and fence-posts.

Animal food: The trees provide both food and shelter to wildlife, and these creatures distribute the seeds in return.

Cultivation: In warm climates the Fan Palm is a favorite tree for urban landscaping and home gardens. It is more drought resistant than most Palms, but still needs regular irrigation. It is not very hardy, and is killed by temperatures below 15 degrees Fahrenheit.

Native Americans used to burn the vegetation underneath the Palms periodically, to clear out overgrown brush, encourage seedling growth, and increase the yield of fruits. This not only provided food directly, but also attracted edible wildlife. These fires also prevented disease and insect pests from becoming a problem in the groves, and played an important role in maintaining the health of the trees.

A characteristic of the Californian Fan Palms is the skirt of dead leaves that hangs down under the crown. Fan Palms growing in Arizona usually drop their dead leaves and so don't have this skirt.

Propagation: Fan Palm is easily grown from seed, though it is quite slow growing. It likes rich soil and an abundant source of water.

Wyethia angustifolia / **Narrow-leaved Mules Ears**
West   *Asteraceae*

These species are close relatives of the Balsamroots (*Balsamorrhiza*) and are sometimes included in that genus. They spread quickly on overgrazed land, and are considered serious pests in some areas, though they might also be looked upon as a symptom of abused land.

Food: The roots can be gathered while dormant and cooked like potatoes. Native Americans often baked them in a fire-pit like Camas bulbs (*Camassia*). The tender, green spring shoots were eaten raw or cooked. The seeds can be used like those of Balsamroot.

Medicine: A tea of the root of *W. longicaulis* was used as an emetic, and as a wash for Poison Oak rash.

Related species:
W. amplexicaulis - **Northern Mules Ears**
W. helianthoides - **White Mules Ears**
W. mollis - **Mountain Mules Ears**
W. helenoides - **Grey Mules Ears**
Used as above.

Yucca species / Yucca

Southwest & locally elsewhere   *Agavaceae*

The Yuccas are close relatives of the Agaves, and can be used in many of the same ways. They are more useful though, as they are commoner, faster growing and don't always die after flowering. They provided the Apaches (and other desert tribes) with many of the essentials of life, and were probably the most important plant resource they had.

These species are pollinated by the Yucca moth (*Tegeticula*) and have a symbiotic relationship with this insect. The female insect deliberately pollinates the flowers and then lays her eggs inside them. The larvae develop along with the fruit, already supplied with food in the form of seed. The larvae don't eat all of the seeds however and some are left to ripen. Plant and insect both benefit from this arrangement, and it explains why the fruits so often contain insect larvae (if you need bait for fishing look inside the fruit).

Food: The Yuccas provide a variety of foods, though their quality varies considerably among the different species. One must experiment to find the best.

Roots: The roots are inedible raw because of their saponin content, but can be eaten if thoroughly cooked. Native Americans often cooked them in a fire pit in the same way as Camas (*Camassia*).

Flower stalk: These species often flower in "Yucca years", when most of the plants in an area flower at the same time. The edible flower stalks appear in early summer and can be eaten up until the flowers appear. These are occasionally eaten raw, but are too bitter for most tastes. Peeling off the outer skin may help to reduce their bitterness to a more palatable level. Even better is to boil the stem as a vegetable. This allows you to eliminate most of their bitterness by changing the cooking water (do this at least once).

Flowers: The flavor of the flowers varies a lot, some are bitter, others are quite good, so sample any you find. The green ovary isn't eaten. The flower buds, and young flowers, can be fried, pickled or eaten raw. Native Americans commonly boiled or baked them in quantity, and then dried them for winter use.

Fruit: Some species produce sweet fleshy fruits, while others are dry and woody. I already mentioned how the fruits are often infested with insect larvae, which makes them unpalatable to most people (though not really inedible). The fruit is also laxative if eaten in quantity.

Fleshy fruit: The sweet fleshy fruits of some species are known as Datil (Date fruit) and are quite good. The immature green fruits contain saponins and can't be eaten raw, but they can be peeled and boiled for 20 minute. The cooked fruit somewhat resemble cooked apple, and can be used to make a pretty good "apple pie". Native Americans often baked them in a fire pit (see *Camassia*). The green fruit will often ripen off the plant.

The fruit ripen in late summer or autumn . They can be eaten raw, but are better cooked. The skins, fibers and seeds are usually strained out, and the pulp is used for pies and preserves. Native Americans used the fruit pulp to make syrup, preserves and drinks. They also dried it in thin sheets for winter storage, and for use while traveling.

Dry types: The dry fruits can be used as above while they are still green.

Seed: The seed was often separated from the fruit and ground to meal for gruel and baking. Soft immature seed can be boiled for ten minutes as a vegetable.

Arthritis

Yucca root was used by Native Americans to treat the inflammation caused by arthritis, a use that has recently been validated by western science. This may take several months to begin working, but it has fewer negative side effects than most other drugs. Positive side effects include reduced cholesterol level and blood pressure.

Medicine: The root was used externally to treat skin diseases such as acne, and again some positive effect has been scientifically proven.

The steroidal sapogenins in the seeds (up to 12%) have been used to make hormones for birth control pills.

Soap: The saponin rich root can be used as a soap substitute like Amole (*Chlorogalum*), for washing clothes, hair and people. This is as effective as commercial soap, but less harsh, and can be used by some people who are allergic to soap.

Native Americans used the root for ritual purification.

Fiber: The leaves have been soaked, split and pounded to separate the fibers (or treated like Flax - *Linum*), which are then used for making cordage, fishing nets, bowstrings, baskets, mats, sandals, brushes, cloth and paper. Some species have been cultivated for their fiber.

Wood: The woody flower stems make good walking sticks. The wood of the much larger Joshua tree has been used for fence-posts, but it isn't big (or common) enough to be commercially important.

Animal food: Livestock has been fed chopped Yucca leaves during drought. The plants provide food and shelter for many desert animals. The Desert Wood Rat uses the spiny tips to fortify its nest.

Cultivation: The Yuccas are adapted to grow in dry desert areas (they use CAM photosynthesis, which is more efficient in hot dry conditions), but some species also do well in cooler, moister climates. They are very pretty when in flower, and some species have been used as ornamentals all across the country.

Propagate from seed (soak for 24 hours before planting - it may take several years to germinate) or by offsets or rhizomes. They like full sun and well-drained soil. They are very rugged and tenacious of life, and it has been said a Yucca will outlive the person who plants it. In the garden they are often killed by over watering, so keep the soil dry around them.

Garden uses: The wide spreading root network makes the plant useful for preventing erosion. Though very drought tolerant, they are quite succulent and don't burn well, so have been planted around buildings to reduce potential fire danger.

Foliar feed: The plants contain steroidal saponins that help them to assimilate nutrients and water and so resist the heat and water stress of desert existence. These saponins have been extracted and used as a foliar feed, to aid stressed crops of various kinds. This can hasten the recovery and growth of transplanted plants and may also improve seed germination. These extracts are available commercially, or a tea of the chopped leaves can be made at home.

Useful species:
No *Yucca* species is poisonous, so you can experiment with any you find. The best include:

***Y. baccata* - Banana Yucca**
This species produces some of the best fruit.

***Y. brevifolia* - Joshua Tree**
***Y. glauca* - Soapweed Yucca**
The flower buds and flowers are good.

***Y. elata* - Soaptree Yucca**
***Y. filamentosa* - Bear Grass**
***Y. schidigera* - Mojave Yucca**
These species have been cultivated for their fiber.

Zamia floridana, Z. pumila / Florida Arrowroot

Florida   *Cycadaceae*
The fern-like Cycads are the most primitive seed bearing plants still in existence. They shouldn't be used casually for food, as they are very slow growing and don't reproduce well. Some species may grow for a hundred years, flower once and then die. These species are more vigorous than most of their kin, but are still rather slow growing.

Starch: The starch in the root was a staple food for the Seminole and other Florida tribes. This starch somewhat resembles Arrowroot, which explains the common name. It is extracted from the fibrous root in much the same way as Kudzu (*Pueraria*). Some species were once cultivated in Florida, and were the basis of a minor starch extraction industry.

Seed: The seed is poisonous in its natural state, but Native Americans found they could make it edible by leaching out the toxic glycosides with water. The leached seeds were ground to flour for gruel and bread.

Fiber: The leaves can be used like those of the Palms (see *Sabal*) for baskets, thatch, mats and cordage.

Cultivation: These species are popular ornamentals in mild winter areas. They may be grown from seed, offsets or division.

Zizania aquatica, Z. palustris / **Wild Rice**

East   *Poaceae*

These species are sometimes both classified as *Z. aquatica*, as the differences between them are relatively minor (they may also hybridize).

This is one of a few wild food plants that has captured people's imagination, and taste buds, and has become a highly prized (and highly priced) gourmet food. For the Menominee, and other northern tribes, Wild Rice was a staple food and was eaten every day. Other tribes planted it on suitable sites, and slowly extended its range to cover most of the eastern two thirds of the country.

Nutrients: Wild Rice is more nutritious than most commonly cultivated grains, containing about 15% protein (with a high lysine and methionine content), 80% carbohydrate and many minerals and B vitamins.

Caution: When gathering make sure that none of the long blackish seeds have been replaced with the purple spurs of the Ergot fungus (*Claviceps*), which is very poisonous.

Gathering: Wild Rice is popular enough that gathering it is often regulated. Before you gather make sure no one else already has the rights to gather from the stand. If

you want to collect the seed you have to be very watchful to get it at the right time, as the ripe seed only stays on the plant for a few days. Too early and the unripe grain is milky and soft, too late and the ripe seed has fallen into the water. Native Americans sometimes tied the individual heads into clumps (before the seed ripens) to reduce bird depredations, and to make gathering easier.

Native Americans collected the rice by paddling canoes among the plants. They would carefully bend the seed heads over the canoe, and beat them to loosen the grain, which then falls into the canoe. On a good day they could collect 50 pounds of seed. In many areas this is still the only legal method of gathering the grain from wild stands.

Crop use

Wild Rice has recently become a commercial crop plant for the first time. The high value of the grain has long made the notion of cultivation an attractive proposition to farmers, but commercial cultivation was uneconomical because the seed shatters and falls over a period of several days, or even weeks. This meant machinery couldn't be used to harvest the seed all at once, and labor costs were too high to make hand harvesting economical. Extensive searching finally located naturally occurring strains that ripen their seeds all at once, and the first large-scale cultivation began in Minnesota.

Cultivation now accounts for about 80% of the Wild Rice available commercially. Most of this is grown in California on conventional farms. The amount gathered from the wild has remained fairly steady, but demand has increased. This is a good example of a wild plant becoming an important crop in a fairly short time.

Preparation: Before the grain can be eaten the outer husk must be removed. Native Americans dried the seed in the sun, and then parched it by shaking it in a basket of hot rocks. In later years they would parch the seed in a heavy skillet, shaking constantly to prevent burning. An easier method is to parch it in an oven at 350 degrees for three hours. The parched seed is then beaten to loosen the chaff, and winnowed to separate it from the seed. The flavor of grain prepared in this way is somewhat smoky, unless you wash it thoroughly in water before cooking. The cleaned rice can be used immediately, or dried for storage.

Use: The grain can be used in the same ways as domesticated Rice, though it is not a close relative. Boil a cup of rice in two cups of water for 30 minutes. It will swell to two or three times its original volume. It can also be cooked with maple syrup and wild fruits as a dessert, or toasted as a snack.

Native Americans ground the grain to flour, for use in gruel, baking (often mixed with an equal amount of wheat flour) and thickening soup. They also popped it like popcorn.

Animal food: Wild Rice is sometimes planted to attract game birds. Muskrats frequently feed on the plants.

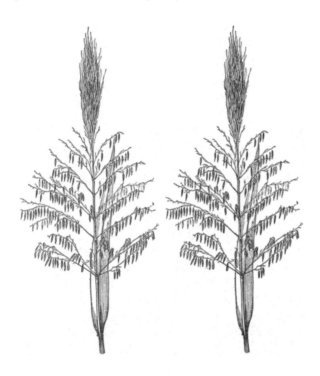

Cultivation: This annual species is grown from seed, planted as soon as it is ripe. Scatter the seed on the surface of the water and it will sink to the bottom (dead dry seed may float) and germinate in early spring. The seed loses viability rapidly if allowed to dry out, so must be kept moist (this is why it is often shipped in Sphagnum moss).

Wild Rice grows naturally along the margins of streams, rivers or lakes, in clear, slow moving water of a fairly constant depth (from several inches to two feet). Water is essential for the plants early growth, and seedlings can't survive on dry land. Older plants don't mind if the water level drops as summer progresses, and often end up growing quite happily in mud. The plants can't compete with such aggressive perennial aquatics as Cattail or Reed, so have adapted themselves to the less hospitable conditions to be found in deeper moving water.

If you want to try growing the plant it is probably a good idea to start on a small scale. Plant a little seed on a suitable site, and if it grows and bears seed, collect this to try again next year on a larger scale. If it fails then you haven't wasted too much time or effort. The plants may grow up to ten feet tall and are graceful ornamentals.

Related species:
Z. texana - Texas Wild Rice
This species is very close to extinction at the present time, though attempts are being made to bring it back from the brink. Obviously it shouldn't be used for food (this hardly needs saying as it is so rare you aren't likely to ever see it). Texas Wild Rice differs from the above species in one very important aspect: it is perennial and has potential as a perennial grain crop.

The only other _Zizania_ species in the world is the perennial Asian species _Z. latifolia_. Like many perennials this species doesn't produce seed reliably, but its spring shoots are useful food. It is cultivated in China for these shoots, which are peeled and eaten raw or cooked. The immature flowers are also eaten.

Zizaniopsis miliacea / **Water Millet**
Southeast   _Poaceae_
Shoots: This perennial species is quite similar to _Zizania_ above, and its seed may be used in the same ways. A closely related Chinese species is cultivated in Asia for its spring shoots. These are gathered as they emerge from the water and are from 3 - 12 inches high. Their tough outer leaves are peeled off, leaving a small white heart about an inch in diameter. These aren't bad raw, but the Chinese always cook them. They are usually used in soups and stews, as they tend to pick up the flavor of whatever they are cooked with.

Starch: The roots might perhaps be used as a source of starch like Kudzu (_Pueraria_).

Zostera marina / **Eel-Grass**
Coasts   _Zosteraceae_
This cosmopolitan plant grows in coastal water all around the Northern Hemisphere from the tropics to the Arctic. It is unusual in that it is a flowering plant, yet grows on tidal mud flats where it is usually submerged in seawater (it has essentially returned to the sea its ancestors left). It isn't a member of the grass family, but superficially looks like it could be. It provides a similar ecological niche as some seaweeds, but differs from them in one important respect; its creeping rhizomes grow in mud, whereas seaweeds can't anchor themselves in mud. It lives in sheltered inlets and bays and slowly traps debris, which builds up around the plants.

Food: This plant has been an important food source for a number of coastal tribes, from the Seri (in Mexico) to the Kwakiutl (in Canada). It has been known as the Wheat of the Sea.

Caution: Don't gather the plants from areas that may be contaminated with sewage, or other human-made pollutants.

Stems: The sweetly flavored young leaves, and stem bases, can be eaten in spring and early summer. Gather them at low tide, or from a boat, peel off the tough outer leaves. They can be eaten raw, steamed or in soups. Older stem bases can be chewed, but are too tough to eat.

Root: The roots can be eaten raw or cooked.

Seed: The nutritious seeds contain about 13% protein, 50% starch and 1% fat. A single plant produces up to 250 small seeds. They are prepared by sun drying, threshing, winnowing, parching, winnowing again and then grinding to flour. The Seri people of Mexico used the flour for gruel and bread.

Fiber: The rot resistant grass-like leaves have been used for roof thatch, basket weaving, bedding, packing material, hats, upholstering furniture, mattress stuffing, paper and building board.

Chemicals: The plants were once burned to produce sodium carbonate for making glass and soap.

Building Insulation

Eel-Grass was once harvested commercially to make building insulation. The dried material was sandwiched between two layers of Kraft paper and stitched together into a quilt known as Cabots quilt, after its inventor. This was quite successful until one of its periodic declines occurred, which caused the grass to disappear for a while.

Energy: These fast growing plants could potentially be used as a source of biomass for producing methane or alcohol.

Animal food: Eel- Grass is vitally important to marine life as food, shelter and habitat. Detritus from rotting plants serves as the bottom of the food chain, providing food for small fish, shellfish, shrimp, crabs and other small creatures, which in turn provide food for other creatures. It also provides shelter for such creatures, and serves as a marine nursery. The seeds eaten by many water birds. Turtles eat the plants.

The foliage has been widely used as fodder for livestock (notably by Julius Caesar's army when he invaded North Africa in 46 B.C).

Cultivation: Eel-Grass has been proposed as a rather unique marine grain crop plant for shallow tropical waters (an environment not noted for its grain production). The plants grow best in clear, warm, brackish water (not fresh and not salt) and can be propagated vegetatively, or by seed. In the wild the plants periodically decline in numbers, and this can have a disastrous effect on other marine life, both animal and plant. It was once thought that a fungus was responsible for this, but it is more likely due to fluctuations in water temperature.

There is some concern that commercial harvesting (or even gathering storm cast material) from beaches could eventually have an adverse effect on marine life.

Fertilizer: Large amounts of Eel-Grass are often washed ashore after storms, and the rain-washed plants make good mulch, compost material or green manure.

More plants

The following plants are those I felt I had to include in this book, but that didn't deserve a more detailed description. Inclusion in this section does not necessarily mean they are inferior to the plants already mentioned. There are many reasons why I didn't give them a longer listing. They might have only one particular use, or be very similar to plants already described at length. Some very useful plants are here because they are not common in the wild, or have only very limited distribution. A few plants are here purely for their historical interest, but aren't really very practical.

Acanthochiton wrightii / Green Stripe
The young leaves of this southwestern species have been used raw or cooked, like those of the related Amaranths.

Achyrachaena mollis / Blow Wives
Native Americans gathered the seed in quantity in early summer, and used it for bread, gruel and pinole. It was gathered and used like Red Maids (*Calandrinia*).

Adenostoma sparsifolium / Ribbonwood
A. fasciculatum / Greasewood
The Cahuilla people ate the seed. A wash or poultice of the leaves was used for skin sores. The wood was used for hut construction, arrows, fenceposts and firewood. The fibrous bark was used for skirts.

Agoseris species / Mountain Dandelion
The young leaves and roots were eaten like those of the related Dandelion. The gum from wounds on the plants was used as chewing gum by Native Americans.

Alchemilla vulgaris / Ladys Mantle
The tender young leaves can be used as a salad or potherb. Older parts contain a lot of tannin, which makes them unpleasantly astringent.

The genus name is derived from the word alchemy and was given because the plant was believed to have powerful medicinal properties. The tannin rich leaves were prized as a wound dressing to stop bleeding (particularly after tooth extraction) and for diarrhea. The common name was given for its value in treating women's complaints, such as excessive menstruation, and as an aid in childbirth.

Aletris farinosa / Stargrass
This tiny plant is often abundant on moist sunny sites. Native Americans ate the small bulbs, but they are too bitter for most people. The same bulbs were used medicinally as a bitter tonic, and for female ailments such as sore breasts and menstrual problems. It was also used to prevent miscarriage. Interestingly they are now known to contain diosgenin, a precursor of the female hormone progesterone.

Alisma Plantago-aquatica / Water Plantain
The entire plant is acrid when raw, and can only be made edible by drying or baking. The edible part is the starchy bulbous base of the stem. This is probably quite nutritious, but is not particularly good.

Allenrolfea occidentalis / Iodine Bush
Like many of its cousins in the *Chenopodiaceae* (*Atriplex, Salicornia, Suaeda* and *Salsola*), this species is very salt tolerant, and can be found on saline desert soils. The seeds have been used like those of Lambs Quarters (*Chenopodium*) for bread and gruel. The succulent young shoots have been eaten as a potherb.

Amoreuxia gonzalesii, A. palmatifida / Amoreuxia
The roasted roots are quite sweet.

Amorpha canescens / Leadplant
The leaves of this shrub can be used to make a pleasant tea. Native Americans smoked the leaves.

Andromeda glaucophylla / Bog Rosemary
Native Americans made a tea by steeping the leaves of Bog Rosemary in boiling water for several minutes. Don't boil as this releases toxins. Some people caution against using any part of any *Andromeda* species.

Aneilema keisak / Aneilema
This Asian species can be used like the related Dayflower (*Commelina*) as a potherb.

Antennaria species / Pussytoes
Native Americans used the resin that exudes from wounds in the stems as chewing gum.

Anthoxanthum odoratum / Sweet Vernal Grass
This naturalized grass smells of new mown hay when dried. It has been used to make tea.

Apiastrum angustifolium / Wild Celery
Used as a flavoring like Wild Celery (See *Apium*).

Aplectrum hyemale / Puttyroot
The corms of this small Orchid are edible, but it is too pretty to be eaten under normal circumstances.

Arbutus menziesii / Madrone
The abundantly produced red berries are considered to be edible, but their value is limited by the large, sharp seeds (large amounts can cause stomach upset), and the fact that they don't taste very good. The berries take a whole year to ripen, so flowers and fruit can be found on same tree. Native Americans ate them raw, cooked, or mixed into pemmican. They are usually insipid and not very good, but vary a lot from tree to tree and some aren't bad, so it pays to experiment. You might try using the berries as a puree, cooked and strained to remove the seed.

The berries were also used to make a drink resembling Manzanita cider (see *Arctostaphylos*). This was considered as good or better than Manzanita cider, and may well be the best way to use the fruits. The curly red-brown outer bark can be used to make a surprisingly good tea. A tea of the leaves was used as a wash for Poison Oak rash.

A. arizonica - Arizona Madrone
A. texana - Texas Madrone
These species are smaller than the above, but can be used in same ways.

Armeria leptophylla / Thrift
The base of the stem has been eaten raw or cooked.

Ascophyllum nodosum / Knotted Wrack
The tender parts can be steamed, fried or boiled. This species is a source of alginates and is one of the best fertilizer seaweeds. See Giant Kelp (*Macrocystis*) for more on the use of seaweeds as fertilizers.

Aster macrophyllus / Large Leaved Aster
The young leaves can be used in salads, or as a potherb. The Asters are good wound herbs, and some may contain an antibiotic in their leaves.

A. cordifolius
A. ledophyllus - Engelmanns Aster
A. spinosus - Mexican Devil-Weed
A. tripolium
 Used as above.

Astragalus crassicarpus / Ground Plum
This species gets its name because the edible seed-pods rather resemble plums in appearance. They don't taste like plums though, being more like a sweet watery pea. The raw pods were commonly eaten to prevent thirst by the Dakota, Pawnee and other tribes. European settlers boiled them as a vegetable (rather like Snow Peas) and also pickled them. No other part is edible.

Caution: The *Astragalus* genus contains a number of toxic plants, so be careful about exact identification.

A. alpinus - Alpine Locoweed
A. mexicanus
A. plattensis
A. succulentus
Used as above.

Athyrium filix femina / Lady Fern
The Fiddleheads have been used like those of the Ostrich Fern (*Matteucia*), but aren't very substantial.

Audibertia polystachya / White Sage
This species is related to Chia (*Salvia*) and its abundant oily seed is equally edible (though not so mucilaginous). Native Americans parched and ground the seed to meal, and mixed it with an equal amount of corn or wheat flour. This was used to make pinole, bread and gruel.

Baeria chrysostoma / Goldfields
Native Americans parched and ground the seed to make Pinole, bread and gruel. They were gathered and prepared in the same way as Red Maids (*Calandrinia*).

Batis maritima / Saltwort
This maritime plant is quite common in salt flats and marshes in warmer coastal areas. The succulent leaves have been used as potherb and salad and are quite good.

Beckmannia syzigachne / Slough Grass
The seed can be prepared by parching and winnowing as for Wild Rice (*Zizania*). The cleaned seed can be boiled like Rice, or ground to meal for bread or gruel.

Beloperone californica / Chuparosa
Chuparosa means Hummingbird in Spanish and was given to this shrub because those birds frequently feed from the nectar-rich blossoms. The cucumber flavored red flowers appear from February to June, and were often eaten raw by the Papago people. You can suck the nectar out of them.

Beta vulgaris / Wild Beet
This is the wild form of the cultivated Beet. It may be found as an escape anywhere in the country, but is naturalized in some coastal areas. The succulent leaves can be gathered almost year round in milder areas, and eaten raw or cooked (so long as they are tender).

Bidens bipinnata, B. pilosa / Spanish Needles
These species may be familiar to you because their barbed seeds attach themselves to clothing and fur. If you get them early enough the young leaves are a passable potherb. The leaves can be used as a wound herb to stop bleeding.

Blechnum spicant / Deer Fern
In spring the small curled fronds (fiddleheads) can be used like those of the Ostrich Fern (see *Matteucia*).

Blephilia ciliata, B. hirsuta / Wood Mints
These small, Mint flavored perennial herbs can be used like the related Mint (*Mentha*) for flavoring and tea.

Bloomeria crocea / Golden Stars
The bulbs are edible, and can be eaten like those of their cousins the Brodiaea Lilies (*Brodiaea*). They are really too pretty to use unless very abundant.

Boisduvalia densiflora, B. stricta / Boisduvalia
These plants flower from June to August, and produce an abundance of rich tasting, oily seeds. These were eagerly sought by Native Americans and used for bread, gruel and pinole. They were gathered and prepared like Red Maids (*Calandrinia*).

Bouteloua curtipendula / Sideoats Grama
The nutritious seed can be ground to flour for baking. This drought resistant species was a major source of food for buffalo on the plains, and is still important as forage for livestock. It has also been used to prevent erosion.

Brasenia schreberii / Water Shield
The leaves are not usually eaten raw in this country because they are covered in jelly-like slime (though they are a popular salad ingredient in Japan). They aren't bad when cooked as a potherb however, and their slime can actually be put to use as a thickener for soup. The leaf buds are also edible. The roots have been cooked and eaten, and apparently starch can be extracted from them in the same way as for Kudzu (*Pueraria*).

Bromus species / Cheat Grass
These grasses are pernicious European invaders, able to exploit overgrazed land where native plants have been weakened. They are almost universally despised, yet make good animal feed when young. Humans have eaten the seed when prepared like Wild-Rice (*Zizania*).

B. tectorum
B. rigidus
B. breviaristatus
All of these species are good.

Bryoria fremontii / Tree Hair
Syn *B. jubata* or *Alectoria fremontii*
Tree Hair lichen gets its common name because it resembles tufts of long black hair hanging from trees.

It is rich in starch and could be a useful survival food if prepared like Iceland Moss (see *Cetraria* for more on the proper treatment of Lichens). The Salish people baked it in a fire pit with wild bulbs such as Camas (*Camassia*) or Wild Onion (*Allium*). After baking for 24 hours the moss turns into a black jelly, which was eaten immediately, or dried in the sun for later use. The dried jelly was soaked in water and added to soups. The lichen can also be boiled for several hours. The flavor has been compared to soap by some, yet others say it is fairly good. Apparently Native Americans in Northern California somehow used it to make bread rise, instead of yeast.

Native Americans sometimes used this lichen to stuff mattresses and make clothing and blankets. It has been fermented to produce alcohol (see *Cetraria*).

B. fuscescens
B. lanestris
B. pseudofuscescens
Used as above.

Caution: Some species are potentially poisonous, including *B. tortuosa.*

Bumelia species / Bumelias
The sweet black fruits are edible raw or cooked and make excellent jelly. These plants are related to the Sapodilla, the tropical tree that is the source of the chicle once used to make chewing gum. Native Americans used the Gum Bumelia as a source of chewing gum, which no doubt explains it's common name.

B. celastrina - Saffron Plum
B. languinosa - Gum Bumelia
B. lycoides - Buckthorn Bumelia
All of these species are good.

Calycanthus floridus / Carolina Allspice
C. occidentalis / Western Spicebush
The aromatic bark has been used as a substitute for Cinnamon. Native Americans used the wood for arrows.

Calyptridium species / Pussy Paws
The tender young leaves can be used in salads or as a potherb.

Calystegia sepium / Bindweed
Syn *Convolvolus sepium*
Apparently the stems and roots of this introduced weed have been eaten. The long twining stems have been used as emergency cord and can even be tied in a knot.

Campanula rapunculoides / Bellflower
This pretty garden ornamental is much tougher than it looks. It spreads aggressively in the garden and out of it, and has naturalized in the northeastern states.

The spring shoots can be added to salads or cooked as a potherb. The fleshy rootstock is the most substantial food from the Bellflower, and is good enough that the plant has occasionally been cultivated as a root vegetable. It is used like its cousin the Rampion (*C. rapunculus*). Young roots are preferable, as older ones can get woody. They are best dug when the plant is dormant from fall to spring. The peeled root is good raw in salads, baked, or boiled for 20 minutes.

C. scouleri -- Scouler's Harebell
A few leaves can be added to salads, or used as a potherb.

Cardiospermum helicacabum / Balloon Vine
The Balloon Vine is grown as an ornamental for its balloon like pods, and has escaped and naturalized in the southeastern states. In parts of Asia and Africa it is cultivated as a potherb.

Carduus species / Thistles
Closely related to the *Cirsium* genus and often classified interchangeably, they are used in exactly the same ways.

Carex species / Sedges

No Sedges are known to be poisonous when young, though mature plants may contain toxins. The use of Sedges as food is limited to the succulent young 3 - 4 inch shoots and stem bases. In spring these are peeled, and eaten raw or cooked. The seeds are also edible, but not often available in quantity.

Some Sedges produce tough creeping rhizomes and were prized by Native Americans as some of the best materials for basket weaving. They are very supple and strong, and can be split as fine as thread. Stands of plants were regularly harvested, weeded and cultivated to encourage the growth of the maximum amount of usable material. The leaves were used for bedding and thatch.

The root network of the Sedges helps to prevent erosion of riverbanks, and they are sometimes planted for this.

Carpinus caroliniana / Hornbeam

Female Hornbeam trees (they are dioecious) sporadically bear crops of small edible nuts.

Cassia occidentalis / Coffee Senna

Some *Cassia* species have been known to poison livestock, but the young seedpods and leaves of this one have been used as a salad or potherb. The ripe seeds have been roasted and used as a coffee substitute, hence the name.

The leaves of several species are cathartic and have been used as laxatives in the same way as their close relative the Senna (*C. acutifolia*) which is an important commercial laxative. They contain the same potent purgative arthraquinone glycosides found in Cascara Sagrada and Rhubarb.

C. tora - Sickle Pod

The nutritious shoots have been eaten as a potherb, after boiling in a change of water to remove their odd smell.

C. angustifolia
C. chamaecrista - Prairie Senna
C. marilandica - Wild Senna

These species are used as laxatives. They are not edible.

Castilleja linearifolia / Wyoming Paintbrush

The red flowers and bracts can be added to salads to give a little flavor and color. The plant may occasionally accumulate selenium and become toxic, so use in moderation and don't use other parts (Native Americans sometimes ate the seeds). Other species can be used in the same ways, but aren't as good.

Caulophyllum thalictricoides / Blue Cohosh

Though the whole plant is reputed to be poisonous, the ripe seeds are said to make a fairly palatable coffee

substitute. Gather the ripe seed in August, roast until dark brown, grind, and simmer for about 15 minutes.

Cenchrus species / Sandbur Grasses

You might be uncomfortably familiar with these grasses, as their spiny burrs make themselves obvious by attaching themselves to clothing, and pricking you as you remove them. In Africa several species are eaten in times of need, though they have to be thoroughly singed to completely destroy their formidable spines. The seeds of all North American species may be ground to meal for baking and gruel.

Centella erecta / Pennywort

This species is closely related to the *Hydrocotyle* species and may be used in the same ways. Related species are sold in markets in Asia.

Cerastium vulgatum, C. semidecandrum / Mouse Ear Chickweeds

These little annuals can be used as a potherb like their namesake Chickweed (*Stellaria*). They are too hairy to be very good raw however.

Cercis canadensis C. occidentalis / Redbud

The young leaves, flower buds, flowers and immature seedpods can be added to salads, or fried in tempura batter. The tasty flowers can also be used in ice cream and wine. Native Americans used the strong durable wood for bows, and the bark for basket weaving.

Cercocarpus ledifolius / Mountain Mahogany

The aromatic leaves and bark of this widely distributed evergreen shrub can be used to make tea, either alone or with other herbs, such as Mormon Tea (*Ephedra*).

Chaemadaphne calyculata / Leatherleaf

The aromatic leaves have been used to make tea like those of its cousin Bog Rosemary (*Andromeda*).

Chamaesaracha coronopus / White Flowered Ground Cherry

This species was once included in the *Physalis* genus. The edible berries are used like those plants.

Chimaphila umbellata / Pipsissewa

Pipsissewa is a relative of the true Wintergreen (*Gaultheria*), and its aromatic evergreen leaves can be used for flavoring in the same ways. The leaves are most often used to make tea, just steep them in boiling water for a few minutes, then sweeten to taste (don't boil them as this will release tannin and spoil the flavor). They are also good for sun tea and root beer. The leaves contain medicinally important *arbutin* (see *Arctostaphylos*) and salicylic acid (see *Salix*). The leaf tea has been used as a urinary disinfectant, diuretic, febrifuge and astringent.

C. maculata - **Spotted Wintergreen**
Used as above.

Chilopsis linearis / **Desert Willow**
This desert tree somewhat resembles a Willow, but isn't closely related. Native Americans ate the large flowers and seedpods. The mauve flowers make this a fine ornamental tree for mild winter areas.

Chrysoplenium species / **Golden Saxifrage**
These perennial species can be found growing in wet soils in cooler climates. They are good as salad or potherbs anytime they are available.

Clarkia species / **Clarkia**
Many California tribes used the small seeds for pinole, bread and gruel. It was gathered and used in much the same ways as Red Maids (*Calandrinia*)

Clethra alnifolia / **Sweet Pepper Bush**
The very young leaves can be used as a potherb in spring. The flowers have been used as a soap substitute like Soapwort (*Saponaria*). The nectar rich flowers attract bees and other insects.

Clintonia borealis / **Bluebead Lily**
C. umbellata - **White Clintonia**
The new spring shoots of Bluebead Lily have a mild Cucumber flavor, and can be used in salads or as a potherb. Older leaves can be used as a potherb up until the flowers appear. The plant is still quite popular as a potherb in rural areas of northern Maine, where it is known as Cow Tongue. The berries are pretty to look at, but unpleasant to taste. They may even be mildly toxic.

Coccoloba uvifera, C. diversifolia / **Sea Grape**
Sea Grape produces edible red fruits that resemble grapes (though it isn't related). These can be eaten fresh, but are most often made into preserves. In the southeast they are occasionally sold in markets for this.

Codium fragile / **Fleece**
In Asia the fronds of this perennial seaweed are gathered for food in spring. They are cleaned in warm water, and used to flavor soups, salads and vegetables. They can also be used for tea. They can be dried for storage.

Coeloplurum lucidum / **Wild Celery**
This very hardy plant was important for Native Americans living in the far north, where green foods are often scarce. The young stems and leaf stalks can be peeled and eaten raw. If their flavor is too strong, boil them in a change of cooking water. Older parts can be used for flavoring like Wild Celery (*Apium*).

Collinsonia canadensis / **Horse Balm**
The leaves have the same citronella odor as the Lemon Balm (*Melissa*), and can be used in the same ways. Horse Balm is also known as Stoneroot, because of its use as a diuretic to aid in the elimination of kidney stones. It was also used to treat water retention, and as an astringent wound herb.

Comandra umbellata / **Bastard Toadflax**
Though this green plant produces chlorophyll and photosynthesizes its own food, it is probably also semi-parasitic, as it attaches itself to tree roots. The small edible nut-like seeds may be eaten any time they are available, though they are at their best while green.

C. pallida - **Pale Comandra**
C. livida - **Northern Comandra**
Used as above

Commelina communis / **Asiatic Dayflower**
This Asian plant is a common garden weed in parts of the east. It gets its common name because the individual flowers open for only one day. In its homeland the Dayflower is a popular salad or potherb, and is actually cultivated for use as food. It is used medicinally as a demulcent and diuretic.

C. erecta - **Slender Dayflower**
The leaves of this native species can be used as above. The fleshy roots can be eaten raw or cooked.

Comptonia peregrina / **Sweet Fern**
This is not a fern, but a shrubby relative of the Bayberry (*Myrica*), as you might guess from the smell of its leaves. The aromatic leaves have been used as a culinary flavoring, but are most often used for tea. To make a tasty tea, steep one teaspoon of dried leaves (or two teaspoons of fresh leaves) in a covered cup of boiling water for ten minutes.

Condalia hookeri / **Purple Haw**
Syn *C. obovata*
The black fruit of this spiny shrub ripen in late summer or autumn. They can be eaten raw, cooked in preserves or dried and ground to flour. Native Americans made a kind of syrup by squeezing the boiled fruit through a cloth (see *Vitis*), and leaving the juice to cool and thicken.

C. lycioides var *canescens*- **Gray Leaved Abrojo**
C. parryi - **Parry's Abrojo**
Used as above.

Conyza canadensis / **Canada Fleabane**
The seedlings and young leaves can be cooked as a potherb.

Coptis trifolia / Greenthread
Syn *C. groenlandica*
This bitter little plant has been used to add bitterness to various beverages. Greenthread was a very important medicinal plant to Native Americans, and was considered to be a panacea, beneficial for the whole body (much like Ginseng (*Panax*).

Cornus canadensis / Bunchberry
The flower cluster produces a bunch of red berries (hence the name), which can be eaten when fully ripe, but they are not nearly as nice as they look (some people say the seeds are the best part).. They are often abundant however, so you might want to experiment with them. Try cooking them with tastier fruits such as Blackberries, in pies and preserves, or boiling with sweetener to make a kind of syrup.

C. nuttalli - Pacific Dogwood
Native Americans ate the fruits, but they must be cooked and sweetened to be at all palatable. Like all Dogwood berries they are somewhat laxative.

C. sericea - Red Osier Dogwood
Syn *C. stolonifera*
The fruits of this species were eaten by Native Americans, but are not very good. Much more important was the greenish inner bark (they discarded the red outer bark and wood). This was dried and smoked like tobacco, and was said to be a much better smoke than Bearberry (*Arctostaphylos*). Apparently it is mildly stimulating, rather like drinking a lot of coffee.

C. sessilis - Miners Dogwood - Fruits eaten as above.

C. mas - Cornelian Cherry - Not native, but widely planted in the east and quite common. The common name is quite appropriate, as the single fruits resemble a sour Cherry and can be used like them. They are actually pretty tasty, and the tree deserves to be more widely planted as a fruit crop. A number of improved cultivars are available.

Coronopus coronata, C. lanceolata / Tickseeds
The Tickseeds are native to the southeast, but their hooked seeds have helped them to spread throughout the east. The new spring leaves can be used as a potherb or salad. The flowers have been used for tea.

Coryphantha vivipara / Pincushion Cactus
Syn *Mammillaria vivipara*
This species is found as far north as Canada. The tasty fruits were eaten fresh, or dried, by the Cheyenne and other tribes. The entire plant were sometimes singed in a fire to remove the spines and cook it. None of these species should be eaten under normal circumstances, as

they are slow growing and under increasing pressure from cactus rustlers (see *Cereus* for more on cactus rustling).

C. missouriensis - Nipple Cactus - Used as above.

C. macromeris - This southwestern cactus contains macromerine, a less potent chemical relative of the hallucinogen mescaline (which is found in the Peyote Cactus *Lophophora williamsii*). Native Americans used it like Peyote to induce visions.

Cosmos sulphureus / Cosmos
This familiar garden annual is locally naturalized in many places. The tender, young foliage has been used in salads, and as a potherb (it was highly esteemed by the Aztecs in its native land). The foliage may cause dermatitis in a few individuals, so use with care. The edible flowers can be used to add color to salads.

Cowania mexicana / Cliff Rose
Native Americans used the leaves and bark to make tea, either alone or with Mormon Tea (*Ephedra*). Cliff Rose tea is also good for washing wounds. The tough wood was used for bows, spears and digging sticks. The bark fiber have been used for cordage, rope and clothing.

Croton corymbulosus / Chapparal Tea
The dried flowering tops have been used as a culinary herb, and (as the name suggests) for tea. This tea is pretty good and is still quite popular. Make sure you have the right species, as some members of this family are quite toxic, and have actually been used as insecticides.

C. fruticulosus
C. monanthogynus - Used as above.

Cunila origanoides / Dittany
The specific name means "like Oregano" and the leaves can be used for flavoring like that herb. The leaves of this aromatic little mint make a nice tea. Steep one teaspoon of leaves in a cup of boiling water for ten minutes. This was said to be beneficial for colds.

Cycloloma atriplicifolium / Winged Pigweed
This annual is a close relative of the Lambs Quarters (*Chenopodium*), and its leaves and seeds can be used for food in the same ways.

Cymopterus species / Camote
These species are closely related to the Biscuit-roots (*Lomatium*), and their roots can be used in the same ways. They are edible raw, but cooking makes them sweeter and improves their flavor. Like Parsnips they get sweeter if exposed to frost, and by early spring they are sweet enough to eat raw. The aromatic young leaves and seeds can also be eaten.

C. fendlerii - **Wild Celery**
C. newberryi - **Wafer Parsnip**
C. purpurescens - **Purple Cymopterus**
These species are all very good.

Cytisus scoparius / Broom
Syn *Sarothamnus scoparius.*
Though most parts of this plant are toxic, the flower buds were once commonly pickled like Capers, and the roasted seeds have been used as a coffee substitute. Some people caution against using any part of the plant, as it contains heart stimulants and vasodilators (it has been used like Digitalis to regulate the heart).

The Latin word scopa means brush, and the flexible twigs of Broom were the original brooms (which is why they are called brooms). They were bound into tight bundles, the butt ends were cut off flush and a handle was hammered in. The bark fibers have been used like Flax (*Linum*) for cord, rope, paper, and even cloth.

Dactyloctenium aegyptum / Crowfoot Grass
The small seeds of this introduced grass have been eaten in bread and gruel in time of famine.

Dalea terminalis / Peabush
The sweetish roots were peeled and eaten by Native Americans, but are quite tough. The dried seeds were ground to meal for baking.

D. emoryii - **Emory's Dalea**
D. lanata - **Woolly Parosela (Syn *Parosela* spp)**
D. candida - **White Prairie Clover**
D. purpurea - **Purple Prairie Clover**
Used as above. The dried leaves of the latter species were used for tea by the Ponca and Kiowa people.

Dasylirion wheelerii / Sotol
D. leiophyllum / Smooth Leaved Sotol
These are close relatives of the Agave and Yucca, and the heart and young flower stalks have been used in the same ways. They are best known as the chief ingredient of the Tequila-like drink Sotol. The leaves were used for baskets, mats and cordage. Like the Agave it should only be used if abundant.

Descurainia species / Tansy Mustards
The young shoots can be used as a potherb, but their flavor is pretty strong (as you might guess if you have ever eaten Tansy). It is suggested that you boil them for 20 minutes, rinse in fresh water, and then boil for a further 15 minutes (which seems like an awful lot of cooking to me). The green seedpods are edible raw or cooked. The ripe brown seed was roasted and ground to meal for use as condiment like Mustard (*Brassica*), or to flavor soups.

Desmanthus brachylobus / Illinois Bundleflower
This nitrogen-fixing perennial is being studied as a possible component of a perennial grain growing polyculture. The seeds are rich in protein.

Dichelostemma capitatum, D. pulchellum / Desert Hyacinths
The bulbs of these Lilies can be eaten raw or cooked, like those of the closely related *Brodiaea* species, but are too pretty to use under normal circumstances. The early European settlers called them Grassnuts.

Dicliptera bracheata / Dicliptera
In spring the young growing tips can be used in salads, or as a potherb.

Dicoria brandegei, D. canescens / Dicoria
The seeds and flowers are edible.

Digitaria sanguinalis / Crabgrass
Crabgrass is notorious as one of the commonest and worst lawn and garden weeds. A single plant may produce 200,000 seeds, which is bad news if you are a gardener, but good news if you are hungry. The seeds have been eaten quite frequently in time of famine. The cleaned seed may be cooked like Millet, or dried and ground to meal for baking and gruel.

When growing unmolested Crabgrass gets a lot bigger than we usually see it on lawns, and it has actually been cultivated as a seed crop in parts of Europe.

Disporum trachycarpum
D. oreganum / Fairybells
The small flowers have been eaten, but are really too small and pretty to use. The sweet juicy orange berries were a favorite of the Blackfoot people. If they are sufficiently abundant, they can be used in pies and preserves. The berries of most related species are unpleasant, or even mildly toxic.

Distichlis spicata / Saltgrass
Saltgrass gets its name because it exudes small globules of salt from its leaves. For some Native American tribes the plant was their only source of salt. They obtained this in quantity by drying bundles of plants in the sun, and then beating them to loosen the salt. Other Native Americans burned the plants and used the ash as a salt substitute.

D. palmerii - Palmers Saltgrass
This Mexican grass is one of only two marine grasses that have been used as a source of grain (Eelgrass - *Zostera marina* is the other). The tasty and nutritious seeds were an important food crop for some Native

American tribes, and they had a number of improved cultivars. It was thought that these were all extinct, until Dr Nicholas Yensen of Tucson found some. Now a number of new improved varieties exist. The ripe seeds sometimes wash ashore in large piles, and can then be gathered in quantity. Prepare them like Wild-Rice (*Zizania*). Saltgrass has been studied as a potential crop for saline soils, or for irrigation with seawater.

Dithyrea wislizenii / Spectacle Pod
The unusual name of this little annual comes from the shape of the pods, which somewhat resemble a pair of spectacles. The young growing tips have been eaten, but they are astringent and not very good.

Dodecatheon hendersonii / Shooting Star
The young leaves and tuberous roots are edible, but the Shooting Star is far too pretty to eat under most circumstances. Native American maidens sometimes made garlands of the flowers to wear at dances (which seems like a much more appropriate use).

D. jeffreyi - Sierra Shooting Star
D. alpinum - Alpine Shooting Star
These species can be used as above, but are also too pretty to use.

Draba species / Whitlow Grasses
The seeds have been used like those of Mustard (*Brassica*).

Dracocephalum parviflorum / Dragonhead
The seeds have been used like those of the related Chia (*Salvia*) for flour and tea. It is also cultivated in the same way.

Dryas octopetala / White Mountain Avens
The leaves have been used for tea.

Dryopteris dilatata / Wood Fern
The edible rhizomes and fiddleheads have been used like those of the Ostrich Fern (*Matteucia*).

D. austriaca - Spreading Wood Fern
D. arguta
Native Americans in the Northwest still frequently eat fiddleheads of these species. They often can them for later use.

Dudleya edulis, D. saxosa, D. lanceolata / Live-Forever
Syn *Cotyledon* or *Stylophyllum* spp
The fat fleshy leaves of this (and some other) species are quite palatable when young in spring. The flower stems were a delicacy to Native Americans.

Echinocactus polycephalus Cottontop Cactus
E. horizonthalonius
E. enneacanthus - Strawberry Cactus
E. stramineus - Mexican Strawberry
Use like *Ferocactus*.

Echinocereus dasyacanthus / Hedgehog Cactus
This species produces tasty fruit, and could probably be cultivated as a fruit crop.

Eclipta alba / Yerba De Tajo
This annual herb is widely used as a potherb in the tropics.

Ehretia anacua / Anaqua
This evergreen tree produces thin-fleshed edible berries. It is sometimes planted as an ornamental in the southwest.

Eleusine indica / Goosegrass
The seed of this common grass has been prepared and eaten like that of the Barnyard Grasses (*Echinochloa*). Some related species are cultivated as grain crops. and improved varieties are available. The young green shoots can be eaten raw or cooked.

Empetrum nigrum / Crowberry
The seedy little fruits aren't particularly palatable, but they are often abundant in the far north, and were commonly eaten by Native Americans in Arctic areas. The berries can often be found on the plants right through the winter, and are improved by repeated freezing and thawing. They don't have much flavor raw, so are usually cooked and strained to remove the seeds. The remaining liquid is sweetened and used for preserves, pies, wine and beer. They are often mixed with tastier fruits such as Blueberry or Cranberry (*Vaccinium*). Native Americans froze or dried the whole berries for storage. A tea of the leaves has been used to treat dysentery.

E. atropurpureum - Purple Crowberry
Used as above.

Enteromorpha intestinalis / Green Nori
E. clathrata - Stone Hair
In Japan this tasty seaweed is eaten raw, stir-fried and in soups. The flavor is improved by toasting it before use.

Epigaea repens / Creeping Arbutus
The flowers of this lovely little plant have been eaten in salads, but it is becoming rare in many areas, so should be left alone. It is often protected by law anyway.

Erechtites hieracifolia / Pilewort
This plant is often common on waste or burned over woodland, and is sometimes known as Fireweed (it's no relation to *Epilobium*). The young leaves can be used as a potherb, if cooked in several changes of water to remove their strange smell. They still aren't very good though. The astringent leaves have been used to treat hemorrhoids, hence the common name.

Erigenia bulbosa / Harbinger Of Spring
The tasty bulbs can be eaten raw or cooked, but they are usually deeply buried in the ground, and hard to obtain in quantity.

Eriocoma cuspidata / Indian Millet
The black seeds were an important food for Native Americans in time of need.

Eriodictyon californicum / Yerba Santa
Two or three fresh or dried leaves can be chopped and steeped (or boiled briefly) to make a cup of very pleasant tea. The leaves have also been chewed to keep the mouth fresh, and are said to taste sweet after one chews them for a while.

This was an important Native American medicinal herb. The leaves were used for colds and other pulmonary complaints, and were once in the USP as an expectorant. It has been used externally as a poultice for bites, broken bones, wounds and sore muscles. The leaves were also smoked for ceremony and pleasure. The common name means Sacred Herb in Spanish

Eriogonum species / Wild Buckwheat
Wild Buckwheats are related to the Sorrels, and have a similar acid flavor (some species are commonly known as Sour Grass). In both cases this is due to oxalic acid, a substance that is toxic in large amounts, so use them in moderation (see *Rumex* for more on this).

There are so many *Eriogonum* species that precise identification can be difficult. Fortunately none are toxic, so the young stems and leaves of any species can be eaten, so long as they are tender. The shoots are best in late winter or early spring, and may be eaten raw or cooked. Native Americans ate the seed, if they could get enough of it.

The roots of *E. jamesii* were reportedly used as a contraceptive by Native Americans. Other species were used as an eye wash, and for female problems (annoying husbands, too much work, lack of money?). The hollow stems of several species were used as pipe stems by Native Americans, and so received the common name Indian Pipestem. They were dried and fashioned into pipes, or a pinch of tobacco was simply burned in the end of the stem, as a disposable pipe.

Eriophorum species / Cotton Grasses
These species would be insignificant as food plants if they didn't grow where few other edible plants can be found. The base of the stem can be eaten like that of the related Sedges (*Carex*)). Native Americans used to take quantities of these from Mouse nests.

Eriophyllum confertiflorum / Yellow Yarrow
The abundantly produced seeds were eaten by the Cahuilla people.

Fagopyrum tataricum / Tartary Buckwheat
Tartary Buckwheat was originally introduced as a food crop, but is now a serious agricultural weed in some areas. The seeds are smaller than those of its cousin Buckwheat (*F. esculentum*), but can be used in the same ways. Gather whole plants as the first seeds ripen, dry in a warm place, then thresh and winnow to obtain clean grain. The seeds can be eaten raw in cereals, boiled whole like Rice, coarsely ground to make a porridge called kasha, or finely ground to meal for baking bread and pancakes.

The seed can be sprouted like Peppergrass (see *Lepidium*), on a layer of soil or on wet paper towels, to produce quick, nutritious salad greens.

Common Buckwheat is widely used as a green manure, and was once a popular small scale grain crop.

Floerkea proserpinacoides / False Mermaid
All green parts can be used as a salad or potherb.

Fouquieria splendens / Ocotillo
This species has adapted to arid climates by only bearing leaves for as long as moisture is available. As the soil dries up, the leaf blades fall off, leaving the leaf ribs to act as spines.

Ocotillo mainly blooms from spring to early summer, though I have seen it flowering in December. The flowers have been eaten raw, fried in tempura batter and used for tea (especially sun tea). The nutritious seeds contain 25% protein and 18% oil. Native Americans parched and ground them to meal for gruel and bread, but they aren't very tasty.

The stems have been used for shelters, fenceposts and torches. If a piece of stem is stuck in the ground it will often take root, and so the plants have been used to make living fences. Wax from the stems has been used for waterproofing cloth. Hummingbirds feed on the nectar in the flowers.

Frasera speciosa / Deers Ears
The large taproot of the Deers Ears is edible. It is best when dug at the end of its first growing season, as older

roots tend to be woody, and not very good. They can be eaten raw, or cooked like Carrot. The leaves have been used as a wound poultice. Native Americans used related species as emetics and contraceptives.

Fritillaria species / Fritillary
These species are becoming rare in many places, due to human activities such as the overgrazing of cattle, so they should be used sparingly, if at all. Another reason for moderation is that they contain substances that may affect the heart if eaten in quantity.

The bulbs can be eaten like Potatoes, though they may be somewhat bitter (their quality varies with species and location). They often bear many small bulblets that look like grains of rice, which is why the plants were once known as Riceroot. It has been hypothesized that these bulblets evolved as a means of regeneration because the bulbs are so often eaten. These bulblets should be replanted if you dig the root. Native Americans gathered the bulbs as the tops died down, and roasted them like Camas (*Camassia*) bulbs. The green seedpods can be eaten raw or cooked.

These pretty little lilies can be used as ornamentals. Propagate from bulbs, seeds, scales or bulblets.

F. kamtchatcensis - **Kamchatka Fritillary**
F. pudica - **Yellow Fritillary**
F. lanceolata - **Chocolate Fritillary**
These species are all very good.

Fucus vesiculosus / Bladderwrack
This perennial seaweed is widely distributed, common and nutritious (it is a good source of iodine). The young inflated tips can be used to make a tea, or a nutritious stock for soups and stews (remove them before serving). The fronds have been dried and powdered like those of Kelp, for use as a nutritional supplement. It is also useful as fertilizer.

F. distichlis
F. gardneri
F. spiralis
Used as above.

Galeopsis tetrahit / Hemp Nettle
This garden plant may be found as an escape throughout the country. In spring the tender young foliage can be used as a potherb.

Galinsoga ciliata / Quickweed
G. parviflora
This South American weed is now naturalized across much of North America and Europe. It is a passable potherb, but a bit too hairy to be good raw.

Gelidium cartilagineum / Agarweed
This species is notable as one of the best sources of the agar (though other species can be used also). The plants have an objectionable flavor when fresh, but this can be removed by drying them in the sun. The dried fronds can be used like those of Irish Moss (*Chondrus*).

Agarweed has been harvested commercially in Mexico as a source of agar. This chemical is used like algin and carragheenan, as a thickening, jelling and suspending agent, in pharmaceuticals and processed foods. It is also used as a laboratory culture medium.

Geum rivale / Water Avens
The roots of this circumboreal species can be used to make a drink. Boil a cup of clean chopped root for 10 - 20 minutes, or steep overnight in cold water. This drink is sour and astringent by itself, so a sweetener and milk are usually added. This drink earned the plant the name Indian Chocolate, though the person who named it must have been deprived of chocolate for a long time, as it doesn't really taste anything like Chocolate.

The astringent, antiseptic roots were in the USP for treating sore throats and diarrhea.

G. urbanum - Wood Avens
The young leaves can be used as a potherb. The aromatic roots have been used to make a drink as above. The roots were once used to flavor wine, and were believed to prevent it going bad. This claim might have some foundation, as they contain an aromatic oil that inhibits bacterial growth.

The roots were once added to potpourri and kept with clothes to repel moths.

G. ciliatum - **Prairie Smoke**
G triflorum - **Long Plumed Avens**
The roots of these species have been used to make tea.

Gigartina stellata / Irish Moss
G. papillata / Grapestone
These seaweeds are another useful source of alginates. Use like the other Irish Moss (*Chondrus*).

Glaux maritima / Sea Milkwort
This species is found on both coasts, and on alkaline soils inland. The succulent leaves have been eaten raw, pickled or cooked.

Godetia albescens / Farewell To Spring
Native Americans gathered, and used, the seeds in much the same way as Red Maids (*Calandrinia*). They were once an important seed crop for Native Californians. The leaves were used as a wash for sore eyes.

G. biloba
G. viminea
Used as above.

Grindelia squarrosa, G. integrifolia / Gumweed

The young spring foliage has been used for tea. Be aware that these species may accumulate selenium, and become toxic, when growing in selenium rich soils.

A tea of the leaves has been used externally, as a wash for Poison Oak and chapped skin. A tea of the flowers and leaves has been used as an expectorant and antispasmodic.

Gymnocladus dioica / Kentucky Coffee Tree

The entire plant contains hydrocyanic acid and is toxic raw. Native Americans ate the roasted seed as a nut-like snack, or ground it to meal for baking. The seeds must be thoroughly roasted at 300 degrees Fahrenheit for three hours to make them edible (this also improves their flavor). They have been used as a somewhat astringent coffee substitute, which explains their common name. This is improved by the addition of milk and sugar and some people develop a taste for it.

Habenaria species / Bog Orchids

Native Americans ate the bulbs of the Bog Orchids, though you probably shouldn't, as they are small and never particularly common. All North American Orchids are edible, but should never be eaten under normal circumstances, as they are often rare. The bulbs are said to taste like frozen potatoes.

Halesia carolina / Carolina Silverbell

The unripe fruits have been eaten as a snack, pickled, or sucked to keep the mouth moist.

***H. diptera* - Two -Winged Silverbell**
***H. parviflora* - Little Silverbell**
Used as above.

Hemizonia fitchii / Fitch's Spikeweed

Also *H. fasciculata* - Tarweed
These species are closely related to the Tarweeds (*Madia*), and Native Americans used their seed in the same ways.

Hesperocalis undulata / Desert Lily

The edible bulb of this lovely (and rather incongruous) desert flower can be prepared and eaten like *Camassia,* but is really too beautiful to eat. The flower is far more nourishing as food for the soul, than the bulb would be as food for the body. If that isn't a good enough reason to leave it alone, it is also hard to dig, as the edible part may be two feet underground.

Hieracium species / Hawkweed

The young leaves have been used as a potherb, though they are rather astringent, and not very good. Native Americans chewed the gum that exudes from wounds on the stems. The astringent leaves were used for diarrhea and as a wound herb.

Hoffmanseggia densiflora / Hog Potato

This plant is closely related to the *Cassia* genus. It can be a troublesome weed in irrigation ditches, but is a useful plant for the forager, as it bears small edible tubers. These are rather too tough to eat raw, but are good when boiled or roasted, and were a favorite food of a number of Native American tribes.

Holodiscus discolor / Ocean Spray
H. microphyllus
The small nut-like fruits were eaten raw, or cooked, by Native Americans.

Honckenya peploides / Sea Chickweed
Syn *Arenaria peploides*
The thick succulent leaves of these maritime plants are rich in vitamins A and C, and were an important food in the far north where few greens are to be found. They are gathered before the flowers appear, washed thoroughly to remove any grit, and used as a salad, potherb and pickle. Icelanders and the Inuit people fermented the chopped, boiled leaves to make a kind of sauerkraut.

Hydrolea species / Hydroleas

These bitter plants have been used as potherbs, though you will probably have to change the cooking water at least once to make them palatable.

Hydrophyllum species / Waterleaf

The common and genus names were given because the plants collect rainwater on their leaves. No species is toxic, so you can experiment with any you find. In spring the succulent young plants of several species are an excellent addition to salads (others are too hairy to eat raw). They can be used as a potherb up until the flowers appear. Later they become too bitter.

Best species include:
H. canadense - **Broad Leaved Waterleaf** - This species also has edible roots, which can be eaten raw or cooked.

H. occidentale - **Squaw Lettuce**

Hypochoeris radicata / Cats Ears

This relative of Dandelion has little of the bitterness of its cousin, and can be used as a salad or potherb any time it is available. It is a good enough food plant to have occasionally been cultivated in Europe.

Hypnea species / Hypnea
This seaweed is a useful source of algin (see *Macrocystis*).

Hyptis emoryii, H. suaveolens / Desert Mint
The mucilaginous seed of these desert plants can be used in the same way as the related Chia (*Salvia*). Native Americans used the parched seed for tea and jelly. They also ground it to flour for gruel. The African Mint (*H. spicigara*) is sometimes cultivated as an oilseed crop in its native land.

Isomeris arborea / Bladderpod
In late spring the Cahuilla people cooked the green seed-pods in a fire pit. The flowers are also edible.

Koeleria macrantha / June Grass
The seed can be ground to flour. Potentially a very useful species.

Laportea canadensis / Wood Nettle
This species is a close relative of the Stinging Nettle (*Urtica*), and resembles it in appearance, habits and uses. The leaves are an excellent potherb. The Japanese cultivate their native species (*L. macrostachya*) as a food crop. The stems have been used as a source of fiber.

Lapsana communis / Nipplewort
The young leaves can be used as a potherb or salad, like those of the related Dandelion (*Taraxacum*). Older plants are usually bitter and unpleasant, but have been used as a potherb after cooking in a change of water.

Larix species / Larches
It's stretching the imagination to think of the Larches as food producers, though the new needles of these deciduous conifers are tender, and make a pleasant enough nibble. The cambium bark layer has been used for food in times of famine. It is prepared and eaten like Pine (*Pinus*) bark. The leafy tips can be used to make a pleasant, vitamin C rich tea, which has been used to treat scurvy. I have used them to flavor water that needed boiling for purification.

Native Americans used the resin as a salve for wounds and treated infected wounds with the powdered bark. Herbalists call the resin Venice turpentine, and use it for wounds, as an expectorant and to treat poisoning. It was collected in commercial quantities by tapping the trees.

Lamium purpureum / Purple Dead Nettle
Some *Lamium* species are implicated with the poisoning of cattle in Europe, though large quantities must be eaten to have any negative effect. In spring the young plants are a nice addition to salads, and can also be used as a potherb. Older leaves can be cooked and eaten. The

Lamium species are important bee plants. The White Dead Nettle (*L. album)* is reported to have the highest nectar yield of any plant in Britain.

L. album - White Dead Nettle
L. amplexicaule - Henbit
Used as above.

Lasthenia glabrata / Goldfields
Native Americans gathered and used the seed like that of Red Maids (*Calandrinia*), for pinole, bread and gruel.

Layia glandulosa, L. platyglossa / Tidy Tips
Native Americans gathered and used the seed like that of Red Maids (*Calandrinia*), for pinole, bread and gruel.

Lecanora subfusca, L. affinis, L. esculenta / Curd Lichens
These lichens were eaten by Native Americans.

Lemna minor / Duckweed
This tiny species is found in sheltered, nutrient rich ponds. It is edible.

Lesquerella species / Bladderpods
The young leaves, and seeds, have been used for food in the same way as Mustard (*Brassica*), but they aren't very good. I have included the plant because some species (*L. angustifolia, L. fendleri, L. gordonii*) are very rich in hydroxy fatty acids, and could have important industrial uses in lubricants, adhesives, plastics and paints.

Leontodon species / Hawkbits
The Hawkbits are close relatives of the Dandelion (*Taraxacum*), and can be used in the same ways.

Liquidambar styraciflua / Sweet Gum
The generic and common names both refer to the sweet resin that exudes from wounds in the trunk. This has been chewed like chewing gum, and is said to clean the teeth and freshen the breath. It is somewhat antiseptic, so Native Americans mixed it with fat for use as a wound dressing. It has also been used as an expectorant.

Sweet Gum is a fast growing tree and coppices well. It has been suggested as a possible candidate for fuelwood energy plantations, either for firewood or as material for making alcohol or methane see Poplar (*Populus*).

Liriodendron tulipifera / Tulip tree
The Tulip Tree is one of the largest trees in the eastern hardwood forest, sometimes reaching 200 feet in height and ten feet in diameter. It gets its common and specific names because its flowers somewhat resemble Tulips. The root has been used to flavor root beer.

Tulip Tree is not great firewood, but it is fast growing, and has been suggested as a tree for energy plantations (see *Populus*). The botanically primitive flowers are an excellent source of nectar, a single tree sometimes providing enough to make several pounds of honey.

Lithospermum incisum / Gromwell
Native Americans ate the cooked roots, though they aren't very good.

The Shoshone used an infusion of the flowering tops, or roots (and those of related species, especially Stoneseed - *L. ruderale)* as an oral contraceptive, to suppress ovulation. The active ingredient (lithospermic acid) affects hormone production, and appears to have few side effects. It is said that if it was drunk daily for six months it could induce permanent sterility. The European Gromwell (*L. officinalis)* has been used in similar ways.

Lobularia maritima / Sweet Alyssum
Syn *Alyssum maritimum*
This species is often grown as an annual ornamental, and in the west it has escaped and naturalized to become a minor weed. This is nice, as it is not only attractive but also edible. The flowers and tender new tips are a spicy addition to salads, or bland potherbs.

Lophocereus schotti / Organpipe cactus
Syn Pachycereus schotti
This species is closely related to the other Organpipe Cactus (*Lemairocereus thurberii*), and can be used in the same ways.

Lupinus littoralis / Chinook Licorice
The fleshy roots of this Lupine are poisonous raw, but have been cooked and eaten in times of famine. They were a common famine food for some Native American tribes, especially in early spring when other foods were scarce. The raw roots apparently cause a kind of temporary intoxication resembling that from alcohol (even cooked roots may have some effect). A number of *Lupinus* species are dangerously toxic, so it's probably best to avoid all of them under normal circumstances.

Some Lupins are important green manure or cover crops, as they fix nitrogen and accumulate phosphorus.

Lycopus species / Bugleweed
Unlike most members of the Mint family, the Bugleweeds don't have strongly aromatic foliage. They are of interest because they bear small edible tubers. These can be used like those of their cousins the Woundworts (*Stachys*). They are propagated in the same ways as those plants, and like the same growing conditions (see *Stachys*).

L. americanus - **Cut Leaved Water Horehound**
L. asper - **Rough Water Horehound**
L. sessilifolius - **Sessile Leaved Water Horehound**
L. uniflorus -**Bugleweed**
L. virginicus - **Virginia Bugleweed**
All of these species are good.

Lygodesmia juncacea / Skeleton Weed
Native Americans chopped up Skeleton Weed stems, and used the gum that exudes from them as chewing gum. The leaves of the Rush Pink (*L. grandiflora*) were used as a potherb by Native Americans, but aren't very good.

Maclura pomifera / Osage Orange
Unfortunately the strange fruit aren't edible. I have included this species because it has long been considered the ultimate wood for making bows. This was sometimes a trade item between tribes. This tree is very hardy and was once widely planted as a shelterbelt tree. It is also very thorny, and makes a good barrier plant or hedge.

Magnolia virginiana / Sweet Bay
Not to be confused with the Sweet Bay (*Persea borbonia*), this popular ornamental has large, sweet scented flowers. The fresh leaves have been used for flavoring like those of Bay (*Laurus nobilis*), but don't really taste the same. The leaves and flowers have been used for tea.

M. grandiflora - **Southern Magnolia** - The flower buds have been used to make a tasty pickle.

Malvaviscus arboreus / Turks Cap
Turks Cap is a close relative of the Mallows, and can be used for food in the same ways.

Mammillaria meiacantha / Pincushion Cactus
The small greenish fruits have been eaten in much the same way as those of the Prickly Pears (*Opuntia*).

Marrubium vulgare / Horehound
This native of the Mediterranean is widely naturalized in milder areas of the west, but is quite rare elsewhere. The aromatic leaves are somewhat bitter, and not to everyone's taste, but they have been used as flavoring, especially for beer and liqueurs. A better use is to make Horehound candy, which was originally intended as a cough remedy, but is good enough to eat for pleasure. Horehound leaf tea, sweetened with honey, was once used as an expectorant for coughs and catarrh.

Matricaria chamomila / German Chamomile
Syn *M. recutita*
This relative of Garden or Roman Chamomile (*Anthemis nobilis*) is cultivated in herb gardens, and is occasionally

found as an escape. The flowers have been used sparingly in salads and stir-fries. The fresh, or dried, flowers are used to make a pleasant tasting tea (this has a mild sedative effect.

M. matricaroides - Pineapple Weed
The strongly aromatic flowers can be used as a culinary flavoring, and to make a tea.

Mentzelia albicaulis / White stemmed Blazing Star
The oily seed was particularly prized by Native Americans. It was gathered and used in much the same ways as Red Maids (*Calandrinia*). It was often used for desserts, or to make a kind of nut butter.

M. involucrata - **White-Bracted Stick-leaf**
M. laevicaulis - **Great Blazing Star**
M. multiflora -- **Yerba Amarilla**
M. puberula -- **Darlington's Stickleaf**
M. veatchiana - **Veatch's Stickleaf**
Used as above.

Menyanthes trifoliata / Bog Bean
This bitter plant was once used to flavor beer before the introduction of Hops. The root has reportedly been eaten, after cooking in several changes of water to leach out their tannin. Apparently in Scandinavia the cooked root was once dried and ground to flour for baking. The dried leaves were commonly smoked, alone or in aromatic herbal smoking mixtures. All of these uses are unimportant nowadays as it is not very common.

Bogbean is often grown as an ornamental in shallow water gardens. Propagate by division.

Microseris nutans / Nodding Scorzonella
The succulent roots are rather bitter, but can be used like those of Salsify (Tragopogon), after cooking in a change of water.

M. laciniata - **Cut Leaf Scorzonella**
Syn *Scorzonella laciniata*
The roots can be used as above.

Mimosa biuncifera / Catclaw Mimosa
This species gets its name for the same reason as the Catclaw Acacia - it is covered in curved spines. The edible pods have been used like those of Mesquite (*Prosopis*), but aren't as good.

Mimulus species / Monkeyflower
The young leaves have been used as both salad and potherb, but become pungent and bitter as they mature. The ash of the burned leaves has been used as a salt substitute. See Coltsfoot (*Petasites*) for more on this use.

Native Americans used the leaves as a poultice for burns.

M. guttatus - **Common Monkeyflower**
M. primuloides - **Primrose Monkeyflower**
Probably all species can be eaten, but these are some of the best.

Mitchella repens / Partridgeberry
The berries of this diminutive eastern plant are edible, but not very good, and hardly worth bothering with. The leaves have been used for tea. The dried leaves were smoked by the Chippewa people

Native Americans knew the plant as Squaw Vine, because pregnant women often drank a tea of the leaves for several weeks prior to childbirth, to make the delivery easier. The same tea has been used as a diuretic.

Mollugo verticillata / Carpetweed
In Central America the tender leaves are used as a potherb.

Monardella odoratissima / Mountain Pennyroyal
This species is used for flavoring like its namesake Pennyroyal (*Hedeoma*). It can also be used to brew one of the best wild teas. Simply steep a single stem in a cup of water until it reaches the desired strength.

M. lanceolata - **Western Pennyroyal**
M. candicans
M. villosa - **Coyote Mint**
Used as above.

Monolepsis nuttalliana / Indian Spinach
Indian Spinach can be used as a potherb in the same way as the related Lambs Quarters (*Chenopodium*). It is a hardy plant and often stays green through the winter. The new growth of young plants is best, though the tender growing tips of older plants can also be used. The Pima people used to fry the boiled leaves. The seeds can be eaten like those of Lambs Quarters.

Nereocystis luetkeana / Bull Kelp
This distinctive seaweed is one of the fastest growing plants in the world, sometimes growing two feet in a day. It grows up to 160 feet in length, and is a component of the great Pacific Kelp forests. It isn't a very accessible plant, though you can often gather the plants that wash ashore, so long as they are still crisp and smooth, not flaccid or wrinkled. Chop the slender (less than three inches in diameter) stipes (stems) into manageable lengths, wash in fresh water and dry. These can be pickled, candied, powdered as a salt substitute, used as a gelatin substitute (See *Chondrus*), or added to soup. They are not good fresh. Native Americans sometimes used them to line fire pits for cooking (See *Camassia*).

The stems were dried and braided to make fishing lines and anchor rope

Nolina microcarpa, N. bigelovii, N parryi / Bear Grasses

The young shoots and hearts have been eaten like those of the related Yucca (*Yucca*). The flowers are said to be toxic if eaten in quantity. Beargrass fiber was very important to Native Americans for weaving baskets and mats. It was also used for brooms.

Nyssa sylvatica / Tupelo

The sour fruits of this common tree contain large seeds and are not very tasty raw. However they are not bad when cooked in preserves and pies. Their quality varies considerably from tree to tree, so sample any you find.

The Tupelos are important nectar producers, and Tupelo honey is considered among the finest there is.

N. aquatica - Water Tupelo

This species gave the genus its name (Nyssa was a water nymph, and this species loves water). The fruit can be used as above.

N. ogeche - Ogeechee Lime -

The fruit of this species is better than the above and has occasionally been sold in markets for making preserves.

Olneya tesota / Ironwood

The only member of the *Olneya* genus, this rugged and long-lived (up to 600 years) shrub is often the dominant plant in an area with relatively few substantial edible plants.

The black seeds of this spiny desert Legume were a prized food of Native Americans, but need special preparation. The pods were pounded to free the seed, which was ground to meal, and then boiled or leached to remove the bitter saponins. The resulting flour was used for gruel and bread. The green immature seeds can also be eaten, after boiling in at least one change of water.

The large seeds are sometimes infested with insect larvae. We find this distasteful, but it didn't bother Native Americans; the insects merely made the seed meal more nutritious. If you can gather, process and eat the seed before the eggs hatch you won't know the difference (or microwave them to kill the eggs).

As the name suggests Ironwood is very heavy and hard. It is used for tool handles and tourist carvings, but not much else because it's so hard it quickly blunts woodworking tools. Native Americans used it for arrowheads and clubs. It is also good firewood, but is not often available in quantity.

Ironwood cannot tolerate frost, so farmers used to plant Citrus groves where it grew. It is an important nurse tree for cacti and other desert plants.

Onoclea sensibilis / Sensitive Fern

The uncurled fronds, and rhizomes, have been eaten like those of the Ostrich Fern (*Matteucia*).

Onopordon acanthium / Scotch Thistle

This species can be used for food like the *Cirsium* Thistles. The leaves are most often used as a potherb, but have also been used in salads (trim off the spines with scissors). The flower stems, flower buds and seeds have also been eaten. A poultice of the leaves was once considered a good treatment for skin diseases. The downy seed have been used like those of Cattail (*Typha*) for stuffing clothing, pillows and bedding.

Oplopanax horridum / Devils Club

Syn *Echinopanax horridum*

This spiny plant well deserves its specific and common names, its vicious spines are horribly devilish and it can be quite a menace to careless hikers walking along stream banks. The young shoots were a favorite food of Native Americans, though they are only available for a short time in spring. They are gathered just before they appear above ground, by pulling up the roots. They don't have spines at this time, and can be eaten raw or cooked. They can also be eaten after they emerge from the ground, for as long as their spines are soft.

This plant is a relative of Ginseng, and was once considered to be a general tonic. The roots have been included in spring tonic mixtures.

Orobanche ludoviciana / Broomrape

This parasite lives on the roots of a number of plant species, especially members of the *Asteraceae* (such as *Ambrosia*, *Grindelia* and *Xanthium* species). It is found almost completely underground, with the exception of its flowers, and lacks green chlorophyll, so is almost pure white. Some members of this genus have caused gastric disturbance in livestock, but they aren't really poisonous.

The tender succulent plants were a favorite spring food of the Paiute and other Native American peoples. They can be peeled and eaten raw, though they are rather bitter, this way. They are better if cooked like Asparagus, or baked in a fire pit.

O. cooperi - **Desert Broomrape**
O. grayana
O. minor - **Lesser Broomrape**
O. pinorum
O. fascicularis - **Pinon Strangleroot**
O. uniflora
Used as above.

Orogenia fusiformis,
O. linearifolia / Indian Potato
The tubers of these early spring flowers are edible, but should only be used when the plants are very abundant. They can be eaten raw, or cooked like Potatoes, and are often very good. The plants are mostly found in mountains, and one can find them through most of the summer by climbing up to where the snow is melting (and it is still technically spring).

Osmaronia cerasiformis / Oso Berry
The fruits are eaten raw or cooked, but aren't very good.

Osmunda cinnomomea / Cinnamon Fern
The curled fronds can be used like those of the related Ostrich Fern (*Matteucia*), but they are somewhat acrid. Native Americans soaked them in a solution of wood ashes to make them more palatable. They are also rather dry unless eaten with a sauce. The woolly fuzz rubbed from the fiddleheads was used as wound dressing by Native Americans.

Oxydendrum arboreum / Sourwood
The generic name means sour tree, as does the common name. The sour leaves can be used as a nibble to keep your mouth moist when out in the woods.

Pectis angustifolia, Pectis papposa /
Lemonweed
These southwestern plants have a strong lemon flavor, and while still young and tender they can be used as a flavoring, potherb or salad. Lemonweed tea is excellent. Aromatic oil from the plant has been used in perfume.

Pedicularis lanata / Woolly Lousewort
The root of this species have been used like Carrot, but should not be used unless very abundant, as taking it kills the plant. The shoots, leaves, stems and flowers are also edible, and this was an important food plant for Native Americans in the far north.

P. arctica - Arctic Lousewort
P. hirsuta - Hairy Lousewort
P. sudetica - Arctic Lousewort
Used as above.

Pellea mucronata. P. ornithopus / Tea fern
The leaves of these evergreen ferns have been used to make a pleasant tea.

Peltandra virginica, P. alba / Tuckahoe
Like many members of the *Araceae* these plants are very acrid and toxic when raw. Nevertheless their large roots (they may grow to six pounds in weight) were a staple of several Native American tribes. It is said that they roasted the roots in a fire pit (see *Camassia*) for two

days, then peeled, dried and ground them to flour for baking and gruel. I haven't tried this so I can't comment.

Peltiphyllum peltatum / Indian Rhubarb
This plant superficially resembles the eastern Mayapple (*Podophyllum*), but isn't closely related, and isn't used in the same ways. It is only of limited use as food. Native Americans peeled the young leaf stalks in spring, and ate them raw or cooked. It is only good for a short time when very young, and quickly gets tough. It doesn't taste like Rhubarb, the name undoubtedly came from its similar appearance.

This plant is widely grown as an ornamental under the name Umbrella plant. Propagate from seed or division, in rich moist soil.

Peraphyllum ramosissimum / Squaw Apple
The Squaw Apple is a close relative of the Juneberries, and its fruits can be used in the same ways (see *Amelanchier*). It isn't nearly as good though, as the fruits are often astringent.

It can be grown from seed or layering, in well drained soil with full sun.

Persea borbonia / Sweet Bay
Sweet Bay is a relative of the Laurel (*Laurus nobilis*), and has similar aromatic evergreen leaves. It isn't related to Sweet Bay (*Magnolia grandiflora).*

The aromatic leaves can be used as a substitute for commercial Bay leaves. These are evergreen and can be used year round, but are best in midsummer after flowering. The leaves can also be used for tea.

Petasites species / Coltsfoot
These species are relatives of the other Coltsfoot (*Tussilago farfara*), and have the same unusual habit of producing flowers before the leaves.

Native Americans used the young leaves and flower stems as a potherb, and for tea. Use in moderation as they may contain toxic pyrrolizidine alkaloids. Some tribes used the leaves of *P. palmatus* for salt. These were left to wilt, rolled up into balls, and put near the fire to slowly turn to ash (or dried and toasted in a frying pan). The resulting ash was then used as a salt substitute.

Generally these species can be grown in most soils, and are propagated by division. Some species are useful as groundcover. They are valuable nectar plants for bees.

Peteria scoparia / Camote-De-Monte
The common name means Mountain Sweet Potato in Spanish, and was given because the roots were eaten raw or cooked.

Phellopterus montanus / **Mountain Celery**

Native Americans peeled the roots of Mountain Celery and baked them in a fire pit. These were then eaten as a vegetable, or dried and ground to flour for baking and gruel. Remember to use caution when identifying it, as this is a member of the *Apiaceae* (which includes some very poisonous plants).

Photinia arbutifolia / **Toyon**

Syn *Heteromeles arbutifolia*

This southwestern species produces edible berries, but they aren't very good, and you have to work to disguise them (sugar helps). Native Americans appreciated them and commonly ground the dried berries to meal for making mush. They can also be used for making a drink like Manzanita cider (see *Arctostaphylos*).

Pilea pumila / **Clearweed**

Clearweed looks like a small, bright green, almost translucent Stinging Nettle without the stinging hairs (it is actually a close relative). The young plants can be used as a mild flavored potherb.

Platanus occidentalis / **American Sycamore**

This tree can be tapped for sap, and used to make syrup, in the same way as the Maples (see *Acer*).

Pleurophycus gardneri / **Kelp**

This Kelp may be gathered from below the low tide mark, or storm cast plants may be gathered from the shoreline (so long as they are still fresh). They can be cooked in soups, or dried and added to salads. It can also be used as a source of algin in the same way as Giant Kelp (*Macrocystis*). The stipes may be dried for storage, and soaked in water overnight prior to use.

Poliomintha incana / **Rosemary Mint**

This little member of the *Lamiaceae* can be used like the Mints (*Mentha*) for salads, sauces, potherbs and as culinary flavoring. It is a good tea plant.

P. longiflora – **Mexican Oregano**

Used as above. It is commonly used as a culinary herb for its Oregano-like flavor.

Polyneura latissima / **Polyneura**

This seaweed can be used in soups and salads.

Polypodium vulgare / **Licorice fern**

This rather bitter fern has a pronounced Licorice flavor, hence its common name. The stems can be used for tea, or sucked to keep the mouth moist while hiking or working in the woods (the licorice flavor gets stronger with prolonged sucking). Don't chew on it too much as this may release a bitter flavor.

P. californicum - **California Polypody**
P. hesperium - **Licorice Fern**
Used as above.

Polystichum munitum / **Sword Fern**

The starchy rhizomes of Sword Fern were roasted and eaten by Native Americans, though they are not particularly good. The starch could probably be extracted in the same way as for Kudzu (*Pueraria*). The leaves were used to line fire pits for cooking.

Pontederia cordata / **Pickerelweed**

The young shoots can be gathered when still tightly furled, and boiled for five minutes as a potherb. The single seed is edible after its outer coat is removed, and can be ground to meal for baking and gruel. It is said to be quite nutritious. Pickerelweed is an important food plant for birds and aquatic animals.

Postelsia palmaeformis / **Sea Palm**

This seaweed is rather inaccessible in its surf-pounded habitat, but can often be found washed ashore after storms. These storm cast plants can be eaten if still crisp and fresh (they are best in spring). The chopped stipes can be eaten raw, boiled, steamed, pickled, in soups or dried.

Ptelea trifoliata / **Hop Tree**

The dry fruits were dried and ground to powder and added to yeast for baking bread (apparently they make the bread lighter). This species gets its name because the bitter fruits were used like those of Hops to brew beer. Native Americans considered it a panacea, and modern herbalists also believe it to have a significant beneficial effect on the whole body.

P. pallida
P. baldwinii
Used as above.

Pycnanthemum species / **Mountain Mints**

These relatives of the Mints (*Mentha*) share their strong mint odor and flavor. They can be used in the same ways, for food, drink and medicine.

Raphanus sativus / **Wild Radish**

This is the garden Radish, escaped and reverted to its natural wild form. It is only of limited used as food, as the root that gives its cultivated counterpart its value has withered to insignificance.

The young leaves can be used like the Mustards (*Brassica*), as a pungent addition to salads, or as a potherb. In mild winter areas the whole plants can be eaten cooked, or raw, right through the winter. The flowers and green unripe seedpods are also good in salads. The ripe seed can be sprouted like Alfalfa, or used as a condiment like Mustard.

R. raphanistrum - **Wild Radish**
Used as above.

Ratibida pinnata / **Prairie Coneflower**
Native Americans ground the oily seed to meal, for baking and gruel. The leaves, and Anise scented flowers, can be used to make a pleasant tea. This species has been used experimentally as a perennial seed crop. A three-year-old plot gave as much as 1400 pounds of seed per acre.

R. columnifera - **Mexican Hat**
The leaves and flowers can be used as above.

Rhexia species / **Meadow beauty**
The tuberous roots can be eaten raw, or cooked like potatoes, and are quite good. The young leaves are nice in salads. Unfortunately the plants aren't very common, so their casual use for food must be discouraged.

Rhododendron pericyclemenoides / **Pink Azalea**
Syn **R. nudiflorum**
Most parts of most *Rhododendrons* are poisonous. This species often produces a growth (probably caused by a fungus) that appears on the leaves and twigs after flowering. These contain a succulent pulp, and are pretty good eaten out of hand, or in salads. The early colonists pickled them.

R. lapponicum - **Lapland Rosebay**
The flowers, and leaves, of this northern shrub have been used as tea, by steeping them in boiling water for a few minutes. Don't boil the leaves, as this will release poisonous andromedotoxins.

Sanicula tuberosa / **Tuberous Sanicle**
The small edible bulbs were a favorite food of the Pomo, and other Native American tribes. They are tasty either raw or cooked.

Sarcobatus vermiculatus / **Greasewood**
Native Americans cooked the tender (if rather salty) growing tips of this shrub as a potherb. It should be used in moderation, as it contains oxalic acid and has been known to poison livestock. In times of famine the seeds were used like those of the related Lambs Quarters (*Chenopodium*).

Sarcostemma species / **Climbing Milkweed**
The edible pods of these pretty vines can be used like those of their cousins, the Milkweeds (See *Asclepias*).

Saxifraga species / **Wild Saxifrages**
The young leaves of several species can be eaten as a potherb, or salad, up until the flowers appear (they are rich in vitamins A and C). Mature leaves are bitter and unpleasant. No species is poisonous, so you can use any that are palatable, so long as they are sufficiently abundant.

S. arguta - **Brook Saxifrage**
S. micrandithifolia - **Lettuce Saxifrage**
S. oregana - **Oregon Saxifrage**
S. pennsylvanica - **Swamp Saxifrage**
S. punctata - **Punctate Saxifrage**
S. spicata - **Spiked Saxifrage**
S. virginiensis - **Early Saxifrage**
All of these species are edible.

Schinus molle / **Pepper Tree**
This native of South America is quite common in the milder parts of California and Florida. The dried, roasted berries are ground and used as a substitute for Black Pepper. It has also been made into wine.

Sesuvium species / **Sea Purslane**
The fleshy edible leaves of the Sea Purslane somewhat resemble those of common Purslane (*Portulaca*) in appearance. The tender young parts can be eaten raw, but many people object to their salty flavor, and prefer to cook them in a change of water. Try pickling them, or adding to soups as a combination vegetable and seasoning. They are rich in vitamin C

The leaves have been used as a poultice for burns, and can be used to treat sunburn if you have been hanging out on the beach for too long.

Setaria species / **Foxtail Grasses**
These plants are often found in abundance, and can provide useful amounts of edible seed. This are prepared like Mountain Rice (*Oryzopsis*), and then boiled like rice, or ground to flour for baking.

Several species of Foxtail grasses have been cultivated for food in the past. Native Americans often scattered the seed to increase the supply.

Sidalcea neomexicana,
S. malvaeflora / **Prairie Mallow**
The tender leaves can be eaten raw, or cooked as a potherb, like their cousins the Mallows (*Malva*).

Silene cucubalus / **Bladder Campion**
The only edible parts of the Bladder Campion are the young spring shoots, gathered when only a few inches high. They can be difficult to find so early in the year. You have to find the dead plants from last year, and

growing nearby will be the new plants. These can be eaten raw, but are bitter due to their content of saponins. They are best when cooked for ten minutes as a potherb.

S. acaulis - Moss Campion
This species can be used as above, but is too pretty for casual use.

Silphium species / Compass Plant
Like many members of the *Asteraceae*, these species contain milky latex, which exudes from wounds in the plant. Native Americans used this as chewing gum, and often wounded the plants to get it.

When growing in full sun the leaves of the Compass plant orient themselves on a north south axis, hence the common name. When growing in, or near, shade they orient themselves toward the strongest light source, so be careful when relying on this "natural compass".

It is suggested that *S. laciniatum* may have potential as a source of hydrocarbons, and fiber for making paper.

Sisymbrium species / Hedge Mustard
There are many *Sisymbrium* species to be found in North America, either native or introduced. The tender young basal leaves can be used in salads, or as a potherb (if they are too bitter, change the cooking water at least once). The seed has been used as a condiment like Mustard.

S. altissimum - Tumble Mustard
S. officinale - Hedge Mustard
S. loeselii - Tall Hedge Mustard
These species are the best potherbs.

Smilacina racemosa / False Solomons Seal
The plant resembles Solomons Seal (*Polygonatum*) hence the name. It can be used in several ways, but you need a lot of plants to make it worthwhile. They should probably be left alone under most circumstances.

If the plant is very common, the thin spring shoots can be used like Asparagus. The young leaves may be eaten raw or cooked, up until the flower buds appear. The starchy aromatic root is prepared by soaking it in a solution of wood ashes for a couple of hours, and then boiling for a half-hour.

S. stellata - Small False Solomons Seal
S. trifolia - Three Leaved Solomons Seal
Used as above.

Sorbus species / Mountain Ash
These trees are mostly found in cool northern, and mountainous, areas. The berries of many species are considered to be edible, but they are usually too bitter to eat raw. They can be used in the same ways as

Cranberries, for sauce, pies and jelly (they are rich in pectin). Native Americans dried and ground the berries to meal for making pemmican. They also used them to make "cider" as for Manzanita (see *Arctostaphylos*). In Europe the fruits were steeped in brandy.

The berries contain sorbitol (named after this genus), a sugar that is poorly absorbed by the body. This is used in diet and diabetic foods, and in "sugar free" chewing gum. It is now synthesized from sucrose, and is used in large amounts by the food processing industry.

Sorghum halapense / Johnson Grass
Ranchers consider this a noxious weed because its fresh foliage is toxic to livestock. Native Americans sometimes cultivated it for its edible seed.

Sparganium species / Bur-Reeds
These species produce hard edible seeds, that stay on the plants well into winter. These can be ground to flour for baking, or roasted as a coffee substitute. The bulbous stem base can be cooked and eaten. Some species apparently produce edible tubers, and were a staple food for the Klamath and other tribes. These are hard to find, but it's worth looking when the plants are abundant, as you might be lucky. If you find any tubers, use them like those of the Arrowhead (*Sagittaria*).

Another potential use for these species (notably *S. eurycarpum*) is in removing pollutants, such as chemical fertilizer runoff and sewage, from water. See *Eichornia* for more on this.

S. americanum - American Bur-Reed
S. chlorocarpum - Green Fruited Bur-Reed
S. eurycarpum - Great Bur-Reed

Spergula arvensis / Corn Spurrey
This small weed of arable fields around the world is a very nutritious food plant. It may be used as a potherb, a salad, or even fermented like sauerkraut. If you can gather enough, the nutritious seed can be ground to flour for baking, or gruel. It has been suggested as a possible oilseed crop.

Spergularia marina / Sand Spurrey
The thick fleshy leaves of this maritime plant have been used as salad, potherb and pickle. In Iceland they have been fermented like sauerkraut.

Sphaeralcea ambigua / Desert Hollyhock
The leaves can be used as a potherb, or in salads, like those of the related Mallows (*Malva*).

Sporobolus species / Dropseed
The Dropseeds are among the most useful edible wild

grasses, because the ripe seed stays on the plant for a while, giving the forager a chance to harvest it. The seed has no attached husk, so can be gathered and eaten with little preparation. The only drawback is that it is small, and hard to gather in quantity. If you can get enough, they may be eaten raw, boiled for gruel, or parched and ground to meal for baking. These are C4 plants, and so very efficient at high light and heat intensities (see *Amaranthus*). They were important to Native Americans in the southwest

S. airoides - **Alkali Sacaton**
S. cryptandrus - **Sand Dropseed**
S. giganteus
S. heterolepis – **Prairie Dropseed**
All of these species are good.

Spirodela polyrhiza / Big Duckweed
This tiny, floating water plant has been eaten.

Stanleya pinnatifida / Princes Plume
The young leaves can be used as a potherb like many other members of the Cabbage family. They often tend to be bitter, unless cooked in at least one change of water. The seeds are also edible.

Staphylea trifolia / Bladdernut
The Bladder-like pods that give the plant its name contain tasty oily seeds. These have been compared to Pistachios, and can be eaten in the same ways.

Streptopus species / Twistedstalk
The Cucumber-flavored leaves and shoots are quite palatable when young, and can be used in salads, stir-fries, and as a potherb. The berries were eaten by Native Americans (they are sometimes known as Watermelon Berries), but are purgative if eaten in quantity.

S. amplexifolius - **White Mandarin**
S. roseus - **Rose Twistedstalk**
S. streptopoides - **Small Twistedstalk**
All of these species are good.

Strophostyles helveola, S. umbellata / Wild Beans
These species are related to the Tepary Bean (they were once included in the *Phaseolus* genus), and their seeds can be used in the same ways.

Symplocarpos foetidus / Skunk Cabbage
Like many members of the *Araceae* this plant contains tiny crystals of calcium oxalate called raphides. These are very irritating to mucous membranes, and if eaten in quantity they cause the throat to swell and close. This can result in death by asphyxiation.

It is written in a number of books that these crystals are destroyed by heat, and that the cooked roots or leaves can be eaten. However in my experience boiling or baking doesn't have any effect all. The tuberous root can be made edible by extended drying, but this takes up to six months (see *Arisaema* for more on this).

Talinum aurantiacum / Flame Flower
The young leaves can be used as a potherb, or salad, in the same way as the related Purslane (*Portulaca*). The roots are also edible.

T. triangulare - This species is found as an escape in Florida (and perhaps elsewhere). It is cultivated as a potherb in the American tropics.

Tanacetum vulgare / Tansy
The entire plant contains a toxic and irritating oil known as thujone (this is also found in Wormwood - *Artemisia* and Arborvitae - *Thuja*). In quantity this can cause convulsions, gastritis and sometimes death. Many people don't even consider Tansy safe for external use.

Apparently Tansy was once widely used as a culinary herb. I find this surprising, as the taste is bitter and quite unpleasant. I suppose if one took the very youngest and mildest leaves available, and added a tiny pinch to egg dishes or salads, you might get to like the aromatic flavor (perhaps).

Tansy was once a popular spring tonic, to cleanse the blood and rejuvenate the body. Maybe it was some perverse doctrine of signatures - if it tastes bad enough, it must be good for you.

The leaves can be used to make an unpleasant and somewhat toxic tea. The best use of this is as a wash to kill external parasites. It was once commonly used for internal parasites also, but such internal use should probably be avoided.

Tecoma stans / Trumpet Bush
The chopped roots have been used for tea in the usual way, or made into sun tea. They have also been fermented to make a kind of beer. The plants have been investigated as a possible source of rubber.

Thinopyron intermedium / Intermediate Wheatgrass
This species has recently been studied as a potential perennial grain crop. Flour made from the seeds can be used like wheat flour for bread, and cakes. A number of improved varieties have been obtained.

Thysanocarpus curvipes / Lacepod
The seeds of this bitter and pungent plant can be used as a condiment, like those of Mustard (*Brassica*).

Tragia species / Noseburn
The stinging leaves of these species have been cooked as a potherb. Use caution, as many members of the *Euphorbiaceae* are toxic.

Trianthema species / Sea Purslanes
These low growing, succulent, maritime plants are close relatives of the other Sea Purslanes (*Sesuvium*), and can be gathered and used in the same ways

T. portulacastrum - Sea Purslane
This is probably the best species, and has occasionally been cultivated.

Triglochin maritima / Arrowgrass
This species is a member of the Rush family and not a grass at all. It is widely distributed around the globe. In this country, it is common along both coasts and on moist alkaline soils inland.

Mature green parts of the Arrowgrass are toxic raw, as they contain cyanogenic glycosides, and they sometimes poison livestock. The young white leaf bases have been cooked and eaten in spring. The seeds can be parched and ground to flour for gruel and baking. The seeds can also be roasted as a coffee substitute.

Triosteum aurantiacum / Wild Coffee
The dried, roasted berries were ground to powder and used as a coffee substitute. Unlike most wild beverages, it is made by adding the ground berries to cold water, and then bringing them to a boil.

T. perfoliatum - Horse Gentian
Used as above.

Tripsacum dactyloides / Eastern Gama Grass
Another native grass that has been studied as a possible perennial grain crop. The seed is high in protein, and can be ground to flour for bread. It can also be popped like popcorn.

Uniola paniculata / Sea Oats
The seeds of this attractive perennial grass are edible and tasty. Unfortunately the plant is rare in many areas, and is protected by law, in which case gathering is rightly illegal. The graceful stems were once widely gathered for use in dried flower arrangements, which is one of the reasons it is now rare and protected. Its dense root network anchors sand dunes and prevents erosion by the wind (this is another reason it is protected). It is now widely planted to stabilize sand dunes, and researchers are looking for improved cultivars with greater sand holding abilities.

U. palmeri
U. virgata
Used as above

Usnea spp / Beard Lichens
These species are edible when prepared like Iceland Moss (*Cetraria*). They contain a medically important antibiotic, and antifungal, agent called usnic acid. The dried plants can be used as tinder.

Uvularia species / Bellworts
The small spring shoots have been used like those of Asparagus as a potherb. However they are not very substantial, or abundant, and you need a lot to make it worthwhile, so probably shouldn't be used under most circumstances. Don't pick more than one shoot from a single plant, or you may weaken it.

U. grandiflora - Large Flowered Bellwort
U. perfoliata - Perfoliate Bellwort
These species are probably the best.

Valerianella locusta / Cornsalad
This very hardy plant may grow right through the winter in mild climates. It is cultivated as a cold weather salad green (especially in Europe), and can be found locally as an escape almost anywhere in North America.

Any tender leaves you can find in spring, or fall, can be used in salads or as a potherb. They are sometimes for sale in trendy vegetable markets under their French name; Mache.

Cornsalad is easily grown from seed in average garden soils, and a number of improved cultivars are available from Europe. It self-seeds readily, and in fact these plants often do better than intentional plantings. It is usually planted in early spring, but in my experience it does best as a fall crop. A spring crop may self sow and reappear in fall.

V. carinata.
Used as above.

Verbena hastata / Blue Vervain
The bitter tasting seed was ground to flour by Native Americans. They first removed the bitter principle by grinding the parched seed to a meal, and then leaching it in water in much the same way as acorns (see *Quercus*). The Omaha (and other tribes) used the leaves for tea.

A tea of the leaves was used as a mild sedative, and to relieve headaches, and menstrual problems such as cramps. Use with caution as it can also be emetic. It was used externally to clean wounds, and as an eyewash for sore eyes (it was also thought to help restore eyesight).

Vicia americana / American Vetch
A number of *Vicia* species have been cultivated for food, the most important of which is the Fava Bean (*V. faber*). Some other species are toxic, so be careful with your identification. Even this species should probably be used in moderation.

The immature pods can be used like green beans. The ripe seeds can be used like cultivated beans. The young leafy tips can be used as a potherb.

The Vetches contain nitrogen-fixing bacteria in nodules on their roots, and so enrich the soil they grow in. Gardeners plant Vetches as a winter cover crop, to prevent nutrients leaching away in winter rains, and to add nitrogen and humus to the soil. They are dug into the soil the following spring prior to planting. They can be very productive plants, and under ideal conditions they have been known to yield 20 tons of vegetable matter per acre. They have also been planted to prevent erosion on bare slopes

These species can be grown from seed, and are not particular as to soil type.

V. cracca - **Tufted Vetch**
V. gigantea - **Giant Vetch**
Used as above.

Caution:
V. angustifolia - **Smaller Common Vetch**
This species is toxic.

Wislizenia refracta / Jackass Clover
This plant has been called malodorous and distasteful, but it has been used as a potherb after cooking in several changes of water. It is more closely related to Beeweed (*Cleome*) than Clover, and can be used in the same ways as that plant.

Wisteria spp / Wisteria
The aromatic flowers of both native, and cultivated, species have been eaten in salads, pancakes, tempura, ice cream and wine.

Wolffia arhiza / Watermeal
This species is one of the smallest of all flowering plants, so small it is hard to identify positively with the naked eye. In nutrient-rich sheltered water it multiplies very rapidly, forming a continuous smooth green mat that resembles a perfect lawn or putting green. It may shade out submerged plants, growing underneath it.

Watermeal is very nutritious, containing up to 20% protein, 40% carbohydrate and 5% fat and also tastes pretty good. In parts of Asia it is cultivated as a vegetable, and has potential as a future crop in this

country. It has also been grown as feed for fish and water-birds.

Xanthium strumarium / Cocklebur
Cocklebur leaves are eaten as a potherb in China, though it is sometimes said that they are slightly toxic. The burrs can be a nuisance as they stick to clothing, but contain edible seeds. These were ground to meal for bread, and gruel, by the Zuni people. They were also cooked like rice, and added to soup.

Xerophyllum tenax / Beargrass
This attractive mountain plant isn't a grass at all, but a relative of the Yucca (*Yucca*). Like many of its kin it is inconspicuous for most of the year, and only really noticeable when in bloom. The root is edible raw, but taste better if peeled and baked in a fire pit like Camas bulbs (*Camassia*). It is a nice addition to soup, as it picks up the flavor of whatever it is cooked with.

The specific name tenax means strong, and refers to the tough fibrous leaves. These were prized by Native Americans as a source of material for weaving, and were even traded between tribes for this. They were used for weaving baskets, pouches, water containers and hats. Native Americans burned the stands of plants to encourage vigorous new growth for basketry.

The saponin rich root can be used as a soap substitute like Amole (*Chlorogalum*). This is why the plant is sometimes known as Soapgrass.

The leaves are prized by florists for making bouquets. In some areas they are gathered commercially for this

Zizia aurea / Golden Alexanders
The flowers can be added to salads. The whole flower cluster can be cooked like broccoli.

Index

Index of Uses

Index of Common Names

About the author

Frank Tozer has been eating and using wild plants for over 40 years. As a child, growing up in Britain, he became fascinated with the idea that plants could be used by humans to satisfy their everyday needs. He roamed the surrounding forests, hedgerows, moors and fields, learning everything he could about the old country ways of living close to the land. This quest continued after a move to the United States, which was largely inspired by a desire to find the plants described by Euell Gibbons, and other great American writers. He has now lived in the United States for over 25 years, during which time he has continued to learn all he could about the plants of his adopted (and botanically much richer) land. He has been growing especially useful wild plants in his gardens in various parts of the country for over 20 years. A passionate environmentalist, he is committed to demonstrating how wild plants can be used to help us live healthier, more sustainable, and more satisfying lives. His international background, and wide practical experience, has given him a very broad perspective on the diverse uses of the plants of two continents. This enormous wealth of knowledge is shared with readers for the first time in this book.

Over the years Frank has supported himself in many different ways; as a carpenter, general contractor, landscaper, organic farmer, painter, baker, jeweler, plumber, gardener, photovoltaic installer, and a writer. He lives in the Santa Cruz mountains in the home he built by himself, with his wife and three children. He spends much of his time in his 2 ½ acre garden, where he tends (at last count) over 250 species (and countless varieties) of edible and useful plants.

Coming soon from

Green Man Publishing
Santa Cruz

☐ ## Using Wild Plants
The companion volume to The Uses of Wild Plants. This is a practical guide to the real life uses of wild plants; in the kitchen, house, workshop and garden.

☐ ## Organic Gardening Handbook
Everything you need to know to grow plants successfully. A complete practical guide to the techniques of organic gardening. A book to take out into the garden and get dirty.

☐ ## The New Cottage Garden
A complete guide to creating a new kind of garden; one that is productive, energy efficient, comfortable, useful and good looking. Combining aspects of traditional cottage gardening, edible landscaping, natural farming, no-dig gardening, Permaculture, Feng Shui, wild gardening and forest gardening, to create a garden that looks after you.

☐ ## Growing Vegetables
An indispensable guide to the serious cultivation and use, of common and uncommon vegetable crops.

See our website **greenmansantacruz.com** for more information on these titles.

Order Form

Green Man Publishing
Santa Cruz
P. O. Box 1546
Felton CA
95018
WWW. Greenmansantacruz.com

Please send me………. copies of **The Uses Of Wild Plants**…………$24.95

California residents please add 7.5% Sales Tax……………………..………2.12

Postage and handling………………………………………………………5.00

Total……………..

Send To:

Name……………………………………………..…………..
Address…………………………………….…………..………..
City…………………………………….State………..Zip………………
Telephone……………………………………………………..
E-Mail…………………………………………………………

Payment type: Check: ☐   Credit card: ☐

Name on card…………………………………

Card Number…………………………………..

Expiration Date………………………………..

Please keep me informed of other Green Man publications. ☐

See overleaf for information on forthcoming books.

584081